PENGUIN BOOKS

INVESTING FROM SCRATCH

JAMES H. LOWELL III is the editor in chief of *The Forbes ETF Advisor by Jim Lowell,* an independent investment advisory service exclusively focused on exchange-traded funds. He is the founder and chairman of The Rankings Service™ (trsreports.com), an independent, objective, third-party research service for institutional clients, providing proprietary review, analysis, and monitoring of individual investment manager performance.

Lowell is also the editor of the multiple award-winning independent newsletter, *Fidelity Investor* (and fidelityinvestor .com), the weekly electronic *Fidelity Sector Investor,* and the customized, independent *401K Focus* service, as well as the founding editor of *The ETF Trader* on *Marketwatch from Dow Jones.* Lowell is the president of the Fund Family Shareholder Association.

Mr. Lowell is also a prolific author. He has written several books on investing, most recently *Smart Money Moves* (Penguin), and *Investing from Scratch* (Penguin, 1997—revised edition in 2005). He is a past editor in chief of America Online's *FundWorks* and of *Funds Net Insight,* a national mutual fund newsletter.

Lowell has written and lectured extensively on investing and personal finance for national audiences, magazines, TV, radio, and online media including Bloomberg (radio and TV), CNN, and CNBC. His market views and opinions appear frequently in such publications as *Barrons, Business Week, The New York Times, The Wall Street Journal, Fortune, Investment News, Money,* and *Smart Money,* to name but a few. He has given numerous speeches, most recently (December '05) to the annual CFA Boston Chapter event and the AAII.

Mr. Lowell is also partner and chief investment strategist of Adviser Investment Management, a private money management fee-only firm advising on over $900 million, based in Watertown, Massachusetts. (Adviser Investment Management receives no fees or compensation from any fund family, nor does it sell or promote investment or insurance products. It is a fee-only firm.) Before joining Adviser Investment Management, Lowell was the chief portfolio strategist for the Boston-based investment division of Adams, Harkness & Hill.

He is also the president of FundWorks, Inc., a financial publishing firm, and was the featured contributing editor for the *Investment Advisor* magazine (ia-mag.com), where he focused on equities, closed- and open-end funds, and exchange-traded funds. Mr. Lowell's columns were frequently used for the CFP (Certified Financial Planner) credit requirement for continuing education. He is also the author of the College of Financial Planning's Exchange-Traded Funds curricula.

Lowell was formerly employed by Fidelity, where he was the senior financial reporter for *Investment Vision* and the formative stages of *Worth* magazine.

Lowell has both his Series 7 and 65 securities licenses. He was educated at Vassar College (BA), and holds master's degrees from both Harvard University and Trinity College (Dublin, Ireland). In addition, Lowell is a published poet, a former teaching fellow at Harvard University, and former lecturer in the Philosophy/Religion Department at Northeastern University College in Boston. He is an accomplished sport fisherman. Mr. Lowell lives west of Boston, Massachusetts—a stone's throw from the hub of the mutual fund industry.

JAMES LOWELL

INVESTING FROM SCRATCH

A Handbook for the Young Investor

• REVISED EDITION •

PENGUIN BOOKS

PENGUIN BOOKS

Published by the Penguin Group

Penguin Group (USA) Inc., 375 Hudson Street, New York, New York 10014, U.S.A.
Penguin Group (Canada), 90 Eglinton Avenue East, Suite 700, Toronto, Ontario, Canada
M4P 2Y3 (a division of Pearson Penguin Canada Inc.)
Penguin Books Ltd, 80 Strand, London WC2R 0RL, England
Penguin Ireland, 25 St Stephen's Green, Dublin 2, Ireland (a division of Penguin Books Ltd)
Penguin Group (Australia), 250 Camberwell Road, Camberwell, Victoria 3124, Australia
(a division of Pearson Australia Group Pty Ltd)
Penguin Books India Pvt Ltd, 11 Community Centre, Panchsheel Park,
New Delhi - 110 017, India
Penguin Group (NZ), cnr Airborne and Rosedale Roads, Albany, Auckland 1310, New Zealand
(a division of Pearson New Zealand Ltd)
Penguin Books (South Africa) (Pty) Ltd, 24 Sturdee Avenue, Rosebank, Johannesburg 2196,
South Africa

Penguin Books Ltd, Registered Offices:
80 Strand, London WC2R 0RL, England

First published in Penguin Books 1997
This revised edition published 2007

10   9   8   7   6   5   4   3   2   1

Graphs from Fidelity Investor

Publisher's Note
This publication is designed to provide accurate and authoritative information in regard to the
subject matter covered. It is sold with the understanding that the publisher is not engaged in
rendering legal, accounting, or other professional services. If you require financial advice or
other expert assistance, you should seek the services of a competent professional.

LIBRARY OF CONGRESS CATALOGING IN PUBLICATION DATA
Lowell, James, 1960–
Investing from scratch : a handbook for the young investor / James Lowell.—Rev. ed.
p. cm.
Includes bibliographical references and index.
ISBN 0 14 30.3684 X
1. Investments—United States—Handbooks, manuals, etc. I. Title.
HG4921.L69 2006
363.25—dc22 2006044825

Printed in the United States of America
Set in Minion
Designed by Victoria Hartman

ACKNOWLEDGMENTS

Investing from Scratch is a handbook to securing your financial future, and it was written by me since I couldn't find any resource that helped me do what I needed to do when I first wrote it: Start!

Since the first edition of *Scratch* rolled off the presses, much has changed both in the markets and in my professional career, which has, almost exclusively, been devoted to investing wisely and well.

I'm fortunate to have many colleagues and friends who are in the business of thinking about and acting on the markets at home and abroad. My right and left hands at FundWorks, Inc., David Cohne and Karen Frost, are two oars in the water without whom I'd be rowing in circles or standing still.

My partners in two significant businesses outside of FundWorks, Inc. are constant sources of new angles and ideas. Dan Wiener, the leading independent authority on Vanguard funds, and the editor of the multiple award-winning *The Independent Adviser for Vanguard Investors* (www.adviseronline.com), is the Lance Armstrong of business cycles and risk-adjusted returns; David Thorne, a quixotic Gandalph trespassing lightly in circles of power and knowing is a mover of molehills and mountains; Dan Silver's mastery of cross-border mergers has created an emerging market he carefully presides over; John Mileszko's ability to pitch any batter puts Kurt Schilling to shame and makes him an easy candidate for any managing director's hall of fame. Bud Sheppard is the most mindfully dogged and determined revolutionary this side of 1776; may his regard for doing what is right meet with the rewards he justly deserves.

All the above lent various degrees of energy and support for this book in particular and my life's work in general, and I remain deeply thankful to each.

At Penguin, there have been so many hands involved in the process that it's hard to single any one person out, but Alicia Bothwell Mancini's editorial and copyediting investment in the revised edition's process were key to getting the book done and delivered.

Finally, I'd like to acknowledge all the readers of the first edition of *Investing from Scratch*; your comments and insights helped shaped this edition. I welcome new readers to comment and help shape the next one!

I can be reached at jlowell@fidelityinvestor.com.

CONTENTS

Investing from Scratch

INTRODUCTION

Investing from Scratch Works!

When I wrote *Investing from Scratch* the first time around (1997), the mood on Wall Street and Main was exuberant—in fact, the phrase "irrational exuberance" was coined in 1996 to describe what many thought was a market bubble about to burst. Hindsight tells us that the definition of such irrational exuberance was early—by four manic market years. In fact, in 1997, 1998, and 1999 the markets went from irrational to zany brainy, and the end result was the most recent example of a market bubble.

Pop!

In 1999 the market took its own version of dot-com ecstasy and soared to higher highs that only Icarus would have dissed. During that rage, it seemed like a monkey could have made more money in a matter of months than any uncle of mine made in his lifetime. And given that, despite evolution's best efforts to the contrary, we're still knuckle draggers when it comes to monkey see, monkey do. The net result of the market bubble of 1999 was that by the end of 2000 many investors opened their year-end statements to the tune of "Yes, We Have No Bananas." And, fittingly, by the end of 2003, Zany Brainy had declared bankruptcy and shut its doors.

THE GLASS IS ALWAYS HALF FULL

Living through a market bubble is an invaluable experience—once you've done that, you ought to be all the wiser (albeit none the richer) for it. That wisdom, put to work in today's (or any day's) market, will not only help you be better at charting a course that can take you from your objectives to your goals—but it can also help you stay the course when the going gets tough. And any chart of the market that incorporates a minimum of five years' worth of history reveals that the going always gets tough. But you'd have to go back to December 7, 1941, to account for the ways in which markets would react to the unexpected terrorist attack on September 11, 2001.

The market was already in bear market mode (having sold off more than 20% from its March 2000 high—10% being the technical indicator of a correction, and 20% loss being the definition of a bear market), when the unprecedented 9/11 attack struck the heart of American business and America. In the immediate aftermath, one didn't have to have a calculator to add up the toll that the event would take when the markets eventually reopened ten days later. But those who rushed to sell on the news of the worst foreign attack on domestic ground in recent American history, surpassing the toll of Pearl Harbor, and directly targeting civilians as opposed to military personnel, assumed that recovery would be years in the making. But history shows that this was a major miscalculation—and that those who wound up selling their shares the day the market opened did so at the worst possible time. In fact, after the first few days of selling pressure in the wake of 9/11, the market staged a remarkable rally that led to a 10.5% gain before 2001's end. True, 2002 was another difficult market—but one could already sense by then that we were building the groundwork for the next bull market. And in 2003, that's just what we got.

The most obvious seeds of the bull market's destruction were sown well in advance of the unexpected attack. In fact, it was sown by an enemy within our own markets: brokerage firms and their hawking of dot-com stocks for no other reason than their insatiable quest for more money in their coffers—and with typical disregard for individual investors' savings. Brokers, it seems, are still consistently good at one thing—leaving their clients broker.

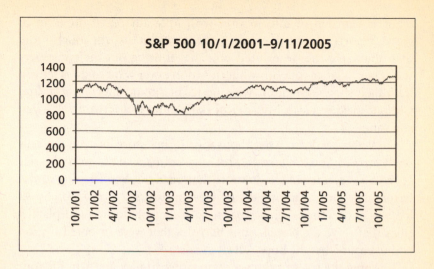

S&P 500 10/1/2001–9/11/2005

Along with the old saw that a rising tide lifts all boats is a counter saw that everyone aboard this titanic vessel was underestimating: A receding tide sinks all boats. Readers of this book, however, should have been more than able to remain afloat during the bear market's ebb tide by virtue of several lessons contained herein—not the least of which is that bear and bull markets happen. There is no such thing as a market that only goes up—any more than there is a market that only goes down. Markets do both every day—which is easy to understand once you know that for every buyer there is a seller and vice versa. Our job as investors is always to ask of the seller, "Why are you willing to sell at this price?" and of the buyer, "Why are you willing to buy at this price?"

Getting answers to these two basic questions keeps tens of thousands of people employed year in and year out. Not that they ever get the answer right. In fact, weathermen have a better chance at getting their forecast right than the seven-figure wunderkinds of Wall Street do with theirs. Such analysis is basically a marketing vehicle with one purpose: to keep you coming back to the store for more. In this case, the store is the brokerage firms whose shelves are stockpiled with stocks they recommend based on their analysis. What they won't tell you is that they get paid whether you win or lose—and that the stock may be in companies that the brokerage got paid to bring to the market in the first place. Skeptical? They'll bring out the research reports: a torrent of information with little advice, all done up in glossy reports that, at the end of the day, aren't worth much more than the paper they're printed on. They'll bring out their salesperson. They'll flatter you. But what they don't ever want to do is let you leave their showroom floor (whether it's brick-and-mortar or online) without making a sale. My advice? Bail. You can do it yourself—yes, you can.

Or, better yet, learn what thousands of investors like you have already learned: You can take control of your financial life, from the get-go, without ever having to do more than read this book. Doing so will ensure that you are among the savviest investors, a group Wall Street loathes since informed investors tend to be able to live and play by rules that serve them well—not by rules that were invented by, for, and to ensure that the house always wins.

Learning the rules of the game, in order to play and win on your own, is what *Investing from Scratch* is all about. As such, it's about liberation, empowerment, and controlling your life's current and future path.

One other major development since I last took pen to paper (okay—mouse to pad) is that the market has been plagued with dirty rotten scoundrels and sensational scandals. Those who tried to be both referee and player racked up some wins against those who did business the legal way, not making up the rules as they went along. Of course, crooks and crooked schemes have as long a history as the market itself—and they usually reach their crescendo at the same time as the market does—so it's not surprising that such scandals were baking inside the market pie long before it was taken out of the bullishly hot oven and put on the regulatory table for all to see.

DISCLOSURE PROS AND CONS

As a result of the scandals of the last bull market, I think we're on the verge of a revolutionary change (for the better) in the way the investment industry does business with us.

Disclosure of Fund Fees and Brokerage Incentives

Charging high fees for poor fund products is a prime example of how brokers leave their clients broker. Furthermore, the truth of the matter is that most brokers are not paid to provide independent advice; they're paid based on the amount of products that they can sell from a product lineup not of their own making. Hence, I do think that disclosing all fees and sales incentives is a crucial aspect of ensuring that investors know the price of what they're paying for—but that alone hardly enables the individual investor to know more about what they own and why they're being told to own it. In fact, fees are only a fraction of the potential cost of investing or not investing in any given fund. For example, you could be paying a very low fee for a given fund but the toll of that initial low fee could be a significantly greater cost in terms of actual losses or missed gains, the result of fund performance. Why not establish a requirement for third-party, independent analysis of all funds sold, along the lines of what is required for stocks, so that investors can rest assured that they're buying on the merits of the product, rather than the salesmanship skills of their "adviser"?

Know all the above and always ask your broker or adviser if he owns any of the funds he's telling you to own. If not, why not? Also, be sure to ask your financial adviser to go on the record—personally, and for his firm—stating that they have never late-traded or used sweetheart market-timing deals for their own benefit, nor invested in hedge funds that did so.

Disclosure of Fund Rating Services' Conflicts of Interest

Unfortunately, I think that the leading fund rating services have a major conflict of interest with the fund firms they're supposed to be independently rating. And they don't disagree with this view. Don Phillips, managing director of Morningstar, states that regarding the "question of potential conflicts, I'd say that most businesses have them. The key is how you manage them."

Bottom line: Rating services ought to disclose the extent to which their business depends for revenues on the very firms they claim to be "independently" rating. Investors who look to rating services with the assumption that they're independent need to know in plain English what the various financial relationships are with the fund firms they're claiming to be independently rating. Also, since rating services are clamoring for disclosure of manager and director ownership of the funds they oversee, it would be interesting to know to what extent such rating services eat their own cooking. Do the owners and directors of such services own their own top-rated funds, or any funds? If not, then I guess all they do is only academic. Trouble is, in the real world, it's nice to know that your adviser can feel your pain—and gain.

Disclosure of Fund Managers' Ownership in Their Own Funds

A good idea in that it lets investors know whether the manager eats his or her own cooking, and with what degree of gusto. But just because a manager owns a large piece of her own pie doesn't mean that, performance-wise, that pie would or should be to anyone else's liking. There are many managers who own a significant piece of their own fund, but its performance nonetheless has been consistently poor relative to appropriate market benchmarks and peer groups. Sour grapes.

Demand manager accountability, but do so with regard to her stock picking as opposed to her personal savings skills. If our phone numbers can be federally mandated to be portable, why can't the career performance numbers of every manager be portable and transparent?

Disclosure of a Fund's "Independent" Directors' Ownership

Also welcome, but again fails to meet the litmus test of what would constitute a worthwhile investment. Just because directors own a piece of a fund they're overseeing doesn't necessarily mean that anyone should want to invest in that fund. More critically, we need to ensure that such directors are truly independent, acting in the best interest of fund shareholders rather than catering to the fund firms that pay them hefty compensation despite their nominal "independence."

Demand that the lion's share of fund directors be independent, but when investing, use such information with a grain of salt.

Disclosure of Manager Performance

We, the investing public, have a right to know all the above information, and I hope that the current investigations, pending regulations, and ongoing restitutions and resolutions will ensure that this is so. However, since the inception of the fund industry, firms have been content to mask individual manager performance records with fund performance numbers for the benefit of the firm, and more often than not, at the expense of the individual shareholder. As Fidelity president Abigail Johnson stated on Marketwatch.com in 2004, "This is a business where you get a chance to build a track record. You do your research, you make your recommendations or you buy your stocks and you live with your moves, and your success or failure against the benchmarks is right out there to be seen." Unfortunately, the fund industry and the major fund rating services don't actually let individual investors ever see these records.

When you get on a Greyhound bus, of course you know that that particular bus has never been totaled, but wouldn't you still care if your driver had never handled a bus before—or worse, had totaled a different bus? Likewise, none of the other types of disclosure mentioned above will likely provide you with the one piece of information you need to know: whether your fund's "driver" has a history of falling asleep at the wheel, or a history of beating his benchmarks and meeting his objectives safely and securely.

Demand complete performance histories of each and every manager you invest in, and demand that it be portable and visible in every fund prospectus. Never let a dollar leave your wallet without it. Also, always assume that every time a dollar does leave your wallet, there's a broker or fund firm eager to tell you where you can spend it. Hopefully, in light of recent developments, you'll be able to tell those who are unwilling to disclose all of the above exactly where they can, er, shove it.

With full disclosure, you can get to the truth about which investments make the most sense for you and your objectives. But before you get there, you need to know the truth about investing itself.

The Truth about Investing

The truth about investing is plain and simple: Investing works! Long term, it can be the smartest move you'll ever make—no matter if heaven or hell has broken loose. And since you spend so much of your life making money, why not have it return the favor in the best way that it can—by growing.

Of course, growing assets doesn't happen overnight. Success isn't guaranteed. Selecting winning investments isn't as easy as some friend's drunk uncle might have you believe. But it's not nearly as hard as everyone wants you to think.

Choosing the best types of investments for your specific objectives requires a solid grasp of some investing fundamentals. And guess what I just happen to have up my sleeve?

SOME INVESTING FUNDAMENTALS

1. *Caveat emptor.* The phrase *caveat emptor,* which means "buyer beware," is written in every investment brick that you select to help you build your portfolio. Over time, investing in stocks has proven to be the best way to grow your money. True, there are other options, and some (bonds, for example), in conjunction with stock-based investments (i.e., stocks or stock mutual funds), can help you reduce the overall risks associated with investing while helping you achieve a decent return on your money—far more decent than a bank CD. But, unlike a bank CD, no investments, not even a mutual fund money market (not to be confused with a bank money market) are insured. If you're not careful, you could end up owning a worthless piece of paper instead of your ticket to a financially secure future.

2. *Risk and return go hand in hand.* Not all investments are created equal—and no one investment is right for everyone. There's a lot you should know about investing, before you invest a single dollar in any one type of investment. But even before you begin to invest, you can begin to envision the probable consequences of your inaction. For example, if your parents had invested $1,000 back when you were born (for argument's sake, let's say twenty-five years ago) in a bank savings account earning approximately 1% per year, it would have been worth more than $1,282 today. That's a sizable sum—enough for a down payment on that Jeep Rubicon you've been eyeing. But what if, instead of taking the safest route in the market, your parents went off-roading and invested that same $1,000 in a stock mutual fund that invested in large-cap stocks (as represented by the S&P 500 index). That $1,000 would be worth $25,563 today—enough for a down payment on a house with a garage big enough for that Rubicon.

Now, think what you can do for your future by investing today. Think big!

3. *Fools don't rule.* There are still no foolproof investment strategies—but there are still plenty of fools. Learning several invest-

ment strategies that have proven to be reliable and successful over long periods of time (accounting for varied market and economic conditions) will help ensure that you can rule the fools, and not be ruled by them. This book will tell you not only which strategies are worth your time and effort, it will also spotlight some of the more common scams that lead too many unwitting investors (and their money) down a dead-end road. One of the best? Diversification (chapter 16). The bottom line is that diversification can work in your favor. What is it? Simply put, it's the division of your assets into several different types of investments. The theory being that when one investment is slipping from favor, another is often gaining ground, the net result being that your gains can offset your losses over time.

4. *Knowledge counts.* A little knowledge can go a long way. You don't need a PhD in economics to invest wisely and well. But you will need to bring yourself up to speed on some of the most prevalent themes that shape the markets you're investing in. Doing so requires a basic understanding of how economies (ours and others') work to shape the various markets where investment opportunities lurk.

5. *Some risks are worth taking—some are not.* The more rapidly you want your assets to grow, chances are the more risks you'll have to take. Some of the risks are definitely worth taking. Others you should absolutely avoid. For example, the risks of small-cap value stocks have been well rewarded, whereas the risks of holding gold bullion have not. This book will help you select the types of investments and strategies that best suit your goals and objectives. (Don't know what your goals and objectives are? Chapter 4 can help.)

6. *Invest in stocks, bonds, and real estate—in that order as you age.* Stocks, bonds, and real estate are the three main categories of investments. Of these three, real estate requires the most money to get started, is the least liquid, and has a history of disappointing those who thought they could rely on property as their primary source of retirement savings. Most bonds also require a lot of up-front capital to get started (although bond funds are a less expensive way to participate). And bonds have (historically) performed less well than stocks over the long run, and are not as safe as many people mistakenly believe them to be. Stocks require the least amount of money to get started in and provide the greatest potential for profit, and are therefore the most appropriate area of the market for you, at this stage in your life, to concentrate your money in—once you know what you're doing!

7. *Risk, liquidity, and return.* Every investment, like every relationship, has three ingredients that you need to know before you jump in.

- **Risk.** What are you getting yourself into? Every investment type comes equipped with its own risks. For example, the risk of a stock investment is that the stock will decline in value from the time you purchase it to the time you sell it. Of course, the value of the stock will fluctuate—sometimes dramatically—over the life of your ownership of it. A higher-risk stock will not necessarily provide a higher return, although it often will, while a lower-risk stock may not give you an adequate return. Knowing how much risk you can afford to take, and keeping your eye on the prize of a self-determined life, will help you create a balanced portfolio of stocks, bonds, and mutual funds.
- **Liquidity.** How easily can you get out if you have to? How easily and quickly you can convert your investment to cash may be an important consideration for those just starting out. For example, a car is a less liquid investment than a stock because you can sell the stock or share in a stock or bond mutual fund in a minute, whereas the car might take months to sell. Of course, the longer you keep your money in a good investment, the better off you will be—at least up to a point. When it comes to a return on your investment, a car won't get you very far, but stock investing will.
- **Return.** What's in it for you? The expected interest and dividends you receive on your investment, plus appreciation (or depreciation), is referred to as the return on your investment. A healthy return is your reward for selecting top-performing investments.

SOME BASIC STEPS TO INVESTING SUCCESS

Make no mistake, investing is the best way to build a better life for yourself. There's no real mystery to investing wisely and well—just the simple truth that you need to do so, now. This book will help you familiarize yourself with the range of investment vehicles you can use to help you get where you want to go (financially speaking)—as well as avoid those "opportunities" that promise a primrose path but deliver dirt. The following eleven-step plan will help you put investing in perspective right from the start.

1. The crowd isn't always wrong, but it's seldom the best thing to follow. More investors begin to invest when the market is at or nearing a peak (the least optimal time to do so, since they're paying a higher purchasing price), and the least number of investors buy at the bottom. Think of it this way: Most investors are like Christmas shoppers—those who purchase wrapping paper for their December 2005 presents in January of 2005 will pay about half as much as those who buy their wrapping paper in the latter months of the year. Same paper. Same function. But one can obtain greater value by purchasing at a lower price.

2. You can make your own investment decisions. And it won't take you two years and a degree to do it. Making your own investment decisions doesn't have to mean spending hours in front of CNBC watching the ticker run on all the exchanges. In fact, such daily nail biting is much more trouble than it's worth. This book will help you focus on the best ways to build a portfolio that can last, with some modifications, for the rest of your life.

3. You know what's in your best interest—and a broker rarely does. Successful investing, whether you invest yourself or use an investment adviser in tandem with your own research, must always be measured in proportion to your achievement of your objectives (the broker could care less if you meet your objectives, since that individual is busy trying to fulfill his or her own goals—with your money). In section 1, you'll find several strategies for developing objectives—and achieving them. Why is it so important to decide what your objectives are? Your objectives will dictate what your investments need to accomplish. (Not vice versa.)

4. The ultimate objective is to reach retirement with all the sources of income you'll ever need—no matter what event arises. Of course, like a sailor who aims to go around the world, you can only plan for so many unforeseen circumstances, together with the foreseen ones. Looking ahead, anticipating obstacles, preparing now to overcome them, that's what you need to do. No one else can or will do it for you.

5. Typically, the best investments aren't the hyped stocks or mutual funds that everyone is talking about. This month's top per-

former is seldom next month's. And while it is true that, in some rare instances, this proves to be the case for a string of months, rarely does the string last long. Look beyond the hype. There are plenty of stocks and funds that have delivered solid results over the long term—far surpassing the spectacular gain of a short-lived darling.

6. Good investments are rarely cloaked. By and large, the best investments are in name brands, known industries, and services and products that have a clear business or consumer demand. Occasionally, a technological revolution and the products (like software for the Internet) that attend it will become profitable. Mostly, it's solid, sober stuff, not the kinds of investments that you have to buy and sell all the time.

7. Always consider the toll inflation and taxes may take. Many investors forget to benchmark the returns they get on their investments to inflation. Others forget to take into consideration the fact that they will pay taxes on their portfolio sooner or later.

8. Use automatic investing and dollar-cost averaging to achieve your goals—both your immediate one of being a more disciplined and regular investor, and your longer-term goal of financial security.

9. Don't confuse saving with investing. In terms of discipline and chicken-and-egg logic, you have to save to invest, but that's where the relationship between the two ends. A savings account may play a role in your overall investment program, but it should be a specific one—relegated to your bill-paying budget and emergency accounts. The lion's share of your "savings" should be invested in order to ensure that your investments will grow sufficiently to help you achieve your financial goals.

10. Patience brings lasting rewards. Always take a long-term view on your investments. Overreacting to current market moves can have devastating consequences to your overall portfolio.

11. Forget slacking. Financial independence is actually getting harder to achieve. That's one reason why investing is more important today than ever before.

Getting Started

To begin with, you need to get your overall financial house in order and develop some clear-cut immediate, intermediate, and long-term objectives. Your ultimate objective should be to increase your investment know-how and maximize your actual investing.

Section 1 will help you review your current financial condition, in order to ensure that you have the right balance between what is immediately due and payable (from your rent or mortgage to your credit cards) and what you hope to achieve in the longer term—for example, home ownership, college funding for any little ones (real or imagined), and yes, a financially secure retirement. After all, if you can't afford to pay this month's bills, you're not going to be doing yourself any favor by investing in some hot stock tip with the hope of striking it rich. (Rarely does this happen.) Instead, focus on a slow and steady pace to win the race.

Section 2 will bring you up to speed on some basic economic and investment themes and strategies. After reading this section, you'll be able to understand why the Federal Reserve chairman is among the most important world leaders. You'll no longer be uncertain about just how a leading economic indicator is akin to a prospector's headlamp when it comes to spotlighting better and worse investments. You'll also develop a better understanding of how uncertainty can work in your favor when it comes to selecting some undervalued or overlooked investment opportunities.

Wrapping your mind around the world of investing in general will lead you to section 3, which covers the best types of investments for your particular objectives. Some of what you read there may surprise you. While the "experts" will tell you that there are three main categories of investments—stocks, bonds, and real estate—they seldom tell you which category is most appropriate for you. Each category does present numerous types of investment opportunities, but the fact is that some are more appropriate for younger, less moneyed investors. The upshot is that most expert advice is generic, canned, and unfocused when it comes to you and your goals. For example, while bonds may be an appropriate part of an overall portfolio for someone who is forty-five years or older, they're seldom right, even in small portions, for the younger investor. Why? They're simply too conservative (a risk you can afford not to take). Real estate is another prime example of a type of investment that's seldom suitable for younger investors—unless it's your primary residence. Investing in real estate costs huge bucks—no matter what those "no money down" gurus try to sell you. (Chances are, they make their real money selling seminars on how to make money in real estate, not on investing in real estate themselves.) However, just because these two categories may not be best for you today, that doesn't mean that there aren't several benefits to learning about them and, in a few instances, perhaps even investing in them.

Stock investments, and in particular, stock mutual funds, are a smart, cost-effective, profit-proven way to invest your money. Mutual funds aren't simply the rage—they're a great way to start and continue to invest in your own future. Mutual funds offer you the ability to get into the market (stock, bond, and real estate) with small amounts of money and, at the same time, participate in a diverse range of investments. Basically, a share in a mutual fund represents a slice of the fund's overall investment pie. The value of your share relates to the total value of the fund's investments. It's hard to say enough great things about mutual funds—especially for younger investors. But there are some pitfalls you'll need to know about in order to ensure that you can avoid them. Ditto exchange-traded funds, which act like a mutual fund, but trade like a stock.

Section 4 will help you become an investment detective. You'll learn how to view each investment idea as if it's a crime scene where the victim could be you. You'll detect clues that will help you solve the mystery of what is (and isn't) a profitable investment. You'll also learn about several ways that you can invest—from hiring someone to do the work for you to controlling your investment decisions to investing in line (and online) with your financial objectives and your ethical intentions.

Section 5 provides the scoop on the best ways to invest in your ultimate investment objective—a financially secure future. Doing so requires that you learn how to select one or more of the several tax-advantaged investment accounts available to you—whether they're offered by your employer (in the form of a 401(k) or 403(b) plan) or whether you offer them to yourself (in the form of IRAs). No matter what, you don't want to miss out on the advantages such plans provide.

Section 6 will help you understand the tax consequences of investing wisely and well—and how you can benefit from investments that have turned out to be duds. While taxes are hardly on everyone's hit list of things to get psyched about, it's in your best interest to know what investment-related tax moves make the most sense for you and your money.

Section 7 will help you cover a new base—your home base in the event that, since reading *Investing from Scratch* the first time, you now have more than your own mouth to feed and your own life to consider when making investment decisions.

Each section of the book, and every chapter, is designed to be read alone or in relation to the others. The latter, holistic approach is the better one to take, since investing is part of your overall financial planning process, and selecting particular investments requires that you understand more than its parts alone. The best way to begin to take control of your financial future is to know which investment moves make the most sense for you—as well as being able to avoid those that don't. Take this book with you to work. Stuff it in your knapsack on your next weekend getaway. Keep it close by. Read it. Why?

The more informed you are about investing, the more likely you will be to achieve the ultimate financial objective: your life on your terms. You can get there from here so long as you understand that investing provides you with the basic ingredients you need to make a better life for yourself—from Scratch.

SECTION 1

A Primer on Your Future Well-Being

CHAPTER 1

Your Life from Scratch

How can you begin to think about investing before you have paid the rent or mortgage—let alone the hundred dollars you owe your friend for last night's low-carb beer binge? Managing your monthly living expenses will no doubt prove to be an ongoing challenge. But it won't be your last financial challenge. Instead, it will be one of many that you will encounter from here on out. The trick is to know what you can do to take the challenge, come out on top, and move on to the next level—a level that challenges you to do more for yourself (rather than for your landlord or banker) by investing in and for yourself.

Your future is not only now—*your future is you.* Knowing what financial responsibilities lie ahead can help you avoid costly collisions between your means and your short- and long-term dreams. No doubt, many financial responsibilities have already arrived on your doorstep. From the onset of adulthood, most of us are hit with the following mundane monthly expenses:

- Student loan payments
- Grocery bills
- Car payments
- Credit card bills
- Rent or mortgage payments
- Insurance bills
- Child care expenses
- Phone bills

In addition to these regular and recurring payments, there are "life experience" events—for example, embarking on a career, going to grad school, purchasing a home, getting married, having children—that can be costly, and without advance planning, troublesome.

Embarking on a career is perhaps your most important life experience, and already one you have no doubt revised several times. Starting a new career path is often a personally and financially exhausting pursuit. Planning for the related expenses of beginning (or changing) your career—from the cost of purchasing matching paper and envelopes for your resume to the cost of the infamous "interview suit" and a new pair of shoes—can help you manage your job search with greater personal and financial ease. This ease should translate into greater personal and hence professional poise. You won't be sitting in an interview wondering whether or not the bubble gum you used to plug the hole in the bottom of your shoe will stay in place, or if you can afford the cost of parking your car in that expensive lot.

The job of your dreams may not exactly enable you to live the lifestyle you most desire. It takes time to acquire a better standard of living, but it also takes planning. For example, knowing the average salary you can expect from your current or future career will help you frame your great expectations within the boundary of financial realism.

How can you get to know what the average salary for your chosen job is? Personal finance magazines (and their namesake e-zines), such as *Money* and *Smart Money* often do an annual survey of career-related pay. But you can do your own informal survey by asking your friends what they make. This is an especially good idea if one or more of your friends is in a field that interests you. Sure, it's a little embarrassing, but, hey, so is asking your parents to help you meet this month's rent. No friends? Just ask the research librarian at your local library for help in getting your hands on the facts and figures you need. They live for that kind of stuff, and the price—free—is right.

What other life experiences can you count on in your life? Take a look at the following list, and check which experiences you have already encountered or think you will more than likely encounter in the near future:

[ ] Renting a more expensive apartment
[ ] Buying a car
[ ] Paying your student loans

[ ] Taking out a personal loan
[ ] Paying taxes
[ ] Saving for a down payment on a home
[ ] Starting a retirement plan
[ ] Taking a vacation
[ ] Changing your job

These financially important life experiences are but a few of many. To make a more comprehensive list of common financial hurdles that you think you will encounter, get together with your friends and see what you can come up with. Distill from that list a more personalized one that details experiences you think you are most likely to meet. To do so, first divide your list into three sections: (1) experiences you're likely to encounter within one year (e.g., student loan payments, rent or mortgage, car loan); (2) experiences you're likely to encounter in one to five years (student loan payments, car loan, mortgage, retirement-oriented investing, graduate school); (3) experiences you're likely to encounter in five to ten years (student loan payments—undergraduate and graduate, car loan, mortgage, retirement-oriented investing, marriage, kids). Once done, take a look at your list and ask yourself the following question: What money-management and investment skills will you need to develop and put into practice in order to meet and master the costs of each event?

Chances are you will need to increase your knowledge of most or all of the following . . .

• Record keeping
• Budgeting
• Spending
• Bill paying
• Saving
• Insuring
• Investing

. . . so that you can increase your knowledge and practice of the following money-management skills . . .

• Balancing your checkbook
• Reconciling what you earn with what you owe

- Living a life you can actually afford
- Maintaining a good credit history
- Setting aside some of what you earn so that you can reach your personal goals
- Covering yourself and your assets from uninsured losses
- Investing in order to control your own financial destiny

Think about the best financial moves to make in the short, middle, and long run so you can win each leg of the race. After all, it's your race.

Segmenting the next ten years into three distinct parts is a great way to begin to map out your goals. The next chapter will go even further in helping you to determine what objectives and goals are, and what your own objectives and goals might be. Subsequent chapters will show you how to acquire and develop the spending, savings, and investment skills you'll need to invest your money wisely and well so that you can take control of your overall financial life and goals. *If you don't do it, no one else will.*

Investing and Your Life

Create an investment plan and stick to it—unless, of course, it isn't working. History has proven that maintaining a relatively stable mix of investments increases your likelihood of succeeding in the stock market. Fables tell us the same thing. Think of Aesop's "The Tortoise and the Hare." Slow and steady wins the race, while a fast pace often courts overconfidence and consequent losses. Prepare yourself for the race of your financial life.

Go.

1. Create an investment plan that relates and responds to your particular objectives and goals. This is crucial to your short- and long-term investment success. Why? Many investments are better suited for shorter and/or longer time frames. For example, if you are planning on returning to graduate school in two years, you don't want to invest in a bond that won't mature until ten years down the road. Instead, you will want to invest in a more liquid (easily sold) investment, like a bond mutual fund. You want to be sure that you are investing in order to meet your goals of a self-determined life.

2. Diversify—invest in a mix of investment types and categories. Diversification is also essential to achieving the best returns on your hard-earned dollars and is one key to investment success. Diversification is based on a down-home notion—never put all your eggs in the same basket. If you do, they might all get scrambled. Instead, spread your investment money around. A portion here, a portion there. Where? Well, you need to decide based on your goals and risk-taking ability. The process of deciding how much money you should place in given types of investments requires that you become familiar with the various available types of investments first. Following this, you will need to make the decision that's best for you. The actual process of divvying up your investment dollars and apportioning them to various investments is known as asset allocation. (For more on this, see chapter 16.)

3. Invest regularly and often. Automatic investing combined with dollar-cost averaging is a great way to ensure that you stay on the investment track that will lead you to your goals. (See chapter 17 for details.)

4. Invest in tax-advantaged IRAs and 401(k)s. They're an even smarter way to put your savings to work. Investing in your own retirement may sound like something you should postpone until you near retirement. But consider this. Suppose you opened an IRA at age twenty-three and deposited $2,000 in your account each year until you reached age thirty ($3,000 is the maximum you can contribute, but chances are that if you're just starting out, that's a sum that would stretch your financial life to the breaking point). You would—assuming you invested your money in mutual funds earning 8%—accumulate as much as someone who waited until age thirty to open an IRA and who put $2,000 aside each year until reaching age sixty-five! How can this be? It's the beneficial effect of compounding.

Here's another eye-opening table showing what the following annual investment earning 8% compounded daily will yield years down the road:

Per Year		You Will Have In	
You Deposit	10 years	20 years	25 years
$500	$8,024	$26,081	$42,333
$1,000	$16,048	$52,162	$84,665
$2,000	$32,096	$104,324	$169,330

Two thousand bucks a year?! Where are you going to get that amount of dough? For one thing, you don't have to come up with the lump sum all at once. For example, you could invest $166 each month (which totals $2,000 in twelve months' time). Think of it as a necessary bill that must be paid along with all your other bills—only this time, you are paying yourself! For another, why not consider getting a second job, the proceeds of which you invest in an IRA? Better yet, if your company offers you the opportunity to invest in a 401(k) or 403(b) plan, take advantage of it. Either way, you give yourself a tax break while at the same time investing in your own future. Good deal. You don't need $1 million to invest in stocks and bonds. You don't even need $100! The fact is that no matter how much or how little you have to invest, the time to start investing is sooner rather than later.

Ready Resources

- *The Complete Idiot's Guide to Making Money on Wall Street,* C. Heady
- *Your Money or Your Life,* Joe Dominguez and Vicki Robin
- *Lessons from the Art of Juggling: How to Achieve Your Full Potential in Business, Learning, and Life,* Michael J. Gelb and Tony Buzan

CHAPTER 2

Your Budget from Scratch

Life without a budget is like a plane without a fuel gauge. Life without investing is like a plane without fuel. If you don't balance your spending with your earnings, you will never save enough to invest, which is a sure way to crash land since you'll never know when you'll run out of juice.

Like a good record-keeping system, a budget is the sine qua non of solid money management, which, as you now know, is the necessary foundation for building a successful investment program. And since building a successful investment program is the only way to guarantee that you won't be homeless come retirement time, budgeting is a critical step in your overall financial and investment planning process. Yet surprisingly few people take time to create a budget—and even fewer take the time to create a budget that works for them in terms of enabling their money to do more for them in the present and not too distant future.

Creating a budget that works is hardly an exact science. First, you'll need to get used to balancing your earnings with your expenses, while at the same time ensuring that you have provided enough room to regularly invest a portion of your income. You should revisit your budget regularly so that you can stay on top of your debts in order to achieve a financially viable self-determined life through solid personal money management and regular investing.

The single greatest hindrance to a successful budget is trying to live on borrowed money. You don't have to watch *The Sopranos* to get the gut-wrenching gist of this. Sooner or later, you will overstep the boundary of reasonable expenditure and end up paying for it by having to drastically scale back your lifestyle or miss out on an opportunity that could change your life—like investing for your future. If you think I'm exaggerating, take a look at your peers. Are most of them happy in their work life? Lovin' every minute of getting up at the crack of dawn to get dressed in "their" new attire (which the department store owns, and which they still owe months of payments on), only to turn the key over in "their" leased car (which the bank owns and which they owe years of payments on), to find they're stuck in traffic making them late for work again, only to get to work to learn that there's a salary freeze going into effect immediately (meaning that they'll still owe a full day's work for no more pay . . . forever). Not!

Okay. So what do you think keeps them bound to the source of their Sisyphean unhappiness? (Freud's "Economic Problems of Masochism" won't furnish the answer—but it's worth reading.) Chances are these poor souls are stuck in the job of their means, rather than the job of their dreams, because they are so mired in debt they can't afford the time to find something more satisfying.

Profit from their example by avoiding their fate!

In fact, there's a good life lesson to be learned from your cash-strapped cohorts. Living beyond your budget can get you into financial trouble, if not downright peril. That's because living beyond your budget usually indicates living simultaneously beyond your income and your debt obligations. Many of us wait until the critical moment—a realization that we've run up our charge cards to the max and can't afford to pay even the minimum monthly amounts on each card—before we realize that the budget bell was tolling for us. In this, we aren't alone. As a matter of fact, we're emulating our elders. As a matter of course, we're living Madison Avenue's version of the American Dream—where the only dreams you can afford are what money can buy.

If you're looking around and wondering how those older than you achieve a lifestyle that they can't afford, the answer is simple. They do it the new-fashioned way—they charge it. Of course, charging what you can't afford to pay for necessarily entails living a lifestyle that you can't actually afford. There's a reason why Carrie Bradshaw was perpetually stressed despite all her sex in the city; she wasn't just trying to find her balance in platform Miu Miu shoes—she was perpetually unbalanced in terms of her zealous spending habits versus her down-to-earth income. Stumble, trip.

Many people who seem to have it all, in reality have very little or worse, only what they owe. This is because they charge everything from the clothes they wear to the DVDs they watch. They "charge" their car. Even their house may be used as collateral for charging such unnecessary items as boats, trips to the Caribbean, a sports car, or a new deck for the new grill for the new friends.

At the end of the day, if you were to add up all the objects that are unpaid for in the stable of what a person claims he or she "owns," you would most likely find that for the sake of truth and accuracy they should replace the word "own" with "OWE." (Visual aid: Rent *Bruce Almighty* and fast-forward to the Post-it scene and you'll see what I mean.)

Unless you buy your car, stereo, or new wardrobe with cash, you don't own what you're driving, listening to, or wearing—your creditors do. In fact, every time someone invites you to take a look at her new car, why not ask her if she has paid for it in full. If she has, fine and dandy. If she hasn't, then perhaps she should come and take a look at what you are doing with your money—i.e., saving it.

That's a far more impressive model.

Your net worth is a big-picture view of your overall financial condition. From this perspective you can begin to view your particular financial situation through the lens of a practical budget.

The following "Net Worth" worksheet will help you distinguish between what you own and what you owe. Note that you need to fill in the total outstanding balances (not minimum monthly payments) when it comes to your current liabilities. Don't be panicked if it's not a rosy picture. You will make it better in short order. I'll help.

First—gulp—you need to know what you're up against.

Your Net Worth Statement

ASSETS		LIABILITIES	
1. Savings	$ _____	1. Mortgage	$ _____
2. Investments (market value if sold today)	$ _____	2. Bank loans	$ _____
		3. Car loans/leases	$ _____

3. Car
   (sale value if owned) $ _____   4. Total credit debt
4. Home equity   A. $ _____
   (amount owed on   B. $ _____
   mortgage minus   C. $ _____
   original sale value   D. $ _____
   multiplied by 80%) $ _____   E. $ _____
                                  Total $ _____
5. Other   5. Income taxes $ _____
   (i.e., trust fund) $ _____   6. Student loans $ _____
6. TOTAL $ _____   7. TOTAL $ _____

NET WORTH
(subtract liabilities from assets): $ _____

Chances are you are in the red. Most people are. Now let's see how we can make your light turn green.

CREATING A LIVABLE BUDGET

A budget is a financial reality check—a check of your actual financial condition and your prognosis for future well-being. Your budgeting objective is to ensure that your expenses do not exceed your income, and to ensure that you save regularly so that you can invest often. If your budget is true to your current financial condition, it will help you see where you have overspent in the past so that you won't have to repeat the same mistake over and over again. It will help you see where you can cut costs and where you can pat yourself on the back for a job well done for putting your money to work for you. In short, the humble budget is an essential lens through which you can not only see your current financial condition, but prescribe a better way to achieve a cost-effective, wisely invested self-determined life for yourself.

Budgeting is elemental. There are two basic elements upon which every budget is based. First, the amount of income that you earn and, second, the ways that income will be put to use. When these two elements are combined, they should provide a commonsense, practical frame of reference for living within your means and investing on a regular basis. Knowing what you spend your money on will help you discern the difference between necessary and unnecessary expenditures. Once this is accomplished you will be better able to restore a balance between your earnings and your spending so that, at the end of the month, your income does not fall short of your obligations, your debts don't obligate you to fall short of your goals, and you have enough left over to invest at least 10% of your take-home pay.

Budget truthfully, sensibly, practically, and clearly. The more closely your budget reflects the actuality of your income and spending habits, the more helpful it will be to you. In fact, the very act of making a budget helps develop your money-management skills. After all, the more you think about your financial condition, the more likely you will be to make it work to your advantage.

The following monthly budget will help you ensure that your income surpasses your expenses so that you can invest the difference. Once mastered, you can rest assured that you will be well on your way to living a self-determined life. Also, remember that the sample budget is a monthly budget. Use your record-keeping file to create a realistic picture of your monthly expenses and income. This means that, unlike the net worth statement above, you need to list the monthly payments due—not the total balance owed.

Subtract your total fixed monthly expenses from your total monthly income to see how much is available to apply toward your irregular monthly expenses. By listing what you make and what you owe, you give yourself the advantage of knowing what you can and can't afford to spend your money on—and what you need to restrain yourself from. For example, if you know that you are going to have approximately $150 a month left over after paying your rent and bills, then you can plan on dividing that sum into the parts of your irregular expenses that you think are most in need. Likewise, if your monthly expenses exceed your monthly income, then you are in a bind unless and until you cut your expenses or increase your income.

Your Budget

Monthly Income
    Monthly take-home pay $ _____
    Other income $ _____

Total Monthly Income: $ _____

Fixed Monthly Expenses
    Rent or mortgage $ _____
    Food (groceries, snacks, Starbucks, etc.) $ _____
    Utilities $ _____
    Phone and/or cell phone $ _____
    Cable or satellite TV $ _____
    Internet $ _____
    Car loan $ _____
    Credit card(s) monthly payments $ _____
    Student loan $ _____
    Bank loan $ _____
    Entertainment (from DVDs to martinis) $ _____
    Gifts $ _____
    Vacation/travel $ _____
    5% of pay to your savings account $ _____
    5% to 10% of pay to your investment accounts:
        Retirement-oriented accounts $ _____
        Other investment accounts $ _____
    Health insurance (yearly cost ÷ 12) $ _____
    Car insurance (yearly cost ÷ 12) $ _____
    Renter's insurance (yearly cost ÷ 12) $ _____
    Other fixed monthly expenses $ _____

Total Fixed Monthly Expenses: $ _____

Irregular Monthly Expenses
    Emergency fund $ _____
    Gas $ _____
    Laundry $ _____
    Clothing $ _____
    Car maintenance $ _____
    Medical/dental co-pays $ _____
    Goals (see chapter 4) $ _____
    Tuition for continuing education $ _____
    Club membership dues $ _____
    Other irregular monthly expenses $ _____

Total Irregular Monthly Expenses: $ _____

STAYING ON TARGET

Luke Skywalker went to manual. Frodo never had a new Palm Pilot. No matter what you do, don't think that someone else is going to be there to give you the answers to your own financial destiny. Instead, take matters into your own hands.

Let the following be your guide.

1. Do track your spending. Review your income, spending, saving, and investing patterns monthly. Discern patterns of necessary and unnecessary spending.

2. Don't carry a wad of cash in your pocket. Carrying a lot of money in your pocket is tiresome. Cash weighs so much that it's plumb hard to walk a mile without lightening the load. Who can blame you? Spend, spend, spend. Carry only what you intend to spend—and know what you intend to spend it on before you withdraw it.

3. Don't carry your ATM card. Don't? How can you live? How can you be expected to go on? No ATM card? What if you pass a café, and are literally dying for lack of your vente skinny triple-shot vanilla latte with two cubes? How can you go on?

Hey. It's your money. Just remember, *what you spend today you won't have tomorrow.* Carrying your ATM card only increases your chances of spending beyond your plans and means. A minirecipe for financial disaster—that's what an ATM card is.

4. Don't shop retail when discounts are available. While it's tempting to stray from your budget—especially when it comes to clothes and clothing sales—if you must stray, stray into a discount or outlet store. Buying retail (and even at a 30% off "sale" in a mainline retail store you're likely to be spending more than at a discount or outlet store) is a quick way to make a sinkhole out of a savings account. Also, don't forget that there's a big difference between saving money and "saving" money by *spending* it on a "sale."

5. Do establish a regular investment schedule that matches your ability to invest. Typically, setting up an automatic investment account (through your checking account or via a money market mutual fund) is an excellent way to keep on schedule. Of course, you'll need to be certain that the resources are in the account to begin with.

6. Do participate in a 401(k) or 403(b) or IRA tax-advantaged, retirement-oriented account. The benefit of the first two plans is that you may qualify for matching funds and have the investment amount (typically from 2% to 10% of your pay) automatically deducted. But if no such plan is available to you, there are solid options. (Section 5 provides the details.)

Remember when you realized that joining the words "now" and "here" spelled "nowhere." That was cool. But no longer. Your future is now, but living in the now, without a budget that accounts for your current income, present debt obligations, and investing to meet your future expenses, will get you nowhere fast. On the other hand, living within the guidelines of your budget will enable you to take corrective action on any existing or potential debt and/or cash flow problems so that you can pick up the pace toward achieving your short- and long-term investment goals here and now.

READY RESOURCES

If you want to get a grip on better budgeting, you might try your library or area bookstores for the following books, which are chock-full of sample budgets.

Budget worksheets (you'll need Microsoft Excel): txstate.edu/osp/budget/budget_index.htm

- *How to Survive in the Real World,* James Lowell
- *The Common Cents Money Management/Workbook,* Judy Lawrence
- *Making the Most of Your Money,* Jane Bryant Quinn
- *The Tightwad Gazette,* Amy Dacyczyn
- *Your Money or Your Life,* Joe Dominguez and Vicki Robin
- *Make Your Paycheck Last,* Jason R. Rich
- *Saving on a Shoestring: How to Cut Expenses,* B. O'Neill
- *Penny Pinchers Almanac Handbook,* Penny Pinchers
- *1001 Ways to Cut Your Expenses,* Jonathan Pond

CHAPTER 3

Your Benefits from Scratch

From your budget (as detailed in the prior chapter), we move on to your benefits in this chapter.

One of the best things you can do for your financial well-being is to get the most out of benefits offered at your job. Many are free or require a minimal contribution to begin to take advantage of what they offer. Other benefits may be offered at a discount. Working for a company means being part of a group, and group benefit plans are often less expensive than individual policies. Picking the right health plan, and dental plan, and life and disability insurance can save you money and increase your peace of mind. That's a good investment by any standard.

It's also crucial to study and take advantage of various retirement and profit-sharing plans. Failing to understand these plans can mean throwing money out the window. And that hardly fits with your goal of taking advantage of what you have now in order to get what you want in the future. Certain benefits may also be offered before taxes, enabling you to maximize your take-home pay and save money.

But that's all well said and not as easily done. The truth about benefits is that they're hard to understand—despite the best-laid plans of office and man. (If you've never had to slog through a benefits plan, you can go to howardcc.edu/hr/Benefits/benefits_guides.htm to see what you're up against.)

Don't worry if you don't fully understand all your benefits or how they work for you. Most of us don't. Don't worry if learning about them seems about as thrilling as having your teeth pulled. It won't hurt a bit. In fact, if I've done my job right, you'll not only have some fun learning about this critical piece of your overall financial plan, you'll also end up with more money in your pocket at the end of this book than when you began reading it. Wow—a course of study that doesn't drain money from your savings but can actually end up putting more money in there? I like the sound of that.

A first step is to stop looking at your employee benefits as separate, stand-alone programs. Sure. One of the biggest reasons you're focused on benefits is that they offer you or your family cost-efficient access to a doctor or a hospital. If you didn't purchase a medical plan from your employer, you would be paying more for medical care or avoiding treatment altogether because it would be too costly. But that's exactly the point of employee benefits—to lower your costs of living so that you have more pay to do with what you want.

Employee benefits can help you achieve a certain quality of life— help you realize your dreams. Benefits offer some amount of financial support from your employer while you're working and after you decide to leave full-time work. When you look at your benefits in this new way—as integrated programs that can save you hard-earned pay today and help stretch your savings to last a lifetime—you're ready to begin to make the most of what your employer gives you or asks you to buy.

The following section will help you see your benefits plan in a new light and offer guidance on how to manage benefits. It will bring you up to speed on all the essential benefit tools—your benefit-planning toolkit. And pay close attention to the *money-saving tips* in this section.

Your employer may not offer all of the tools described—and even if you do have access to them, you may not need to use all of them. But in order to know what specific tools are right for you, you'll need to know something about what each can accomplish. Once done, you'll be able to build yourself a better benefit plan—one that will help you save more money and, hopefully, help you put that money to work for you and your future goals.

Let's get started.

Health Benefits

The Right Level of Medical Coverage
to Meet Your Unique Needs

A health plan helps cover some of the expenses you incur as a result of an accident, sickness, or pregnancy and protects you from serious financial setbacks in the event that you or a family member should become ill. You save money by being part of a group health plan. Whatever savings the group, or company, reaps gets passed on to you in the form of lower health care premiums, a portion of which employees must usually pay. Group health insurance is almost always less costly than individual insurance.

The types of services typically covered by a group medical plan include:

- Doctor office visits
- Emergency care
- Hospital stays
- X-ray and lab services
- Surgery
- Maternity care
- Substance abuse treatment
- Prescription drugs

To be covered under your company health plan, an employee must meet certain eligibility requirements, such as a minimum number of hours of work per week. You may have to fulfill a waiting period before you are added to the plan. In addition, your spouse and children, including those attending college, may be eligible for coverage. In rare instances, a parent or grandparent may be eligible for coverage under your plan.

A domestic partner may also be eligible for coverage. To meet the typical definition of a domestic partner, the person must be over eighteen, living with you, unrelated to you, and have joint responsibility for your household. The person must also not be married to a third party.

Whether a domestic partner of the same sex can be covered under the plan depends on your company. Some recognize only partners of the opposite sex.

If you are married or have a domestic partner, you should do your homework when it comes to health benefits. Study your spouse or partner's health-care options. Depending on the various costs and benefits, you may choose to opt out of your own employer's plan and join your partner's plan. Or you may find it's beneficial to each enroll in your own plan.

If you elect to be covered in both places, remember there will always be "coordination of benefits." That means you won't ever be able to get the same bills paid twice. You may, depending on the plans, get certain covered expenses on one plan that you don't get on the other. Compare the plans carefully to decide the best course.

There are different kinds of health plans in the market. Your employer may offer you a choice. The three basic types of plans are:

- Indemnity plans. These cover a certain percentage of expenses, charge annual deductibles and coinsurance, and cap your out-of-pocket expenses at a certain point. You can generally go to any doctor you choose. You must file claims for reimbursement.

> **Example:** Say your plan had a $200 deductible, 80/20 coinsurance, and a $500 out-of-pocket cap. On a $1,000 bill, you'd pay the first $200, plus 20% of the next $800, or $160. As the year progressed, if you paid $500 in expenses, the rest of your expenses that year would be covered by the plan.

- Managed-care plans: HMOs (health maintenance organizations). These are groups of doctors, hospitals, and health-care professionals who offer a wide array of services. As a member, you can seek care anytime you are sick, with few out-of-pocket costs. Most doctor visits involve a $10 fee, for example, instead of a deductible and co-pay. You must visit doctors and hospitals within the HMO to receive benefits (except in emergencies). There are no claim forms.
- Managed-care plans: PPOs (preferred provider organizations). These permit you to use a provider network (like an HMO) at a discounted cost or to obtain medical services out of the network and incur indemnity-type deductibles, co-pays, etc.

You'll need to consider your own family's needs before choosing a plan. And you will probably want to see the list of doctors and hospitals in the HMO option, to make sure they are convenient for you.

Find out how much each option costs you per paycheck to be in the plan. Don't forget to look at the out-of-pocket expenses you may be asked to pay each time you access a health-care service or buy a prescription. Now is a good time to begin to track the out-of-pocket dollars you spend on health care year to year. By doing so, you'll be in a better position to estimate which options may help you lower expenses when you're asked to sign up for next year's benefits.

If you change jobs, or lose your job for any reason other than gross misconduct, you can continue your group coverage through COBRA at your own expense for eighteen months. (COBRA stands for Consolidated Omnibus Budget Reconciliation Act of 1986, a law that was passed so you wouldn't be left high and dry without coverage between jobs.)

You can continue your COBRA coverage for longer than eighteen months under certain conditions. If the employee dies or divorces, or if a child ceases to be a qualified dependent, the employee's dependents may continue their coverage for an additional eighteen months. Coverage may continue for a total of twenty-nine months (eleven months on top of the original eighteen) if the employee becomes disabled.

Your plan may also cover care for mental health and substance abuse. These can be important benefits when it comes to treating a variety of conditions, from anxiety to marital problems to eating disorders, chronic mental illness, or addiction to drugs or alcohol.

Depending on your needs, you may find broader mental health coverage under a managed-care plan than under an indemnity plan.

Prescription drug benefits should also figure into your choice of health coverage. Medicines are covered differently under indemnity plans and managed-care plans.

- Under an indemnity plan, prescription drugs are subject to the employee's deductible and coinsurance. Say you had a $200 annual deductible and you'd had no doctors' visits or other medical expenses yet that year. If a $25 prescription were your first expense of the year, you'd have to pay the cost completely, and it would be applied to your deductible.

Indemnity	Managed Care
Psychiatrists	*Psychiatrists*
Psychologists	Psychologists
Social workers	Social workers
Hospitals	Hospitals
	Social workers with MSW degree
	Substance abuse treatment centers
	Halfway houses
	Group homes
	Intensive outpatient treatment centers
	Other

- Under a separate, employer-sponsored prescription card program, an employee can fill prescriptions for just a $5 or $10 co-pay. You must typically use a pharmacy that's preapproved and part of a specific list. This type of plan can be part of an indemnity or a managed-care plan.
- Mail-order prescription plans can also be offered with any type of health plan. These are best for people who need maintenance drugs that can be ordered in large quantities.

Note: Not all drugs are covered under any of these plans.

Vision care is an additional benefit offered by some employers as part of the overall health-care package. They provide payment toward the cost of routine eye exams, lenses, frames, and fittings. If you or your family members wear glasses or contacts, this could be a cost-saving benefit for you.

Depending on the type of plan your employer offers, vision plans typically cover services by:

- Vision-care vendors
- Eyewear providers

- Optometrists
- Ophthalmologists
- Opticians

Under an indemnity-type vision plan, your vision benefits would be subject to the usual deductibles and coinsurance. You could go to the vision-care provider of your choice.

Under a vision PPO, you could choose an eye-care provider within the network and pay just a small co-pay per visit, of $5 or $10. If you chose to go outside the network, you would be reimbursed at a set rate for the services. Deductibles and coinsurance would apply to the out-of-network benefits.

Under a vision HMO, you would see a provider within a given network and pay only small co-pays of $5 or $10 per visit.

With all the different benefit options that might be presented to you, it's clear why you need to calculate what's valuable for you and your family. It would be wasteful to pay for vision benefits if no one in your family wears glasses. But if you take a medication regularly, it could well be worth your while to elect prescription drug coverage.

Do the math. Add up what your contribution to the health-care plans you're considering would be over the course of the year. Weigh costs against benefits. Choose those plans that will help you save money, not just up-front but if you get sick.

How to Determine the Right Level
of Dental Coverage

The chief goal of dental plans offered at work is to encourage employees to take care of their teeth and to seek routine preventive care, to head off dental problems. Beyond cleanings and X-rays, dental plans help pay for more costly procedures like fillings, crowns, or root canals. As with medical care, there are managed-care and traditional indemnity options in dental care.

Under an indemnity dental plan, you may see any dentist you choose. Expenses are generally subject to a deductible, and then the plan pays a certain set amount toward the procedure. There may be a calendar-year benefit maximum. And, if excessive dental work is needed, you might have to budget for it since your plan may not cover all the expenses.

Like an HMO, a dental maintenance organization is a network of dentists from whom you can seek services. There are typically no payments for diagnostic, preventive, and most restorative procedures. There are co-pays or fees for major procedures.

With a dental PPO, you can choose between HMO-like coverage with the network dentists or pay more out of pocket to use out-of-network dentists. Deductibles are lower within the network, and coinsurance rates are more favorable than outside the network.

You can bring more of your paycheck home if you choose your dental plan well. If all you typically need is preventive care, such as cleanings and X-rays, you might be best served to enroll in the least expensive plan your employer offers. On any plan, most of your services will be covered.

If you have a dentist you see regularly and like, find out if he or she is on the list of HMO or PPO providers. You'll save a lot of out-of-pocket money on fillings and other care if your dentist is on the managed-care list. You may consider switching dentists to take advantage of lower costs within a dental HMO or PPO, especially if you have kids and you want to keep dental costs down.

Health-Care and Dependent Care Savings Accounts

Another great benefit for employees who expect to incur significant expenses on health care or dependent care: flexible spending accounts. These accounts allow for pretax money to be set aside to cover eligible health-care expenses like deductibles, your portion of medical bills under indemnity plans, or day care. Because the money is taken from your pay before federal and state taxes, flexible spending accounts can help take the bite out of hefty medical or day-care expenses.

Medical savings accounts permit you to set aside money, through payroll deduction, to cover most expenses not covered under your medical or dental plan. To use these plans effectively, you need to have a handle on your out-of-pocket expenses. If you use an HMO, for example, your expenses are minimal—usually $5 or $10 per visit. If, on the other hand, you're enrolled in an indemnity plan, you could shell out thousands of dollars a year for you and your family, depending on your health plan. To set aside the right amount of pretax money in your account, you should track your medical bills. If you have last year's bills, add them up. If you don't, then estimate what your medical expenses will be this year. For example, if you know your son has to have his tonsils out, or that you have to undergo knee surgery, find out how much the bills are likely to add up to, then reduce that by the amount that should be covered by your insurer. The rest is yours to pay, and you're better off paying it with pretax dollars than taxed money.

Only set aside what you think you'll need in these accounts, however. Any money you don't use in a year is forfeited.

Between the money you save on taxes and what you save on medical bills, you'll come up with a decent little pile of cash. Perhaps you need that money to help make ends meet. If not, you might consider putting it away in your 401(k) plan—saving today can help make your future better.

Dependent-care spending accounts can be used toward the costs of day care, summer day camp, preschool, adult day care, or in-home child care. You can set aside as much as $2,500 as a single or $5,000 if you're married for dependent care.

Be careful to set aside in these accounts only those dollars you believe you will spend next year on health or dependent care. Track your out-of-pocket expenses for each. Then, estimate a similar or reduced level of spending for next year. Put these dollars into your flexible spending accounts. You also may want to estimate how these accounts can boost your take-home pay. Consider moving the pay you saved into your 401(k).

DISABILITY BENEFITS

How to Preserve Your Pay if You Become Disabled

Disability is an area of the insurance world that baffles most folks. Do you need it? How much? And what should it cost? Why bother?

Well, if you're a construction worker and you break your leg in a skimobiling accident, how will you work? If you can't work for three months, how will you pay your bills? Disability is the area where most experts say workers are underprotected.

Disability insurance can protect you financially when you can't perform the normal duties of your job due to a physical or mental impairment. It can also be important if you become physically or mentally unable—according to a doctor's diagnosis—to do any job at all.

There are five basic kinds of disability plans:

1. Short-term disability
2. Long-term disability
3. Workers' compensation
4. Social security disability
5. Accidental death and dismemberment

With each type of disability, there are waiting periods to receive benefits and maximum lengths of time in which to receive payments. Disability payments are always less than the amount of your full working pay. A doctor must usually verify the worker's condition.

Short-Term Disability (STD): This provides protection against temporary loss of income to a disabled employee, usually for three months to a year. Payments kick in after zero to eight days of disability under most plans; waiting periods are generally waived for hospital stays or accidents. And normal sick days often cover the waiting period in other instances. Typical payments are 50%, 60%, or 66⅔% of pay.

Long-Term Disability (LTD): This picks up where short-term disability ends. For example, a long-term disability plan with a three-month waiting period would typically be paired with a short-term disability plan that ends at three months. The intent is to have continuous coverage, whether long-term disability picks up at three months, six months, or twelve months.

What LTD costs: You typically buy LTD at a cost per $100 of earnings each month. Say you made $1,000 a month and the cost was 55¢ per $100. Divide $1,000 by $100 and you get 10. Ten times 55¢ is $5.50 per month.

Long-term disability plans typically cover disabilities due to accidents or illnesses that last a long time. The plans usually replace 50% to 70% of a worker's pay. Payments can last until age sixty-five or seventy, depending on the plan. If Social Security or workers' compensation benefits apply, the LTD payment would be reduced by that amount.

For example, long-term disability would typically pay 60% of a worker's monthly earnings. If that worker earned $2,000, that would mean a benefit of $1,200 (0.60 × $2,000). If Social Security paid the worker $500 a month, the plan would reduce its benefit to $700. That way the worker still gets 60% of his or her pay—and has an incentive to return to work.

After eighteen months or two years, the definition of total disability tightens. At that point, a worker may have to consider taking on a job other than the one he previously performed to receive benefits. Total disability at that point would mean the worker was incapable of being trained to take on any job.

If disability is partial, arrangements may be made for the worker to do part of the job and get a partial disability payment.

Workers' Compensation: This covers work-related accidents and illnesses. The idea is that employees should not have to bear the cost of medical treatment or time lost at work due to an injury or sickness they acquired on the job. Employers pay the full cost of this insurance.

Social Security Disability Benefits: This is for people who cannot work at all due to disability.

The Social Security Disability Income Program is paid for through regular withholding of taxes from all workers' pay, along with the other benefits provided by the government Social Security program, like retirement benefits and survivor benefits. The disability benefit equals what the worker's retirement benefit would be at age sixty-five.

To be eligible for the Social Security disability benefits, the worker must:

- Be insured.
- Be under age sixty-five.
- Have paid Social Security taxes at work in five of the ten years before the disability.
- Be disabled (or be expected to be) for at least twelve months, or have a disability that's expected to end in death.
- File an application with the Social Security Administration and wait five months (unless waived).

Accidental Death and Dismemberment (AD&D): This coverage provides a payment to a worker who loses a limb or eyesight due to an accident. If the worker dies in the accident, the plan will pay his or beneficiaries the benefit.

AD&D coverage may include several options:

- Coverage for loss of speech and hearing
- Coverage for paralysis
- Special education benefit if the employee dies
- Dependent coverage for the employee's spouse and children
- Waiver of premium if the employee is permanently and totally disabled

A typical AD&D plan would pay the following benefit amounts:

- Death: full death benefit
- Loss of two or more body parts: full death benefit
- Loss of sight or one body part: 50% of death benefit
- Loss of thumb or index finger: 25% of death benefit

Death Benefits

Taking Care of the Ones You Love after You're Gone

You know what they say about the only two certain things in life. We've already mentioned taxes several times. The other one is death. There are bascially two kinds of life insurance products:

- Term life
- Group universal life

The point of life insurance is to secure a sum of money for your beneficiary (or beneficiaries) if you die. A death benefit can be modest, meant merely to cover funeral expenses, or it can help pay off a mortgage or finance your children's education. Single workers with no spouse or children have the least need for life insurance.

Another benefit of being part of a group plan is that you may be eligible for life insurance without medical exams or a lot of paperwork. Term life insurance is often provided by the employer at no cost to the employee. Under some plans, the employee can elect to purchase additional life insurance. If you leave your job, your term life policy ends.

Group term life plans provide for "accelerated benefits" in the event of a terminal illness. If an employee is expected to die within twelve months, he or she could elect to receive payments before death.

Group universal life is another option. Considered a "permanent" plan, it provides a death benefit plus the option of cash build-up.

The employee picks an amount of term coverage under the plan, usually a percentage of salary or a flat dollar amount. By payroll deduction, the employee pays the insurance premiums on the policy and can make cash contributions to the plan. The value of the cash in the account grows at a certain rate. Employees can withdraw money from the account at any time or take loans against it. In addition, you can take the policy with you when you change jobs, and continue paying premiums directly to the insurance company.

Retirement Benefits Dos and Don'ts

1. Do Know What Your Monthly Pension Check Will Be When You Finally Decide to Leave Full-Time Work.

Once a cherished fixture of American retirement, the traditional pension plan is becoming rarer all the time.

These "defined benefit" plans provide retirement income to workers, generally after working for a large company, or for the government, for a number of years. Such plans are entirely employer funded. Benefits are based on pay or job type and years of service, according to a set schedule. There is typically a minimum required length of employment before an employee is eligible for a pension plan.

There are four main types of defined benefit plans:

- *Flat benefit:* Annual benefit is based on a flat, predetermined sum times the number of years of service.

Example:
$120 × 30 years at the company = $3,600 payment per year.

- *Career pay:* Annual benefit is based on the sum of the benefits an employee earns over all years with the company.

Example: Benefit formula is 1% of pay, and total pay over all the years is $1 million.

So $1 million × 0.01 = $10,000 annual benefit payment. I'll take it.

- *Final pay:* Annual benefit payment is based on the employee's average pay in the three or five highest-paid years and the length of service.

Example: Benefit formula is 1% of final average pay times 30 years of service. The five highest consecutive years of pay add up to $250,000, making the average pay $50,000.

So ($50,000 × 0.01) × 30 years of service = $15,000 per year. Sweet.

- *Cash balance:* Annual benefit is based on salary, benefit credits, and interest. The employer invests the money, but the employee can see how much it's accumulating each year.

Example: Benefit credits are 4% of annual pay; annual pay is $50,000; and interest is 8% a year.

So the account balance at end of year one is: ($50,000 × 0.04) × 1.08 = $2,160. Not bad!

2. Do Get to Know How Much Retiree Health-Care Coverage You Will Have to Lower Your Costs of Living in Retirement.

Your health coverage ends on the last day of the month in which you retire. But you may be eligible for retiree coverage, or to continue your coverage temporarily through COBRA, by paying the required premiums. At least one year prior to your retirement, you will need to map out how you will maintain adequate coverage—and what the costs of doing so will be. This is a critical piece of your overall retirement planning, and one that is best done well before you pocket your gold watch.

Find out from your employer or benefits company how much you will receive from your pension each month when you retire—and at what age you'll be eligible for full pension benefits. Find out how much retiree health-care coverage you can expect. You'll want to factor these anticipated dollars into your retirement planning. This will help you figure out how much more or less you will need to save on your own—in a 401(k) or IRAs—in order to reach the annual income goals you've identified for each of your retirement years. If having access to a pension permits you to save less in a 401(k) or IRAs, shift those dollars into other shorter-term savings vehicles, such as a discount brokerage or bank account.

3. Do Plan and Buy the Right Level of
Long-Term Care Coverage.

Even a big nest egg can be gobbled up quickly by nursing home costs. Long-term care plans permit you to pay premiums, based on your age, toward a set daily benefit in the future. These policies generally cover nursing home costs, convalescent facilities, adult-care centers, and in some cases nursing care in your own home.

Nobody likes to think about being in a nursing home. But it's important to think about it ahead of time. Round-the-clock care can cost $30,000 to $70,000 a year, and more. If you're around fifty years old, you should at least consider this benefit, especially if you don't have large investment and savings accounts to cover nursing home costs. If you don't, you risk spending all your money on nursing care—a potentially huge problem for your surviving spouse, who could be left penniless in old age.

Remember, Medicare does not cover nursing home costs. Long-term care coverage comes in the form of a dollar benefit per day. There is also a waiting period to choose. You can keep your costs down by waiting three or more months before you want coverage to kick in; you'd pay the bills out of your own savings during the waiting period.

You may also be able to purchase long-term care coverage for your parents.

4. Don't Plan to Live off Social Security.

Everyone has heard the concerns about the health of the Social Security system and questions about how long the fund will endure in its present form. No matter what your politics or your point of view, it's best to think about Social Security as part of your retirement—certainly not the whole plan. For most people, Social Security checks won't cover the lifestyle they've grown accustomed to in their working years. Everybody wants to be comfortable in retirement, and not to worry about paying the bills after age sixty-five.

There are several proposals being floated now by politicians, think tanks, and private firms on how to reform Social Security. One way would be to continue Social Security benefits as currently structured for everyone over a certain age—say those who are retired and people less than ten years from retirement at age sixty-five. Current budget surpluses could cover those benefits for many years.

All newer workers entering jobs would set aside the 15.3% of their pay they (and their employers) now contribute to Social Security. Instead of going into a low-return, government-run fund, from which Social Security checks are cut, the money would go into mandatory individual accounts. Those accounts would be invested—at least in part—in market instruments like stocks, helping even lower-income workers build sizable retirement accounts for the future.

The American Association of Retired Persons and other groups representing seniors are against this approach. They want to keep the system the same and charge that the poor would be left in the cold under an individual account system. Clearly, there would still need to be a safety net for the elderly poor.

The fact is, Social Security, in its current form, covers only a slice of the income retirees give up when they stop working.

5. Do Plan on Investing in Your 401(k), 403(b), or 457(c).

The 401(k) retirement plan (it's equivalent in non-profits is a 403(b), and in government plans it is a 457(c)) has gained widespread popularity this decade. It's a savings and investing vehicle for workers that is administered by your employers because, frankly, your employer doesn't want to have to shoulder the burden of ensuring a secure financial retirement for you. While there are many benefits to investing in these tax-advantaged plans (most of which are explored in chapter 23), here we'll look at the nuts, bolts, and utilitarian benefits of them.

Unlike a traditional "defined benefit" pension plan, the 401(k) is made up chiefly of pretax money from your own paychecks. You decide how much to set aside from each check and that amount will be automatically deducted from your pay by your employer (or the employer's payroll company).

There's a big benefit not to be missed here: These 401(k) contributions come out of your check before federal and state (except Pennsylvania) taxes. That helps you save more. And it means the dip in your take-home pay will be smaller than your actual contribution.

Look at this example for an employee earning $30,000 a year:

	Without 401(k)	With 401(k)
Salary	$30,000	$30,000
Pretax 401(k) contribution	0	1,800
W-2 gross income	$30,000	$28,200
Federal income taxes	4,500	4,230
FICA taxes	2,295	2,295
Total taxes	$6,795	$6,525

(Source: CIGNA, "Understanding Your Retirement")

That's another $270 of savings on taxes. As a result, 401(k) contributions make a smaller dent in your take-home pay than the size of your contribution ($1,530). It certainly affects your pay less than saving after taxes.

Following the chart above:

Net pay	$23,205	$21,675
After-tax savings	1,800	0
Total take-home pay	$21,405	$21,675

In a 401(k), your money also grows faster than it would in a taxable plan, because you don't pay taxes on the gains on your investment until retirement after age 59½, or when you pull the money out.

Under IRS rules, the maximum amount of pay you can direct into your 401(k) plan annually is $10,000. Many employers match some portion of the employee contribution, adding significantly to your portfolio. The maximum combined employer and employee contribution to a 401(k) is $30,000 a year, or 25% of the employee's taxable compensation, whichever is less.

One of the chief differences between traditional pension plans and the 401(k), or "defined contribution," plan is that here, you, the employee, control all the investment decisions. At the same time you decide how much money to set aside each pay period, you also will choose how to invest the money within the plan. Typically, you will choose from a menu of professionally managed mutual funds.

You should make these fund selections based on your age (how many years away you are from retirement) and risk tolerance. As we discussed earlier, the younger you are and the further away from retirement, the more aggressively you should invest. As you approach retirement—and get closer to needing to withdraw funds from the account—you may choose a more conservative approach.

Depending on your plan, you may be able to borrow from your 401(k) plan in case of an emergency, like coming up with a down payment on a house or paying a child's college tuition, without paying taxes or penalties. Loans of up to 50% of your vested account balance, or $50,000—whichever is less—may be taken out to help finance your primary residence or for a general-purpose loan.

But be very careful with this option.

You may think it's harmless to "borrow from yourself," and in some cases it may be worth it. But when you borrow the money, it's not earning the valuable investment returns you need over time to reach your goals. You'll be setting yourself back as long as the money is pulled from the account. General-purpose loans must be repaid, with interest, within five years, which could become a hardship without careful planning. Loans for homes may be outstanding for longer.

There are cases in which an employee who is still working may withdraw assets before retiring. Such "in-service" withdrawals are most common if an employee reaches age 59½ and wants to take money out of the plan, or in the case of financial hardship. To demonstrate financial hardship, an employee must be in one of the following circumstances:

- Need help in buying a primary residence
- Need money to pay for college
- Be facing extraordinary medical bills
- Need the money to prevent foreclosure, or eviction from, a primary residence

Withdrawing from a 401(k) plan early, as with an IRA, is expensive. Not only do all the ordinary taxes on the income hit, but the employee will be subject to an additional 10% penalty tax. It's obviously best to avoid handing over such a big chunk of your hard-earned investment portfolio unless it's absolutely necessary.

If an employee dies, his or her beneficiaries would receive the account assets free of the 10% penalty tax.

The plans are also portable, which means they go with you when you change jobs, unlike a traditional pension plan. The plan should be "rolled over" into a new 401(k) or IRA, not withdrawn, to avoid the 10% penalty tax and a 20% withholding tax.

The 401(k) is widely seen as the best tool American workers have for setting aside money—and growing it—for retirement. Such plans have made more than a few middle-class workers into millionaires.

6. Do Invest in Profit-Sharing Plans.

Profit sharing is a way for companies to share a portion of their gains in good years with their employees. It's a valuable benefit that costs workers nothing. And it helps make employees feel they are part of the success of the company.

A company may determine the size of the profit-sharing benefit every year, at its discretion. Or it may promise to pay a set yearly amount, as a percentage of net profits or of the employee's compensation. The maximum annual profit-sharing benefit is 15% of an employee's compensation.

7. Invest in Workplace IRAs.

IRAs are similar to the 401(k) in that they allow for tax-deferred growth of investments. But they are individual instruments; you don't need to be part of a group to get one. The money a person invests in an IRA has already been taxed. You can contribute as much as $4,000 annually, as long as you are under age 70½. A married couple can invest $8,000 a year.

As with a 401(k), an individual decides how to invest upon opening an IRA account. They can be as conservative as bank savings accounts or money markets, or as aggressive as a growth stock fund. IRAs can help you save more for retirement beyond your retirement account at work.

IRAs are popular in part because they offer a tax break to some investors. If you don't have a 401(k) plan at work, you may be eligible to write off your entire $4,000 IRA contribution, depending on your income. If you do have a 401(k) plan, you may still invest in an IRA but you may not take a write-off on your taxes.

You have probably heard all the talk about the relatively new Roth IRA (see chapter 24 for details). With a Roth, there is no up-front tax write-off. But nor are there taxes to be paid upon retiring—a huge new benefit. You can open a Roth if you are single and earn less than $110,000 or if you are married, filing jointly, earning less than $160,000. You can contribute the full $4,000 if you are single and earning less than $95,000 or if you are married, filing jointly, and earning less than $150,000.

Another benefit of the Roth: Because the money was taxed before you invested it, there are no mandatory withdrawals at age 70½. With a regular IRA, it's crucial to start withdrawing money from your account by the April 1 that falls after you turn 70½. If you don't, believe it or not, the IRS will zap you with a whopping 50% tax.

Now that we've reviewed the basics, you've got the tools and the knowledge to tackle the next step. We're going to zero in on your own situation. The following chapters lay out key benefit decisions and savings and investment roadmaps for you at every stage of your career and life.

Ready Resources

This chapter is as good as it currently gets in this department.

CHAPTER 4

Investing from Scratch

Once you figure out where you stand, financially speaking, that is, the next step is to determine where you want to go. Doing so entails knowing something about the possibilities that lie ahead of you—from graduate school to home ownership to retirement. (Your life in the nutshell called life.)

Thinking about all the possibilities can easily drive you to the funny farm. How can you begin to think about your retirement when you're not even sure that your current job at Banana Republic isn't the be-all and end-all of your career advancement? How can you begin to contemplate home ownership when you're still trying to figure out where you want to live—in the Aleutian Islands or downtown New York? How can you begin to think about investing, if you have just bought a car or a home? Why can't you put off today what won't happen for many more tomorrows?

Let me put it to you this way. You can.

But when do you think you should start to plan for the mega-events that will happen in your life, let alone those events you can't exactly schedule into the calendar year five- or thirty-five years hence? If you answered "Today" you can read on. If, however, you answered "Later," you better return to chapter 1 for a refresher course on just how little time you have to plan ahead.

Remember that a sign of your needing to get your financial house in order is easy to spot—if you don't know what you owe, stop here before you go.

Unless you have the perfect job, the perfect place to live, and the perfect place to retire to, all expenses paid (in which case, I'd like you adopt me), then you're like the rest of us. Not exactly dazed and confused, but not in perfect harmony when it comes to the reality of our current financial state and the utopia we dream of living in sometime in the near future. In short, you want to move from where you are to where you most want to be. We all do. And, for the most part, we can all do it.

Personal Goals and Investment Goals Are Directly Related

The good news is that, no matter how old you are, and no matter what stage of life you're in, and no matter what state your finances are in, there are many ways in which you can plot a course to achieve short-term skill-building objectives that will in turn help you reach longer-term, more self-fulfilling goals without sacrificing your current and future financial security.

To begin with, you need to be clear about the difference between a goal and an objective.

Goal: Determine who you are and who you want to be. Think of a goal as a vision of yourself—who you would most like to be, what you would most like to achieve, what you would most like to do. Your goal might be to rise to the CEO's chair in a major corporation or to become a tenured professor at a small Midwestern college or to simply take a backseat to all that pressure and work in a fairly anonymous job. Whatever road you take is fine—so long as you can live within your means and invest enough money to ensure that, thirty-odd years from now, you can retire in relative security as opposed to having to start another career, like the guy who picks up the gold balls after the driving range closes, or the woman who could be your grandmother serving up Mighty Meals.

Objective: Compared to a goal, an objective is a practical step that moves you closer to your goal. An objective is a thing that is within your grasp to achieve. Objectives entail specific ends, definite time frames, and achievable goals. You won't be able to achieve your personal goals without concrete objectives—any more than you will be able to meet your investment goals without concrete investment objectives. Let's take your personal objectives and goals first, and then we'll look at the more essential investment objectives and goals which you need to achieve.

Personal Goals

Even if you are not sure about what your ultimate goals are, you can determine specific objectives that can help you on your way to discovering who you want to be and where you want to go.

Examples of objectives you ought to set:

- Create a savings account
- Increase your marketable skills
- Pay off as much existing debt as possible
- Apply to graduate school
- Build your current savings
- Invest for your retirement

You should consider adding more specific objectives to this list, ones that will help you get your financial—and personal—house in order. Take a look at the following objectives:

- Save more regularly
- Establish a good record-keeping system
- Ensure adequate health insurance coverage
- Increase your income
- Increase your savings
- Learn to invest
- Invest—your ultimate objective

Investment Goals

Make your shorter-term objectives work toward your ultimate objective of investing regularly and wisely. In order to get the hang of this, try the following. Pick one of the objectives from the above list. For example, saving more regularly. Notice that this objective is different from save more money—although that's always a wise thing to do, too.

"How do I save more regularly?" I'm glad you asked. The answer is simple. Create a savings plan. What does a savings plan entail? A schedule for depositing a portion of your earnings into an account that you don't use to rent videos, buy cappuccinos, or debit for groceries and gas. (Determining the best place in which to put that slice from your pay's pie is detailed in chapter 6.)

Try again, and again—until you design a savings schedule that works for you. Start with a plan that corresponds to your income and expenses. At first, don't worry about how much money you deposit, though 5% of your take-home pay is a good place to start. Do focus on the objective of regularly depositing a portion of your pay (all the while keeping the goal of your savings in mind, whether that goal is the discipline of saving itself or the more advanced form of the savings goal, namely, saving for something other than saving itself—investing!).

You say to yourself, I need to save more if I am going to ensure that I can invest more. Why? The last thing you want to do is to have to tap into your investments in order to pay for current obligations. Instead, you should have an emergency savings plan to help you meet the unforeseen circumstance of a forced layoff (for example), or to help you better decide about your financial ability to change career paths, go back to school, or tell your boss to take a hike.

Of course, you'll need to open a savings account—any bank will do as long as it's FDIC insured. Before you open this emergency savings account, turn to chapter 6, which will teach you the basics of smart banking. If you already have a savings account for this purpose, check out chapter 6 anyway. You'll find there a tip or two relating to fees that can be avoided (and so should be). Once you have your account, you'll need to figure out what time of the month is best for making your deposit. If you're paid biweekly, the beginning, middle, or end of the month may be appropriate. If you are paid on a monthly basis, the end or beginning of the month will probably prove best. But keep in mind that your bills may not all fall within the same time frame. So, don't let your saving plan collide with your bill paying; instead, plan ahead. (Also, if you find that you have difficulty paying bills at different times of the month, try asking your creditors to switch their billing date to match your system. Many will do so.)

From Saving to Investing

Once you have proven to yourself that you can save more (by building up an emergency savings account that will cover six months' worth of your living expenses), then you can really turn up the volume of your ultimate goal—investing more. Determining your investment goals in advance of your actually investing will help you achieve them. However, many of us began investing (in a retirement plan, for example) based on the consensus that this is the right thing to do. The truth is that it is the right thing to do—but there are better and worse ways to invest. Planning ahead of time (or revisiting your current pattern of investing) will help ensure that the goals you achieve are your own—and not some generic goal.

Of course, you'll need to open an investment account—and as with the several types of banks that are out there waiting for your savings dollars, so there are many places, including banks, that are in the business of vying for your investment dollars. (But, unlike most banks, brokerage firms and mutual fund companies are not FDIC insured.) Before you open your investment account, turn to chapter 18, which will teach you some brokerage basics. If you already have an investment account, check out chapter 18 anyway, since it contains all kinds of cost-cutting moves that you can make—and, in so doing, enable more of your investment dollars to go to work for you. If you are already participating in a retirement plan—a 401(k) or pension plan, for example—turn to chapter 23 to maximize your plan's potential to deliver the ultimate reward: a retirement nest egg that won't leave you scrambling for night watchman jobs at age seventy-five. If you aren't participating in a retirement plan, don't miss out on this golden opportunity. (Again, turn to section 5 for details.)

Once you have your account, you'll need to figure out whether you'll be investing on a monthly, quarterly, or annual basis—and when. Typically, investing smaller amounts more regularly (i.e., having the money automatically deducted from your paycheck and invested in a mutual fund, or two or three) is the best way to go since it ensures that you won't spend the money in the here and now. As with setting aside money for your savings account, plan ahead so that your investing plan doesn't collide with your other payment obligations.

Setting objectives can be easy: the hard part is fulfilling them. However, if your objectives move you closer to the ultimate goal of being able to invest a portion of your paycheck, it will be easier to discipline yourself. Why? Because you're doing something for yourself!

For those of you whose financial troubles are threatening your immediate life, let alone your distant future, take heart. There are solutions to almost any problem—and cumbersome debt is no exception.

In fact, chapter 2 explained in detail the ways in which you can pay your debts on a timely basis while increasing your current cash flow and boosting your investment income (sections 2 and 3 will help you accomplish this second feat). No matter what your immediate concerns are, stay focused on the ultimate objective of being able to invest in yourself. In order to accomplish this, you'll need to plan for it.

The following worksheet will help you jump-start your way to investing in a better future for yourself today.

Your Investment Goals

Goal:	Turn to:
Learn about money management	Section 1
Save more regularly	Section 1
Establish an investment record-keeping system	Chapter 5
Learn to invest	Chapter 4
Get invested	Chapter 18
Buy a stock	Chapter 12
Invest in mutual funds	Chapter 14
Learn the best ways to invest	Section 4
Take advantage of retirement investing plans	Section 5
Understand investment tax strategies	Section 6

Now, let's set some goals. The following suggestions will help jump-start your own thinking about investing your way to a better life.

Short-Term Goals (within the next six months)

1. Learn more about money management
2. Learn more about investing
3. Establish a savings strategy with the intermediate-term goal of investing

Intermediate-Term Goals (six months to five years)

1. Select the best tax-advantaged retirement plan for you
2. Select the best type of investments for you and your objectives
3. Open a brokerage (preferably discount) account

LONG-TERM GOALS (five years and more)

1. Increase retirement-oriented investing amount to at least 10% of salary
2. Review portfolio's adequacy for new financial obligations (e.g., college for kids)
3. Assess probability of buying (larger) home within the next five years

INVESTMENT GOAL ONE:

Target Date:

Estimated Cost:	*Invested:*	*Need to Invest:*
$_____	$_____	$_____

INVESTMENT GOAL TWO:

Target Date:

Estimated Cost:	*Invested:*	*Need to Invest:*
$_____	$_____	$_____

INVESTMENT GOAL THREE:

Target Date:

Estimated Cost:	*Invested:*	*Need to Invest:*
$_____	$_____	$_____

MONTHLY AMOUNT TOWARD GOAL: $

Note: You will probably need to expand this worksheet to encompass all your goals!

BUILD YOUR OWN PYRAMID

Think of investing as building toward a better future. You might start small—but someone had to place the first stone that launched the Great Pyramid.

The base of your pyramid represents where most financial experts—from financial planners to investment counselors—suggest you place the money you want to keep safe. It's easily accessible, at a low risk, and shows a predictable return. The middle of the pyramid comprises investments with higher risk and potentially higher return. The greater potential for growth is essential if you want your money to work for you and beat inflation rather than lose its purchasing power to inflation. Mutual funds, high-quality stocks, and bonds are what this part of the pyramid is made of. The peak of the pyramid represents high risk and high potential for loss, but the profits can be extraordinary. Commodities (pork bellies and the like), options, penny stocks, and other very risky investments are found here.

Keeping track of your investing progress is what the next chapter is all about. If you don't develop a way to track your progress from your immediate goals to investing wisely and well in order to achieve your ultimate goal of a financially secure life, you are working against yourself. On the other hand, establishing a way to track your progress will not only help you get to your ultimate goal faster, it will also help you reduce the potential anxiety that awaits those who have no clear idea of where they are heading—or why.

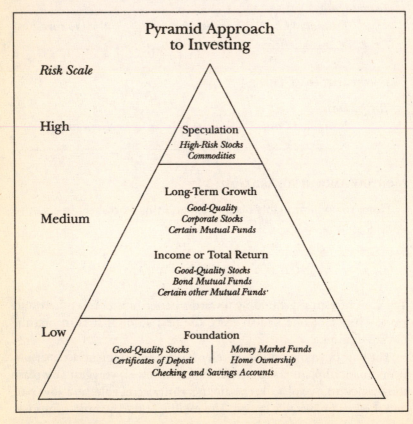

Pyramid Approach to Investing

Risk Scale

High

Speculation
High-Risk Stocks
Commodities

Medium

Long-Term Growth
Good-Quality
Corporate Stocks
Certain Mutual Funds

Income or Total Return
Good-Quality Stocks
Bond Mutual Funds
Certain other Mutual Funds·

Low

Foundation
Good-Quality Stocks   *Money Market Funds*
Certificates of Deposit   *Home Ownership*
Checking and Savings Accounts

CHAPTER 5

Your Success from Scratch

Successful investing relies on a foundation of solid money management. Everything to do with money management relies upon your being fully informed about your current financial condition. A record-keeping system that incorporates your personal finance and investment-specific transactions is the best way to keep track of the financial information you need in order to meet the demands of our money-centered culture. Those demands range from paying bills to keeping track of your investments' performance in order to ensure that you're on track in terms of achieving your objectives. If you can't find the bill you need to pay, and if you can't locate the proper documentation to back up your assertion that an error has been made on one of your investments, you can find yourself incapable of paying what you owe, and earning less than you deserve.

To begin with, a record-keeping system will help you collect and organize the necessary financial information and documentation relating to your current financial obligations. A record-keeping system will also help you review and revise your budget. It will enable you to avoid untimely and potentially costly searches for documentation. Also, as mentioned above, a record-keeping system will help you rise to the challenge of keeping tabs on your investment transactions. That's all pretty obvious, but a good record-keeping system can help you do much more. Come tax time, for example, your filing system will help you to have all the documents you need at your beck and call.

This means you will be able to fill out the forms easily, accurately, and promptly—good news whether the IRS owes you or vice versa. (Why? Either you will get your refund sooner or you will avoid paying a penalty for underestimating your tax bill.)

With your financial life well organized, you can spend more time thinking about how to successfully invest your time and money, rather than wasting time searching for paperwork you need and spending money to correct errors that otherwise could have been avoided.

Organization is half the battle, but organization alone won't do. In fact, you will need to develop a system that is shaped, in part, by your inclination to be disorganized. That's right: one way to ensure that your record-keeping system will work for you is to structure it according to your record-keeping weaknesses (as well as your strengths). In other words, focus on aspects of your money-related record-keeping habits that you are least likely to follow through on. If you're someone who never balances a checkbook, organizing your monthly checks would be the obvious place to start. Address your weaknesses, then move on.

Creating Your Own System

There are many different ways to create a record-keeping system that can work for you. A good "system" will be divided into two main categories: personal finance and investing. And it will have two main components: an active file and an inactive file.

Straightforward enough.

But making this system work for you is a more complicated matter—in fact, it's as complicated as you are.

Ask yourself, are you the kind of person who meticulously puts your bills and investment statements away as you receive them? Or do you just toss them in a drawer in your room? Perhaps you scatter them all over the place. Maybe you even throw out bills as soon as you pay them. If there are two of you, this process can be twice as difficult to manage. If you choose to set up an online file, the difficulties can surpass the more mundane paper chase, since it's more difficult to enter all the data you need if you aren't organized and disciplined. No matter what record-keeping habits you have (from meticulous to mercurial), the following suggestions should help you develop better record-keeping skills.

- Keep the files easily accessible.
- File away bills and investment statements as they come in—not on a weekly or monthly basis. This is the best way to keep track of what you have spent, what you owe, and when the bill is to be paid, as well as how well you are paying yourself in terms of investing wisely and well.
- Always write the date and amount paid on the bill. Then file it in its appropriate active file. Writing the date and amount on the bill will help you keep track of your own payment history so that, come the next statement time, you can check and make sure that the company received your payment and recorded it. If you use personal finance software (see the personal finance software resources at the end of this chapter) to pay your bills, you may think you are off the bill-filing hook. What happens if you lose the program? That's right: it happens. You should print out your bill payments and file the hard copy in your active file.
- Buy a small calendar specifically for bill paying and investing. How many times have you sent in a late payment—or missed a payment altogether? Every time you do, you set yourself back in two ways. First, you are either assessed a late fee or charged interest on a needlessly high balance; plus, you may find that your delinquency is reported to credit agencies, which, in turn, can make it harder for you to obtain a loan down the road. A bill-paying calendar will help you help yourself to pay each and every bill on time—or to warn creditors in advance that you will be unable to do so on time. If you have an automatic investment plan (a smart move), then you have solved one potential problem that many investors fail to overcome—regularly investing a portion of their income. Still, it's a great idea to make a note in your calendar as to the date (and amount) of your automatic withdrawal so that you don't accidentally overdraw your account. It's also a good idea to mark down significant investment dates, for example, for a quarterly review of your 401(k) portfolio so that you are prepared to research and make potential trades in due time (rather than rushed time).

Keep the calendar at the front of your active file, and when you receive a bill, open the calendar and mark in red when the payment is due. By the same token, you can use one of the many personal finance software solutions to scheduling and planning your payments and investment statements. Just be sure you keep a backup file.

- Reserve one drawer in one place for your active files. That way you'll always know where they are so you'll never have to throw your bills on a chair and then forget where you put them. And, perhaps more importantly, you won't have to wonder about how your investments have been doing—and just what you're invested in. Also, set aside a large enough drawer to accommodate what can become sizable folders.
- Buy an alphabetized accordion folder—or buy loose folders, and label them: one folder per credit card, bank, or insurance company. Sounds simple—works great! (Cost: $20 max. Less than a late payment fee that could have been avoided if your records were organized.)
- Keep some extra space set aside for a "research" folder in which you can keep information on your investments, or news that pertains to them, as well as information on changes in your overall personal financial landscape.
- Buy a fireproof box for your most valuable documents: passport, birth certificate, naturalization papers, etc. Also, keep copies of your most important papers in your active record-keeping system.

Heeding the helpful hints for setting up a record-keeping system is a good first step. Now you need to take the practical application plunge. You need to know what documents to file and where to file them.

Your Active Files

Bank statements (including recently canceled checks), charge card, credit card and loan statements, paycheck stubs, and insurance bills are just some of the items to keep in your active personal finance file. Investment statements, annual and semiannual reports, trade documentation, and written memos of any conversations you have had with your broker, financial adviser, or customer representative are some of the items to keep in your active investment file.

Active Personal Finance File

The following are some sections you might consider:

- Banking
  — Most recent bank statements

— Deposit/withdrawal/ATM slips
— Automatic investment slips
— Canceled checks

• Credit Cards
— Monthly statements

• Food and Entertainment
— Grocery bills
— Liquor bills
— Restaurant/bar tabs

• Insurance
— Health insurance payments
— Car insurance payments
— Renter's or homeowner's insurance payments

• Loans
— Bank loans
— Car loan
— Student loans
— Mortgage

• Receipts or Purchase Slips
— Clothing
— Furniture
— Appliances
— CDs, DVDs, etc.
— Other (such as pharmacy bills)

• Rent and Utilities
— Electricity bill
— Phone and/or cell phone bill
— Gas bill
— Heating bill
— Cable or satellite
— Internet bill
— Fitness club bill

• Transportation
— Gas
— Car repair receipts

— Car insurance
— Commuter ticket or monthly card

• Taxes
— Tax statements

Active Investment File

• Investments
— Mutual fund statements
— Brokerage statements
— Retirement plan statements
— Account memos*
— Annual reports
— Most recent semiannual reports on funds and companies you invest in
— Most recent quarterly statements

• Research
— Magazine reports on your stocks, bonds, and mutual funds
— Industry reports that affect your investments
— New investment ideas

Notice that there is no "temporary" or "to-be-filed" file. Such "temporary" files all too easily become a permanent pain in the bill payer's (your) and investor's (also your) derriere. As with most events in life, you should never put off doing today what you think you will do tomorrow. Tomorrow comes, chaos remains.

Your Inactive Files

An inactive file is a mini financial library where you can research your spending, saving, and investing history. Your ability to research your own questions is not only the best way to ensure that you get the answer

---

*While the above investment statements are relatively self-explanatory, many investors neglect to keep an accurate record of the time, date, person's name with whom they spoke, transaction request, and response. You should do so every time you call your broker, brokerage, mutual fund company, or human resource department so that you are certain you have an accurate record to defend your side of the story—should something go wrong.

you are looking for, it's also money saved. If, for example, you call your bank or brokerage and ask the company's staff to research a transaction that you think may have taken place seven months ago, the company will be more than happy to oblige. More than happy, because it'll charge you at least twice what it pays the clerk who actually researches your account to come up with the noncommittal answer that somehow costs you more money. If, instead, you create an inactive file, you will be able to do most or all of the work yourself.

Another significant advantage of an "inactive" file is that you can activate it, in terms of researching how well your investment portfolio has done over time. Many investors become so caught up in the day-to-day performance of their portfolios that they forget to look at the cumulative success (or failure) of their history of investments. You know Santayana's saying, "Those who forget the past are doomed to repeat it"? Learn from the history of your own actions. Also, use the history of your investments contained in this file as a sounding board for future investing strategies.

Write the following labels for your inactive file:

- Financial Papers over Three Months Old
  — Bank statements
  — Canceled checks
  — Past tax returns
  — Brokerage and/or mutual fund slips

- Loans and Other Obligations over Three Months Old or Paid in Full
  — Student loan statements
  — Car loan
  — Personal loan
  — Credit card statements
  — Canceled credit card/charge card paid bills

- Personal Papers
  — Adoption papers
  — Birth certificate
  — Citizenship papers
  — College diploma
  — Passport
  — Social Security card
  — Veteran's/ROTC papers

- Ownership Papers
  — Automobile title
  — Other

Just do it. Once you have created your active and inactive record-keeping files you will no doubt need to discipline yourself to actually use them. What makes this difficult is easy to understand. It requires no effort not to file a bill or investment statement. It requires some effort to do so. But the effort it requires to file one statement is minimal compared to the effort it will take to file several all at once—or to find the one statement you need in a pile of papers that have been accumulating over the past few months.

You can develop a good record-keeping system for your personal finance and investing areas. You can perfect your own record-keeping skills. If at first you make a mess of things, try to set it right. Just about everything in life requires work, revision, more work, and more revision. Most man-made systems are prone to occasional screwups, so it should come as no surprise that you will need to tinker with your record-keeping system on a regular basis. You will know that you have finally got it right when you don't have to search for bills when you want to pay or question them, or wonder what the total return of your investment portfolio is or what percentage of your investments you have in stocks, bonds, cash, foreign markets, and pork bellies. Practice makes perfect.

Ready Resources

The following money-management software will help you plot your financial course to your ultimate investing goals. They will also help you cover most of your bill-paying needs, and some will help you establish a record-keeping system for all your financial concerns—from personal finance to investing.

- Quicken
- Managing Your Money
- Microsoft Money
- Kiplinger's CA-Simply Money

SECTION 2

Selecting the Best Markets Is Essential to Your Overall Investment Success

CHAPTER 6

Smart Banking from Scratch

Understanding some basic ingredients that create money and markets, economies and economics before you start investing from scratch is the only recipe for success. It's one we all could put into practice on a more regular basis. The truth is most of us don't like to think about money, since it's something we know we lack a lot of. And who likes to think about what they lack?

This section is designed to give you a full course on investing basics even before you get acquainted with the basic categories of investments. While this may sound backwards, it isn't. Many investors spend so much time focusing on individual stocks and funds that they fail to see the forest of events that affect their investments—from creating a better way to bank their money to learning which economic factors and cycles affect various markets to understanding which markets are most likely to yield the most consistent, successful investment results.

Each chapter will serve you like a stepping-stone across a river of investment opportunities that await you on the other side—in section 3. True, you can try to jump across, but don't blame me if, in so doing, you wind up getting soaked by an economic cycle or volatile market you could have learned to avoid had you only taken your journey step by step.

. . .

Banks are the traditional cornerstone of one's financial house. In fact, for many of us, banks will hold the key (and the right to take it back) to our actual home—typically the single biggest investment we will make (or have already made) in this lifetime. That's why, when it comes to growing your money, you need to become as smart about banking as you will become about investing. The tricky part is that banks are no longer the places they once were. For example, not only can you deposit and withdraw money from banks, you can open up an automatic investment account, invest in a bank-related mutual fund, receive investment information, invest in a host of funds from many different fund families, and, when it comes to some banks, you can do it all online. On the other hand, you can also do everything that a bank used to be the sole proprietor of without ever having to open up a bank account. You can open up a checking account at your brokerage or mutual fund firm. You can take loans from a variety of nonbank sources, including your own 401(k) plan. You can get a mortgage from a mortgage broker rather than a bank—the broker sells your mortgage to a bank down the road.

Additionally, all banks are not created equal. Some are safer than others. Some are more convenient than others. Others offer greater interest on accounts than their competitors do on the same types of accounts. Still others offer a wider range of products and services. All these differences could work to your saving and investing advantage—or, in the event of an uninsured bank closing, the loss of some of your cash.

Most of us have basic banking needs, but the question concerning whether or not we need a bank to fulfill them is getting more interesting these days. For one thing, it's unclear that we will need banks in the near future since, with the advent of mortgage brokers and money market mutual funds with check-writing, debit, and credit card privileges, the main staples of a bank's fee-based diet are offered on other menus. Besides, many of us are already used to doing most of our banking automatically (with automatic transfers, ATMs, and even online transactions with a PC).

What role should banks play in your life? But before we get ahead of ourselves, perhaps we should review what today's bank can do for you. After all, most of us do have a bank checking account—and should have a savings account (wherein three months of our take-home pay is stashed for cash-based emergencies). What's more, a bank is the place many of us will go to get our first mortgage (or refinance the one we've got). And for the lucky few who bought real estate in the early 1990s and have seen some appreciation in equity, a second mortgage or equity line of credit is perhaps a worthwhile consideration. Other bank-related services: automatic teller machine (ATM) transactions, new car loans, bill consolidation loans.

Today's banking environment is a jungle of products and services. Many of those products and services are worth considering while others are money pits to be avoided at all costs. In your search for overall financial independence it's critical that you become an informed banking consumer so that you will know how to shop for the bank that best meets your current and future financial needs.

Banking Basics

How did you choose your bank? When it comes to banks, most of us let banks choose us, rather than the other way around. Here's how it works. You graduate from college or change your career. You move into a new or familiar town. You need to have checks with your name and address on them and you need them now. You look out your window. No bank in sight. You walk one block. There, within walking or easy driving distance to your new digs, is a bank. Your new bank. "How convenient," says a devilishly persuasive voice within your head. "Let's just set up an account here and be done with it—we've got better things to do than fiddle around in bank lobbies all day!" It is a most convincing voice. But is it the voice you should be listening to?

If you ask yourself what should you be looking for in a bank, chances are convenience won't top the list, but with today's online banking services, maybe it should be—but not at the expense of quality. Low-cost service, the variety of services, and then geographical or virtual convenience should be your concerns.

Looking for all the above takes little time and effort and, at the same time, it can actually save you money before you open up a new account. Five steps to take to set you out in the right direction:

1. Familiarize yourself with the types of banks that are in your area.
2. Familiarize yourself with the range of services they offer.
3. Choose the one bank that provides the services you need at a cost that is competitive with other banks.

4. Make sure that the type of bank account you choose enables you to bank online and invest automatically. Remember, there are several types of banks. It's not the size that counts. It's the level of savings safety (FDIC insurance), product range, and quality of cost-effective service. The key is to bank where your money will be the safest and where you will be best served.

5. Make sure you are comfortable with your bank's ethical practices (see page 76).

In addition to banks, credit unions are often good places to do business, if you are eligible to join. A credit union is a banking cooperative operated for the benefit of its members. Most credit unions are sponsored by an employer or an association—meaning they aren't open to the general public. Workers' unions—from teamsters to teachers—tend to offer this alternative form of banking. If you have the opportunity to join a credit union you should consider it. Typically, credit unions offer better rates—on both savings accounts and consumer loans. One drawback to credit unions, however, is that they're a bit behind the times when it comes to online services. While this will no doubt change rapidly in the year(s) ahead, you may find that even your local bank provides greater electronic access.

Above all, be sure that your deposits are federally insured—by the Federal Deposit Insurance Corporation, or FDIC, as it's more commonly known. It won't be hard to tell whether or not your bank is FDIC insured. For one thing, if it is, it will likely be posted on every teller window and then some. If you don't see any signs to indicate FDIC insurance, you can ask the branch manager—and ask for positive proof. (Word of mouth may be a great way to decide if you're going to go see the new John Travolta flick, but it gets two thumbs down as a way to recommend a bank.) If you don't make sure your bank is FDIC insured, there's not much to ensure that the money you deposit tonight will still be there come sunup.

To find a bank that's right for you, you can do it the old-fashioned way: Get your hands on the Yellow Pages and call several banks that are convenient for you to get to. Call each bank, and ask for the following information:

A. FDIC insurance: [ ] Yes   [ ] No

B. Types of checking accounts: 1. _____

                                      2. _____

                                      3. _____

                                      4. _____

C. Types of savings accounts: 1. _____

                                      2. _____

                                      3. _____

                                      4. _____

D. Interest rates on B and C: 1. _____   1. _____

                                      2. _____   2. _____

                                      3. _____   3. _____

                                      4. _____   4. _____

E. Fees for B and C: 1. _____   1. _____

                                      2. _____   2. _____

                                      3. _____   3. _____

                                      4. _____   4. _____

F. Location:

The new way to select a bank that's best for you is to go online. While the details of online banking are provided in a special section below, it might surprise you to know that you can actually shop for all your basic and even most of your more complex banking needs without standing up. As long as you're linked to the World Wide Web, the world of banking is literally at your fingertips. True, it's a small world, right now. But you can bet that banks will proliferate in virtual reality at a warp speed similar to their ATM installations during the last decade. Why? Customers are the driving force of their business—and many of their customers are finding it increasingly difficult to do their banking during banker's hours. The Web gives banks twenty-four hours a day to catch new customers. Many customers are already banking online with services like Quicken.com and Microsoft Money.

Shopping for a bank that provides all the services you need at a comparably competitive cost has been made considerably easier of late—and not just because banks have gone virtual. Most banks—big and small—offer a host of service-related incentives to new customers, often waiving monthly fees for new checking and savings accounts. Since average annual service fees can easily cost over $100, this is no small deal. Of course, the deal may be short-lived. For example, "No annual fee for the first year." But that still represents money saved and money in the bank in your account.

When it comes to mortgage lending, banks have also become more competitive—some will waive closing costs (all or in part) and many will be less turned off by a spotty credit history. The reason? For one thing, there's more competition from mortgage companies vying for your business. And there are fewer of us, meaning that banks have more to lend—and since lending is their business, it behooves them to find ways to maintain a steady pace. Now, this rosy condition may not last forever. Low-interest-rate environments are the best time to buy a home. When rates are at historical lows, you can buy more house for your buck. The merits of buying a home, versus renting one, aren't as straightforward as they used to be. The bottom line: Think of your house as a home—not as an investment. Chances are you'll qualify for a larger tax break if you "own" your home, but building equity in your home will take longer, on average, than in previous years (the drawback of a low inflationary environment). Moreover, since you don't really own your home—your mortgage lender does—if you are thinking of moving within the next five years, consider renting as an option. Or consider a two-family home as a possible investment. (For more on real estate investing, turn to chapter 13.)

Select a bank based on services needed, not on services provided. A bank is basically there for taking money out (from your checking account, which can also be the base of your automatic investing account, and as loans and mortgages) and putting money in (to your checking and savings accounts).

No matter which bank you select, be sure to stick with the most essential criterion of all—the safety of your money. After you are certain that the bank is federally insured, then you can begin to match your search for cost-effective service and best interest deals with your sense of what constitutes a higher purpose.

ETHICAL BANKING

One of the commonly overlooked aspects of selecting a bank is whether or not your bank practices a business ethic you believe in. Like ethical investing (see chapter 21), there are criteria you can use to rate your bank's social conscience. Not that you have to. Most investors are not concerned with the social responsibility of the companies they invest in. Most banking consumers are, likewise, uninterested. However, we're the new generation of banking consumers and investors. Maybe it's time to become more of an ethical activist and less of a consumer passivist when it comes to where our money is deposited and how it is invested on our behalf by the bank we do business with.

The following criteria will help you rate a bank's commitment to social responsibility.

- Community development: How active is your bank in terms of community development projects? How can you find out? Since 1977, banks have had to file a community reinvestment statement—under the Community Reinvestment Act mandate—in which the bank's distribution of loans among all members of the community is disclosed. Not that numbers tell the whole story—high denial rates among specific minorities may be an indication of an underqualified applicant pool. Nevertheless, requesting a copy of this statement—yours for the asking—from your bank will help you jump-start your thoughtful engagement with the institution that not only holds your money, but also invests it in projects you may or may not agree with.
- Community involvement: Economic commitment to the community as a whole is one thing. Community involvement is another. Use the following criteria to rate a bank's commitment to its community:
  — Does the bank locate branches in distressed areas? (Some banks are opening ATM machines inside area police stations in order to keep banking opportunities open to all, even in high-crime neighborhoods.)
  — Are bank officers active in local charities and community organizations?
- Who owns the bank? Minority-owned banks are one way to go. In opening your account in a minority-owned bank you may be helping to promote lending in less developed areas in your community. It's not a guarantee that you are. To find out if there is a minority-owned, FDIC-insured bank in your area, contact the National Bankers Association (nationalbankers.org).

BASIC BANKING ACCOUNTS

To open your bank account you will need the following four items: money, your Social Security number, an address, and some form of positive identification—a driver's license should be just the ticket. Not surprisingly, putting money into the bank is easy. However, deciding which accounts suit your needs likely will prove more difficult.

Savings Accounts

Although there are many variations on the savings account theme, most savings accounts share a basic motif: its purpose—you put money into a savings account in order to build up a cash reserve while earning (a modest amount of) interest on it.

Banks calculate interest in three different ways. This means the interest you receive on a similar account may differ from bank to bank depending on how each calculates its savings account's interest. Day of deposit to the day of withdrawal, average daily balance, and the lowest monthly balance are the three ways in which the amount of money in your savings account may earn interest. Day of deposit, which means you earn interest on money from the day it is deposited to the day it's withdrawn, will earn you the most interest; average daily balance is less attractive because it pays interest on the average balance in your account; and the lowest balance method is the least attractive since it pays interest on the smallest balance in your account during the month or quarter.

Earning interest on your hard-earned money is one advantage of a savings account. Another, less obvious benefit is that the act of setting your earnings aside in an account specifically earmarked for savings is, in itself, a positive money-management development. A savings account can also allow you to create an emergency fund—a sum of money set aside for the purpose of providing cash should your monthly resources prove inadequate to meet life's little (but costly) surprises, like a flat tire or a wisdom tooth removal.

Is there a downside to a savings account? You bet. Naturally, you assume that the hard-earned money you've deposited in the account will earn enough interest to make it a worthwhile investment. But guess what? Chances are, unless you use your savings account only as a temporary parking place for your cash, the money deposit there will decline in value on an inflation-adjusted basis. This is because the amount of interest earned in a typical savings account is usually lower than the rate of inflation.

Inflation affects the value of each and every dollar you earn, save, and/or spend. If the rate of inflation is 3.5% and the rate of interest you're earning on your savings account is 3.25%, then your dollar's purchasing power—what it used to be able to buy versus what it can now buy—has lost ground, not gained it. That's why a savings account is strongly recommended for one specific function: the establishment of an emergency reserve fund for life's unexpected surprises. Otherwise, your money can be put to better use earning higher interest.

Passbook or Statement Savings Accounts

The one basic type of savings account is the "regular savings" account. There are two subspecies of the regular savings account, which differ only in the way your transactions are recorded. One is the passbook savings account and the other is the statement savings account. In a passbook account all your deposits and withdrawals are recorded in an actual book—a "passbook." In a statement savings account, the bank records and stores your transactions in its database and sends you a monthly printout of your account activities (including deposits, withdrawals, and ATM use). Traditionally, passbook accounts were the standard type of savings account. Thanks to computerization, however, statement savings accounts are now the more common form of regular savings account. A statement savings account provides you with a detailed monthly review of all your account transactions, which can be a handy way to review your savings account's progress.

Passbook accounts are easier to use and easier to keep track of. Every time you make a deposit or withdrawal, it's there in black and white. On the other hand, a passbook can get lost or left behind. If you do not have your passbook with you when you go to deposit or withdraw money you may be in for some time-consuming hassles. The signature card that most banks require clients to fill out will have to be accessed, and the clerk will have to scrutinize your word against your signature. This is time consuming as well as annoying.

A statement savings account will take a bit more effort on your part. If you have a statement savings account, you should receive a monthly account transaction summary that details your deposits and withdrawals, including any ATM-related use. It's important to read through the statement when it arrives and to match its account history with your own version of the truth. You may, for example, find that it lists an ATM transaction that you don't remember making. If this is so, you will be thankful that you saved your ATM slips for the past month. If you didn't, there's still a chance to reconcile your version with the bank's. You will need to call the bank and request a review of the suspicious item. This request may cost you, so be sure of your doubts before you call.

You have to pay to save. Banks charge you fees for the privilege of depositing your money with them. Fees for similar accounts may differ from bank to bank. That's why it's important to find out whether or not, and how much, you will be charged for each and every type of bank account you open. For example, a basic savings account might run you $4 to $8 per month. Ditto for checking. One way around paying a fee is to open an account that waives fees (as long as you keep a specified minimum balance). However, if there is a minimum balance required in order to waive the fee, find out what it is, and make sure you're not likely to go below it. Also, check and see whether or not there are withdrawal fees. Some regular savings accounts might assess a withdrawal fee based on an allowable monthly withdrawal limit. In both instances, the fees can easily negate the gain in interest your savings have made—so be sure you know what the fees are, and that you know that you can live within their limits. Moreover, since there's a dramatic difference between interest earned in one bank's savings account as opposed to another's, the fees imposed on the savings account will affect your savings goals to a greater or lesser degree. For example, if Bank A offers 3% interest but charges you $8 a month for the privilege, you would be better off going with Bank B, which offers 2.5% interest but charges you only $4 per month for the privilege. How much better off would you be? Suppose you deposited $250 in both Bank A and Bank B. At the end of a year, your account at Bank A would contain $161.50, while the one at Bank B would hold $208.25. Bank B is $46.75 better. But, expenses considered, your motives could have been better. Herein lies a basic investment lesson: pay attention to any and all types of fees and the toll they can take on your hard-earned dollars.

Checking Accounts

These are the preferred accounts of young people, for good reasons. First, like a savings account, a checking account enables you to deposit your earnings. Second, a checking account enables you not to carry a wad of cash on your weekly trip to the supermarket. Third, and perhaps most important, a checking account serves as a convenient and cost-effective way to pay your monthly bills. (For your best options on how to pay your monthly bills, see chapter 5.)

Having said all that, with the advent of the debit card and electronic bill paying, you can also access the money in your bank account with the touch of a keystroke or the insertion of a debit card. Look into the possibility of taking advantage of electronic banking. To help you do so, go to [yourbanksname].com (by which I mean, type your bank's name and attach a *.com* to it—or Google it). Chances are you'll find online services that give you the ability to pay your bills with the touch of a keystroke, apply for a loan, even complain to the branch manager. Most of these programs and services will cost you nothing—since, effectively, you're acting as a temporary employee every time you do the bank's work for it. Be sure to keep as accurate a record of your online wheeling and dealing as you would any other hard copy financial transaction—if you don't, and something gets lost in e-translation, you may end up paying more for electronic banking in the short run since the bank will charge you to research the problem.

Most likely, your bank offers you at least three types of checking accounts: regular checking, NOW (Negotiable Order of Withdrawal), and Super-NOW. A regular checking account typically earns no interest and often comes with a small monthly fee—$4 to $8—whether or not you write a check. As with savings accounts, there is a way around paying this monthly fee. You will need to keep enough money in your account (on an ongoing basis) to provide the minimum balance requirements—usually $500 to $2,500—in order to waive the minimum monthly fee.

There are other advantages to the NOW and Super-NOW accounts besides being potentially fee-free. Both pay interest on your deposits. (A Super-NOW account will pay more interest, but you'll have to keep a higher minimum balance in the account.) Moreover, both NOW and Super-NOW accounts let you write a certain number of checks per month for free (some accounts even give you unlimited check-writing privileges). It's important to know the limits so that you can avoid being charged a fee for each check you write over the specified limit. You can easily double or triple your monthly account fee by ignoring this limit.

These two types of NOW accounts may also make you eligible for small discounts on same-bank loans, free traveler's checks, and discounted or waived fees on bank credit cards. The catch? If you fall below the minimum required balance you'll pay a fee that is higher than the one you would pay in a regular checking account. If you think you will have some trouble keeping the minimum balance required of a NOW or Super-NOW account, stick with a regular checking account. Chances are you will come out ahead of the game if you do since the higher monthly fees associated with not keeping the minimum balance in a NOW or Super-NOW account often outweigh the amount of interest earned plus the small monthly fee for a regular checking account.

There's one surefire way to save money with a checking account. Order your checks—the actual item—from a source other than your bank. It makes sound financial sense to do so since it can cut the cost of getting checks—typically about $9 per 200 from your bank—by about 50%. And it's easy to do by ordering your own checks from independent printers right over the phone—or, if you have the software, you can print your own. Checks in the Mail (checksinthemail.com) charges $5 for a book of 200 checks (with your name, address, account number, and the same bar codes that appear on your current checks).

Balancing Your Checkbook: A checking account is a simple, comprehensive account designed to handle all your day-to-day personal payment needs. Opening one is easy. Writing a check is easy, too. On the other hand, balancing a checkbook—and keeping it balanced—is as likely an occurrence as finding Ozzie Osborne in church.

Yet, *balancing your checkbook is one of the most important financial moves you can make.* If you don't, you run the (expensive) risk of bouncing a check. Even if you don't bounce a check, you will waste valuable time worrying about whether or not you might. Moreover, if you don't balance your checkbook on a regular basis, you'll have no way of knowing if the check you're writing is swinging you over the edge of your budget's precipice. Then there's the matter of keeping track of the dents you make in your checking account via your ATM. It's easy to see why balancing a checkbook can be difficult. But, with a little know-how, it can be quite simple.

To balance your checkbook subtract the amount of the check you are writing from the existing balance. Or add the amount you are depositing to the existing balance.

You tell yourself that you can subtract and add. But, believe me, the tricky part is actually doing it. This is so tricky, that few people ever go through life with a balanced checkbook, and many experience the costly embarrassment of a bounced check. Why is it so tricky? People assume that they can put off balancing their checkbook to the end of the week or month. That's the trap. Here's how you can avoid it:

1. Balance your checkbook every time you write a check.
2. Balance your checkbook every time you make a withdrawal from your checking account with your ATM card.
3. Always subtract the applicable monthly fee for the account from your existing balance.
4. Get a "top-stub" checkbook. A top-stub checkbook may cost you a few pennies more, but it will make keeping your checkbook balanced a whole lot easier. Basically, a top-stub enables you to record your transaction and update your balance each and every time you write a check. The more traditional back-end balance checkbook adds a wrinkle to the process—you have to turn to the back of the checkbook to record and balance your account. That wrinkle turns out to be the tsunami of checkbook balancing. There's no way to ride the wave—so why not opt for a different, more effective checkbook instead?

Following these four steps is the best way to keep your checkbook balanced. It requires minimum effort and brain power—and it can save you a bundle. If that's not enough incentive, consider the major effort it will take to balance your checkbook at the end of the month.

If you already have a checking account and you are unsure of what your balance is, there are several ways you can find out. But first, don't write another check. The next step is to get your hands on your most recent bank statement, your bank's toll-free customer service phone number, a calculator, and a piece of scrap paper. On the piece of scrap paper, create five columns to record the following information:

1. Checks Accounted for on Most Recent Bank Statement
    Check Number _____   *Check Amount* $ _____
2. Checks Unaccounted for on Most Recent Bank Statement
    Check Number _____   *Check Amount* $ _____
3. Checks Unaccounted for since Most Recent Bank Statement
    Check Number _____   *Check Amount* $ _____
4. ATM Withdrawals since Most Recent Bank Statement
    Amount $ _____

5. Ending Balance on Most Recent Bank Statement
    Balance $ _____
6. Complete (1). Subtract (2), (3), and (4) from (5). You're done.

If you can't locate your most recent bank statement, don't panic. You can call your bank and ask when you can expect to receive your next account statement. If it's only a matter of days, wait it out—unless you are convinced that you have overdrawn your account. In this case, or in the event that the next statement won't be arriving for a week or more, you can contact your bank's customer service department and request the information listed above.

Make sure you have your checkbook, pen, paper, and calculator set up and ready to go. Also, be prepared to have to muscle your request through a reluctant account representative. While most are user-friendly, some suffer from politeness deprivation. If you find yourself up against a snotty clerk, don't feed his Napoleonic urge by letting him know you're aggravated. Simply insist that you speak with his superior. Say it exactly like that, too: "I want to speak to your superior." When you get someone you can talk to, let him know that you're having trouble balancing your checkbook and that you'll need the above information to help you out. Once you've gathered all the above information, it will take you under five minutes to balance your checkbook. Go.

If your version differs from your bank's get the answer without delay. If your balance and the bank's balance aren't identical twins, cross-examine yourself. For example, did you forget to list a check or ATM transaction? Did you remember to subtract the monthly fee owed to the bank? Did you enter a check amount incorrectly—$3 for $30 worth of CDs? Did you include the same check twice—#347 for $23 × 2 = $46? Did you transpose numbers—$34 for $43—when writing in or balancing your checkbook? If all these questions are answered and you still aren't able to square your account, then call your bank to help reconcile your account.

If you seriously think—or find out—you're overdrawn place a stop payment order on each check that has crossed the line. A stop order, or stop payment order, can be placed on any check that you write—for a fee. If, for example, you write a check and lose it, or write a check and don't want the person or store to whom it was sent to be able to cash it, then for a fee (typically $15) you can place a stop payment order on that check. Since your bank likely will charge you much more for bouncing a check ($25 per bounced check), and since you will also be assessed a processing fee (typically $5) from the merchant to whom you wrote the check, it makes financial sense to place a stop order. It also makes personal sense—you will spare yourself some of the attendant check-bouncing embarrassment. ("Manager to checkout counter nine. Manager to checkout counter. Hey, Morty—that couple who bounced a check last week are back again!")

If the check was written within the past two weeks, you can place the stop payment order over the phone. To place a stop order, you'll need to know the check number, name of the person to whom the check was written, and/or amount of the check. In most cases, if you don't have the check number, the bank may hem and haw about being able to honor your stop payment order. This is because it makes it very difficult for the bank to detect the particular check. Be persistent. In the end, as long as you can tell them the amount of the check and to whom it was written, they will be able to honor your request. After all, you're paying them good money to do so.

Reconcile your monthly checking account. Once you balance your checkbook, keep it balanced. Like a game of Concentration, you need to be sure that you can match every check that you write with every check that is processed.

Money Market Accounts

Instead of a savings account or checking account, you may prefer a money market account. This type of account (not to be confused with a money market mutual fund, discussed on pages 202–3), is a higher-yielding hybrid of a savings account with check-writing privileges. Interest is earned on the amount you have in your account, and you can write checks—sometimes as few as four checks per month, sometimes as many as you wish. However, the minimum balance required to waive the monthly fee is often much higher in this type of savings account—typically over $1,000. Also, the check-writing privilege needs to be viewed for what it is—a fee trap, for most people. This is because the limits fall below the average check writer's usage per month. Think of how many bills you have that you will want to write checks for. Chances are the number exceeds four to six checks per month—and that's not including the checks you write for groceries, or the ATM use for dinner and a movie. The bottom line is that few people write so few checks that they won't trespass the limit boundary of a money market account.

Solution: Use a money market account as the place for your emergency money supply. Use a checking account for check-writing related business. That way you can take advantage of a money market account over a savings account—slightly higher interest rate—without being taken advantage of, in the form of fees levied for excessive check writing. If you are contemplating the best possible location of immediately accessible emergency money, the money market account is a great way to go.

Tools You Can Use

Banks offer a variety of account-related and credit-related services. Consider the following to be some of the most practical and useful banking tools.

1. Overdraft protection. If you bounce a check—that is, write a check for more money than you actually have in your checking account—you will damage your financial condition in two ways. First, you will be socked with a hefty fee ($15 to $30 per bounced check) from your bank and the $5-or-more fee from the proprietor to whom you wrote the check. These fees could easily total $100 or more if several checks are bounced at once. Second, you may be blacklisted—the bank or store at which your check bounced may put your name on a list that is either specific to the establishment where you wrote the check or, worse, a general list of bad-check writers that's sent to several retail establishments. In short, you will have trouble writing a check—and you'll always be worried about doing so. The only surefire way to avoid such a situation is always to balance your checkbook to the penny. Another fail-safe way to avoid this problem is to check out something called overdraft protection for your checking account. Many banks now offer you and your wallet some peace of mind in the form of an automatic line of credit. This line of credit automatically funds your checking account should you inadvertently overdraw your account. Typically, there's no annual fee for this service—however, there's an interest rate that is charged on any unpaid line-of-credit balance. That rate will be high—very high. The result: overdraft protection is an excellent idea so long as it's used to protect you from the expense of bouncing checks. Used incorrectly, i.e., as a source for borrowing money, it's a recipe for debt distress.

2. ATM, or "debit," cards. Chances are you have an automatic teller machine (ATM) card. ATM cards provide you with the convenient benefit of being able to withdraw and deposit money twenty-four hours a day, in nearly every locale in the country, as well as abroad. To do so, you simply pick and memorize a PIN (personal identification number), then find an ATM machine that is part of (or linked to) your bank's data network. (You will likely be charged a fee for nonmember bank-related machines. You may even be charged a fee for bank-related ones.) To find the nearest machine you can use, find a phone both and call the toll-free number on the back of your card. That's it. You are off and running. And, no matter which kind of transaction you're making—whether deposit, withdrawal, account balance inquiry—you will get a printed readout of your transaction. Don't throw that slip away. Instead, pocket it. Bring it home. Put it in your active banking file. Then, when you receive your statement at the end of the month, you can match your slips to the statement's record of your ATM use. Once it all checks out, you can toss the slips—in your circular file, of course.

But hold on a minute. Do you really want to use that card? Can you afford to? How will taking money out today affect your budget for tomorrow? Convenience can be a drawback. For one thing, all those convenient locations invite you to use your ATM card often. However, with your increased use comes the potential for increased service fees. Anytime you use your ATM in a network not affiliated with your bank, you may be charged a fee of $2 or more. Also, ATM use may be hazardous to your health. According to the FBI, ATM-related crime has increased as steadily as the proliferation of the machines themselves. Be aware of your surroundings when using your card. For example, ATM booths located at the back of the bank, in an alley, or in any poorly lit street should be avoided. Also, be aware of who is around you when you enter and when you leave an ATM booth. You are a picture-perfect target for a thief—there in a well-lit glass booth counting your money for all to see.

3. Super ATM, or debit, cards. You may also notice a variation on the ATM theme that allows a regular ATM card to be used in place of a check or anywhere a major credit card is accepted. In fact, this is a debit card by another name. A debit card works in the following way: each purchase you make with it is automatically deducted from your checking account. All uses of both types of ATM cards will appear on your

monthly bank statement, making it easy to keep track of your use—and target any overuse patterns before they get out of hand.

4. ATM machines. You can now use your ATM card to access mutual fund investment information and, if you are investing in mutual funds through your bank, you can obtain prices and account balances and even buy and sell shares. (To buy more shares, you simply authorize a transfer of cash from your savings or checking account.) At the end of your transaction, you will get a printout of what you have done—just the way you do when you make a normal deposit or withdrawal.

5. Secured cards. This is a new variation on an old theme. But it also provides the answer to an old riddle, namely, how can you get a credit card if you have no existing credit card history, and how can you get an existing credit card history if you have no credit card? With a secured card, the bank will require you to place a specific sum of money (typically $500) in a secured credit card account. That money then will serve as your secured card's credit limit. Every "charge" you make will be debited from the balance. Every payment you make will be credited to it. This may sound like a loathsome deal—but it's a great way to establish a credit history.

6. Bank cards. A bank card is a bank-issued credit card. There may be an advantage to taking out a bank card at your bank as opposed to another bank. Lower interest rates and lower or no annual fees top the list. However, you will need to do your homework when comparing the actual cost of a bank card with other sources. For one thing, specially promoted low rates may also have a less well promoted short life span—e.g., for the first six months only. The same holds true when comparing the benefits of transferring your existing credit card balances to a bank card or other credit card touted to save you money. It may end up costing you in the long run. How? The low, low interest rate for a transferred balance typically applies to that balance only. Additional charges on the card are typically socked with a much higher rate of interest.

7. Loans. Banks are often thought of more as a place to take out a loan than as a place to put money into. Nearly every bank on the planet has a host of ways to lend you money. (Chapter 7 will cover some loan basics. You can also visit eloan.com to get the loan you need at e-speed.)

8. Investments. Banks are now offering a host of investor-related services and products. Bank mutual funds are increasingly common. As with direct-marketed or broker-sold funds, the variety and type of bank-marketed funds can be overwhelming at first. This is especially

true if you are unsure about investing basics, let alone facts about mutual fund investing. For more on these topics, turn to section 3. There, you'll find the investment information you will need in order to select the best mutual funds to invest in.

A New Age of Banking

There are a number of ways that banks are using new technology to make banking easier for you (and for themselves). Some of these technologies aren't even so new:

1. Direct deposit. Social Security checks, veterans' benefits, and, more relevant to you, paychecks can often be directly deposited into your account. Everyone involved saves time. Just find out if your employer participates in such a plan.
2. Automatic investment and withdrawal. If you invest regularly, design a schedule for automatic transfers from your savings account to your mutual funds and/or IRAs.
3. Online banking. Today, you can satisfy most of your banking needs online—opening accounts, looking up your balances, transferring funds between accounts, paying bills, investing, even shopping and qualifying for a mortgage. What do you need to open up an online account? A computer, modem, and access to the Web or one of the online services (AOL, MSN), for starters. From there, it's a breeze, especially if you are using Quicken or Microsoft Money, which will let you download your bank account information directly into your own personal financial plan.

In the late 1990s, it was estimated that the number of banks that were accessible on the Web doubled every day. As you read this, there are thousands of banks online which you can choose from. Those banks that aren't online will be harder pressed to compete with those that are. But the evolution of banking online swiftly led to online banks—*virtual* banks that will likely take the market by force, just as banks that invested in the ATM biz did in the 1990s. Why? Convenience has taken on a whole new meaning. Today, convenience can save you time and money—and more. Netbank (netbank.com) is one of the best of this virtual bank breed. And the laundry list of Netbank's services include all the bells and whistles of your brick-and-mortar bank, from free checking to global ATM access to FDIC insurance. Online banks offer more than meets the eye. They're not just providing you with a more efficient way to bank, pay your bills, and buy a home—they're providing you with a host of relevant, timely financial information that you can put to good use in your overall financial planning and decision-making processes.

A prime example of a "Net bank" is Security First Network Bank (SFNB)—a virtual bank (in that it can only be accessed via the Internet) owned and run by a small Kentucky-based bank. SFNB can be tapped into at sfnb.com. There you'll find a virtual bank that mirrors one you might find in your hometown. Everything from an information desk and an account rep to a personal finance area and the bank's president are at your disposal.

Traditional banks are also online. These are the banks that will dominate the Internet. Currently some large and small banks are out there with excellent sites. From the mega Bank of America (bankofamerica .com) to the mini Salem Five Cents Savings Bank (salemfive.com), services and bargains abound. And while the current level of discounts might fall away, the level of services is likely to continue to increase. In fact, if you go to Bank of America's online site, you'll find a host of interesting avenues to travel—from loan and budget calculators, home loan rates, mortgage applications, and credit card applications to the more mundane transaction-based services.

You will also, no doubt, find more and more banks on the paid online services. There, in a simple menu-based format, you can shop for a bank, then open an account, which you can visit any time of day or night.

Still need to know how to write. Currently, opening an account still requires a signature (for most banks), some paperwork, and a stamp. But once you mail in the necessary items, you can fly on the Net bank to your heart's content—for a fee.

There are two types of fees you'll need to note when it comes to online banking. The first is the fee you're assessed for accessing the Internet. The second relates to the way the bank charges you for the privilege of doing online business with it. Many banks are currently waiving such fees. Fees are banks' bread and butter. Chances are, you'll be charged real-world rates for your virtual account—perhaps similar to the ones you're currently charged for your use of ATMs. Check and make sure that you know and understand all the fees involved.

There are security concerns related to online banking. First, there's the question of a hacker's ability to explode the code—whether your bank's or yours. Is there a way to ensure that your account is being safeguarded from such an event? Yes. You can make sure that your bank is using one or more of the following services: encryption, which ensures that the data feed between your PC and your bank's server isn't corrupted; private/public key cryptography, which ensures that your data is (a) yours and (b) heading to its correct destination; and a proprietary authentication method, which double-checks the first two steps. The second area of concern ought to be every banking consumer's primary concern: making sure the online bank is FDIC insured.

No matter which browser you use, definitely use it to check out some of the bank sites available. Finally, banking is shedding its boring cloak and donning an interesting, interactive mantle that will provide you with more efficient means to your money's ends.

A Final Reminder

After opening up your account, go home and set up a record-keeping file for it. If you already have an account, make sure you have an active file for it in your current record-keeping system. Don't make the common mistake of thinking you don't really need a file for this. An organized file will make such matters as balancing your accounts and checking errors on your accounts a breeze—without it, this can become very time consuming.

Furthermore, if you don't keep accurate and accessible information on your banking accounts, you could be making a costly mistake. Costly? That's right, when it comes to resolving clerical errors, most banks make you foot the research bill. However, if you do go home and set up that file then you will have the information you need to detect and prove an error. Make your life simple. Keep meticulous records of each of your accounts.

Ready Resources

- Bankrate.com
- *The Bank Book*, Edward F. Mirkvicka
- *Money, Banking, and Credit Made Simple*, Merle Dowd
- *Money Is My Friend*, Philip Laut

CHAPTER 7

Useful Economics from Scratch

Economics? Wasn't that a useless course you took once—together with hundreds of others in an air-conditionless auditorium where the only sounds you could hear were those of your fellow sufferers snoring? What was that professor's name? What was it he said about how one day you would find that you were living the lessons he was droning on and on about?

While you were busy studying economics, I was cramming ancient Greek in an effort to increase my understanding of the roots of what we call knowledge. Studying philosophy and Greek had some hidden advantages, not the least of which is that I know the philosophical and etymological derivations of *economics*. It's from the Greek, *economoi*, meaning to take care of one's household. And so we come eons later to our modern-day sense of the necessity of a balanced budget, living within one's means, in order to ensure that we're able to run our own household in a sensible manner—well, some of us do. Others, in their quest to build a castle, get caught in their own labyrinth of debt. There are ways to strike a livable balance between senseless spending and obsessive saving, and this book will touch on several. (If you want my complete personal finance road map, you'll have to grab a copy of *How to Survive in the Real World*.)

Back to economics. Let's say your econ professor suddenly appeared at your doorstep today. Chances are you'd be far more interested now in his theories on supply and demand, not to mention how purchasing power is directly affected by inflation—and how inflation itself can affect your current and future lifestyle and standard of living. Hey, you can always go back and sit in on a class or two—he didn't notice when you weren't there, and it's doubtful he'd notice you were there now. But there's a simpler way to refresh yourself on some basic economics. Read on.

Economics, like psychology and many other intellectual disciplines, professes itself to be a science. But like those 1950s sci-fi flicks where science goes terribly wrong and unleashes ants the size of school buses on a hapless little town in Lonersville, Nevada, economic theories can often do as much harm as good—especially if you take them to be absolute answers in a conditional world. The best way to proceed when it comes to wedding economic theory to real-world facts is to understand some of the basic themes and areas in the overall market that most theorists use in order to establish their predictive prowess.

Fortunately, so much of what you need to know and keep yourself up-to-date on is readily available in easily accessible newspapers, financial magazines and newsletters, TV, and the Web. But the abundance of information, like the abundance of potential investment vehicles, can prove to be a stumbling block in and of itself. First, the amount of information can be so overwhelming as to discourage all but the most stalwart researcher. Second, when it comes to reading the business section of the daily paper, most of us tune out—unless it's to hunt for the mutual funds that we own. To begin with, then, you need to determine a manageable number of sources of information regarding the economy and the markets. From that viewpoint, you can see how easy it will be to read the financial pages that come across your desk daily (just how is detailed in the following chapter), as well as how to scan for information that relates directly to your investments.

When it comes to economics, you're the expert. In fact, chances are you already have firsthand knowledge of how a growing or faltering economy has affected you, a family member, or a friend. A growing economy makes it easier to, among other things, find a job that pays well. It also makes it easier to feel good about spending what you have earned. But be careful. Everything that rises must mimic Icarus and plummet featherless and bloody back to earth. Don't fall under the spell of sunny days without preparing for rainy ones.

During tough economic times, jobs are as easily lost as they were to find in better times; thus, unemployment climbs, and as unemployment climbs employers may reduce wages. This means they can expect to get the same level of work (because there's competition for the job) for less. For you, this means the same amount of work will earn you less. If that's not bad enough, it's also harder to stretch a dollar to buy what it used to buy. Examples abound. Think of how there's no such thing as penny candy anymore. Or, take the way Jimmy Dean could never go back to a five-and-dime—they've all turned into Buck a Books or the $1 stores you see on the fringe of most suburban malls.

You don't have to have PhD in economics to become a savvy investor. Instead, you can familiarize yourself with some of the most common terms and frames of reference used by analysts, journalists, and investors alike—in a matter of minutes. I call it economics in a nutshell. And it's founded on the most basic and commonsense principle of all: supply and demand. Supply and demand and scarcity and production, that is. Here's how it works.

The greater the demand, the less the supply and the greater the incentive to increase production (supply) to satisfy demand. If the resources needed to produce the item are themselves scarce, then the limited supply will self-regulate the demand by pushing the cost of the item above the means of the majority of those who want it. In this situation, profit is made by targeting high-end consumers. Likewise, if the resources needed to produce the item are plentiful and commonplace and the costs of production aren't high, then production can easily meet the demand to the point where the price of the item will be reduced in order to entice the majority of consumers who can afford it—and not just those who need it. In such an instance, profit is made by volume sales.

Supply and demand is easy enough to understand. But there are a host of other terms you will need to know in order to grasp what this economy of ours is all about. The following rates, indices, and stats will help introduce you to some of the most significant economic data that's readily available for your investment research.

Big-Picture Numbers

The Prime Rate

The prime rate is the lowest lending rate available at a bank. The lower the lending rate is, the greater the temptation and the ability to borrow is. Moreover, greater borrowing usually translates into greater spending, which is good for the economy even if it's not so good for you.

Unemployment

One of the most watched figures on Wall Street and, no doubt, your street. The higher unemployment is, the worse off the economy is likely to be or soon become. Why? In economic downturns, fewer people have money to invest and purchase new items like cars, homes, and stereos. They're too busy trying to pay the rent or mortgage. The flip side isn't 100% rosy either. The lower unemployment is, the more nervous the bond market gets. The greater the number of people at work, the greater the demand for consumer goods. This increased demand usually drives up prices, creating what economists call an inflationary environment. During the past decade or so, stock investors have generally been as afraid of inflation as their colleagues on the bond side.

THE CONSUMER-DRIVEN ECONOMY

The following three figures will help reveal the state of the consumer-driven economy that we live in. In fact, two-thirds of all economic activity in the United States is consumer driven. The days of a manufacturing-based economy have gone the way of NAFTA. In the future, we may run the risk of outsourcing new consumers, a critical part of our economy's health, to the countries where the outsourced jobs land. For now, consumer-related data remain the bellwether indicator of the state of our economy—and they are usually reflected in the price levels of the market. Result: These numbers tend to be robust in times of economic prosperity, and the market tends to be up as well. Inversely, these numbers tend to flag in time of a slowing economy—down and out in recession, with the markets being down and out, too.

Retail Sales Figures

Selling consumer items is good for the economy. This figure relates to just how good things seem to be. How so? Look at it from your own perspective. The more you buy, the more optimistic about the economy, your job prospects, and your continued employment you seem to be. (Of course, you may have just been laid off and gone on a buying binge to compensate—bad move, and, hey, you're messing up the statistics!)

Auto Sales

You can check this out for yourself based on the number of "sales" and the amounts of the rebates being offered that you see listed in the automotive section of your paper every day. Chances are, when "sales" are at their loudest and largest, actual sales of cars are at their slowest. Now, it's true that the auto industry is not simply cyclical, it's also seasonal—with more sales coming at certain times of the year. But, during a slowing economy, and especially during a time of high unemployment, new car sales tend to tank.

Housing Starts

New housing starts signal the strength of the economy and bode well for specifically related industries like building product manufacturers, banks, and mortgage companies. These industries tend to be knocked down like a house of straw, however, when housing starts slow. Ditto for another housing-related number: existing home sales.

FUNDAMENTAL FACTORS

These comprehensive indices that make megacalculations (crunching sales and earnings numbers from hundreds or thousands of, for example, real estate agents or car dealerships) to produce very small numbers.

Consumer Price Index (CPI). This index is composed of over 100,000 goods and services that we buy—including food, energy, cars, clothing, and new homes. As such, this index can be seen to present a picture of the overall cost of living. The Federal Reserve keeps a very close eye on this index, and uses it to help determine whether short-term interest rates should be raised (to slow borrowing and so reduce the chance of inflation) or lowered (to increase borrowing and so help spur spending, which, in turn, is a boon to the economy). It's an important index since your salary and your potential raise (and its amount) are likely to be directly affected by this figure.

Producer Price Index (PPI). This figure reflects the direction of product prices. When this index rises it signals that businesses are raising the prices of the products they sell. While rising prices might seem like an obvious negative, this isn't necessarily so. In fact, often while businesses are raising their products' prices, the markets in which those products are found are offering rebates, coupons, or discounts to offset the potentially negative effect on sales.

Manufacturers' New Orders. New orders (of inventory) are how manufacturers gauge the relative strength and weakness of their business in the near future. Since new orders represent a demand for products (or lack thereof), this number can also be used to gauge the short-term future strength and weakness of a particular industry. Can the manufacturer meet the demand or will it have to spend in order to remain competitive? Overproduction is the real negative here, however, since overproducing (whether of cars, cereal, or software) can lead to inventory that can't be sold for love or money.

Industrial Production. Industrial activity, the efficient production of basic materials required by manufacturers to produce their products, can serve as an advance warning of a market peak or valley. If industrial production is running at capacity, and materials are being purchased by manufacturers as fast as they can be provided, then the economy is ticking along nicely. If, on the other hand, the capacity that's being produced isn't being purchased at the rate of production, then inventory piles up, and layoffs occur.

Purchasing Managers' Index. This index shows how much and to what extent industrial materials are being bought by manufacturers. When these manufacturers are buying, it's good news for the industrials. When they're not, you better have a voice like Sissy Spacek in *Coal Miner's Daughter* if you want to keep food on your plate.

Leading Economic Indicators. The US Department of Commerce compiles a monthly report based on what it considers to be twelve leading indicators of the economy's strength (or weakness). Taken as a whole, these indicators are used to help forecast the future climate for businesses in general. A monthly change is rarely significant (although it can reflect an anomalous event, such as bad weather that unexpectedly devastates crops). However, when the leading twelve indicators composite shows consistent gains (good for the economy) or consistent losses (bad for the economy) some investors feel inclined to raise their spinnakers (to capture the fair wind) or batten down the hatches (to help secure them against a downturn).

As with the Dow Jones Industrial Average (defined and detailed in the next chapter), few people know what the Department of Commerce's twelve components are.

1. Average work week of production workers.
2. Layoff rate in manufacturing jobs (see "Unemployment" above).
3. Value of manufacturers' new orders for consumer goods and materials (detailed above).
4. Index of business information.
5. Standard & Poor's 500 index (see the next chapter for definition and details).
6. Contracts and orders for plants and equipment.
7. Index of private housing units authorized by local building permits.
8. Vendor performance (percentage of companies reporting slower deliveries).
9. Net change in inventories in hand or on order.
10. Change in prices of raw materials.
11. Change in total liquid assets.
12. Money supply.

Hold on. What is money supply, and how does it affect the economy and you? Good question. And one that brings up an important distinction—between fiscal and monetary policy. Fiscal policy is shaped by the raising or lowering of taxes, which negatively or positively affects our demand (and ability to pay for) goods and services. Monetary policy, on the other hand, is governed by the Federal Reserve board, which uses it to control the direction of the overall economy by managing the supply of money in circulation—including what you have in your pocket and what's in your checking account. The supply of money in relation to the production of goods and services affects the pricing of products and services, as well as inflation. Too much money and too few goods can dampen interest rates but increase prices and inflation—and vice versa.

MARKET PSYCHOLOGY

Who said the market is fundamentally driven? Well, of course it is—in part. But, as with all things human, psychology plays a significant role as well. The following indices help track this phenomenon as they relate to the market's relative strength or weakness.

Consumer Confidence. When times are good, consumers spend (typically beyond their means, with the confidence that they'll still be employed long enough, and still earn enough, to pay off the new car, boat, porch, and sixty-four-seat home surround-sound theater they just charged on their Sears card). When times are tough, consumers cease to spend on fun, in order to concentrate their earnings on the staples of life—food and shelter.

Investor Sentiment. When the majority of investors (or invest-ment advisers, depending on which sentiment index you're looking at) are bullish, it's time to get bearish. When the majority of investors are bearish, it's time to reconsider your cash position and look to get-ting fully invested. This index helps gauge the herd instinct, which is typically a more lemminglike (i.e., suicidal) path to follow than your own hard-nosed, analysis-driven stock buying. Still, momentum in-vestors (those who look to where the herd is heading and try to get there slightly ahead of the masses) would argue that this index can be used to help gauge the directional flow of money into various sectors within the market.

Business Confidence Index. In 1996, *Fortune* magazine changed from an annual to a monthly survey of corporate America's "Fortune 1000"—one thousand top chief financial officers and treasurers (the people who need to be on target when it comes to how well their busi-ness is actually doing). Review this index regularly, because this index is based on a monthly questionnaire and because those surveyed have their fingers on the pulse of the economy as it relates to their particu-lar business as well as how it relates to the consumers who enable their business to thrive, survive, or be tested by tough times.

TOO MUCH OF A BAD THING,
TOO LITTLE OF THE GOOD

Installment Credit (Debt). Okay. This may be hard for you to believe, but people use credit cards to purchase what they can't otherwise afford to buy outright. And the very same people use home equity loans and other sources of installment debt to buy a lifestyle that, without the debt, would be beyond their reach. You know from your own personal experience just how problematic this type of living can be. Sleepless nights and peanut butter for breakfast, lunch, and dinner for one week a month, after the paycheck runs out—or, better yet, bar snacks, which are (a) free and (b) require no cleaning of dishes. This index shows just how overextended consumers have become—and believe me it's not a pretty sight. In fact, it's a great way to see just how addicted to overextending ourselves through credit debt we've become. For nearly two years after the 500-point stock market crash in October 1987, consumers reduced this figure quite dramatically. Now, we're way over the highest level attained back then. (The first step toward a cure is to admit the addiction.) Taken together with the percentage of savings (under 4%), this number can spell tough times ahead for the two-thirds of our economy that depends on our ability to buy more and more and more stuff. Add to that the perilous job market and things look kind of shaky.

Personal Income. If your income (in terms of annual raises) is rising ahead of inflation, it bodes well for industries that rely on your purchasing power—like retailers and car companies. If, however, your income doesn't keep pace with inflation, then your purchasing power is declining—bad news for the same industries.

MARKET MOMENTUM

Fund Flow. Flow of money into (and out of) mutual funds serves as an indicator of investors' interest in the various markets (stock, bond, foreign) as well as which industries they're interested in. Momentum investors often use this figure to determine their own flow of funds into the market (or out of it). However, since so much of the money coming into mutual funds (over 75% of new money in 2003, for example) is retirement related—in the form of 401(k) or IRA money, for example—flow of funds may no longer be as telling as it was once believed to be. After all, retirement money is long term in nature—so the real story of the recent flow of money into mutual funds is that investors have woken to the fact that they need to invest in their own future. Of course, this begs the question of what will happen to the stock market when these investors begin to withdraw their money to meet their retirement income needs. The answer may not be as devastating as you might think since, after all, these investors will need to continue to grow the lion's share of their capital in order to fend off the inflation tiger. And what better way to do so than to stay invested in stocks? Still, you should mark on your calendar the year 2020—the year in which the demographic boom is likely to be at its widest. After that date, all bets in the markets are off (with the exception of stocks in funeral homes, that is).

SIGNS OF THE TIMES

Economics isn't a theoretical kingdom; it's the realm of the real world. If you know where to look for the signs, you might be able to track down some interesting investment leads. If nothing else, it will make the next trip to the supermarket, mall, or Gap Outlet shift gears from a dull trip to an informed shop. After all, you can readily gauge the retail side of the economy by looking for early and drastic sales on clothing you bought just last week for full price. What else? When you swing into your local gas station for a refill before you get to the mall, check out the pump prices—have they risen or fallen since your last visit or from a month or so ago? Don't know? Take notes and track what you pay for a gallon of gas each time during the months ahead—there may be an energy investment idea there. As always, keep yourself attuned to the world around you. It's not just a Zen way of being—it's a way to tap into some of the more obvious investment ideas in town.

There are other, more standard real-world measures of the overall economy. The following few suffice to show you how to improve your own index of real-world economic activity.

1. NYSE seats. In order for a broker to be able to buy or sell the shares on the exchange, he or she must have a "seat." There are a limited

number of these seats, so the price of the sale of one seat can taken as an indicator of investment professionals' bullishness or bearishness—which, in turn, can be read as a contraindicator. How so? In 1987, the record sale of a seat on the NYSE was set at $1,150,000—one month before the October crash. Little wonder, then, that in early 1999, when the market had set record territory on top of record territory for over twelve months, the sale of a seat for $1,500,000—a new record—was met with mixed emotions. Some saw it as a bullish sign (that a firm would be willing to spend so much for the seat seemed to say that the firm was convinced the market would support the price through increased business). Others were far more cautious, remembering the history of the last record-breaking sale.

2. Cab medallions. Demand for the limited number of New York City cab licenses (or your city's) drives their price—sometimes up (when business is expected to remain robust) and sometimes down (when the economy tightens, consumers walk). The price for a medallion is easily found by calling city hall. For a price history of medallions, city hall would be the best starting place, although they may direct you elsewhere. Once you have that price history in hand, you can match its pattern to the market's and see what you see.

3. Read between the lines! Investors must always be on the alert for potential economic benefits from far afield—as far afield as China, for example. In early 1996 the Chinese government issued a demand that every Chinese have not one, but two eggs for breakfast. Before you go thinking about one billion people in need of a cholesterol drug, think about what it takes to get chickens to double their production. (If you said "more chickens," you're half right.) In fact, it turns out that grain is a key ingredient. But China had already ramped up its grain imports—signaling its inability to produce the necessary grain to meet the new edict. The result was that US grain producers looked like the golden goose.

This chapter could go on to be a book in itself. But you now have enough tools to begin to build your own frame of reference for potential investment opportunities that come about through the changes in our economy, and in the global economy in which our markets participate. Of course you'll want to know more about the markets that corral the securities that you might want to invest in—and that's what chapter 8 is all about.

READY RESOURCES

- Economy.com
- *The Making of Modern Economics*, Mark Skousen
- *Forecasting Interest Rates*, J. Schwartzman
- *Using Economic Indicators to Invest*, E. Tainer

CHAPTER 8

The Markets from Scratch

When it comes to understanding the markets—stocks, bonds, mutual funds, real estate, commodities, precious metals, and more—it's easy to understand why many people shy away. After all, so many markets, so little time, not to mention the risks of making a wrong decision that could not only wind up costing you money—but could even erase the savings you've worked to accrue. That doesn't exactly add up to a welcoming invitation to learn how to succeed in the market, let alone dip an investing toe in it. But, like learning some of the basics of economics that affect the markets you can invest in, coming to terms with the various markets—and market terms—and staying up-to-date on these ever-changing and potentially profit-making areas is pretty easy to do, and necessary.

As we saw in the previous chapter, the marketplace has gone global. So too have the stock and bond markets. In fact, the average US stock fund holds around 10% in foreign stocks. The average large-cap company found in the S&P 500 is actually a "multinational" conglomerate with anywhere from one-third to one-half of its overall revenues derived from sales into foreign markets of Europe and Asia. The upshot is that you need to keep tabs on markets both at home and abroad. For example, take a look at the following chart. It illustrates how well the US market did in comparison to the foreign markets from 1993 to 2003. Historically, foreign markets have played a positive role in building a successful investment portfolio (as detailed in chapters 11 and 14). The role of this chapter is to help you get to know

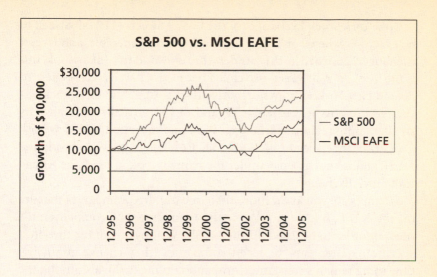

the several markets and their wares, as well as the best ways to gauge their value.

(The S&P 500 is the best broad measure of the U.S. large company market, while the EAFE is the best broad measure of stocks traded in the international markets.)

When it comes to mastering the world and its markets it's no wonder you feel overwhelmed. As with the raw economic data we found in abundance in the previous chapter, information on the various markets, let alone the geopolitical ebb and flow that sustains them, is plentiful—as are the pundits who extol the virtues of some markets over others. But we'll avoid the hype in favor of getting up to speed on the basics. Knowing where each market stands (in terms of potential investment opportunities that suit your needs) is the best way to determine where you want to invest.

THE MARKETS

The following brief history of our major exchanges will help you wow an uninitiated or two at your next brew pub tasting. But, more importantly, it will help you get a sense of the differences between the three major exchanges and their US and global counterparts, as well as get a better sense of the types of companies you'll find listed on them.

New York Stock Exchange (NYSE). Wall Street—11 Wall Street, to be exact—is where you'll find our oldest, most venerable, and largest exchange. Launched in 1817 under a buttonwood tree (okay, look, this is the lore) on Wall Street—so called because of a wall erected there to defend New Yorkers from northerly attacks—the New York Stock Exchange grew to its current size and shape virtually unrivaled by smaller, more regional exchanges, with one exception, the New York Curb Exchange (begun in 1842). That exchange grew alongside the NYSE and is known today under the name it took in 1953, the American Stock Exchange.

Chances are you know more than one hundred companies that are on the NYSE, but do you know the requirements a company must meet in order to be listed on the NYSE? Visit nyse.com for the latest specific requirements for listed companies (they change annually). One thing remains constant: Companies on the NYSE are among the bigger companies. In fact, the lingo is "large-caps," or companies with large capitalization (typically in excess of $3 billion). But big doesn't necessarily mean better. You know the expression the bigger they are, the harder they fall? There are plenty of Goliaths on the Street.

Okay. Biblical metaphors aside, what goes on at the NYSE on a daily basis? The buying and selling of stocks, of course. But what does a typical day on the NYSE look like? Outside of the image of pandemonium and paper chits flying everywhere, business as usual takes the following course: The gavel comes down and trading begins at 9:30 AM Eastern time and the gavel comes down again signaling the end of trading at 4:00 PM Eastern time. Rarely does the market miss a scheduled beat. In between the gavels, a blizzard of millions of transactions takes place. Typically, one transaction will take the following path: An order to buy or sell comes into the broker, and the broker gets busy. He or she either manually or electronically writes the order and places it with the brokerage firm whom he or she represents. The order is then sent to the floor clerk, who in turn passes the order to the brokerage firm's floor trader. This floor trader tracks down another floor trader with an opposite interest (to buy or sell, since for every buyer there must be a seller, and vice versa). The two traders meet and agree on a price. The order is agreed upon, written down, and returned to the floor clerk, who files the order and price of the transaction with the order department. This department issues an execution ticket to the brokerage firm's representative who, in turn, lets the original broker know the transaction has transpired—and for what price. The broker then calls the client with the deal—and the client then receives a trade confirmation that, like a receipt, details the transaction.

If all the above sounds like a lot of leg- and paperwork, you're right. But for orders of 1,200 shares or less, trades are handled on the DOT (Designated Order Turnaround) system, which is a computerized way to trade efficiently. Currently the DOT system accounts for more than 50% of NYSE trades. To learn the best ways to place an order, turn to chapter 12.

American Stock Exchange (AMEX). Known as the market for mid-cap companies, the AMEX is based on Trinity—rather than Wall—Street, and is often referred to as the NYSE's little brother. AMEX-listed companies must meet certain definitional requirements (found at amex.com), but are often mid-cap companies (companies that tend to have market capitalizations of $1–$5 billion). As we go to press, the AMEX is facing an uncertain future—and could be merged into an existing exchange or acquired outright.

National Association of Securities Dealers Automated Quotation System (NASDAQ). The NASDAQ celebrated its thirtieth anniversary in 2001—at the same time that its listed companies were struggling for dear life in the pit of the last bear market. Needless to say, there wasn't much celebrating goin' on. But, having grown from a tiny, electronically traded, over-the-counter stock service with one hundred companies in 1971 to its current three-thousand-plus universe of stocks ranging from mega-Microsoft to microcompanies struggling to stay aloft, it's an exchange with a future. As a result, the NASDAQ is known as the market for small-caps (companies with capitalization under $1 billion). In fact, many investors think that the NASDAQ is all small-company stocks, but the truth is that as the NASDAQ has itself grown from puny to gigantic, so have many of the companies that list there, including Amgen (one of the few biotech companies to actually post earnings), Cisco Systems, Intel, and Oracle.

If some of its early comers have grown up, the NASDAQ is still a market for smaller companies that can't (yet) list on "the big board" (NYSE) or AMEX. Like an auction, trading is done on a bid/ask basis, and is conducted by dealers who are members of the NASD (National Association of Securities Dealers)—electronically. The NASDAQ exists in virtual reality as opposed to on one street.

COMMODITY EXCHANGES

Some exchanges provide a place to buy and sell contracts on everything from stocks to pork bellies. Commodities are typically agricultural products: coffee, sugar, and corn are all commodities. Investors in commodities are placing bets on their future value. For example, if there has been an ice storm in Florida, orange juice contracts become very expensive since there will be fewer oranges to satisfy consumer demand for orange juice. The following commodity exchanges dominate the field. They are defined by the type of instruments their contracts are based on.

Chicago Board of Options Exchange (CBOE). This market serves as the most prominent source for auctioning puts and calls on NYSE stocks, S&P 100 and S&P 500 futures, and Treasury bonds. (For more on puts and calls, turn to chapter 17.)

AMEX Options Exchange (ACC). This area of the AMEX is specifically designated for trading puts and calls on NYSE and OTC (over-the-counter) stocks.

Chicago Board of Trade (CBT). A major market for futures contracts on commodities (from coffee to pork bellies to soybeans), interest rate securities, and more.

New York Cotton Exchange (NYCE). This exchange is dedicated to trading futures in cotton and orange juice.

REGIONAL MARKETS

In addition to the more famous stock and commodity exchanges, there are several regional exchanges, which typically list smaller, more localized companies. The exchanges' names, for the most part, are based on their location. So, for example, you have the Boston Stock Exchange, as well as exchanges in Cincinnati, Chicago, Philadelphia, and San Francisco (known as the Pacific Stock Exchange). If you live nearby, stop in for a quick look at how a trading floor works. You might have to call in advance (or, if you have a broker, ask her for an entree).

INTERNATIONAL MARKETS

Foreign markets offer investors the chance at some thrills—and spills. Not all foreign markets are created alike, however. Some, like the London Stock Exchange, are as solid as the White Cliffs of Dover, while others, like the Italian Market, resemble the frangible dunes of Cape Cod. The following table provides a list of established markets and their performances. You can see a wide divergence based on this table alone, as well as come to see how many markets there are. (For more on the benefits of investing in foreign stocks, and there are some, see chapter 14.)

Returns around the World

	10 Year
MS EAFE	47.9
MS World	71.3
MS Europe	100.2
MS Japan	−8.8
MS United Kingdom	68.3
MS France	131.8
MS Germany	79.9

*As of 12/31/05

If foreign markets can sometimes throw investors for a loop, emerging markets are like a roller-coaster ride on a Möbius strip—unending volatility. While there are ways to minimize the risk of investing in emerging markets (for example, investing in a well-diversified emerging markets fund—or, better yet, investing in a well-diversified international fund that itself invests a small portion of its assets in emerging market securities), there is no way to bring the volatility of these markets in line with our own. Are the rewards worth the risks? Well, as the following table illustrates, not only are there several emerging markets to choose from, but, as is always the case, one or more of them delivers eye-popping returns in any given period.

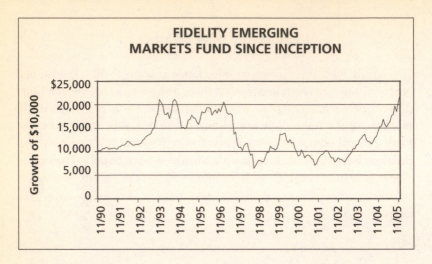

Emerging markets are currently considered to be: Argentina, Bolivia, Botswana, Brazil, Chile, Columbia, Czechoslovakia, Ecuador, Egypt, Greece, Hong Kong, Hungary, India, Indonesia, Jamaica, Jordan, Kenya, Malaysia, Mexico, Morocco, Nigeria, Paraguay, Pakistan, Peru, the Philippines, Poland, Portugal, Singapore, South Korea, Sri Lanka, Taiwan, Thailand, Turkey, Uruguay, Venezuela, and Zimbabwe. Some markets in these countries are more established (in terms of longevity) than others. More new markets, especially from the former Soviet Union and China, are likely to emerge in short order. The commonality? Volatility in terms of the market, economy, and political maturity of each country.

Because these markets are emerging, rarely will you be able to time their periods of stability well. And failing to do so can leave you on the slippery slopes of a disastrous downside. (My recommendation is to avoid them; else, keep your total exposure in them to under 10%.) Not surprisingly, when it comes to investing, most of us would be better off listening to Dorothy. She was basically right, there is no place like home.

However, some funds, for example, hedge their foreign stakes, and by doing so neutralize the effects of fluctuations between the value of the US dollar and the value of foreign currency. But before you rush out and invest only in those funds that fully hedge their currency (and there aren't many that are fully hedged), you should know that doing so can make the fund vulnerable to a strong US dollar.

Currency Concerns

When investing in a foreign market, you need to be aware of how well the investments are doing relative to the market and country in which they're located, as well as the currency in which they're denominated. The question is, what are your (or a fund's) investments worth in US dollars—since, after all, it would be hard to buy this week's groceries with a bag of bhats or rupees. While the performance of various world markets is listed in easily accessible sources—from print to the Web—the performance of individual stocks, and the performance of those foreign stocks held by a domestic fund, are less easy to track down, and to track. However, there's a shorthand way in which you can keep tabs on the potential negative or positive effects of currency markets worldwide. How so? The value of the dollar relative to most major international currencies is listed in all the right (i.e., accessible) places. The question is, is a stronger dollar good or bad news for the foreign stocks you or your fund own?

Answer: A rising dollar relative to other currencies will translate into bad news for any investments that are denominated in those foreign currencies that are weaker by comparison—they will be worth less, but not worthless. If, on the other hand, the dollar is weakening relative to other currencies, then the value of the investments denominated in those foreign currencies will be worth more in dollar terms. If two funds, for example, were invested in the same stocks, in the same foreign markets, and one fund was fully hedged, and the other was unhedged, then the following would happen: If the value of the US dollar is falling, the unhedged fund outperforms the hedged one. If the greenback is strengthening, the hedged fund will suffer less than the unhedged fund, and so fare better by comparison.

Keeping tabs on the strength of the US dollar versus other currencies is easy to do, and, as the above shows, a smart thing to do. However, just because the dollar spikes up or trips down, don't sell on short news. Instead, consider the prospect of the dollar's value over a longer-term time frame before making any moves.

OUR REGULATORS

The Securities and Exchange Commission (SEC) was begun in 1934 to counteract numerous stock-trading schemes that were plaguing the market and threatening its integrity. The SEC is the markets' watchdog—and it's got federal teeth to back up its regulatory bark. Its job is to ensure that the integrity of a market is maintained—as well as prosecuting those who violate the rules and regulations that govern fair and honest market practices. The trouble is that the history of the SEC is one of reparation, not forecasting or forewarning. As such, the SEC has rarely been able to to anything other than react to a scandal, rather than prevent one. Now, after successive market scandals, the SEC began in 2003 to attempt not only to prosecute wrongdoers—from brokerage firms to fund companies to CEOs of publicly traded companies—but to write into the code of business practice and conduct more stringent rules of the game. While you might assume that that's all good news, I'd be more cautious about any intervention by any agency in our markets' ability to remain free. Greater disclosure, accountability, and liability are three excellent pillars to build on—but the best way to run a business is a still the old-fashioned way: ethically.

The SEC needs to work to ensure that investors are fully and accurately informed about the securities on the market. In the late 1990s, the greed that turned brokerages into brothels left the SEC with many wrongdoers to contend with. But the wrongdoing will always persist. So be forewarned: the SEC doesn't guarantee that you are informed. You need to do your own homework to learn how anyone's hype relates to the real promise behind the numbers.

The Industries

There are several ways to break the overall market into the constituent parts that participate in it. The following main industries or "sectors" are commonly agreed on, while the ninety-plus subsectors may be viewed more subjectively and creatively.

To begin with, you'll need to get to know each major industry. From there, you can begin to unpack the constituent sectors and the companies that compose each sector. Most companies concentrate in one or a few related industries, and so their stocks can be similarly categorized by industry or sector. While you can break down industry into over a hundred narrow categories, I feel the following ten broad sectors allow a more useful overview of the market's action.

1. Basic Materials. Basic materials are the raw materials that manufacturers use to produce their goods. Aluminum, chemicals, paper and forest products, and steel (commonly referred to as "deep cyclicals") are prime examples. Companies that harvest and produce such raw materials tend to have their peak earnings in the later stages of an economic recovery, when increased demand for manufactured goods (from cars to homes) begins to outstrip the supply of raw materials (e.g., aluminum and lumber), resulting in price increases that go straight to a basic materials company's bottom line.

2. Cyclicals. Housing and auto manufacturers top this industry list. Sensitive to economic cycles, this group tends to rise quickly in economic upturns, and slide back just as quickly during downturns. The success of each sector relies on the consumer's willingness and ability to purchase durable goods—which, naturally, slows during tough times and increases during better times.

3. Noncyclicals. Also referred to as consumer staples, the industry includes food, tobacco, and sometimes drugs—the three staples for surviving in the real world. (While drugs are often included in this category, most listings put them with other health-related companies.) Name-brand products have recently come on far stronger than generic products (although this wasn't the case in the early 1990s), and are likely to remain constants in the universe as more sales go overseas and more consumers want the prestige associated with brand names. But loyalty aside, the companies in this sector tend to produce basics we all need and would find it hard to do without.

4. Energy. Energy is a big enough sector that it's usually considered separate from the other commodities making up Basic Materials. Energy companies are involved in oil, natural gas, coal, and/or energy services (oil exploration and pipeline equipment and service suppliers). As this is a commodity industry, supply and demand fundamentals heavily impact profits. Since oil producers can't count on OPEC to drastically cut production a third time (remember the 1970s?), the more typical good news for this industry comes from economic recoveries in established markets and strong growth in emerging markets. Emerging markets are providing an increasingly positive picture for this industry—in terms of their rapidly growing demand for cars and plants and the need to fuel them.

5. Financial. Banks, savings and loans, brokerages, mutual fund firms, and insurance companies (life and property/casualty) make up

this industry. While mother nature can wreak havoc on property/ casualty insurers, she can also benefit banks that are called upon to loan money to rebuild. As a whole, this industry is sensitive to interest rates. Rising rates are typically a negative, while falling rates tend to be positive. Why? Higher rates can dry up loan demand, while lower rates tend to encourage greater borrowing, increasing demand for loans, and are good for the securities markets. Economic growth also tends to bode well for banks and brokerages via increased loan and investment demand.

6. Health Care. This industry includes those companies that make or sell products or services used in health care, with products primarily consisting of pharmaceuticals (prescription and over-the-counter) and medical devices, and services ranging from hospital and nursing home chains to HMOs and other medical insurers. The health-care industry is susceptible to politics (in the form of federally mandated price controls), as well as rising pressure from HMOs and other large purchasers to keep prices lower.

7. Media and Leisure. This conglomeration includes everything from TV broadcasting, newspapers, and advertising to restaurants, casinos, hotels, and cruise lines. What do these two very different areas have in common? They primarily exist to help people spend their free time. (Each is also too small to give its own category.) While people don't give up watching TV during a recession, ad revenues do decline, hurting media companies across the board. Leisure spending is at least as sensitive to changes in people's discretionary income.

8. Retailers and Wholesalers. Another smallish category, these firms include major discount chains such as Wal-Mart, as well as department stores, specialty retailers, and "category killers" such as Toys R Us. For the last several years, many retailers have been hurt by a major slump in apparel purchases. (Apparently, everyone bought all the clothes they needed in the 1980s, and with workplaces going casual, there's even less need for expensive replacements.)

9. Technology. From semiconductor and computer manufacturers to software producers and telecommunications, this industry is likely to be a long-term success. All the major technology sectors should prove to be excellent long-term performers, benefiting primarily from the constantly improving performance of these products. Multimedia is the way this world is heading—but expect volatility in this high-growth sector.

10. Utilities. These companies move electricity, natural gas, or data (e.g., phone messages) into homes and businesses. Because they tend to be stodgier, low-growth, high-dividend-paying stocks, they are generally most suited for more conservative equity-income investors. Because of their high, stable dividends, they are often held as bond substitutes, and they move closely with the prices of long-term bonds, making them the most interest-rate-sensitive sector. However, some of the telecommunications companies do have higher growth potential, with some of the newer areas (e.g., cellular) often categorized with the technology stocks.

Don't forget to unpack an industry into its constituent sectors. For example, with finance, you can examine each sector—banks, brokerages, and insurance—in order to scrutinize the performance prospects of the industry, sector, and individual companies. From there, you can ferret out those funds that are most committed to the particular companies and sectors within one industry. And you can then measure that company's or fund's past and potential performance against a pool of its peers, as well as against an adequate market benchmark.

The following table reflects an accurate mosaic of the types of industries that most publicly traded companies participate in. Why is knowing this important? For one thing, it's interesting in itself to see

S&P SECTOR INDICES			
		Annual Returns	
Symbol	**Name**	**2004**	**2005**
xly	S&P Consumer Discretionary	12.9	−6.6
xlp	S&P Consumer Staples	7.6	2.8
xle	S&P Energy	34.0	40.2
xlf	S&P Financial	10.9	6.2
xlv	S&P Health Care	1.3	6.4
xli	S&P Industrial	17.7	2.7
xlb	S&P Materials	13.5	4.1
xlk	S&P Technology	6.0	−0.3
xlu	S&P Utilities	23.6	16.4

just how multifold our markets are, and our world is. For another, especially when it comes to mutual funds, sector concentration may be the closest you can come to current weightings in any given fund. Knowing where a fund is concentrated will help you judge its performance in light of what you know about the sectors. And it will also help you avoid owning two funds that are invested in the same way (for more on the significance of determining your fund's "correlation," turn to chapter 14). Likewise, when scanning the globe for new investment opportunities, you'll be far better off knowing in advance what industries are out there to choose from—so that you can wed what you know about the economy (for example, its cyclical nature) with your buying and selling strategies.

As you can clearly see, in a given year, even an unusually positive one, some industries fare better than others—and some stand head and shoulders above the rest.

While you will need to select your investments based on your objectives and the investments' fundamental promise, you will also need to heed the dominant industry themes of the day. Known as top-down investing, it's basically a bird's-eye view of the forest (as opposed to a forester's view of each individual tree). First, you'll need to familiarize yourself with the major industry categories as well as their related subsectors. From that vantage, you can look at how those sectors relate to the overall economic and market environments. Doing so with respect to a particular company provides you with one way to gauge its prospects relative to the market and its industry peers. For example, GM is a car manufacturer that tends to do well earnings-wise in the later stages of an economic recovery, when people are more willing to pay for big-ticket items.

With respect to mutual funds, sector weightings are perhaps even more critical, since a fund's investment character can be reflected in its sector weightings as much as in its stock selection. Not surprisingly, stocks in the darling industry of the day (for example, technology stocks, and within technology, software issues) and funds with strong weightings in technology (and, in particular, in software companies) tend to outperform those that are less focused in that industry and subsector. Sector analysis may sound difficult to wrap your mind around—but, thanks to the many user-friendly resources at your peck and call (peck, in terms of using online services), it's become much easier to note top- and bottom-performing industries and sectors as well as top- and bottom-performing stocks and funds.

MEASURING A MARKET'S PERFORMANCE

The science of measuring market performance is mathematically based, and so less susceptible to error than analysis relating to each market, industry, and company. However, there's a lot of room for judgment in terms of what gets included in an index—and what gets left out. The following indices reflect the most commonly accepted ones in use today by experts and novices alike. You'll note that, not surprisingly, not all the indices are US-focused. After all, since many of us invest abroad as well as at home (directly through buying ADRs [Automatic Depository Receipts] or indirectly through buying shares in an international or global fund), it's a good idea to get a grip on how the foreign markets we're investing in are performing.

The Major Indices

Dow Jones Industrial Average. It's the most common, publicly accepted daily measure of the overall market. You've heard about it. You've seen it. You've talked about it. You've ignored it. But do you know what it is—the Dow Jones Industrial Average (DJIA), that is? Don't worry if you don't. Most people assume it's a good market indicator, and leave it at that. But it might surprise you to know that many market experts feel the Dow doesn't accurately reflect today's overall market. Critics of the Dow point to the fact that, for example, the thirty stocks that compose the Dow are a slim reed on which to hang a daily picture of the more than eleven thousand publicly traded companies. Still, I think it's a reliable index of the market (I'll explain why shortly). For one thing, the Dow's 2004 inclusions of Microsoft and Intel answered its critics who claimed its narrow band didn't include the ever-widening playing field when it comes to new industries, most notably, technology. You be the judge: Let's take a look at the thirty companies that make up the Dow Jones Industrial Average.

Dow Jones Industrial Average Companies

Alcoa	Boeing
Altria Group	Caterpillar
American Express	Citigroup
American International Group	Coca-Cola

DuPont

Exxon Mobil

General Electric

General Motors

Hewlett-Packard

Home Depot

Honeywell International

Intel

International Business Machines (IBM)

JPMorgan Chase

Johnson & Johnson

McDonald's

Merck & Co.

Microsoft

Minnesota Mining & Manufacturing (3M)

Pfizer

Procter & Gamble

SBC Communications

United Technologies

Verizon

Walt Disney

Wal-Mart Stores

Aside from what the DJIA doesn't include, critics charge that what it does include biases it toward large-cap companies. One final argument against using the Dow as a standard by which to measure the market is that the way it calculates the average of the thirty companies is itself problematic, since it gives more weight to higher-priced stocks than to lower-priced ones. So, should the Dow be replaced? NO! Here's why.

Since 1896 (when Charles Dow introduced this index), the Dow has served to accurately reflect the movement and mood of the overall market. In fact, compared to the broader indices that the Dow's critics propose as adequate replacements, the Dow withstands the test of time and accuracy. For example, when compared to the S&P 500 (a market-weighted capitalization that does in fact better reflect the market and, perhaps as important, serves as the benchmark against which many money managers and fund managers gauge their performance) the Dow shows little divergence—and the same can be said when the Dow is compared to other popular and significant indices like the NASDAQ Composite and the Russell 2000 (discussed below). The bottom line on the Dow, then, is that it continues to serve as an accurate and, thus, adequate measure of the market. It's worth paying attention to, but not exclusively so. It's best used in conjunction with other indices that better reflect their particular markets.

S&P 500. Charles Dow created the first standard to measure the markets, and it was the only commonly accepted measure until 1928, when Standard & Poor's created a market-weighted index based on ninety stocks. Twenty-two years later, the S&P 90 had become what it is today—the S&P 500. Over 70% of all US equity is tracked by the S&P 500. That's why it's perhaps the most broadly used benchmark to gauge one's successes and failures versus the overall market. The index is a "market value–weighted" index, meaning that it's calculated based on stock price times the number of shares outstanding, with each stock's weight in the index proportionate to its market value. The S&P 500 is a tough performance standard to live up to—but don't buy the index fund hawkers hype—many managers beat the index time and again. (We'll get to how you can aim to do so in chapter 9.) The S&P 500 index consists of four hundred industrial companies, forty utility companies, forty financial companies, and twenty transportation companies.

NASDAQ Composite. The NASDAQ Composite index is a market value–weighted average of 3,700 domestic OTC (over-the-counter) stocks. This index is becoming synonymous with the leading technology companies it comprises (like Microsoft, Oracle, Cisco, and more). As such, you've no doubt seen this index gain wider acceptance as a market indicator everywhere you look. It's an excellent indicator of this sector of the market, although it can no longer be viewed as an exemplary small company index since so many of its one-time small companies have become huge.

Other Indicative Indices

The following indices will help you cover the markets of the United States and the world in more detail. The more refined you become in terms of benchmarking the performance of your individual investments (stocks, bonds, and mutual funds) the more interesting these indices become.

Russell 2000. This index is used to measure small company performance. The two thousand companies in this index are also the smallest companies (in terms of capitalization) in the related Russell 3000 index. Russell provides both a growth and a value 2000 index, which further refine your view of the stocks included in the small-cap universe as expressed by investment style.

Russell 3000. An excellent overall stock market standard, it comprises the three thousand largest US companies (defined by market capitalization). This index takes a broader view than the Dow and S&P 500 indices. The companies in this index represent over 95% of the total US stock market. Another excellent stock market index is the Wilshire 5000.

Standard & Poor's MidCap 400 (S&P 400). If its larger sibling is used to represent the overall market, this index is used to help investors gauge the performance of midsized companies (which are typically found on the AMEX). Another mid-cap index to watch is the Wilshire MidCap 750.

Wilshire Top 750. The 750 largest US stocks make up this index. If you're looking to get a take on the overall health of big-time corporate America (as reflected by their stock performance) this is a superior index to scout out.

International and Global Indices

The most popular benchmark for international markets is commonly referred to as the EAFE, which is short for Morgan Stanley Capital International Europe, Australasia, and Far East (MSCI EAFE). MSCI has over three thousand indices, but the following are the most generally relevant ones for most investors. Moreover, while Dow Jones provides equally useful international and global indices (found in the *Wall Street Journal* and online, among other places), the following Morgan Stanley Capital International (referred to as MSCI) indices will help you know what to look for when you're looking at most market indices. Some are self-explanatory, as with MSCI Europe, MSCI Pacific, MSCI Latin America, and MSCI Japan, while others, like the MSCI Free indices (which include most markets in those countries that nonresidents can invest in, including the United States), and MSCI World (which comprises sixteen larger world markets, including the United States) are less so.

Note that, whether the United States is included in the index or not, when it comes to comparing international market returns you need to ensure that the returns translate to US dollars as well as local currency—typically, this is listed.

US Bond Indices

Lehman Brothers cornered the bond index market—and remains the most generally used litmus test for taxable and tax-free bond performances in the United States. The Lehman Brothers Corporate Bond is a bond index that includes all publicly issued, fixed-rate, non-convertible, dollar-denominated, SEC-registered, investment-grade corporate debt. Lehman Brothers Government Bond does for US Treasuries and agency bonds what the above index does for corporate. The Lehman Brothers Government/Corporate Bond combines the two. And the Lehman Brothers Muni Bond compares the performances of long-term, investment-grade, tax-exempt municipal bonds. And yes, Lehman provides indices for high-yield (junk) bonds and mortgage bond funds.

MARKET TRENDS

As with economic cycles that can directly impact companies' performances (as well as funds that invest in those companies), so there are some interesting historical trends that have proven over time to affect markets or specific types of stocks within those markets. Two recurring and more prominent trends are the January Effect, named for the fact that January has historically been a very strong month for small-cap stocks—as have the early winter months; and the Election Effect, based on the historical trend (since WWII) in which the election year and the third year of a president's term tend to beat the market's (S&P 500) average return.

• • •

No matter what resources, cycles, trends, indices, or industries you turn to to ferret out risks and potential rewards, this section should have put you on a more focused path toward your goal of understanding the economy and markets in a more comprehensive and useful manner. The next section will help you further distill your investment education by helping you tell one investment category from another, one investment from another, and one fund from another—in order to help you tailor your overall investment portfolio to your specific objectives.

READING THE FINANCIAL PAGES

Of course the Wall Street lowdown is available via your broadband superhighway (and chapter 22 clicks into this essential route to being an informed investor). But there's still something to be said for getting your investment hands dirty the white-collar way: with ink.

You step into the local unwired café with a *Barron's* or *Wall Street Journal* under your arm. You walk up to the coffee bar and ask for the mug—black. You pull up your stool and lay the paper down just like a miner from the Old West with a prospector's chart. The absence of a six-gun strapped to your side shows that prospecting for gold has become a lot tamer than in the past—but it hasn't become all that much easier to strike it rich. Sure, there are the lucky few who play the lottery and win. But, since you're like the rest of us, chances are you'll have to do it the old-fashioned way—earn it, save it, invest it. But if you don't know what you're looking for, chances are you won't find it.

To begin with, you will need to find a paper that lists stocks, bonds, and mutual funds. Most major papers do—in the business section, of course. If you can't locate a paper that has an adequate business section, visit your local library or purchase today's *Wall Street Journal* or take a look at the Ready Resources below. (And, yes, there's a quicker way to do this research online—turn to chapter 22 for the scoop.)

From there, you will want to locate the exchanges on which your stocks and funds are located. Note the following similarities: companies, bonds, and funds are listed alphabetically. Names are abbreviated—IBM, for example, for International Business Machines.

Funds are listed by their family name first, then their proper name. For example, if you're looking for Fidelity small-cap funds, you would find the following: Fidelity, then Fidelity Small Cap (meaning the Fidelity Small-Cap Fund).

The following key will help you decipher the most meaningful investment information in your paper's financial pages.

Stocks

- 52 Weeks Hi/Lo (the highest and lowest price per share of the stock during the past 52 weeks)
- Stock (the name of the issuer)
- Sym (the stock's trading symbol)

- Div (the latest annual dividend paid by the stock)
- Yld (the stock's latest annual dividend expressed as a percentage of the stock's price on that day)
- P/E (the price-to-earnings ratio—the price of a stock divided by the issuing company's past four quarters of earnings)
- Hi/Lo/Close (the stock's volatility expressed in terms of a single share's price movement; the close is what the price of the stock will open at on the next trading day)
- s *or* x (these symbols may appear in the left-hand column; an "s" indicates that the stock has split or the company issued a dividend within the last year; an "x" stands for "ex-dividend," meaning that new investors won't receive the next dividend)

Bonds

- Issue (the issuer's name)
- Coupon (interest rate at which the bond was issued)
- Mat (maturity date—the year in which the bond matures)
- Price (the price the bond closed at; for example, a price of 98¾ means it closed at 98¾% per $1,000 of par value, or at $988)
- CHG (change reflects the amount the bond closed at compared with its previous day's closing)
- BID YLD (the bond's yield to maturity)
- CV (the issue is a convertible bond; i.e., it can be exchanged for a fixed number of shares of common stock from the issuer)

Mutual Funds

- NAV (net asset value—tells you what a share of the fund is worth today)
- Offer price (what you would pay per share were you to purchase shares in the fund that day)
- p (the fund charges a 12-b1 fee)
- t (the fund charges both a 12-b1 fee and a redemption fee: 12-bl fees are fees levied by the fund on its shareholders to market the fund to potential new shareholders)
- NL (no load, meaning there are no up-front sales charges)
- r (redemption charge; some are as high as 6%! A redemption fee is also called a "back end load"; a fee charged if you sell the fund before a specified holding period, typically 30 days)

- x (ex-dividend, meaning that new share buyers will not receive the fund's next dividend payout)
- Note: A fund can either have a "p" or an "r" symbol listed next to it and still be called a no-load fund. However, a fund with a "t" can't be so listed.

READY RESOURCES

As this whole section has amply demonstrated, when it comes to investing, information is never in short supply. The following barely scratches the surface (or airwaves or virtual space)—but it will help you unearth some of the best (i.e., useful and potentially profit-producing) information around. Moreover, purchasing some of the following could be tax deductible. That's right, you may be able to take a tax deduction for every investment-related book and magazine you purchase. What about CNBC and your cable TV? Don't count on it. Online time? If you feel adventurous, you might explore this new territory for a possible partial deduction.

Caveat emptor (and caveat viewer and listener): Many of the sources below should be scrutinized by you much the way you would scrutinize a potential investment. Some provide more hype than true type. Others provide insight for a price that can be beat or can't be met—after all, if you're eking out $100 per month to invest, spending $100 for a source isn't exactly in your scope. (Hint: Focus on your library.) Nevertheless, most of what you'll find below are acceptable sources for furthering your own research. Never become reliant on one. Question all. Distill what's useful to your investment objectives.

TV and radio pundits. Just as it's difficult to select the best stock or fund from the overabundant crop, it's difficult to know who among the many television and radio pundits is worth listening to (and who should be avoided). But, when time is short, there are several shows worth watching, and, of course, those that plainly are not.

The late-night hucksters with their no-money-down schemes are good for a laugh, but little else. To begin with, anyone who is trying to sell you something that sounds too good or easy to be true is probably telling a lie. Next, there are those who try to sell you something you simply don't understand. Avoid investing in anything—and anyone— you don't completely understand.

The more meaningful question is who can you listen to—and here, you're in luck. Of course there's CNBC throughout the day for market updates and the occasional economic news. In addition, two of the best daily financial shows occur every night on TV: *Nightly Business Report* and *CNBC Market Wrap*. In radio land, dial into *Marketplace* (National Public Radio, nightly) and profit from news that any investor can use.

Magazines. I strongly recommend that you subscribe to one of the following personal finance magazines. They're listed in order of my preference—but I recommend that you go to your library to compare them before subscribing to the one that seems best for you. *Kiplinger's Personal Finance Magazine, Money,* and *Smart Money* are some of the best. Not only are they an excellent resource for a broad range of investing information, they're also a great source of new money management, investing, and overall personal finance ideas.

Newspapers. The best daily source of investment news you can use is the *Wall Street Journal.* It provides the best reporting on business in the business. Economic and market analysis, stellar and bombing bonds, the funds to watch and the funds to invest in—all are scrutinized. The *New York Times* business section is a close second for 100% of your daily dose of recommended financial news and advice. The eminent financial weekly *Barron's* is worth pursuing at your local library. In fact, since these papers cost a bundle to receive, you may want to subscribe to a monthly magazine and make a biweekly visit to your library for one or more of these excellent papers.

Newsletters. They don't exactly come for a dime a dozen—it may even cost $100-plus for an annual subscription to one—but a handful of the many investment newsletters out there are worth considering. Hulbert's Financial Digest (on marketwatch.com) tracks the portfolio performances of over 150 independent newsletters and ranks them accordingly. Morningstar.com is an obvious stock and fund information warehouse—and deservedly so for its data. But take Morningstar with more than two grains of salt when it comes to the performance merits of its vaunted star rating system. Morningstar's free service is worth the price of admission—but don't get tricked into paying for anything. The truth is that its five-star fund rating system has been proven time and again to lag the market dramatically over any meaningful time period. Plus, I don't think it can be called "independent" since Morningstar receives payment from the fund companies it claims to be independently rating.

Fidelity Investor is my own award-winning independent newsletter (check it out at fidelityinvestor.com). It has proven to deliver consistent outperformance. And I have never taken a dime from Fidelity. (See page 129 for a chart on how my model growth portfolio fared during the best and worst of times for the stock and bond markets— 1998 through 2005.)

Annual reports. Every company publishes a year-end review of its financial health. You can get hold of an individual company's annual report—typically free for the asking—by calling the company and requesting it. Of course, there will be a lot of hype, but there will also be some interesting narration and numbers, such as changes in management, marketing plans for the future, and profit and liability statements, all of which will help you gauge your potential investment in that company.

Analysts' recommendations. Brokerage firms pump more pulp than most paper companies. Literally thousands of recommendations are produced by a handful of companies in a year or less. Nevertheless, analysts' reports are usually easy to understand and fact-based in spite of healthy doses of salesmanship in the rhetoric. As with an annual report, an analyst's recommendations should be taken with a grain of consumer-savvy salt. To get your hands on a report about a particular company, call a brokerage house and request it. Even if you have no intention of opening an account with the brokerage it may be happy to serve you—so that it may be able to serve you again.

Standard & Poor's stock reports. Provide detailed performance analyses on thousands of stocks. Standard and Poor's also publishes a monthly stock guide, which tracks the performance of more than five thousand stocks. Both the reports and the guide are available in larger libraries and are useful sources for examining a company's stock's history of performance and potential future value.

Value Line Investment Survey. This survey covers 1,700 stocks and provides what some consider to be the best analysis in the investment industry. Your library should have it; if not, ask your library to get it. It's too expensive to buy on your own. (But you can access much of the info online—or in your local library.)

Internet. Participate in the information revolution—it just may enhance your investing skills and profit potential. America Online, Marketwatch.com, and Yahoo Finance provide easy-to-access and -understand online economic, investment, and business information as well as the ability to buy and sell stocks, bonds, and mutual funds online.

The Internet offers the widest range of raw data and wild opinion on all facets of the economy, markets, and investing. A lawless global village, it can be as easy to wind up with less than zero (especially after you calculate the cost of searching) as it is to hit a fountain of information that can change the way you think about an industry, fund, or company. Chapter 22 details some of the best methods for finding information on the Web. Turn there before you turn your modem on. But before you go, take note of the sources listed below for further focusing your watchful eye on the markets here and abroad.

bigcharts.com	money.com
barrons.com	morningstar.com
marketwatch.com	riskmetrics.com
google.com	smartmoney.com
investopedia.com	wsj.com

- *Security Analysis,* Graham and Dodd
- *Hulbert Guide to Financial Newsletters* M. Hulbert (available at Marketwatch.com)
- *How to Profit from Reading Annual Reports,* R. Loth (out of print, but if you dig in your library, you'll find it)

CHAPTER 9

Beating the Benchmarks
from Scratch

You're about to settle into a quiet single malt when a man with the smell of stale cigars and too much Polo saunters up to you and begins to tell all about his latest winning investment. The *one* that knocked the socks off the average return. The one anybody could have picked if they just paid enough attention to what the world was telling the Street. The killing this guy made could have made you a fortune. But there you are. No back door to the wall you're propped against. You have to respond. You have to say something clever and competitive. You're scanning for the right investment—the one that delivered unbelievably good results. You can't think of one. In fact, you can't think of how to begin to measure what a truly good result is. What, after all, does beating the market really mean? Is it a good thing? Is it a necessary thing?

There's a lot of talk about beating the market. There are a few good books about it (including *Beating the Street* by Peter Lynch). And while this chapter may be short, its lesson is critical to your overall investing success. Its lesson, in short, is that you must set mileposts to measure your portfolio's progress—or the lack of it. Failure to do so will mean that, like living without a budget or a financial plan, you're the investor equivalent of Casey Jones riding that train.

When it comes to beating the market, you have to be careful that you know which market you're referring to—and to what extent it is accurate to use that market as an adequate benchmark of your investment's success. The truth is that, while it's important to judge a particular investment by the index it is most closely related to, there are two solid milestones that you want to keep in mind at all times: one is a market index (the S&P 500) and the other is an economic index that relates to your wallet (the rate of inflation).

BEATING THE MARKET

For the most part, when people talk about beating the market, they mean beating a specific market index, which they use as a benchmark for measuring the success or failure of a particular investment, and of their overall investment. Typically, this benchmark is the S&P 500—not the father of all benchmarks (which, once upon a time, was gold, and is now, in popular use, the Dow Jones Industrial Average). The S&P 500 could be more correctly viewed as the mother of all indices. If your investment portfolio has been keeping pace with this index, let alone staying ahead of it, then you have been ahead of the majority of investors and their portfolios. Here's a chart of a model growth portfolio taken from yours truly's newsletter (fidelityinvestor.com) for the five-year time period between 1998 through 2005—when both stock and bond markets saw the best and worst of times). It illustrates one simple point: You can beat the market.

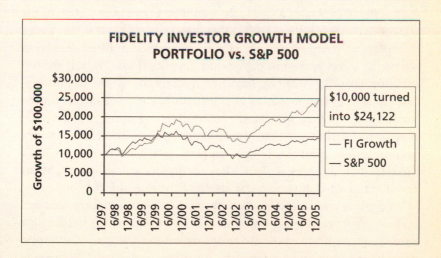

BEATING INFLATION

Inflation is a nemesis—no matter how "controlled" it seems to be today. That's why it's essential that, in conjunction with all the more fancy benchmarks out there, you understand how inflation affects your money at the core of its value, namely, its purchasing power. What is purchasing power? Think of it this way. You know your uncle who has told you countless tales of the value of the nickel in his day. You know how with nothing but one dollar in his pocket he could wine and dine a girl, take in a movie, and fly to Brazil for a wild overnight gambling spree, and still have enough left over to buy himself a breakfast special at the Blue Diner come Monday morning. Seriously, not. But the value of that dollar in your uncle's day was far greater than it is today. George looks the same, but his purchasing power has been eaten away (just like those missing teeth that keep George from smiling). What reduced the value of the dollar (in terms of its purchasing power)? Inflation. The purchasing power of $1 is reduced by 50% every fifteen years or so. This means that $1 today will be worth almost nothing in thirty years' time thanks to inflation's slow but persistent nibbling. In fact, if you look at the value of $1,000 put in a conservative CD (among the least impressive investments, in terms of performance) versus putting the cash in a drawer for the time period from March 1984 through February 1996, the results tell the tale: Your $1,000 would be worth over $3,000 in the CD—but worth less than $300 in that drawer.

Fortunately, investing—in stocks and stock mutual funds in particular—has proven to be the only consistent way to beat the toll inflation takes on your pay. Investing in common stocks has historically proven to be the way to beat inflation's corrosive effects on the purchasing power of your hard-earned dollars. Failure to invest your money in instruments that beat inflation will result in your money becoming less valuable. If this happens, you'll be forced to live a lifestyle of diminishing returns. The only way to beat inflation is by increasing the value of your dollar ahead of the rate of inflation.

As long as your investments outpace the rate of inflation, you will be fine. It's when they fail to do so that you know you're heading for trouble. Determining how far ahead or behind the rate of inflation your interest-earning or investing accounts are is easy. Watch the nightly news and listen for the rate of inflation. Compare that to what your investments are earning. For example, if you are earning 8% on your average stock funds and the rate of inflation is 3%, then you're doing all right. If, however, your bank CD is earning 4% and inflation is at 6%, you are fighting a losing battle.

BEATING BOTH THE MARKET AND INFLATION BY NOT DEFEATING YOURSELF

It gets a little more complicated. You need to ensure that your overall investment portfolio is beating inflation as well as being in step with (or preferably ahead of) a meaningful market benchmark. For example, if you are earning 8% on your average stock funds and the rate of inflation is 3%, then you're doing all right so long as the S&P 500 isn't delivering a 10% return. You will also want to keep an eye on each individual investment in terms of its inflation-beating, market-beating, and industry- (or peer-) beating results. If it is falling behind on one point, it still may receive a passing grade. But if it's falling behind on two or more, you better get to the heart of the matter before your portfolio suffers the consequences.

Ultimately, if you invest in good stocks for the long haul—you don't panic sell at market bottoms or impulse buy at market highs (or any time, for that matter)—you will likely keep ahead of inflation and, if you've done your homework, be within reasonable proximity of meaningful market benchmarks. While this may seem like a facile way to comfort oneself, the truth is that those investors who brag most about their "timely" successes are also those who are most prone to the negative effects of market timing—buying and selling at the wrong time, as well as buying the wrong type of investments.

There are those who say the market is a game. Others who call it a horse race. And for some it may be. But there's enough room for knowledge to play a key role in successful investment decision making to encourage those who are thoughtful investors.

CHAPTER 10

Uncertainty, Risk, and Reward from Scratch

You're at lunch with a colleague. She asks what you did last weekend. You say, "Nothing much," while trying to repress the image of yourself sitting at home playing Blade & Sword, followed by a Jackie Chan binge that left you craving some Szechuan. But it was raining out; the roads looked kind of slippery; and the Joy Luck wasn't delivering. So you turned the heater up. Walked to the fridge. Pulled out an Ultra. Made some popcorn. Slipped in *Hellboy.* "Nothing really," you repeat. "How about you?" Her eyes light up. She plunges into describing a weekend you thought only Hollywood could manufacture. She was up before dawn, throwing instant coffee, two raw eggs, orange juice, and a papaya into a blender. She wanted a jolt. She needed to be fully alert. She had a plane to catch—but this plane would toss her out at ten thousand feet and leave her behind in midair, howling at the rising sun as she and her parachute plummeted toward the good ship earth. The rush of it. The lift and plunge of it. Your heart is pounding, and all you can say is "No effing way."

Taking risks is something all of us do—to a greater or lesser extent. And therein lies the rub. Some of us are more risk averse than others; we look both ways twice before crossing. Of course, taking risks for the sake of taking risks is a psychosis, not a challenge. The truth is that, when it comes to taking risks, even the most adventurous risk taker looks before he leaps—and believes there's a better than even chance that he'll make it to the other side.

When it comes to investing, a critical point to remember is that risk, in and of itself, is not necessarily bad. In fact, some risks go hand in hand with potential rewards, meaning that, for some investors, the risks inherent in some investments may be worth taking. On the other hand, some investment risks are simply not worth taking. Each type of investment has its own specific risks, and there are also risks shared by each major category of investments. Those risks are examined in detail in section 3. In this chapter, you will:

- learn the several definitions of investment risk
- test your own level of risk tolerance
- learn how to manage risk
- understand how to benefit from risk taking
- see how to avoid losses from unnecessary risks

If you are going to remain in control of your investments, you will have to learn to manage the risks involved in investing. While this may sound trite, the truth is that too many savers are swayed by their risk aversion to avoid investing altogether (which leaves their money prone to the damage inflation can do) and, perhaps more commonly, too many investors are often enticed by sky-high returns on a current fund or promised by brand-new stock on the market. Sure, there's the middle ground of investors who have made the transition from saving into investing, who have not overcommitted themselves to extremely risky types of investments. Chances are, that's where you find yourself. But, and this is important to note, the majority of investors who are new to the market haven't experienced a full market cycle—from good to bad to good again. More than any other factor, an investor's risk tolerance is put to the test by a protracted down market since, as my uncle Ralph says, when the tide goes out, all the ships drop. In a down market, most securities are affected, although some are certainly more affected than others. That's why many investors, as part of their overall investment portfolio, select defensive stocks or funds that invest in them. For you, however, a young investor, your best defense is a solid offense of growth-oriented stocks. Why? Time is on your side—time enough, that is, to weather a market downturn and ride the upsurge.

Not all tests are so severe. You might find yourself being tested by one or a handful of investments that you thought were sure things only a matter of months or weeks ago. What made you change your mind? Chances are it had something to do with a drop in the stock's or fund's performance. What made you select the investment to begin with? Chances are, if it was a fund, past performance would have played a decisive role in your decision. The unexpected drop in performance simply serves to underline the way risk adheres to performance. In fact, risk simply defined is a measure of how consistent and predictable a stock's or fund's returns are. Has a stock price risen steadily month to month, or has it swung in wide arcs? Does a fund deliver similar returns from month to month, or do returns look like they are attached to the pendulum of an overwound clock? Of course, as long as the up periods last longer and/or are substantially stronger than the down ticks, even a risky investment like small-company stock funds can prove to be more rewarding than a less volatile large-cap growth fund (of course, the reverse can be true, too).

So why doesn't everyone invest in them? For one thing, small-company stocks are most appropriate (in large doses) for younger investors precisely because of their volatility—the older you get, the more defensive of your principal you'll become. But, for now, you want to focus on investments that build your principal. For another thing, the intemperate nature of small-company stocks increases the risk that an investor in them will sell in a down market (the worst time to get out—unless something has fundamentally changed with the fund itself). If you've done your research, then chances are the reasons you bought the stock or fund in the first place remain reasonable enough to hold on to it. Don't panic. Don't sell during a steep downdraft. Learn to tolerate risk—by testing your risk tolerance and matching investments to your understanding of the risks involved.

Risk Tolerance Test

Okay, this isn't exactly a scientific experiment here. But the following risk quiz is designed to help you gauge your risk tolerance as well as your ability to take the right kinds of risks—in life and when it comes to investing. What does one have to do with the other? Chances are you are already somewhat familiar with your risk-taking skills and desires when it comes to such things as driving a car—speeding or not, lane changing or not, driving on fumes or never letting the gauge drop below half a tank.

1. Would you ever consider trying a sport like bungee jumping or parachuting?
   (a) yes   (b) no   (c) maybe

2. Have you ever decided to do something without knowing the potential consequences?
   (a) yes   (b) no   (c) almost

3. Have you traveled abroad?
   (a) yes   (b) no

4. Do you go to the ATM machine at night?
   (a) regularly   (b) sometimes   (c) never

5. Without looking at the top ten companies one of your funds invests in, can you name:
   (a) all ten   (b) more than five
   (c) one   (d) none

6. How often do you check the air pressure in your tires?
   (a) regularly   (b) sometimes   (c) never

7. If the pilot light in a gas stove isn't working, do you:
   (a) light it
   (b) stand by while someone lights it for you
   (c) leave the house

8. If you had to rank your current investments from most to least risky would you score:
   (a) A+   (b) B   (c) C   (d) F

9. Does the probability of losing 10% or more of your total invested savings make you:
   (a) not want to invest   (b) invest a modest amount
   (c) ignore short-term dips

10. If you inherited a lump sum of money, say $25,000, would you:
    (a) invest it all at once   (b) gradually invest it
    (c) put it in a CD

11. Do you feel more comfortable when you're:
    (a) in total control   (b) sharing decisions
    (c) being told what to do

12. Would you risk everything for a potentially huge return?
    (a) yes   (b) no   (c) maybe

13. Which strategy suits you best?
    (a) taking your time to get to trust someone
    (b) trusting someone before you know them
    (c) trusting no one

14. Rank the following professionals in order of how much you would trust them:
    (a) car mechanic
    (b) hair stylist
    (c) real estate agent
    (d) banker
    (e) airline pilot

15. The last time you pretended to know something, but didn't, was:
    (a) just yesterday
    (b) about one year ago
    (c) never

16. You would rather:
    (a) impress your friends
    (b) impress yourself
    (c) impress your best friend or spouse

17. When you were applying for your latest job did you:
    (a) tell everyone you thought you would get it
    (b) tell only a handful of people
    (c) keep it to yourself, until you actually got it

18. If you had to rate the riskiest thing you have ever done on a scale from 10 (the most risky) to 1 (the least risky) which best matches your answer?
    (a) 10   (b) 7   (c) 5   (d) 3   (e) 1

19. If you weren't guaranteed to get all your money out of the bank account it's now in, would you be less inclined to keep it in that bank account?
    (a) yes
    (b) no
    (c) I'd keep only the amount I was guaranteed to get back

20. In general, do you think that compared to the stock market, banks are:
    (a) safer places to keep your money
    (b) better places to keep your money
    (c) safer and better
    (d) safer, but not necessarily better

21. Do you think the stock market is:
    (a) too risky to invest in
    (b) too expensive to invest in
    (c) too risky and expensive
    (d) worth the risks

22. When standing in line at the airport, do you check to ensure you have your ticket:
    (a) once   (b) twice   (c) three times
    (d) more than three times
23. When it comes to long-term commitments would you say that you are:
    (a) unshakable
    (b) mostly committed
    (c) susceptible to change
24. Are you easily influenced by others when it comes to making decisions about your well-being?
    (a) yes   (b) no   (c) sometimes

SCORECARD

Remember when your teacher told you that you could grade your own exam? Well, that's not in the cards. Instead, you'll need to score yourself based on the following:

	A	B	C	D		A	B	C	D	E
1.	1	.5	0		13.	1	0	0		
2.	0	1	.5		14.	0	0	0	.5	0
3.	1	0			15.	0	0	0		
4.	.5	1	0		16.	.5	1	.5		
5.	4	2	1	0	17.	0	.5	1		
6.	.5	1	0		18.	1	1	.5	0	0
7.	1	.5	0		19.	.5	0	1		
8.	.5	1	.5	0	20.	1	0	0	1	
9.	0	.5	0		21.	0	0	0	0	
10.	1	.5	0		22.	1	1	.5	0	
11.	.5	1	0		23.	.5	1	.5		
12.	0	0	1		24.	0	1	.5		

20 or more. You are a well-rehearsed risk taker who knows how to set reasonable limits in accordance with realizable goals. Not unwilling to try to take on a new challenge, you are also against leaps of faith for faith's sake. Chances are you could be a successful entrepreneur, which, by the way, is the same profile it would take to be a successful investor. You're willing to take charge of a new situation in an informed, objective way while at the same time able to recognize the potential pitfalls and calculate the consequences. You're also able to spot trouble before you're in it. To be a successful investor, you need to be able to tolerate and accomplish all of the above without being overwhelmed by second doubts. You're on your way.

10 to 19 points. Depending on where your score falls, you are either more or less likely to take risks with a greater or lesser degree of probability that there will be a reward waiting for you on the other side. You have tended to either take too much risk with too little advance thinking about the possible consequences, or too little risk without understanding the potential downside in terms of gain. As an investor, you will need to learn more about the potential risks and rewards in order to ensure that you flourish, rather than founder, when it comes to new investments that are better suited to your age and objectives. You will need to learn more in order to take on more risks, which, in turn, will help you increase your long-term chances of successfully achieving your investment objectives. In the chapters ahead, pay particular attention to the sections on each investment category's particular risks and potential rewards.

0 to 9. You are, in varying degrees, either too willing to take risks without knowing and understanding the consequences or too unwilling to take on necessary risks in order to achieve reasonable objectives. As a younger investor, you'll need to come to terms with the fact that some risks aren't worth taking—while others decidedly are. Familiarizing yourself with appropriate risks and rewards for each type of investment vehicle within each investment category will help you overcome your timidity and/or tame your overconfidence when it comes to taking risks.

OVERCOMING UNCERTAINTY

Being uncertain is a natural condition, but so is growing beyond uncertainty. If it weren't, no child would crawl, no adolescent would survive into adulthood, and no adult would commit to self-determination when it comes to career and family. As in life, so in investing, accepting uncertainty as a starting point—not as an end in itself—is a condition you'll need to evolve from. And like psychological growth, when it comes to investing you'll need to come to terms with (and so take control of) your own past and present investment experience (or lack thereof) in order to reasonably ensure a more fulfilling future for yourself.

Knowing that investing in certain types of securities has proven effective in the past is one way to overcome any sense of foreboding you might have in the present. The best way to do this, I think, is to look at what would happen if you had made the wrong moves. Taking the worst-case scenario in terms of investing in common stocks at market highs, rather than lows, might help. After all, conventional wisdom has it that this is the worst way to invest. Most investors won't ever repeat such a poor performance record of investing new money into the market at exactly the wrong time—but it's important to know that it can happen to anyone.

What is immediately apparent is that, had you invested at the wrong time, you would have come out well ahead of where you would have been had you not invested at all (i.e., stuffed your money in a mattress). Making a classic mistake still turns out to be rewarding enough to make the move from saving to investing. But note the type of stocks you would have had to have invested in: the more liquid, large-company stocks, right? Well, yes. But you would have fared better in small-company stocks over the same time period.

This information is meant to help those who are reluctant to enter the market overcome their aversion. However, the truth of the performances lies in a hidden fact—that the money wasn't pulled out of the market on the downside. Your ability to commit to the market for the long term is of paramount importance when it comes to reaping the potential rewards investing has to offer. In fact, every category of investment tends to diminish in terms of its volatility (swings from positive to negative returns) over time. In fact, time may be the single most important ingredient you can add to the recipe of what makes a successful investment.

What exactly is volatility? It's a relative term. In fact, the term is more accurately phrased "relative volatility," and it refers to the history of a security's or mutual fund's range of rise and fall over specified time periods. To calculate the standard deviation—or "beta"—for a stock mutual fund, for example, divide the fund's standard deviation by the standard deviation of the S&P 500 index for the same period. A standard deviation sounds highfalutin, but its derivation is down-to-earth: it uses a security's past performance as the standard by which to calculate its deviation from its own norm (or average) as well as its deviation from a benchmark (like the S&P 500). If, for example, the S&P

500 is determined as the benchmark, or 1.00, then a stock fund with a standard deviation of 1.45 is 45% more volatile than this benchmark, and a fund with a standard deviation of 0.85 is 15% less volatile.

Calculating a security's or fund's standard deviation or beta requires some doing, but there are several sources that do this for you for stocks and stock funds. Morningstar, Value Line, and several investment newsletters provide this figure. Yours free, at a local library.

While this may be sounding like Greek 101, it's really Risk 101. Whereas a beta refers to a security's performance in terms of its volatility, a positive alpha is, well, positive—since it relates to the extra return received for taking a risk, instead of accepting the market's risk and return.

MANAGING RISK

If you lift weights, or haven't repressed the memory of high school gym class, chances are you have heard the expression "no pain, no gain." Something similar applies to investing, although it's translated as "no risk, no return." And since risk is a constant in the investment universe, you'll need to learn how to adapt to it—and use it to your best advantage. You've already assessed your risk-taking tolerance. Now you need the know-how to gauge whether your risky investment has real potential for reward.

Managing risk is only partially possible—no matter what some experts would like you to believe. But the fact that it is somewhat possible should drive you to learn how. The following tips will help you cover some of the risk-related bases that can arise unexpectedly, leaving one or more of your investments vulnerable to an unwanted degree of new risk, or threatening your conviction in an investment even though that risk has not fundamentally changed:

1. Know past performance. Even if you don't have the resources to find or calculate a beta or alpha, chances are you can locate a security's or fund's past performance and get a relative sense of how it has performed over time—in good and bad markets, economic environments, and industry cycles. Doing so will help you avoid investments that have performed poorly on a consistent basis (a risk not worth taking) and, hopefully, discover some better performers that, over time, have provided a market-beating return.

2. Understand how the performance was derived. Some securities may have a spectacular record for a few months, one year, maybe even a bit longer. But, unless they've consistently done so over three or more years, chances are they took substantially more risk than their peers to deliver the wide margin of performance-related difference.

3. Find out any significant changes in the economy, market, industry, and company (if it's a fund, such a change could be a new manager). While subsequent chapters will help you discern these qualities, it's worth keeping in mind that changes in any of the above categories will necessitate a review of the individual risks that may be increased (or decreased) as a result.

4. Review your objectives. If your objectives change, and your time frame for achieving them changes, then you have injected a degree of risk into your overall investment plan that did not exist when you put your portfolio together. Chances are you will need to review and revise your portfolio in light of the changes and the risks they bring to your portfolio.

5. Review your portfolio's risk. Each security or fund in your portfolio has a degree of risk which, when combined with the other securities or funds in the portfolio, creates an average risk of your overall mix. You want to be sure that this risk remains in line with your tolerance and ability to manage it.

You Can't Avoid Risk. But you can live with it—and even profit from it so long as you can understand it and know how to look for ways to manage it to your advantage. In 1987, a year that saw one of the worst days on Wall Street, even bearish investors (those who think the market will fall on their heads at any moment) made money—so long as they remained invested and didn't panic sell. That's what you'll need to do to be able to comfortably take appropriate risks in order to increase your potential to achieve your objectives. Sometimes it will be more difficult to stay the course—especially during intemperate markets. But the markets have never been dead calm, and will likely never be. The result is that you need to assess investment risks in relation to their specific rewards and particular potential in terms of your overall portfolio. That's the best way to avoid losses that uncertainty can yield, and to maintain your prime directive: to invest in a better future for yourself.

SECTION 3

Know the Basics
Before You Invest

CHAPTER 11

Bond Investing from Scratch

What is a bond? Think of a bond as an IOU. When you purchase a bond, you're basically acting like a bank, which lends money in return for (a) some interest and (b) ultimately the return of the total principal amount that was lent. When you buy a bond, you are "lending" the corporation or government the price of the bond (its face or "par" value). In return, you are hoping to receive either one or a combination of: a high rate of interest, tax advantages, and/or safety of principal.

The following chart gives you a bird's-eye view of bond performance over the past ten years. You'll note the distinction between long-, intermediate-, and short-term bonds—a key factor in a savvy bond investor's selection process. What does it refer to? The term of a bond, also referred to as its maturity, is the time the IOU becomes due and payable. The longer out that pay date is, the greater the risk of price fluctuation tends to be. The shorter the term, the less the bond's volatility. While long-term bonds perform better over time, shorter-term bonds can offer you a greater degree of certainty that your money will be returned to you when you need it.

As with stocks, there are numerous different types of bonds to chose from, and it's in your interest to familiarize yourself with them. Since many mutual funds hold some percentage of their assets in bonds, familiarizing yourself with the various types of bonds that are available to the investing public will help you better understand the risks and rewards each type lends to mutual fund portfolios. Even

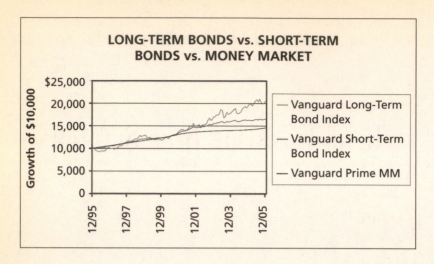

stock funds often have some bonds in their mix, and growth and income funds often have upwards of 30% of their assets in bonds or other types of fixed-income instruments. Finally, bonds are barometers of Wall Street's take on the overall economy and particular parts of it. Learning to "read" bonds will help you grasp more than their own worth; it will help you see some underlying signals that the economy is sending to bond traders.

BOND RISKS

If stocks are often viewed as a walk on the wild side of investing, bonds are often viewed as a walk on the safe side, supposedly offering more moderate (but inflation-beating) rates of return with lower risk than stocks or stock mutual funds. As a result, conventional wisdom suggests that bonds can and should play an important balancing role in most investors' portfolios. However, before you buy some bonds for your portfolio, be aware that there are two problems with the rosy picture of bond investing mentioned above. First, bonds are not generically "safe" investments; there are risks inherent to each type of bond you can purchase. Second, and contrary to conventional wisdom—most of which is written from the perspective of those over age forty-five—bonds shouldn't necessarily be a part of your portfolio. In fact, if you're under age thirty-five, they should rarely play a role in your portfolio. You've got the need and the time to risk short-term losses in your search for capital appreciation of your long-term investments. For shorter-term objectives, on the other hand, you can make a case for some types of bonds for objectives that fall within a two- to three-year time frame.

As with stock investing, there are risks associated with bond investing. But, while no bond is risk-free, some are far safer than others. There are three main risks associated with bond investing; they should all be taken into consideration before you purchase any type of bond. It's important to keep in mind that, as in life, taking risks can be very rewarding—or downright punitive. Investing in some types of bonds is like taking new back roads to a familiar destination, while investing in others can be like trying to jump fourteen flaming buses with your mountain bike. Keeping the following risks in mind should hopefully help you avoid getting burned.

- Interest rate risk. If there's one thing about bonds that you need to know it's this: When interest rates rise, your bond's value declines, and vice versa. Thus, interest rate risk is the risk that your bond's market value will fluctuate with changes in interest rates. To be attuned to the overall interest rate scene, all you need to do is to tap into one of the online services for a bond market update or interest rate forecast. Failing that, read the business section of your paper—there you'll likely find where short-term interest rates are at as well as where they've been. If they're significantly lower than one year previous, you should probably stay away from bond investments.
- Call risk. While rising interest rates hurt bonds, falling rates are good for bonds, sending prices above face value. However, in many cases a bond's issuer may "call" the bond prior to maturity, at par value or only a slight premium to par value. This, of course, limits the upside potential of the bond in the face of falling interest rates. When a bond is called, the bottom line is you will have to reinvest in a new bond paying you less interest. Most bonds are callable, with the exception of Treasury securities, most of which are noncallable. The bond's fine print should spell out whether the issuer can call the bond as well as spell out any premiums required, or date limitations of the call. If you decide to invest in individual bonds, be sure to inquire about this often-overlooked feature of bond investing.

- Credit risk. This is also known as default risk and it is the risk bond investors fear most—and most often hear about in the press thanks to the likes of junk bond king Michael Milken and, more recently, the Orange County, California, bankruptcy. Credit risk is the risk of losing your investment due to the default by the bond issuer. Issuers default for several reasons, typically because their business fails. And it is new or high-risk businesses (such as retailers) that are typically more likely to go bust or enter into bankruptcy than, for example, the federal government, which can always raise taxes (or print money) to help pay you back. But during the federal budget impasse of 1996, the federal government came under scrutiny from bond rating agencies, suggesting that even the US government may no longer be a safe bet. The best way to safeguard yourself against default is to invest in high-rated bonds. While this is no guarantee, it has proven to be the most successful way to hedge your bets.

Moody's and Standard & Poor's are the most highly respected agencies in the bond rating business. Each firm provides a rating scheme designed to underline the degree of credit risk a potential bond investor is getting him or herself into. Among the ratings categories used by Moody's and Standard & Poor's are the following:

Moody's	Standard & Poor's	Meaning
Aaa	AAA	Best quality
Aa	AA	High quality
Baa	BBB	Medium quality
B	B	Minimal quality

Anything rated less than BBB/Baa is a junk bond.

Typically, lower-rated bonds offer a higher yield, but they also pose greater risk of defaulting. On the other hand, higher-rated bonds provide lower yields but greater chances of seeing full payment of interest and principal.

Bond Types

Like the various portrayals of James Bond, bonds have differing characteristics and don't act in the same way. The following types of bonds will help you sort through an investment category that many people invest in, but few know much about. Even if you never invest in a bond (and this may be a good idea) you will be able to impress your friends with some hip market talk and save yourself from investing in something that is often touted as safe but is, in fact, potentially rife with risks.

Treasury Bills

The US government regularly borrows money to fund its projects. Treasuries—also commonly referred to as "T bills"—are issued at a discount to the investor and redeemed at face value ($10,000) on maturity. (Face value is $10,000, so you need to invest almost as much per bill, depending on maturity and interest rate.) Treasury notes and bonds have longer terms and pay interest semiannually at a fixed interest rate. All are as free from credit risk as a bond can get. (More on that below.) While yields are lower than on other bonds (other than municipals), Treasury yields are free from state and local income taxes (but are federally taxable), so you may not be giving up much in yield to get a Treasury's ultimate safety.

Treasury Inflation-Indexed Securities

More commonly referred to as "Treasury inflation-protected" bonds or "TIPs," inflation-protected debt securities were created and launched by the Treasury in October 2001 (simultaneous to their suspension of the issuance of the thirty-year bond). With an emphasis on US Treasuries, it can invest in federal agencies, and even corporate and foreign (if they're dollar-denominated) bonds with an average maturity of about fourteen years, but the bonds' inflation protection gives them, under most market conditions, the volatility of a much shorter-term bond fund. (They're susceptible to changes in real interest rates, but not to the bond market's bugbear, inflation.) TIPs are exempt from state and local income taxes, but subject to federal income taxes.

US Savings Bonds

Safe. Secure. Stable. Solid. Although they don't offer the highest rate of return—4%—savings bonds are a sound introduction to bond investing. With a required minimum investment of only $25, it's easy to start.

Mortgage-backed Bonds

Backed by pools of mortgage loans, these bonds have names that sound like a long-lost relative—Ginnie Mae, Fannie Mae, and Freddie Mac. These bonds offer high rates of interest but require high investment minimums to get in. Moreover, in times of lower interest rates when people refinance their mortgages (billions of dollars of refinanced mortgages swept the market in 1993 and 1994), mortgage-backed bonds are paid off sooner than many investors expect or desire, and investors' principal has to be reinvested at the new, lower rates.

Adjustable-rate Mortgage (ARM) Bonds

If you're looking for a bond investment to help you hedge your portfolio against rising rates, this is a better bet than most. This is because as rates rise, so do the payments of ARM mortgagees. These increased payments allow ARM funds to hold up relatively well compared to other fixed-income securities. ARMs can offer the safety of a short-term bond, but they typically pay a fairly low yield—like a short-term bond.

Corporate Bonds

Corporations are often in search of capital-issue bonds. In return for your investment the company pledges to repay you the value of your investment at some specified future date, in addition to making specified interest payments. However, corporate bonds vary in quality from AAA-rated bonds (almost as safe as Treasuries) to the lowly junk bonds (euphemistically referred to as "high-yield" bonds).

High-yield (or Junk) Bonds

Junk bonds offer higher yields to compensate for lower credit ratings, based on the uncertainty of the company's ability to repay the debt.

One real advantage of junk bonds is that they are less affected than most other types of bonds by rising interest rates (although they still are hurt by them). Their prices are more closely tied to the issuer's and the economy's well-being rather than to interest rate levels. However, credit risks generally outweigh the slim benefits of interest rate risks here—if you can spell junk, you can spell default. Historically, these types of bonds have promised higher yields for their higher risk—but sometimes the promise hasn't been kept, leaving investors holding thin air.

Preferred Stocks

A preferred stock is like a bond in that it pays a fixed dividend. It is called preferred because its dividends must be paid before any dividends will be paid to common stock holders. But unlike bonds, the issuing company has no absolute obligation to pay the dividends. (Preferred stock holders, unlike bondholders, cannot force the company into bankruptcy.) For that reason, many preferred stocks have a fair amount of credit risk, like a junk bond.

Convertible Bonds

Convertible bonds offer you the option of converting your bond into common stock at a predetermined price. If you think the company is growing and that the price of its stock will rise, then a convertible will enable you to capitalize on the company's growth rather than be locked in to a lower rate of return. The price you pay for the conversion privilege is, however, the fact that convertible bond yields are lower than for other, "straight" bonds. The yield is, however, generally greater than on the same company's common stock. (Mutual funds known as "equity-income" funds often invest in convertible bonds.)

Municipal Bonds

"Munis" are sold by states, counties, cities and towns, and other governmental and quasipublic authorities to finance everything from road construction to sewer systems. But before you flush this option down the toilet, consider the following fact: income from munis is federally tax-free, and in-state bonds are generally free of state and often local income taxes. Munis offer lower rates of interest, but their tax-free aspect increases their value. Like corporates, munis range in quality from AAA to junk.

BOND VALUES

Since a bond's value fluctuates and is not necessarily close to its par or "face" value, to determine the return on your investment you must take both principal and yield into account.

For example, a $1,000 bond bought at par, with a term of five years at an interest rate of 5%, held to maturity, and sold, would realize a return of $250:

$$
\begin{array}{l}
\$1,000 \text{ (par)} \\
\underline{+250} \text{ (5\% interest} \times \text{5 years)} \\
\$1,250 \\
\underline{-1,000} \text{ (original cost)} \\
\quad \$250 \text{ (return)}
\end{array}
$$

Taking a more complicated case, where the bond was bought at $950 and sold five years later for $1,050:

$$
\begin{array}{l}
\$1,050 \\
\underline{+250} \text{ (5\% interest} \times \text{5 years)} \\
\$1,300 \\
\underline{-950} \text{ (original cost)} \\
\quad \$350 \text{ (return)}
\end{array}
$$

A bond's current yield is easily derived by dividing the annual interest payment of the bond by its price.

When the bond is at par:

price: $1,000
annual interest: $50
yield: 5%

When the bond is selling for $950:

price: $950
annual interest: $50
yield: 5.26%

A bond's yield is what you actually earn on your investment only so long as its price holds steady. Remember that as a bond's price rises its yield falls, and as a bond's price falls, its yield rises.

Treasury Bills

There are some advantages to buying individual Treasury bonds. First, with Treasuries you needn't worry about diversifying to minimize credit risk. Second, there is generally a yield advantage. This is mostly because you're not paying a mutual fund's annual expenses. Moreover, when rates are trending up, the money market you might buy is already holding lower-yielding securities, while you're free to buy Treasuries at the market rate.

Also, with individual Treasury bills you can generally go out a bit further than the sixty-day maturity typical of a money market without taking on any real interest-rate risk (so long as you won't be needing the money before the Treasury bill matures). Similarly, but unlike a bond fund, any individual bond matures on a specified date. Regardless of where interest rates are at maturity, the par value of the bond will be paid (assuming there isn't a default). Bond funds never mature. They are managed within a certain average maturity band and are redeemed at the prevailing market price of the bonds held in the fund. If you've designated your money for a specific purpose, it may be useful to know exactly how much money will be available on a specified date; an individual bond can give you this security.

In most cases, you'll want to buy a maturity matching your need for the money. If you expect to be buying a house in six months, buy a six-month CD or Treasury bill.

Treasury bills are issued by the US government in amounts of $10,000. They mature in three months to one year and are sold at a discount. That means you buy the bill at less than its face amount, and receive its face amount at maturity.

Recently, Treasury bills were yielding slightly more than 5% (three-month bills) to around 5.5% (one-year bills). Moreover, they're free of state and local taxes, so their tax equivalent yield is generally somewhat better than a CD. But if you buy Treasuries from a broker you'll be charged for the service—typically a $50 charge, or 0.5% on a $10,000 investment. (Instead, you can buy directly from the Federal Reserve—for more info call the Federal Reserve Bank in New York at (212) 720-6619.)

US Savings Bonds

These are another ultrasafe option. Under new legislation recently passed, savings bonds purchased and held for six months to five years will pay a rate equal to 85% of the yield of six-month Treasury bills, adjusted every six months. (For bonds held five years or longer, the interest rate will remain the same: 85% of the five-year T-bill yield.) Savings bonds are nevertheless a reasonable alternative to money markets and CDs. Also note that a savings bond's interest is free of state and local taxes (thereby boosting its tax-equivalent yield). The interest may even be federally tax-free if the proceeds are used to pay for college education. (Check with your accountant—okay, check with your uncle who is one.)

Two disadvantages of savings bonds are that you can invest a maximum of $15,000 per year, and they aren't redeemable in the first six months, unless you can prove you have a financial emergency. Furthermore, if bonds are redeemed on any date other than their anniversary issue date or six months from the date of issue, accrued interest will be lost.

Bond Funds

Some bond funds perform better than others in a rising rate environment. But that performance is typically based on a loser's game, and not a winner's game. That is, they still go down, just not as much.

You can also look for super-short-term bond funds—funds with average maturities of less than one year. The advantage to investing in super-short-term bond funds is twofold. First, in a rising rate environment they'll be able to guard against the low or negative returns of (comparatively longer-term) short-term bond funds. Second, because interest rates on securities with a maturity of six to twelve months are significantly higher than a money market's securities, which have about a one-month maturity, super-short-term bond funds will outperform money markets under most conditions; that is, when rates fall, remain steady, or rise slowly.

BOND INVESTING STRATEGIES

The following general strategies are designed to help you invest in bonds. While bonds are often too expensive for the young investor to get involved in via direct ownership, you might find yourself in the position of being able to do so. Even if not, the strategies below will stand you in good stead if you decide to take the more affordable and often as profitable option—investing in bonds through a bond mutual fund (discussed in detail in chapter 14).

- Follow interest rates. Bonds may be attractive when they beat inflation, but they're plug-ugly when they don't. To get a handle on where inflation and interest rates are headed, stay informed about the markets and the economy.

    If you think interest rates are going to head up, purchase the shortest maturity bonds (e.g., one year or less). If you think rates are going to fall, move into longer-term bonds (five years and up). But watch out. No one can predict the direction of interest rates with 100% accuracy, so you probably shouldn't try to jump back and forth between one-year and thirty-year bonds. When in doubt, keep the bulk of your income securities on the short end (three years or less). You've got plenty of time to practice on these before you lock into a long-term bond that even Houdini couldn't get out of.

- Ladder maturities. "Laddering" or "staggering" maturities means investing in a variety of maturities—some short-term (less than three years), some intermediate-term (three to ten years), and some long-term bonds (ten to fifteen years). (Forget the thirty-year stranglehold for now.) This will help you hedge your bond market bets by reducing the risk of being mistaken about them. Another advantage to laddering is that it will give you a leg up in terms of being able to match your investments with your goals. For example, if you're planning on going to law school in a few years, you would do well to invest some or most of your assets in short-term bonds that will mature around the time you will enter.

- Buy quality. When it comes to investing directly in individual bonds, top-quality bonds (rated AAA or AA) are the best way to go. Individual investors rarely have the time or expertise to really investigate bond safety, or the assets to sufficiently diversify against default risk. The last thing you want to have to do is confess to your friends that you can't go out tonight because (a) you invested in bonds, and (b) those bonds turned out to be junk.

- Diversify. As with stock investing, diversification is a bond investor's prime directive. Don't put all your eggs in one basket! This is very hard to do with direct bond investing, because of the cost involved. For this reason, you will probably be better off focusing your early investment attention on mutual funds—stock mutual funds for sure, and perhaps a bond fund or two. And that's what chapter 14 is all about. If you do want to directly own bonds, stick to a US Treasury (if you're only holding one or a few bonds) or maybe AAA- or AA-rated munis or corporates (if you're holding several).

Short-Term Investing Strategies

The following specific strategies are designed to help you invest in bonds and their fixed-income equivalents. While bonds are often too expensive for the young investor to get involved in via direct ownership, many fixed-income investments (like bank CDs or money market accounts) are affordable and advisable for short-term places to park your cash (while being assured that the money you parked won't be towed away in the interim). In addition to these most conservative types of fixed-income investments, the strategies below will help you understand the ways in which you can put your knowledge of bond risks and types to good use—i.e., making you some money. Regardless of the fact that you'd probably be best served by avoiding bonds altogether (for the time being), the following specific strategies will help you wed your bond-investing ideas to real-market scenarios. Also note that, in chapter 14, you'll come to learn about a more affordable option—indirect bond-investing through a bond mutual fund.

Chances are that the closest thing you've come to in terms of investing money for a substantial short-term gain was either the office football pool or a Publishers Clearing House free-for-all. When you need to safeguard a sizable sum (like the amount needed for the down payment of a house), you'll need to build it over three to five years by investing it wisely and then, two years before you go knocking on the home-buyin' door, play it safe by putting your money in short-term investments.

If you need the money within two years, short-term CDs and money market accounts are the safest place, and super-short-term bond funds a possible alternative.

Bank CDs and money market accounts offer you the following: a reliable place for short-term cash, and a better hedge against rising rates than more speculative short- and intermediate-term bonds. While it's true that a money market mutual fund delivers these as well, it fails to deliver one potentially important thing: a federal guarantee.

A bank certificate of deposit (or CD) that is federally insured has several advantages over betting—for one thing, it's not against the law, and for another, bank CDs are usually federally insured (i.e., safe) up to $100,000. (Look for the FDIC label on the door of your bank or on the teller's window.) But while CDs are often a good temporary parking place for your cash, there are other equally or more attractive short-term investments that are worth considering.

When it comes to long-term performance, most varieties of bonds outperform the more staid CD. But remember, CDs are much less volatile than bonds: a CD investment is more appropriate if you're looking for a short-term parking place for your capital.

Let's look more closely at volatility. As noted, the chart on page 146 illustrates the often overlooked fact that investing for the short term (less than three years) in longer-term bonds (and bond funds) can be a losing proposition—and that rising interest rates decrease the value of bonds and the funds that invest in them, just as declining rates increase the value of bonds and the funds that invest in them.

Look at what happened to bonds, for example, in 1994 and 1995, when their prices showed wild gyrations. This period is a great example of interest rate risk—and how it affects bond prices. Rising interest rates, which are always bad news for bonds, took their toll in 1994 as the Federal Reserve continued to raise short-term rates. CDs or money markets would have been a better place to be. Super-short-term bond funds (with a duration of less than one year) also held up well— since these types of bonds are the least interest-rate sensitive. In 1995, thanks to a succession of Fed interest rate cuts, longer-term bonds more than quadrupled the return on a CD or super-short bond as yields hit new lows and prices rose dramatically.

Some bonds (and bond funds) are less interest-rate sensitive than others. Historically, the least interest-rate-sensitive fixed-income investments deliver lower returns in exchange for the benefit of reliability of income. But while CDs, money markets, and super-short-term bond funds may be the best way to defend your fixed-income investment against the toll from rising interest rates, they won't really help you guard against the toll inflation will take on the overall purchasing power of your invested savings.

The bottom line on bonds is that they are best left out of your overall investment portfolio for now. For one thing, the expense of investing in bonds is prohibitive. For another, they're hard to track, analyze, and purchase. And you have two better fixed-income alternatives: CDs (for the short term) and bond mutual funds (for the long term). Finally, when it comes to investing your hard-earned savings, there's a better investment alternative: stocks and stock mutual funds.

READY RESOURCES

- bondsonline.com
- investinginbonds.com
- ustreas.gov

- *The Bond Book,* A. Thau
- *Bond Markets Analysis & STR,* third edition, F. Fabozzi
- *Bond Markets,* second edition, F. Fabozzi
- *The Bond Market,* C. Ray

CHAPTER 12

Stock Investing from Scratch

Investing your money is the best way to grow it reasonably well over meaningful time periods. While this declarative sentence is this book in sum, it's loaded with conditional elements that make practicing what *Investing from Scratch* preaches a life's work. For one thing, you have to be extraordinarily selective about which investment vehicles you invest in. For another, you need to determine what "meaningful time periods" means. Growth at a reasonable rate is no small achievement—and before you get to the end, you have to determine the best means to get you from here to there. That's where this book, and this chapter in particular, come to bear. Not because I think individual stocks are the best place for individual investors like you and me to place their money—but because you need to know the ins and outs, ups and downs, whys and wherefores of individual stocks before you become a savvy mutual fund investor.

What's a mutual fund? A stock mutual fund is a pool of individual stocks held in one professionally managed portfolio. And, make no mistake about it, I'm a much stronger advocate of investing in mutual funds (chapter 14), where managers with proven career records of being able to grow their investors' money well, in tough and smooth-sailin' times, make staying the investment course not only rewarding but possible since knowing that such managers fared well in tempestuous times before will ensure that you won't be tempted to abandon ship when the going gets rough. (The going always gets rough before it gets better. The worst time to abandon any ship is in the middle of a storm-tossed sea—that way you guarantee you'll never make it to a safe harbor.)

So forget those trendy cybercafes where jazz and blues are the buzz—or better yet, when you get to a cybercafe, tap into Wall Street online or via one of the several sources listed at the end of this chapter. (See chapter 22 for details.) While you're there, look around for some better investing ideas. In fact, from here on out, you should keep an eye open for making your money grow the old-fashioned way: investing it.

TAKE STOCK OF YOUR WORLD

To start with, take a look around you. If you're in a café, for example, consider where the coffeemaker (the machine, not the server) is manufactured. Who provides the raw materials (the metals and plastics) for its construction, for the cup's construction, for the building's construction? Where do the beans come from? How is the price of a plain cup of joe determined? Who owns the joint? (Chances are, you should own a portion of it, given the amount of money you pour into it. And if you had invested $100 in Starbucks stock back when you started drinking the stuff—say ten years ago—that $100 would be worth around $180,000 today!) When you step outside are there other retail stores that are more (or less) crowded? What's the average age group in each store you browse? Do they have money to spend? Are they spending it on full-price items—or waiting for a sale? Are there more stores on the street or in the mall where you go for your cup o' joe today compared to a year or two ago? And what about all those cybercafes springing up—how will they all survive? If only a few do, which ones will it be and why? And who needs to get wired on java when you can keep yourself frantic just trying to look at the world through an investment perspective?

Personally, I find this way of thinking exhilarating. Poetic even—since what it helps you do is to look for rhythms in the market and world. Okay, they're called trends within industries and economies, but I like to think of investing as an artful form of analysis as opposed to a solely quantifiable, statistically based dissection of things.

To begin with, every investor needs to ask two basic questions: What's really going on? And how can I profit by finding out? The first

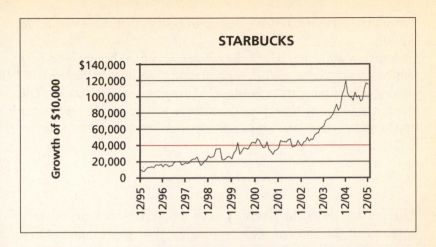

answer to these two basic questions is itself basic—namely, that what's really going on is that the best way to profit (in terms of increasing the current value of your savings) is to invest regularly, wisely, and well. But chances are you know this. The question then becomes—where to invest!

This chapter is all about understanding different types of stocks, why investing in certain types of stocks—preferably pooled together in a well-managed mutual fund—is the best possible way to grow your money, what some of the best stock investing strategies are, and how to invest in them. Getting into the stock markets—either directly through owning individual shares of a company's stock or indirectly though purchasing shares in a stock mutual fund—makes particular sense for you and for everyone else young enough to have an investment horizon measured in decades. But before you leap, let's take a look at some of the real risks of stock investing.

THE RISKS

The risks of stock investing are straightforward: The potential for decline in the stock's price (you buy a stock at $10 and it drops to $3) and/or elimination or reduction of dividend income. If you bought the stock at $10, loss occurs when you sell your stock for $9.99 or less. Selling may still make sense—and it may not. In fact, since most stocks fluctuate in price, it may be best to hold tight and ride out the downward curve if you have reason to believe that there will be an upside.

Right. Now that you have a clear picture about the benefits and risks of investing in stocks or stock mutual funds, let's unpack the stock investing trunk from start to finish. Read this chapter in its entirety. The modest amount of time you spend here will be amply repaid, for stocks and stock mutual funds will top your investment list.

STOCK GUIDE

This stock guide will help bring you up to speed on the types of stock investments that are out there waiting for your green thumb. Once you familiarize yourself with them, you can begin to practice the fine art of making your money grow (while accounting for the risks you need to know) by implementing one or more of the stock investing strategies detailed below.

A common stock represents ownership of a (small) share in a company. Think of a share as one vine in a vineyard—whether a very large IBM vineyard, wherein your one plant amounts to a tiny portion of the harvest, or a small Netscape vineyard, wherein the one plant is a somewhat larger part of the whole. Depending on how well the vineyard grows its vines and prepares the harvest, and how many grape plants you own, you will either be able to live off the harvest or have to look elsewhere for sustenance (unless you want to live off raisins). Note that you could do well in the large vineyard or in the small (at either place, one vine makes about the same amount of wine), but the large vineyard may better rebound from bad weather, while the small vineyard may have more room for expansion in good conditions.

The following list of stock types is comprehensive, but not all-inclusive. Consider these the most common apples in the barrel—and realize that in each type there are likely to be a few rotten individual stocks. The good news? Knowing what to look for and diversifying will help ensure that one rotten apple doesn't ruin your overall portfolio.

Blue Chips

Blue chips are large-cap stocks and are traditionally thought of as the highest quality of all common stocks. Blue chips are typically larger, solid-performing, dividend-yielding companies. Examples of blue chips are Coca-Cola, General Electric, and Microsoft. I say traditionally, because these giants can fall as mightily as the small. For example, let's take a look at IBM's performance over the decade between 1995 and 2005.

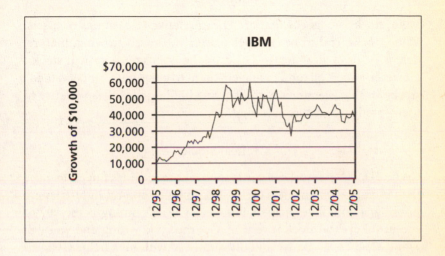

As you can clearly see, you could have easily lost money owning shares in IBM at the wrong time. Fortunately, it's just as evident that, had you sold at the high and bought at the low, you would have done very well for yourself.

Blue chips, like all other types of stocks, are characterized as a growth, a value, or a cyclical stock (or they can be somewhere in between). The difference?

Growth Stocks

Growth stocks present investors the opportunity to invest in companies that promise to increase their stock's market value through earnings growth. They tend to be smaller companies and/or in rapidly growing industries. (But they could, like Wal-Mart, be large players expanding market share in a mature industry.) Because investors expect their earnings to grow, growth stocks tend to be expensive relative to their current earnings. Growth stocks typically rise in value more than other stocks, but they are far more volatile and subject to greater declines in price too. Growth stocks should be the choice of your generation: they're more exciting, can be more rewarding over the long term, and are less likely to get you caught in the web of trying to time a specific economic cycle—and you can afford the greater risk for the potentially greater reward.

Value Stocks

Value stocks are stocks that are cheap relative to earnings or assets. Value stocks tend to be stodgier players in slower-growing, mature, defensive, or cyclical areas—basically the opposite of growth stocks. However, almost all fund managers claim to be seeking "undervalued" stocks, or that even their highest-flying holdings are cheap relative to their (predicted) future earnings.

Cyclical Stocks

Cyclical stocks are stocks in companies whose earnings fluctuate more than average with business cycles. Examples of cyclical industries are housing, automobiles, paper, and steel. Correct timing is the key to successful cyclical stock investing. Get the cycle wrong and you will know what it feels like to land on your head without a helmet. Crash! As with growth versus value, the cyclicality of stocks is a continuum. Some stocks are in the middle, and might be considered cyclical by some investors and not by others.

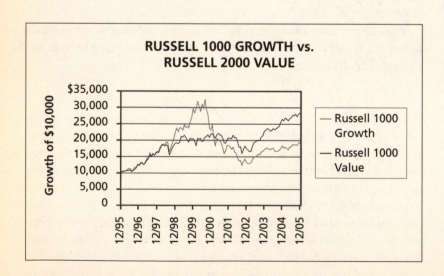

There are other ways of categorizing stocks by other distinct characteristics which it behooves the potential stock investor to know more about.

Income Stocks

Dividend-paying stocks, these pay a substantial or above-average dividend income. Income stocks are most often value stocks; stocks in companies that are typically in more stable, mature industries. The stability enables these companies to provide steady dividends—a source of income for many retirees or, more relevant from your vantage point, a source of reinvestment capital. (See chapter 17 for more on the benefits and strategies of dividend reinvesting.) Examples of income stock industries would be utilities, telecommunications, and energy—but even many pharmaceutical companies (not exactly a stodgy industry) fall into this camp.

New tech to phone tech to nanotech to no tech—there's a revolution or two underfoot these days. Dial up the communications industry as an example—whose caveats you can apply to other new, new stocks based on new, new tech. In the communications industry, you can plug into both the telecommunications and the utilities industries. On the one hand, telecommunication companies are getting into developing new modes of communicating (cellular as opposed to cable, satellite as opposed to cellular) so look for some increased volatility in the decade ahead—as well as the potential for greater profit in this group. But watch out, the new technology is leading to significant downsizing and consolidation in the industry—a plus if you're on the right side of the investment, but again, added volatility will have to be weathered. The revolution in utilities is a far more sleepy affair involving both regulatory changes on the federal and state levels as well as industry consolidation. While I wouldn't recommend such a conservative type of stock for you, I would think that, with some diligence, you could track down smaller companies that stand to benefit from this old world industry's change from coal burning to cleaner, more efficient gas fuel. (For example, who manufactures gas turbines, and who makes the necessary parts for those turbines?) Ditto for biotech, or nanotech—who makes the equipment and systems for their brave new world pursuits? Finding out the answers could provide you with a no- or low-tech way to play these high-tech sectors—without taking on the risks of one company's failure—since all the companies in a given sector need the tools of their trade to produce their wares.

Preferred Stocks

A preferred stock is really more like a bond, performance-wise (yawn!) in that it pays a fixed dividend. These "stocks" are generally more appropriate for income investors—i.e., the blue-haired, denture-driven, Ex-Lax cocktail crowd. Use the tooth index on this one—if you have 100% of your teeth (apart from the hockey accident), then you can avoid this group 100%.

Penny Stocks

Penny stocks, so called because you can often buy them for under $1 per share, are highly speculative. Danger is the name of this investment game. Investing in speculative penny stock entails investing in a company with way above average share price fluctuations, and a higher risk of loss for all or most of your investment compared to most other types of stocks. (Many penny stocks are also the creation of less than scrupulous brokerage firms.) While the lure of these stocks is that with relatively little money you can own a lot of them, this is one case where more is decidedly not better. Often, they are like holding a wheelbarrelful of coal instead of a handful of diamonds. Invest only what you can afford to lose—or better yet, avoid these stocks altogether. If you want to be a high roller, concentrate on a very volatile but often more promising group of stocks known as IPOs.

Initial Public Offerings (IPOs)

IPOs are new issues of new companies' stocks. Such companies issue stock in order to generate capital to expand their business (and/or to buy out company founders and venture capitalists). Bottom line: Be forewarned. One of the reasons why IPOs come so highly recommended is that the investment bankers who back their launch, as well as the brokerages who have come in line, need to sell their inventory of shares in the IPO (just as much as the IPO needs to sell more of whatever it makes in order to sustain itself as a viable company).

Flashy new stocks are also often flashes in the pan. Nevertheless, every stock was, at one time, an IPO. As a result, you needn't avoid IPOs on principle—the way you should avoid penny stocks. Instead, concentrate on the individual promise of the company and its long-range profit potential. It certainly helps if you are familiar with the company's products, or know someone who is. That's a great, grassroots approach to starting your investigation. It can also lead you to become overenthusiastic, since you might feel that the product is so good it can't help but do well. (If that always held true, then Apple Computer would probably be doing better than Microsoft and Intel.)

Foreign Stocks

Many foreign stock markets have outperformed the US stock market in the long term—and many haven't. As the economy goes global, foreign stock investing will likely provide choice investment opportunities. The difficulty will be in selecting the right stocks in the right country at the right time—and how best to invest in them. Since the country and company may be foreign to our language and frames of usual stock-investigation reference, you'll be up against difficulties that you would not normally face when investing in the United States. Nevertheless, taking advantage of stocks in a foreign country such as France, Great Britain, Japan, or Germany can make sense. After all, they have well-established stock markets, and information abounds on these countries and their companies. But when it comes to hot emerging markets such as Hong Kong and Taiwan, you may experience information deprivation. In which case, be fearful.

There are four ways to invest in foreign markets: (1) directly through a foreign stock holding, though that's pretty hard to arrange; (2) directly through American Depository Receipts (ADRs, see below); (3) indirectly through shares in US-based multinational companies (like Procter & Gamble, Bausch & Lomb, and Kellogg's—since 40% of their total sales are derived from foreign markets); and (4) by buying international and global mutual funds (see chapter 14).

What exactly is an ADR? ADRs are receipts for shares in a foreign corporation that are traded in American securities markets such as the New York Stock Exchange. These tend to be larger foreign companies in established markets (blue chips). Examples include British Airways, Honda, and Toyota. (To find out more, go to adr.com.)

Stock Ownership

You can own stocks directly and indirectly. Direct ownership means that you "hold" an actual stock certificate or serial number that designates the number of shares purchased. (Actually, stock certificates are a thing of the past—although you may have inherited a handful or more, which can be the sole proof of your ownership; nowadays, electronic ownership is the rule in the US market.)

Indirect ownership refers to owning shares in a stock mutual fund. The advantages of indirect ownership are examined in the chapter on mutual funds, so for now suffice it to say that mutual funds offer individual investors several advantages over direct ownership. Mutual funds (as you may already know, but will certainly come to know more about in chapter 14) can be composed of a pool of one or more of the following: stocks, bonds, cash, and/or options. For the purpose of this chapter, I'll talk about those mutual funds which are primarily composed of stocks—and, with this in mind, the benefit of indirect ownership of stocks through a stock mutual fund is that, with a small amount of money, you can purchase shares in a well-diversified portfolio of stocks.

Specific Stock Analysis

You'll need to know what to look for in an individual stock that may have piqued your interest. The following questions will help you begin the process of determining the possible profit and risk potential of a given stock. Keep them in mind whenever you are thinking about a particular investment.

- Is the company in a growing industry?
- What are the industry's prospects for future growth?
- Does the company have, or have the potential to get, a significant share of its particular industry's market?
- How successful has the company been in its industry?
- Does the company have a history of profitability that is above average for its industry?
- If the company is relatively new, has it shown that it is likely to be successful in the industry?

There's more to reviewing a particular stock than a general feel for its potential. The following will help you get acquainted with some analytical fundamentals, as well as refresh your mind about those you visited in chapter 8.

- Dividend. A dividend is a cash distribution a company makes to its shareholders. At many companies, dividends can be reinvested in more shares of stock (good), but even if you do so, they count as taxable income. A stock's dividend yield is its annual dividend divided by its share price.
- Earnings per share (EPS). A company's net income divided by the average number of shares outstanding. A company that reports income of $1 million with one million shares outstanding would have an EPS of $1.
- Price-to-earnings ratio (P/E). The price of a stock divided by its actual or estimated earnings. The P/E ratio is used by most investors as one way of determining whether a company's stock is fairly valued. Not surprisingly, companies with little or no earnings tend to have sky-high P/Es—but, as in the case of many newer, smaller companies, this may be acceptable, if earnings seem likely to take off. If a stock sells for $20, and it has $2 earnings per share, it has a P/E of 10.
- Debt-to-equity ratio. An often overlooked source of risk, since a company with sizable debt may be unable to compete—whether in terms of research and development, or in ability to withstand a slowdown—against a rival that's debt-free. Sound like you and your best friend?

You can dig deeper! Look at the company from the bottom up. Doing so will require that you get your hands on its latest annual report—as well as any analyst reports you can find. (Be careful to weigh your own analysis on a par with the "experts." Often, experts are best used to direct your questioning process rather than for answers to adhere to.) Look for the following key markers when analyzing an individual company's annual report:

- How much long-term debt has the company taken on? If it's greater than 40% of capital (or high relative to its competitors) tread lightly. Heavy debt can prove to be a severe competitive handicap in a slow economy, since competitors who are cash-flush can continue to grow their business unhindered by debt payments.

- How much working capital does the company have? The more it has, the better able it should be to stay competitive within its own industry (although that industry itself might still be one to avoid).
- How old is the company's plant and equipment? If it's brand new and paid for, so much the better. If, on the other hand, the factory was built in the Etruscan Age, then updating costly equipment has to be factored in to your estimate of the company's short-term growth capacity.
- Review the following ingredients in the company's annual report in order to spot performance trends, strengths, and weaknesses within the company:

  — Sales—the backbone of any company, comprising three basic elements: volume, product range, and selling prices. Are the company's sales volumes increasing? Are they increasing at an above- or below-average rate compared to its competitors'? Is volume being moved because prices have been slashed (and how does this affect overall profitability)? Are comparable products competitive, and competitively priced? How does the company's price-to-sales ratio (share price divided by per-share sales) compare within the industry?

  — Profits. The sine qua non of business. Is the company making any money on its sales? Do profit margins compare favorably with the rest of the industry? What is the stock's P/E ratio (price divided by trailing—i.e., the past twelve months—twelve-month earnings)? Is it reasonable compared to its competitors and/or its prospects for growth in profits?

  — Cash flow—generally defined as net income, with depreciation and amortization charges added back (since these aren't real cash expenses). Cash flow is the amount of cash the business is generating for management to reinvest, service debt, and pay dividends. It's a useful indicator of a particular company's ability to provide its own capital while maintaining a desirable earnings or dividend record without having to borrow money or sell additional stock.

  — Book value—the stated value of all the company's assets. How many times book value (the price-to-book ratio) is the stock selling for, and how does that compare within the industry? Don't necessarily avoid paying several times book value; many assets may be grossly undervalued (for example, at cost, when they were bought forty years ago, or when they can annually generate more profits than their stated "value").

How to Cut Your Losses

Dissecting a company's profit potential can be a fascinating exercise in and out of itself but it won't guarantee that you will be able to select a winner. Combining all your research, from the broad questions of economic cycles and market competition to the particulars of patents and earnings reports, will at least help you avoid the pitfalls of an impulse investment. As in shopping, where impulse buying rarely gets you what you need or want, in investing you need to be cool, calculating, and clear about what you are buying and why.

Everyone concentrates their energies on how to buy stocks—but there's an equally significant and often overlooked piece to this investing puzzle: knowing when to sell. As with buying, there are no guaranteed ways to always sell when the stock has hit its high or is threatening to become a fallen star. But there are warning signs. For example, if the company whose stock you are investing in cuts its dividend, stops dividends, or does not increase its dividends when others in its category are doing so, then it may be time to sell. Another sign to sell may be when the stock hits a high that is equal to or ahead of even the rosiest projections for it, or when its price gives it an absurdly high P/E ratio. Such peak performance can foretell a precipitous fall. However, it may be only a temporary one—as long as you have tied yourself and your investment dollars to a strong company. If not, you might be better off cutting the cord and hoping for a soft landing in another stock or mutual fund investment.

Although there are no foolproof methods for selling (or buying) stocks, the following suggestions and guidelines should be kept in mind. It's inadvisable to try to time the market by buying a stock today that you think you can make a killing on in a few tomorrows. A good rule of thumb is to avoid investing in a stock with the intention of selling it in the next two or three years. Instead, concentrate on those stocks that potentially provide longer-term rewards.

Every investor gets bitten by the hand they thought would feed them. If one of your golden opportunities turns out to be worth less than a plug nickel, then you've missed the opportunity to sell at a livable loss. Some stocks will catch even savvy investors by surprise and plummet almost overnight. But most solid-seeming stocks don't vanish instantaneously. Instead, their demise tracks out over a long enough period of time that, with the proper diagnosis, the attentive investor will have enough advance warning to get out before suffering truly painful losses.

How can you spot a "rotting" stock in your portfolio's barrel of good ones—before it turns rotten, that is? One way is to see how it performs relative to its benchmark. If, for example, you own a stock whose benchmark is the Russell 2000 (a small-cap stock index), and it has not kept up with this index's average over three or more consecutive quarters, then start asking why. But don't jump to conclusions—selling too soon is often the way investors wind up losing money by missing out on a big gain. Instead, go back to the drawing board that led you to select the company in the first place. Are the fundamentals still as believable now as they were when you first bought the stock? What has changed in the company or industry that could account for the glitch in performance? Is the change temporary or a trend toward worse times ahead?

There's another important aspect to selling a stock that is easy to overlook—especially if you have determined that you want to sell. That aspect is the individual stock's position in your overall portfolio. If the stock plays a particular role—for example, it's your only exposure to an industry that you continue to believe will do well—then by all means hunt for another company within the industry to purchase with the proceeds of the sale of the fallen-from-favor stock.

Finally, always evaluate the selling of a stock in light of your capital gains and the taxes you'll have to pay on them. Often, there are more (and less) beneficial times to transact the sale of a stock—and you could wind up saving (or losing) yourself some money if you take (or fail to take) the tax factor into consideration. (For more on tax strategies, see chapter 25.)

INVESTING STRATEGIES

There's more that you'll need to know in order to become an informed investor. The following approach to stock investing will help you and your investments keep on course—no matter how bumpy the ride.

- Think before you buy. Too many first-time (and some experienced) investors leap before they look. Hot tips, a cover story, a fast-talking broker can all conspire to trick you into buying a stock you don't know much about. Be sure to tie your shoes before walking down the road to a new investment. Request and read the company's annual report and Form 10-K before investing. (You can obtain these documents directly from the company, from your broker, or on the Internet.) Also, stay informed about the economy, markets, industries, and subsectors that could potentially affect the performance of the company and its stock.

- Know why you're buying. Buy stocks that fit your investing plan—and not someone else's idea of what's a good thing. While you want to be convinced there's a "story," or a plausible scenario for an improved earnings outlook, beware of "sure things." Look for companies that have dominant positions in their fields, or are likely to become dominant in the future. Also, examine each stock's performance history to see whether its potential volatility is acceptable to you.

- Scan for promising industries. Target industries that seem most likely to succeed—and don't be fooled into thinking that the industries that are on top today will be there tomorrow. If the industry of a company you're thinking of investing in seems likely to fail or become moribund, give it Das Boot. If, on the other hand, it seems like it's ahead of its time, you may be able to ride the stock to the top. If the industry has long-run promise, it's that much easier to find stocks (and time periods) that will prove profitable.

- Diversify. The key to successful investing. You've heard me say it before: Never put all your eggs in one basket, but beware of over-diversification, too. Overdiversification, especially with smaller amounts of money, can lead to nothing more than a record-keeping, fee-paying headache. It's easier to keep track of a dozen stocks than a hundred; and a dozen stocks, if they're sufficiently different, can provide sufficient diversification.

- Buy low and sell high. If you haven't heard this maxim yet, wait another minute and you will. Every expert will tell you this—and it's as obviously true as it is difficult to achieve. Remember, when the market is hot everyone wants to get in—but that's when prices are high. Try a contrary approach—researching companies you want to invest in and hoping for a temporary dip in their prices—then lock in.

- Keep your eye on the market. As discussed in detail in the previous chapter, keeping tabs on the market's current and expected condition requires little effort and can provide maximum gains. But when it comes to investing in an individual stock your vigilance can really pay off. For example, if your stock falls with the market, but you're convinced its fundamentals are sound, you may want to buy more shares. If, on the other hand, the stock rises to above fair value on the strength of a bull market, you may want to sell.

- Invest for the long term. Buying and holding on to your stock investments is a historically proven smart money move—but it's harder to do than most investors realize. The difficulty comes with market volatility and individual stock price volatility. It's hard to hold on to what you've got when its value is taking a nosedive. Still, if you have reason to believe in the fundamental strength of the future promise of the company, then stick to your guns. Generally, you'll come out ahead—as the market has so far continued to gain over time. Consider a holding period of ten years or longer a time-proven way to earn inflation-beating returns. Concentrate on knowing what to buy since buying well will reduce your need to sell. Also, remember that investing for the long term is in your best interest—so long as you have selected stocks in quality companies with quality management.

READY RESOURCES

There's no shortage of stock investing books on the shelves of your bookstore and library. There are also dozens of stock investing newsletters—some great, some useless. The following list includes both books and newsletters. I recommend requesting newsletter samples and borrowing books from your local public library before making any purchases.

- *Beating the Street,* Peter Lynch
- *One Up on Wall Street,* Peter Lynch
- *How to Buy Stocks,* Louis Engel and Brendan Boyd
- *Fundamentals of Investing,* Lawrence J. Gitman and Michael D. Joehnk
- *Investing in Growth,* Philip B. Capelle

- *Classics: An Investor's Anthology,* Charles D. Ellis, ed.
- *Buying Stocks without a Broker,* second edition, Charles B. Carlson
- *Free Lunch on Wall Street,* Charles B. Carlson
- *Dividends Don't Lie,* Geraldine Weiss
- *Dictionary of Investing,* J. Rosenberg
- *All about Commodities,* R. Wassendorf
- *How the Options Market Works,* J. Walker

CHAPTER 13

Real Estate from Scratch

Whoever said a home was a castle didn't have to scrounge to pay rent for a one-bedroom apartment, let alone make the leap into actual home buying. But, despite the difficulty of saving up a sizable enough down payment, many of us cross the threshold from apartment dwelling to home ownership before we turn thirty-five. True, fewer of us do so today than in the generation before us—and it's not because we're slacking. For the most part, it's because we're lacking (the money) to make the move. So why bother to buy a home? Why not stay put and let the landlord do all the snow shoveling, painting, plastering, and lawn mowing? Well, from the day we were old enough to differentiate between our playpen and the home we shared with our benefactors, we've been told what a great investment a house is—just about any house, but "location, location, location" should ring some repressed bells.

Is a home a good investment? Well, not as good as your parents might want to have you believe. What about those no-money-down gurus who hawk their sun-splashed success on late-night TV? Nope. They've got it wrong, too. This chapter will help you distinguish between the value of buying a home and the potential value of investing in real estate. But don't you confuse the two. They're not the same, and rarely do the twain meet when it comes to buying a home and making a good investment.

BUYING YOUR HOME

A home may not be the good investment it once was, but home ownership is still likely to top the list of the single biggest investment you ever make. (Moreover, if you can't afford to buy a home, you shouldn't consider investing in real estate.) Since this is so, you should anticipate the costs that you will incur when it comes to buying your new home. That's the best way to avoid the money pitfalls that many others have encountered. It's also a great way to avoid having to sell some of your longer-term investments to meet a short-term need.

Coming up with a down payment, which typically runs from 5% to 20% of the cost of the home, is a first hurdle many would-be home buyers fail to get over. For example, a $150,000 house will likely require a down payment of anywhere from $7,500 to $30,000. In addition, you can count on paying from 1% to 3% of the mortgage amount in closing costs (including "points," the charge for preparing the mortgage).

Of course, you'll also need to estimate how much home you can afford to buy. After all, if you can't afford the mortgage payments on a $150,000 home, there's no need to build up a savings amount of $30,000 before you start looking. That's why, before you start looking, you should come to terms with how much house your income can legitimately support.

There are several ways to estimate how much mortgage you're likely to qualify for. These days, most banks and mortgage lenders (and personal finance software) will be happy to do this for you. Typically, your monthly mortgage payment shouldn't exceed 28% of your net (posttax) monthly income or 32% of your gross (pretax) monthly income. Including the mortgage payment, lenders look at your total monthly debt obligations—from credit cards to car and student loans. The line in the lending sand: your total monthly obligations shouldn't exceed 36% of your gross monthly income. Obviously, the less debt you owe, the larger the mortgage and/or the better the rate you'll be able to qualify for.

You can estimate what your monthly mortgage payment will be by using the following table. For example, if you're thinking of qualifying for a $150,000 thirty-year mortgage at 6.5%, multiply 8.71 by 150— your monthly principal and interest payment will be approximately $1,306.

Monthly Payment per $1,000 of Loan

Interest Rate	15 Years	30 Years
4.0%	$7.40	$4.77
4.5%	$7.65	$5.07
5.0%	$7.91	$5.37
5.5%	$8.17	$5.68
6.0%	$8.44	$6.00
6.5%	$8.71	$6.32
7.0%	$8.99	$6.65
7.5%	$9.27	$6.99
8.0%	$9.56	$7.34
8.5%	$9.85	$7.69
9.0%	$10.14	$8.05

Ensuring that your home ownership plans are part of your investment plan is the only way to go. Not only will buying a home be the biggest deal you're likely to make in this lifetime, but, once purchased, you'll need to view the potential benefits of refinancing your existing mortgage if rates dip 1% or more below the rate of your mortgage. Your home mortgage is very much like a fixed-income (bond) investment, in that it can and should be actively managed from the standpoint of interest-rate sensitivity. As you can see from the chart above, even a 1% change in your mortgage can make a significant savings to your pocketbook.

Investing in Real Estate

Traditionally, real estate has been one of the more common foundations on which people have built wealth. But, as many veteran homeowners will tell you, it is also possible to lose a great deal of money in the real estate market. Like all good investments, real estate opens the door to risks as well as potential rewards. If you own your own home, you may be troubled by deteriorating real estate markets or delighted by stable or rising prices—and if you own your home for long enough (ten or more years) chances are you'll run the gamut of those emotions, since real estate values tend to move in long-term cycles based on shifts in demographics and unemployment.

Location is one way to hedge your bets. A solid locale, one with a well-diversified mix of ages, incomes (tending toward the higher end), in a stable work environment with good schools is hard to beat—and harder to find. But, if you're flexible, and are able to move beyond either coast (inland, and/or to the South) you might be able to find a way to turn your home into a viable investment. If you are a potential real estate investor—tempted by the "bargains" flooding the market in some locales—educate yourself thoroughly before buying. There's one golden rule of real estate investing (which I just made up): If you can't afford to buy your own home or condo, forget about investing in one!

Many investors think that they know enough to invest in a piece of property simply because they know the area. And while that's a great start, it will hardly drive you toward the most successful real estate investments (in your area, or beyond it). When it comes to investing in real estate—either in the form of your own home or in potentially income-producing properties, there is one critical drawback compared to stocks and bonds (and mutual funds). That drawback is that you are putting money into an illiquid investment, namely, one you can't simply sell overnight if you need the money or want to get out. In fact, unlike, say, a mutual fund, where you can sell if you don't like the new fund manager or the fund's increased concentration in a particular industry, if you buy or invest in real estate, you can be hamstrung by bad news—all the way to ground zero if it so happens that the building burns to the ground and you let your insurance lapse, or the ground turns out to be a hazardous waste dump site, or the local factory or military base shuts down, sending property prices plummeting. In such worst-case scenarios you'll find it hard to recoup your down payment—and you still owe the bank the money you borrowed.

Fortunately, most of us won't run into worst-case scenarios. Instead, when it comes to our homes, we're more likely to see the value inch along with the rate of inflation. Not a great investment, but at least you'll build a part of your retirement savings successfully so long as the home's value does at least keep pace with inflation.

Real estate investors may also find more bargains on the lot than in previous years. In the 1970s, as inflation took off, housing prices jumped, and many homeowners with low fixed-rate 1960s mortgages saw windfalls. But the late 1980s and early 1990s saw many property values plummet back to earth from these lofty levels. Markets have come back, but the hardest hit segments of the real estate investment market, like condominiums, might still provide some hidden gems that can actually produce income for the smart investor.

Let's move on to each real estate category, and don't forget that, when it comes to real estate investing, let caveat emptor be your guide. Or better yet, come to terms with the following ways to evaluate a potential real estate investment first, then consider if there are any viable options in your neck of the woods. But before you open the door to potential real estate investment opportunities, be sure to slam the door closed on the following:

- Most real estate limited partnerships (i.e., those not publicly traded)
- Time-shares
- No-money-down real estate seminars
- Unimproved land
- Uninspected property
- Foreign property

Younger investors (who don't have enough money to buy a whole apartment building) invest in residential rental property in order to produce more income for themselves. A typical investment might be purchasing a single condo or a two-family house. Both can potentially provide a steady secondary source of income while at the same time increasing in value. The location and condition of such properties will affect the price of them—as well as your ability to obtain a viable rent from them. But there are several other factors you need to consider before making such a significant investment, including the zoning laws and renter population. Chances are, buying near a large university will net you a steady flow of willing renters, but the wide pool of potential renters may prove to be a shallow one in terms of their ability to pay the rent you need (for the investment to succeed). Also, with students comes the increased potential for hassles and transience.

Be sure you get to know the place before you invest in it. For example:

1. Is the property in a location with a solid history of appreciating values?

    [ ] yes   [ ] no

2. Have you researched the socioeconomic factors (employment, roads, taxes, zoning laws, demographics, transience) that can affect the property's value as well as the property's ability to generate a consistent cash flow?

  [ ] yes   [ ] no

3. Is the property conveniently located for prospective renters?

  [ ] Public transportation
  [ ] Grocery store
  [ ] Retail shopping
  [ ] Recreation
  [ ] Schools

4. When was the last time the roof was done (choose the closest)?

  [ ] Fifteen or more years
  [ ] Seven to twelve years
  [ ] Less than five years

5. Have you received the following?

  [ ] Complete rental history
  [ ] Complete history of utility costs
  [ ] Complete history of water billing
  [ ] Complete history of maintenance
  [ ] Complete history of tenant complaints
      and legal actions
  [ ] Complete history of the electrical or heating systems
  [ ] Complete history of reported crime
  [ ] Complete history of property damage and repair costs

Remember that the real estate agent is representing the seller—not you. As a result, you'll need to be reasonably assured that the agent isn't "bumping to market." Bumping to market is basically replacing actual rent with what it "ought to be" according to the agent's sense of the overall market level. Don't even think about it.

The following method for evaluating a property's potential merits (or lack thereof) will help you see the investment of a lifetime through the more realistic lens of financial viability. The method is called the "rent multiplier" and it enables you to evaluate a property by comparing the total price you'd have to pay for it with its current gross annual rent (not just last year's but over its rental history). Note that it's also important to see if the property's rental history shares common ground with apartments in the same location (same size and condition), as well as any significant demographic or economic changes in the area. Each, or all, could affect the ability of the history to repeat itself.

The main problem with investing in real estate for income is that it is difficult to locate properties that are priced low enough that the rental income is sufficient to cover the cost of your investment. Of course, there's no guarantee that a property that passes the rent multiplier test will deliver the goods, either. In investing, uncertainty is the constant. The rent multiplier is the selling price of the property divided by its gross annual rent. The traditional rule of thumb for this multiplier is that any property selling for more than seven or eight times its gross annual rental will be unlikely to deliver sufficient rental income to cover your costs (mortgage and maintenance expenses), let alone make you a profit.

Here's how it works: Say a two-family house selling for $210,000 generates $18,000 in annual rent. Dividing 210,000 by 18,000 gives you a rent multiplier of 11.66.

In other words, the property is selling for 11.66 times its annual rental income. This is probably not going to be a good investment. Of course, you can ensure a positive cash flow by sinking a large down payment into the property—but you'll only be scuttling yourself. First, you're already having to compensate for the property's lack of inherent value. Second, and perhaps more important, you're tying up your cash in a negative investment—as opposed to investing it in a positive one, like a stock mutual fund.

There are tax benefits to direct ownership that must be considered, such as maintenance costs, depreciation, real estate taxes, and mortgage interest allocable to rental use, which can all be claimed as deductions and subtracted from rental income. This can be a significant sum, but it still may not make the property a better-than-average investment.

Despite the fact that there are better investments out there, many younger investors are drawn to real estate as a potential source of secondary income. Some achieve this goal truly and well. In fact, I have a friend who spent ten years building a small kingdom of multifamily rental properties, which he in turn used to help finance his graduate school costs (for himself and his family of three). His costs were substantial (he went to Harvard business school), but unlike many of his fellow students, he didn't have to overburden himself with loans. But, for every successful real estate investment story, there is probably one about losing some, most, or all of the initial investment—or more. If you think the risk is worth taking, then by all means familiarize yourself with the following real estate investment options that are out there waiting for you.

1. Single home, condominium, cooperative, or apartment. Investing in a single-family home rarely works to your advantage. In fact, I'd avoid it since it's among the most costly and least flexible forms of real estate investment. On the other hand, investing in a condo, co-op, or single apartment could pay off—especially if you buy during a low. Generally cheaper than equivalent single-family homes, condos provide you with the benefits of direct ownership. However, there is a lack of overall control with this type of investment, which should give you some cause for concern. For example, despite the fact that each unit is individually financed, if one owner defaults on his or her condo, the other owners may have to assume the defaulting owner's share of operating expenses.

As with a house, when it comes to owning a condo there are more expenses involved than the mortgage. There are condo fees, and there are meetings to attend. The condo association (typically made up of the owners) oversees common areas like entranceways, yards, and parking lots, which are typically owned by the condo owners. They, or the majority of the owners, not just you, will decide what money to spend on maintenance and improvements. There are also potential problems when it comes to wanting to change the outward look of your condominium.

Despite the drawbacks, condos can make solid sense for rental purposes. To test a potential condo's worth, make sure the renters are there and that the rental income is sufficient to support your ownership costs by employing the rent multiplier method shown above (or a more detailed analysis of all expenses).

2. Multifamily. Two-, three-, and more family homes that are often owner occupied can provide you with positive cash flow, increased tax advantages, and a roof over your own head. You might even be able to live "rent free," although you'll have to ensure that the mortgage payments are made in full. Multifamily dwellings require a greater initial investment (it's a bigger building), but the cost per unit can be lower than with a single condo, and your ability to qualify for a mortgage is based on rental income as well as your ability to pay. Down payments can be a problem, but lenders have become more flexible in

recent times. All the other potential pitfalls are multiplied by two, three, or more times (from tenants to the costs of insurance)—but so are the potential benefits. One generic drawback might be location, since multifamilies abound in lower-income and more transient neighborhoods. But this can work in your favor since there are typically a greater number of renters and lower property values in such neighborhoods.

3. Second home. The demand for second homes (particularly those near the water) is likely to increase as the boomers age and look for places to retire to. One of the more interesting ways to invest in this phenomenon is to consider buying a second home that can serve as an investment rental property in season, be a place to get away to during the off-season, and has long-term potential for increased resale value. Note that if a vacation home is rented for fewer than fifteen days a year, the resulting income need not be reported to the IRS. If, however, the residence is used solely as a rental property, all income must be reported.

Don't invest in a second home for the short term. Most likely, the rental income you'll receive will be insufficient to cover your total expenses. Instead, consider it as a long-term investment—so long as the location and demographics are likely to materialize buyers down the road.

4. Land. You know those ads that promise forty acres of hunting, fishing, fields, and forest? Well, these deals typically don't tell about the lack of water, electricity, sewage, and roads. Land doesn't generate any income; your cash that could be invested elsewhere is staked to it; financing is difficult to arrange for unimproved land and likely to be costly once arranged; and the current value is likely to remain the same (i.e., a bad investment) unless there's a potential for development (in which case there would likely have been a long line of developers ahead of you). Zoning and environmental issues can wipe you out overnight. Avoid the forty acres, or chances are you'll wind up looking like a mule's relative.

5. Commercial property. Chances are commercial properties—office buildings, malls, industrial plants—are beyond your direct financial reach, but you could invest in them via either a real estate limited partnership, real estate investment trust (REIT), or REIT mutual fund (see below).

REAL ESTATE INVESTING STRATEGIES

1. Sole ownership. Becoming a landlord isn't all it's cracked up to be, but when it comes to the potential for the best returns—and the most risks—owning an investment property by yourself is the way to go. If this is the way you want to go, make sure you are ready for the monetary, legal, and psychological demands that even a single investment condo can rain down upon you.

2. Real estate limited partnerships. Real estate limited partnerships pool money from a group of investors in order to purchase larger properties like a mall or apartment building. There are some advantages to real estate limited partnerships, from purchasing (you get a prospectus and send a check to the general partner), to smaller initial investments, to no management responsibility. It's the general partner's responsibility to find tenants, fix the sink, unplug the toilet, get and bank the rent, file the tax reports, and all other management duties. Moreover, unlike owning a property outright, your legal liability is limited to the total amount you have invested in the partnership, so your other assets are not at risk.

You can estimate the worth of a potential limited partnership investment by doing the numbers in advance of your actual investment. To do so, use a method called a capitalization rate, or "cap rate." To determine the cap rate of a potential investment property, you can use the following formula:

Capitalization rate = Net operating income ÷ Total amount invested

For example, a limited partnership investment in a mall requires a total investment of $1,500,000 and has an estimated net operating income of $125,000. The cap rate is 125,000 ÷ 1,500,000—or 8.3%. A cap rate of 8% or greater is considered desirable. So is this investment worth it?

Don't get too excited. There are several disadvantages—beyond a forecasted soft commercial real estate market for years to come—including the fact that you are basically giving up control of your investment to the general partner. For this reason alone, investing in real estate limited partnerships makes less sense than direct ownership, but there are other reasons why this particular way of investing in real estate makes less sense for those just starting out, including your inability to generate the kind of cash flow you could generate from direct ownership. Why? The general partner takes a cut for commissions paid to set up the partnership, to operate the property, and, upon liquidation of the partnership, to sell the property.

Remember that the people who sell you these partnerships are the ones who stand to make the most money from the deal—not you.

3. Real estate investment trusts (REIT) and REIT mutual funds. REITs are companies that invest in a pool of real estate or mortgages, and their shares trade on major stock exchanges like the New York Stock Exchange. Buying shares in an REIT means you can avoid the pitfalls of illiquidity and other drawbacks that dog direct real estate investments and limited partnerships and, similar to a mutual fund, it lets you participate in a diversified portfolio of real estate (or mortgages) you couldn't afford to get into by yourself. Moreover, like investing in a mutual fund, REITs offer the prospect of professional management. Of course, there are drawbacks—like the unavoidable fact that REITs suffer from bad real estate markets just like the other types of real estate investments available to you. If only you could buy a mutual fund that invests in REITs, maybe you'd be able to enjoy the benefits of an even more diversified portfolio of real estate investments, which just might stand a better chance in a down market— and still capitalize on any boom. You're in luck. (See the next chapter.)

CHAPTER 14

Mutual Funds from Scratch

Mutual funds are by far the most popular form of investing today. And that's not too surprising, given their many benefits and low cost, especially relative to investing directly in stocks and bonds. In fact, they're the single best avenue for your investing plans—at least in the beginning. But in addition to the many positive features that funds offer most investors, there are some pitfalls you'll need to avoid—not the least of which is the common mistake of thinking that mutual funds are guaranteed to deliver positive results. (They're not.)

Mutual funds remain a decidedly great way for you to gain entree to the market via a diversified portfolio of stocks that you couldn't hope to own by yourself right off the bat. And for those of you who have been (or have just begun) investing in funds, take note: there are many ways you can enhance your control over your overall mutual fund investment portfolio. This chapter will show you how. In fact, this chapter will help you see:

- The many distinct trees in the overall fund forest
- The clear-cut differences between fund types
- The benefits of investing in mutual funds
- The drawbacks of investing in mutual funds
- Which funds suit you and your objectives best
- What to look for in a prospectus

- Why knowing who is managing a fund is a key factor in fund
  selection
- What the main fund investment styles are

What exactly is a mutual fund? A mutual fund is a professionally
managed, diversified portfolio of stocks, bonds, money market instruments, or other securities. Each fund is composed of many investors'
money, pooled by the fund manager or managers to purchase these
securities. "Pooling" the money gives you the potential benefits of a
larger and more diversified portfolio than your money alone could
purchase.

However, you'll still need to know what is in the pool, since otherwise it's easy to get in over your head without realizing that that's what
you've done. Mutual funds don't magically protect you from the market's eddies. The value of your fund shares still depends on the value
of the stocks and/or bonds owned by the fund. And the value of the
stocks and/or bonds the fund holds still depends on the market risks
they are subject to (as discussed in the previous chapters).

It used to be that mutual funds represented an easy way for investors, large and small, to avoid the complication of picking a large
portfolio of stocks and/or bonds. Even one decade ago there were under 500 mutual funds and well over 3,000 stocks trading on the NYSE.
Today, there are still over 3,000 stocks trading on the NYSE. However,
you must now choose the best mutual funds from a selection of over
7,000 mutual funds—1,000 new funds in 1995 alone. This chapter
will help you do just that—as well as introduce you to a new, user-
friendly, optimal way to buy mutual funds. But first, let's take a look at
why funds should play such a significant role in your portfolio.

Funds, like the stocks they hold, haven't exactly delivered a smooth
ride—but it's clearly been a very rewarding ride for those who've sat
in their seats for the entire journey. And while you'll hear me say this
time and again, it's worth reiterating now: investing for the long term
is the best way to ensure that, down the road, you will have created a
secure financial environment for your retirement.

MUTUAL FUND ADVANTAGES

Selecting the best mutual funds to invest in has become quantitatively and qualitatively more difficult. And, while we'll sort this out together below, it's important to note that the advantages of investing in mutual funds remain the same today as when they were first introduced back in the early 1940s. For example:

- Performance has been a principal strong point. Beating inflation as well as a comparable market index is one objective every investor must come to terms with.

  The average stock mutual fund has delivered a solid inflation beating return. But, and this may come as a surprise to you, the average stock fund hasn't outperformed the S&P 500 index. Some significant down years in the early 2000s set funds back a bit—but that's not the real story. The real story is that the majority of fund managers fail to beat the S&P 500—although they don't fail to take their seven-figure paychecks! Even your local weather forecaster has better averages (and a much lower paycheck). That's why it's crucial for you to learn how to select the best funds based on the managers that run them. And, you're in luck—this chapter will help you to do just that.

- You can invest in a fund even if you only have a small amount of money—some funds have no or low minimums (i.e., under $1,000) while others, it's true, have minimums that range from $1,000 to $1 million. Note that the minimum amount for opening a tax-advantaged account (like an IRA or Keogh) is typically $500 or lower. The majority of funds offer a low-cost way (i.e., around $2,500 for taxable accounts and $500 for tax-advantaged accounts like your IRA) to start investing today.

- Diversification is the mutual fund's principal benefit. Mutual funds are a low-cost way to diversify a small amount of money in a broad range of stocks, bonds, or other securities, in various industries, markets, and/or countries. The advantage of diversifying is twofold. First, it helps reduce the overall risk of your investments. Second, it can enhance your total return.

- Convenience is another plus. Mutual funds make it easy to invest regularly, through automatic investing, dollar-cost averaging, and their presence in your 401(k) plans. Taken together with twenty-four-hour-a-day toll-free numbers, Internet websites, and the advent of mutual fund networks, in the past few years convenience has been further enhanced (see pages 278–79 for more on mutual fund networks).

- Researching your own funds is within your grasp. Mutual funds are relatively easy to research (compared with other types of investments). Current information abounds—so much so that it may take you a while to locate the funds you own in the business section of your paper. You can re-create your portfolio on the Internet and get a nightly update as to where you stand. (Nightly, since most mutual funds' values are determined at the close of market each day.) And, yes, you can also order an electronically personalized version of the *Wall Street Journal*—to be delivered to your e-mail address—which can ferret out your funds from the reams of otherwise overwhelming data.

- Information is as close as your phone, modem, and library. Performance records, fund manager interviews, commonsense and detailed analyses of potential risks and returns (as well as past strengths and weaknesses, which might affect your funds in the future), and the year's top performers and dogs—all are daily, weekly, and monthly topics for the dizzying number of sources available to you. In fact, as one quick glance at chapter 22 shows, the Internet provides some of the best information available.

- Professional management. Mutual funds are managed by experienced investment professionals whose business it is to perform well for their shareholders; failing could be harmful to their current job and career path, not to mention your hard-earned money. But keeping track of fund managers has become about as difficult as tracking professional baseball players. If they perform well, they themselves become a hot commodity. That's why it's important to know who is managing your fund (and what his or her past fund records have been)—and who was managing your fund prior to the current manager. Why? The fund's performance record might be attributable to someone else—which, depending on that record, could bode ill or well for you. One more ingredient in the manager's mix is his or her credentials. While performance, like action, tends to speak louder than words, some managers who are new to the scene may share some professional traits in common with veterans—namely professional designations like Chartered

Financial Analyst (CFA), which is the most highly regarded certification in mutual fund town. (Chapter 19 has the lowdown on this and other professional designations—as well as a review of the range of financial advisers available to you.)

- Wide range of investment choices. As you will see in the section below, there are dozens of types of mutual funds to choose from. And while this range of choices makes it easier for you to select funds that match your objectives, it can also make it harder to determine these objectives in the first place. Fortunately, if you have access to a personal computer, there are a bevy of automated resources at your beck and call. (You can create a mutual fund screen to quickly sort through the abundance in order to locate the best funds for your objective and your particular portfolio.)

- Liquidity. You can place orders to buy and sell mutual fund shares over the phone twenty-four hours a day. (The actual trades are made once a day.) This investment is, for the most part, as liquid as water, which is a good thing if you want to get in or out of the market. However, there are instances where selling your funds (or buying them) can prove to be a difficult proposition—and one in which you can lose big money—by untimely delays. The section below on buying and selling your funds will help you avoid such pitfalls—or, in the worst case, be forewarned about them.

MUTUAL FUND DISADVANTAGES

What? There are disadvantages to investing in mutual funds? Oh, come on. What are you, some holdover commie looking to destroy the very fabric of our God-given country? Sorry. But there is potentially bad news on mutual funds:

- Fluctuating value. Okay, so this isn't really a disadvantage—it's just the nature of the game. But many investors mistakenly think that mutual funds are a safe house for their money. The reality is that some funds are built of brick and mortar—and others are made of straw soaked in gasoline. And while we'll talk about ways to discriminate between marketing huff and puff and down-to-earth facts for most types of funds, you'll need to keep in mind that mutual funds, like the securities they invest in, have risks. A fund's value can fluctuate with changing market and/or economic conditions, the same risk as if you buy individual stocks and bonds.

- Fund fees. If you buy $1 million worth of shares in a fund, you might be able to wrangle a free lunch out of the company—otherwise, get used to the fact that you'll pay some amount for investing in most funds. But just because you have to pay something, it doesn't mean you should pay the highest amount possible. There are no-load funds (which charge no up-front sales commission, but may include one on the back end if you sell shares before a specified date), low-load funds, and load funds (which can charge a sales commission of up to 8.5% of the money you invest). These are not the only fees you need to watch out for, and both these and others are outlined on pages 211–13.

FUND PERFORMANCE

Performance is attractive (but can be deceptive). When it comes to determining whether one fund's performance is better or worse than others, this chapter will help. There are two performance terms you need to know inside and out: net asset value and total return.

- Net asset value (NAV). A fund's net asset value is determined by adding all the fund's holdings (its assets in securities and cash) and dividing by the number of shares outstanding. For a no-load fund, the NAV is the share price you see listed in the paper—and the price per share you would pay (to buy) or receive (if sold).
- Total return. Total return tells you how well your investment is doing. It measures the fund's total investment performance by adding the fund's yield (dividend or interest distributions) and capital gains distributions to any undistributed capital appreciation (change in NAV).

TYPES OF MUTUAL FUNDS

Mutual funds come in two distinct flavors: open- and closed-end. Open-end funds are by far the more popular. They're the funds you find in the mutual fund section of the newspaper, and they number in the thousands. Closed-end funds are listed in the stock pages of your paper (and trade like a stock, while acting like a bond), and they number under two hundred.

There are many types of open-end funds to invest in, but the funds themselves invest in one or more of the three core investment categories: stocks, bonds, and money markets. Of course, each core category itself is made up of dozens of investment vehicles.

1. Stock funds. A stock fund, also referred to as an equity fund, invests in individual stocks of large and/or medium and/or small companies, here and/or abroad. A stock fund is characterized by the kind of companies it invests in, and by the fund's specific objective. You can use stock funds to jump-start your investment plan.

2. Bond funds. A bond fund invests in bonds of companies or governments as varied as those the stock funds invest in. Bond funds tend to be more conservative when it comes to risk and growth. Invest in bond funds down the road—when you reach middle age. And then, invest only a small portion (no more than 20%) of your money in bonds. You'll gradually increase this percentage as time goes on, but for now, you're young and stand to benefit most by investing in good stock funds.

3. Money market funds. Money market funds are the investment world's equivalent to a bank's money market deposit account or savings account. A dollar in is typically worth at least a dollar out. Money market funds may not really make you money (after taxes and inflation), but are a good place to store your short-term cash because they offer liquidity (easy access to your cash) and stability of principal (least risky).

4. Real Estate Investment Trust (REIT) funds. REIT funds invest in REITs—which are corporations that invest in real estate or mortgages—and they trade on the NYSE. REIT funds aren't numerous, and are more suitable for more conservative investors as a source of income.

5. Closed-end funds. Unlike open-end funds, closed-end funds issue a fixed number of shares, and trade just like a stock on the New York Stock Exchange (NYSE), American Stock Exchange (AMEX), or the NASDAQ. Since they're traded like stock, you don't go through a mutual fund company to purchase or redeem shares in closed-end funds. Instead, you purchase them through your broker—and pay him or her a commission.

All of the above categories are detailed in the pages ahead.

·

Fund Managers

Consistency is the key to our short- and long-term success.

Among diversified funds, fund management is the most important determinant of fund performance—and the single most important factor in picking a fund for your portfolio. But with the narrowly drawn sector funds, the managers' performance record is relatively less important than the funds' investment objective. You wouldn't want to invest in or avoid a sector fund based primarily on its fund manager when management factors are swamped by other issues.

Looking overseas, although the choice of a single-country fund should generally depend more on the country than on the manager, choices among similar regional funds and among the diversified international funds should rest primarily on the fund manager. (The most important difference is not to be found in the funds' prospectuses or objectives, but in the funds' managers.)

The Good News

In a world where, statistically, half of us have to be below average, some managers continue to produce above-average numbers. Those who consistently beat their benchmarks, and/or the market as defined by the S&P 500, are worth finding. In a batting-average business, where numbers are key to our portfolios' lineup, some managers do deliver superior active management daily, weekly, monthly, and year in and year out.

The Bad News

Good managers are not easy to find. And the flip side is that the vast majority of managers underperform.

Become Your Own Fund Watchdog

Without regulations requiring fund firms to provide the portable history of the total career returns of their fund managers, and with Morningstar complying with the fund firms' desires by promoting a rating system that is based on a fund's performance—not its managers'—you need to ask some hard questions before you invest in any fund. TRSreports.com provides this crucial information—but it ain't free. In fact, most sources of fund investing information focus solely on a fund's past performance relative to "similar" funds, or one market index (typically the S&P 500 index of large-cap domestic stocks) to deliver a vague sense of its strengths or weaknesses. Others simply exhort you to "buy the manager, not the fund," but without giving you the data to do so. Both of these approaches are fundamentally flawed, but they're easy to do, taking much less time, thought, and due diligence.

First, here's what I know: It's rare that a solid stock picker suddenly loses his or her talent and touch—just as it's rare for a poor stock picker to suddenly bat above average. Consider Will Danoff at Fidelity Contrafund, my top choice for a core, diversified, large-cap fund. His numbers tell the tale that he's a Buy in a bull or a bear market. Why? Less risk is more fulfilling. Take a look at his career chart.

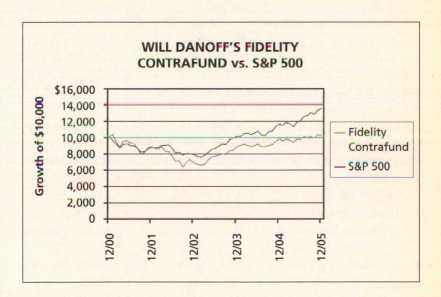

The Best Managers

The best investment you can make is in a manager who has beaten his or her benchmark with relative consistency (especially without making big "macro" bets outside the benchmark) and whose funds have not shown significantly more volatility than the benchmarks. A steady hand at the helm, even if the market and the fund are skyrocketing, is essential to delivering sustainable, long-term risk-adjusted returns. It will also provide a greater degree of certainty in terms of knowing how successful the manager you're investing in is likely to be when the going gets tough.

A manager's record relative to closely correlated benchmarks is a more useful performance measure than simple returns, or even returns relative to "the market" (usually the S&P 500 index), or returns relative to other mutual funds within, for example, a Lipper grouping. (The Lipper groupings of mutual funds by investment categories are often too broad, especially in the case of Fidelity Select funds, many of which have no real direct competitors, and may be grouped with a large hodgepodge of "unaligned" specialty funds.) If you compare manager records to unmanaged indices, it's also a much tougher standard than Morningstar's fund rating system or Lipper's, since indices do not have trading or management expenses.

Of course, one way a manager can beat (or lag) his or her particular benchmark is to make a bet outside of that index. If such bets pay off (or fail) then the manager deserves credit (or blame) for the resulting performance. Similarly, if a manager's individual stock picks beat (or lag) the benchmark average, he or she also deserves the credit (or blame) for that. But you don't want the manager to get credit for showing a "good" performance if he's merely tracking his benchmark or, more important in a bear market, to be blamed for a "bad" performance if it's really his benchmark that has been losing ground.

It's important to grasp whether, how much, and how consistently your fund managers have beaten the most relevant market indices—and with how much risk. If you're considering a fund that's had the same manager for five or ten years, it's usually a relatively simple matter of gauging the fund's (and thus the manager's) performance against competing funds with similar holdings and risk. What about newer managers who may be totally unfamiliar to you—or new funds with a manager who has a record you should know about? The right questions—but the answers are not as simple as last year's return.

If you include the results of each manager's long- and shorter-term performances, including a long-term "risk-adjusted" relative return number, you'll get closer to the information you need. Risk-adjusted return is a figure that permits comparisons between the total return of funds (and/or investment models or indexes) of varying levels of risk, by factoring out differences in volatility. A fund's risk-adjusted return is the return one would obtain with a portfolio holding the fund and enough cash reserves or similar zero-volatility investment (or, for low-risk funds, enough margin) to maintain the risk level of the S&P 500. For a fund with a relative volatility of 1.25, a portfolio would be constructed of 80% of that fund and 20% of a cash position, giving the portfolio a volatility of 1.00. The returns for this portfolio are that fund's risk-adjusted return. For funds compared to an index other than the S&P 500, risk-adjusted return is also calculated for that index. (The risk-adjusted return for the S&P 500 is the same as its actual return, since its relative volatility is by definition exactly 1.00.)

A manager's risk-adjusted career relative return is his return after factoring out both the investment parameters of the fund (e.g., by comparing Fidelity Select Paper & Forest to a paper and a forest index) and the level of risk the manager has taken on relative to that index. Thus, a "neutral" manager would earn a rating of about 0.0%. Any positive number would mean very successful active management, while a negative number would mean relatively unsuccessful active management. That said, industrywide, most managers would earn significantly negative numbers due to fund expenses (often over 1%), brokerage commissions, and bid/ask spreads.

STOCK FUNDS

Stock funds are the most appropriate place for you to invest your money and for you to concentrate your investing dollars. As you get older, you'll want to shift more money to bond and money market funds because bonds typically show less short-term volatility than stocks. However, in your youth it's best to focus on investments that present the opportunity for substantial growth. Stock funds are your answer. They should be the choice of the new generation—that's you.

- **Aggressive growth funds** invest in stocks of new companies and industries and/or more speculative stocks in an attempt to achieve very high returns. Objective: maximizing capital gains.
- **Growth funds** invest in somewhat more established companies whose earnings are expected to steadily increase. Objective: achieving a rate of growth that beats inflation without taking the

risks necessary to achieve occasional spectacular success. Risk factor: high.

— Large-cap stock funds invest in name-brand multinational companies like Coca-Cola, McDonald's, Intel, and Pfizer.

— Mid-cap stock funds typically invest in companies you know— like AutoZone and Outback Steakhouse. They're companies with real products, real market share, real management—and possibly even real earnings—but whose market capitalization falls between $1 billion and $5 billion.

— Small-cap stock funds invest in smaller companies (under $1 billion market cap) whose earnings are expected to steadily increase—companies like Corrections Corporation of America (which runs hoosegows) and Steel Dynamics (a mining company). Volatility is the byword.

- **Growth and income (G&I) funds** tend to invest in more-established companies whose stock tends to pay significant dividend income. They may also hold some assets in bonds. These funds vary in aggressiveness, but tend to have less growth potential than the previous groups. Objective: Significant price increases combined with current income.

  G&I funds will no doubt come to serve a central, centering force in your overall investment portfolio. However, for now, these funds generally present a too-timid approach to the markets, investing in overly conservative securities, and should be used as a small, stabilizing percentage of your overall portfolio. For example, you could place 10% to15% in an S&P 500 index fund. Often classified as growth and income funds, these funds try to match the S&P 500 index which, over time, has performed better than the average stock fund. An index fund could be the first and best G&I fund you ever own, but keep it under 15% for now—or better yet, give yourself a G&I fund down the road—for your 40th birthday, perhaps.

- **Income funds** generally invest about half their portfolio in dividend-paying stocks and the rest in convertible securities and bonds. Objective: Current income is the primary objective, and long-term price increase is a secondary one. (Not generally suitable for younger, more aggressive investors.)

- **Balanced funds** invest in common stock, preferred stock, and bonds. Objective: Current income, growth, and lower-than-pure-stock-investing risk. (Not generally suitable for younger, more aggressive investors.)

BOND FUNDS

Bond funds have limited potential for long-term gains and are generally more suited to retirees than to investors who haven't yet moved to a golf community. My suggestion: avoid bond funds altogether for the time being. Unless you're within five years of funding a child's college tuition or within ten years of retiring, stick to stock funds. Nevertheless, as an informed investor you ought to know all your options—bond funds included.

Bonds funds are often mistakenly thought of as safe, sure-thing income-producing investments. Except for funds that invest solely in shorter-term government bonds, this simply isn't so. Bond funds have a significant degree of risk, particularly from rising interest rates reducing the value of the instruments they invest in.

Only by examining both interest rate and credit risk in relation to how they affect a fund's performance in different market environments can you be assured that the bond fund you've selected matches your overall investment objective.

A fund's duration reflects its sensitivity to interest rates—its "interest rate risk." This is an important factor to consider, given that different bond funds hold bonds of widely varying durations. For example, if interest rates were to rise by 1%, a fund with a duration of ten years will (all other things being equal) fall 10%, while a fund with a duration of six months would fall only 0.5%. (When rates decline, bond prices rise, and a fund with a ten-year duration would appreciate 10% in response to a 1% decline in rates.)

A reliable way to recognize the speculative and/or conservative nature of the bonds in a given fund's portfolio is to note the letter ratings from Moody's and Standard & Poor's as well as the economic health of the companies.

- **Short-term bond funds** invest in a mix of government and corporate bonds with maturities of one to five years. Objective: income with limited exposure to interest rate risk.

- **Intermediate-term bond funds** invest in a mix of government and corporate bonds with maturities of five to ten years. Objective: higher immediate income.
- **Long-term bond funds** invest in a mix of government and corporate bonds with maturities of fifteen to thirty years. Objective: steady source of income.
- **High-yield bond funds (a.k.a. "junk" bond funds)** invest in below-investment-grade-quality bonds that offer potentially high profits but at higher risk. Needless to say, these can be volatile. Objective: higher-than-average yield.
- **Municipal bond funds (better known as "munis")** invest in bonds of state and local governments. Objective: tax-free income. Note: Muni bond prices are hard to find. Muni bond fund prices are not.
- **Single-state funds** invest in bonds only from one state. Since interest earned from these funds is free of state (and often local) as well as federal income taxes, single-state funds often provide the highest tax-equivalent yields (yields that, when the tax advantage is calculated, let you compare tax-free and taxable bond funds). Objective: double tax-free income.

INTERNATIONAL FUNDS

An essential subset of stock and bond funds is international and global stock and/or bond funds:

- **International stock funds** invest only overseas in the stocks of several countries or regions. Objective: to take advantage of foreign stock market opportunities.
- **Global stock funds** invest in a combination of foreign and US stocks. Objective: to take advantage of both foreign and domestic investment opportunities, often hedging against currency risk.
- **International bond funds** invest in foreign government or corporate bonds. Objective: income, diversification, and hedge against a depreciating dollar.

International stock funds, like growth and growth and income funds, present a wide variety of investment opportunities and, yes, risks. Some international funds concentrate their assets in established

European markets, others in a combination of European and Japanese securities, while still others participate in whole or in part in the combustible emerging markets. Taken together with the economic, political, and currency risks that investing abroad visits upon you, you'll need to keep your eye on the country-by-country issues as well as your own portfolio diversification in order to rest assured that you've selected the best international fund for your particular portfolio.

Why invest abroad at all? It's profitable, to a degree. A globally diversified portfolio can help you guard against a potential US market correction, as well as benefit from a rebounding market beyond the US. In fact, as the chart on the following page shows, investing a portion of your assets abroad long-term can land you risk-adjusted returns that prove to be better than a purely US portfolio. But it can also place your portfolio in harm's way if you attempt to time the markets or you overconcentrate in one market. First, let's look at the potential benefits of diversifying your US portfolio to include some international exposure—to do so, we'll use an "efficient horizon" chart. This is a graph showing risk and return for portfolios with varying amounts (0% to 100%, in 10% increments) invested overseas. The return figures (vertical scale) are in a straightforward arrangement, with returns lower the more you have in foreign investments. It shows that over the last ten years (through 12/31/03), the S&P 500 index of large-cap US stocks is up 186%, while the Morgan Stanley Europe, Australasia, and Far East (EAFE) index of established foreign market stocks is up a mere 55%.

Nothing can change the fact that, for this period as a whole, one would be better off sticking to domestic stocks rather than a diversified foreign stock offering. However, over different periods foreign markets certainly can go up more than the domestic market. And a more timeless truth also emerges from this graph: adding a small to moderate position in overseas investments to an all-US stock portfolio does not add to your portfolio's risk; it actually decreases risk slightly, even to US investors. (In fact, for this ten-year period the lowest volatility comes at 60% invested overseas, but in other periods this least-risk position is more commonly at 30% to 40% invested overseas.)

The same benefits of diversification apply abroad as well as at home. But with an international or global fund, you'll need to focus on country as well as stock diversification. When it comes to diversification and international funds, investors often think of global funds. These

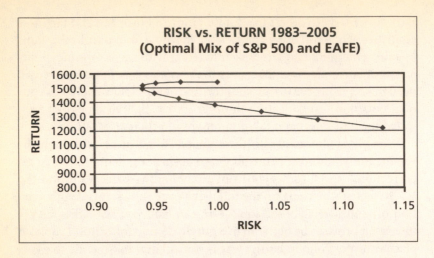

RISK vs. RETURN 1983–2005
(Optimal Mix of S&P 500 and EAFE)

funds tend to deliver less stellar returns but with less risk than a straight international fund. Geographical diversification is their main benefit. You can also add to your diversification by putting together two or more narrowly drawn international funds, but in that case you'll need to determine how closely the international funds correlate. Of course, funds with "Europe" in their name tend to perform relatively similarly, and downright differently from, for example, Japan or emerging market funds. However, while this is the case for the most part, it's not always as clear-cut—especially among funds with the generic "International" or "Worldwide" designations.

MONEY MARKET FUNDS

Money market funds invest in a variety of short-term interest-earning securities. Objective: preservation of capital, liquidity, and as high an interest rate as can be achieved without sacrificing the first two objectives.

Until Orange County, California, got squashed by its wrongheaded speculation in derivatives (which, simply stated, are a bet on the way interest rates will go), money market funds were considered to be the bastion of safety and stability in the mutual fund industry. Since that fiasco, a number of money market funds have suffered from derivatives. (For the first time in sixteen years a small institutional money market fund fell below $1 per share). All of which may lead you to ask how safe money market funds are today. Answer: not as safe as an FDIC-insured bank money market account—but still, pretty close. The key is to ensure that your money market fund isn't propping itself up on a house of derivative cards. How can you tell? The following should help you answer this question for yourself.

1. Does your money provide an unusually high yield? If it does, or if it has high expenses (as revealed in the prospectus) then it could be using derivatives. Call and find out.

2. If your fund does use derivatives, what types does it use? Steer clear of funds that are swollen with exotic varieties of interest-rate floaters such as capped, CMTs, dual-index, inverse, leveraged, and ranged floaters.

3. Regardless of what your money market invests in, the best thing you can do is stick with a fund that is part of a large fund complex. A large firm is more likely to have the financial strength to compensate a fund for any losses. But more importantly, a large fund group would have a bigger incentive to help out a troubled fund, if only to pacify its existing clients in other funds.

Closed-End Funds

As I mentioned earlier, mutual funds are open- or closed-end. Open-end funds are the funds you find listed by the thousands in the mutual fund section of your paper. Closed-end funds are listed in the stock section and are bought and sold like stocks on the NYSE, AMEX, or NASDAQ. And you purchase them only through your broker, with a commission.

Unlike open-end funds, closed-end funds issue a fixed number of shares. While closed-ends tend to perform like whatever type of stocks or bonds they invest in, moving up or down with the net asset value (NAV) of their investments, there is no guarantee that you will be able to buy or sell a closed-end fund at this price.

Closed-end prices are set by supply and demand in the market. Often, closed-end funds trade at significant discounts or premiums to the actual value of their portfolio—i.e., with a closed-end you can often pay "too much" or, just as often, get a bargain. With an open-end fund, new shares are created whenever a new investor steps up to the plate—and you buy shares in an open-end fund directly from the fund company (or through a fund network, bank, or brokerage) at the NAV price (although often with some load or other fee charged). With a closed-end fund, the number of shares is limited, and, unless you get in on the initial offering (more on that below) you don't really buy closed-end shares from the fund company, you buy them from another investor who is selling.

The only time you're likely to be solicited to buy shares in a closed-end fund is during its initial offering. Why? That's when the brokers can make a big commission. Typically, for every $100 you invest, commissions eat up around $7, and only the other $93 goes to work for you. It rarely, if ever, makes sense to buy a new closed-end fund at this time. Unless you want to reward your broker for exemplary service and advice, wait until after the fund has been available for a while and buy it on the open market. Then the commissions will be more like 1%, not 7% or more.

How should you judge a closed-end fund? First, if the fund doesn't meet your investment objectives (e.g., for growth, or for stable income) you must avoid it. Second, if the fund's management has shown a poor record and/or management expenses are out of line with the norms for open-end funds, you should probably stay away. (Stock funds' expenses shouldn't exceed about 1.5%, with some leeway for aggressive small-cap growth funds and international funds, while bond fund expenses should be well under 1%, again, with some leeway for funds investing in junk bonds and convertibles.) Finally, even if the underlying fund looks good and appropriate, if it's selling at a significant premium to the value of its holdings (its NAV), you should stay away, at least for the time being. Remember, there's probably a no- or low-load open-end fund that's just as good.

When is a good time to buy a closed-end fund? Closed-end funds are generally attractive when they are selling at a significant discount to their NAV. (This information can be found in *Barron's* magazine each week.) You can often buy $100 worth of assets for $95 or less. Optimally, you can buy discounted shares in a closed-end fund when its investment niche is out of style; then, when the area recovers, you'll make money from both a higher NAV and the elimination of the discount. (You may even sell your hot fund for a considerable premium!)

There's some truth to the cynical interpretation that closed-end funds exist largely because there are brokers willing to sell a new closed-end fund for a fat commission. But closed-end funds do have another, more legitimate reason for existing. The managers of many funds, particularly specialized funds that invest in illiquid securities like stock in foreign companies (or small domestic companies), have to spend a lot of time waiting for the right securities to come on the market at a good price. If they have to dump these securities to meet shareholder redemptions one day, they may have trouble finding similar replacement securities when their shareholders are buying a week later. To avoid such problems, many open-end funds levy redemption fees on short-term traders, but that is only a partial solution to the problem of shareholder redemptions. If half a fund's shareholders sell out in the same month, it will be little consolation to fund management (or the other shareholders) that they had owned their shares for more than a year!

The manager of a closed-end fund, on the other hand, has complete confidence that he won't have to be dumping illiquid securities and raising cash to meet shareholder redemptions—because there aren't any redemptions. This gives him the freedom to concentrate assets in promising, but illiquid, securities.

Closed-end investors who dump their shares at the same time will suffer exaggerated market losses because (unlike open-end fund investors) they lack the power to force the fund's management to buy the shares back at their NAV. But paradoxically, shareholders in general benefit from their lack of power, because it allows the closed-end fund's managers to invest in these promising but illiquid securities in the first place, and to avoid dumping the securities at sensitive times.

For this reason, closed-end funds make the most sense as a vehicle for investing in narrowly defined portfolios of illiquid securities, and many of the most notable (and worthy) closed-end funds are single-country funds. In fact, if you look up the name of just about any European, Pacific Rim, or fast-growing emerging-market country in your newspaper's stock tables, you're likely to find a closed-end fund or two (e.g., the Japan Equity and Japan OTC funds on the NYSE).

MORE FUND TYPES

The following funds can offer you the possibility of investing in a single country, industry, market, or new fund. While this may sound like an advantage, the truth is that these funds often present the highest degree of risk, since they focus their investing on a single area, industry, or market. Nevertheless, these funds also present potentially higher returns than most other funds.

- **Sector funds** invest in the stocks of a single industry, such as biotechnology, electronics, health care, utilities, and so on. If, for example, you think an industry is about to take off or rebound, then a sector fund may prove to be the best way to invest your money, as opposed to buying stocks in companies in the industry directly. Because they focus on a single area or industry, sector funds behave more like individual stocks. Also as a result of this focus, sector funds often top the list of the highest-performing mutual funds for the year. Unfortunately, the same funds that top one year's list are often found at the bottom of the next year's.
- **Index funds** invest in an index, such as the Standard & Poor's 500 or the Wilshire 4500. Objective: duplicating a broad section of the market in order to safeguard investors against below-market returns (but also eliminating the possibility of above-market returns). Pros and cons of index funds are discussed in depth in chapter 15.
- **Socially responsible funds** limit their investments to companies considered to be socially responsible. (For more on creating a criterion checklist that will help you screen funds with a conscience that matches your own, see chapter 21. However, be sure that your conscience isn't your only guide, so that you research and screen out poorly performing funds, too.) Objective: to achieve an adequate return without sacrificing the moral imperative.

  There is no common definition for social responsibility. As a result, each fund's holdings will differ. Some, for example will base their investments on companies to avoid (e.g., tobacco, alcohol, defense) while others will base their investments on companies to include (e.g., those that tend to promote women, or that provide health insurance for the partners of gay employees). But perhaps the biggest concern ought to be the performance of such funds, historically, versus "conscienceless" funds—after all, your money is used in a more focused manner when you actively support the charities you believe in through tax-deductible donations, as opposed to purchasing an investment product that supposedly does the work for you.

- **New funds.** While not a "proper" category, new funds are a phenomenon within the overall industry that you can't avoid—and so need to know about. Like IPOs (initial public offerings) in the stock world, new funds present investors with a dilemma: whether to invest or not to invest, that is the question. New funds can provide investors a substantially rewarding investment opportunity. But with over one thousand new funds started up in 1995 alone, it's hard to know where to look for the most promising new funds to invest in.

  All funds were new funds at one point in time. But investing in new funds can be a risky business. Unless, that is, you can afford the time to do your research and find those funds that offer real promise. Many investors view new funds from the largest fund families as their only source of new funds. Here, logic dictates that if a company has produced some of today's top-performing funds, their new progeny will prove to do likewise come tomorrow. But the fact is that new funds from even the most successful families can wind up losing you money. In short, fund-family name-recognition isn't the best way to scan the fund horizon for the best possible new fund investment opportunities.

- **Single-country funds.** While most international and global funds invest in several countries on one or more continents, single-country funds focus on one particular country's stocks and bonds. By far the most volatile of the bunch, single-country funds are generally best avoided unless, as in the case of Japan, the country is the largest market outside the United States, with well-established markets, industries, and accounting practices.

  You'll still have to do your research on such funds, however, since funds with the same single country can invest in different types of markets—as well as hedging or not hedging their bets against currency fluctuations.

- **Emerging market funds.** While the majority of international funds invest in countries with well-established markets and economies, emerging market funds concentrate in developing markets, countries, and economies. We discussed some of the issues related to emerging markets in chapter 8. The results of these funds can be spectacularly good (or bad).

HOW TO TELL ONE FUND FROM ANOTHER

Every fund publishes a prospectus. The prospectus designates the type of fund (aggressive growth, balanced, etc.), details the specific objective of the fund and its past performance, states how the fund will be managed, and much more. To lay your eyes on a fund's prospectus, you can go directly to the fund firm's website and download a pdf (or upload an html) version of each fund's prospectus. To get your hands on a fund's prospectus, simply call the fund company and ask for it to be sent to you. Once it arrives—and it will arrive quickly, since you're their business—you may be a bit shell-shocked by the bombardment of information contained within each prospectus. (For a thorough understanding of how to read a mutual fund prospectus, Google this query: "reading a fund prospectus" and find references to the Investment Company Institute [ici.org] and the Securities and Exchange Commission [sec.gov] for some plain English on prospectus gibberish.)

The SEC has instituted a "profile prospectus" requirement, which is a two-page fund profile that serves as crib notes for prospectus readers and includes: the fund's objective, investment strategies, the types of securities in which the fund will invest, any special investment practices, risk factors, expenses, and past performance. When asking for a fund's prospectus ask for the profile prospectus, too.

Why is a fund's objective so important? Although it's only a paragraph or two long, a fund's objective tells you most of what you need to know. The objective indicates what types of investments the fund invests in, what the fund manager's goals are, and what the manager's investment strategies will be. Risk, reward, and your personal objectives and goals can be measured against this objective.

SELECTING A FUND
THAT'S RIGHT FOR YOU

Selecting the mutual funds that suit your investment means, objectives, and goals is not a simple task. Neither was learning to ride a bike, but I'm sure you mastered that pretty quickly. The trick is partly in choosing the right vehicle and partly in getting the balance of the thing. Once you have these two in check, you will be able to select a suitable group of funds that will help you stay in the investment seat no matter how bumpy the market ride gets. First, you will need to make sure that your investment vehicle is in working order, then you will be able to map out a course that puts your investing know-how to the real-world test.

The following questions will help you keep focused on the answers you most need:

- What is the fund's objective?
- What is the minimum investment?
- What loads and other fees are charged?
- How well has the fund performed relative to its peers and index?
- How long has the fund been in existence?
- How is the fund managed?
- Who is the fund manager and how long has he or she been at the helm? (Did he or she manage a fund prior to this one, and how did it do?)
- How can you purchase and redeem shares?

Mutual fund investors all share one basic goal: to make more money. Yet making more money won't help you achieve financial independence if the money isn't slated for specific goals and objectives. It is your goals and objectives that should dictate not only how much money you're investing in mutual funds, but also which types of funds you're investing your money in. The following fund analysis primer will help you do just that.

Fund Analysis for Diversification

Stock funds can be parsed by their investment style (value versus growth), their capitalization (the size of the company the fund invests in—large-cap [over about $3 billion], mid-cap [$1 billion to $3 billion], small-cap [under $1 billion], or micro-cap [under $500 million]), as well as their industry concentrations. Knowing each of these parts helps you picture the fund as a whole, as well as how one fund is likely to correlate with another. Remember, you don't get added diversification when you buy two funds that invest in the same things!

1. Investment style. Value-style managers focus on stocks that are currently selling at low prices relative to their book value and/or earnings (price-to-book and price-to-earnings ratios). Value-style funds

typically invest in mature, slower-growing stocks, like industrial equipment manufacturers and financial service companies. Growth-style managers, on the other hand, seek out rapidly growing businesses—even if the company's stock price is higher than the general market. That's why you'll find technology, health care, telecommunications, and other rapidly growing industries in growth-style funds. Value-style funds typically tend to outperform growth funds in periods when the economy is recovering from a low point. (Economically sensitive stocks, like capital goods manufacturers, benefit as other companies expand capacity.) In a maturing economic recovery, growth funds tend to gain ground. Companies in these funds aren't hurt as much by an economic slowdown as are companies found in value funds.

2. Capitalization. Many investors mistakenly think that value-style funds are inherently less risky than growth-style funds. You'll have to dig deeper to get at the real risk-related difference between these two investment styles—since a fund's average market capitalization often reveals more about its inherent volatility than does its investment style. In fact, if you took two value funds with similar industry concentrations, you might be surprised to find a wide divergence in terms of their volatilities. One way to explain this is to look at each fund's holdings. Is one large-cap oriented (focused on steady, reliable, liquid performers), while the other focuses on more volatile, small-cap issues? Chances are, the answer is yes. Similar investment style and industry weightings don't necessarily mean similar volatility.

3. Industry concentration. Investment style determines the types of stocks a growth manager is most likely to own, as well as the fund's industry concentrations.

4. Correlation. Your ability to put together a well-diversified portfolio depends on your ability to discern such similarities and differences as described here. The "correlation matrix" (page 212) illustrates the performance similarities, or the correlation, among a representative group of funds. (The table compares monthly total returns over the past three years.) If you do hold two growth funds with a high correlation, chances are the growth portion of your overall portfolio isn't as diversified as it could or should be. On the other hand, if you own two growth funds with a very low correlation, you've achieved added diversification. This table clearly shows how closely the growth funds' returns correlate with one another. Simply put, for any two funds,

there is a number, called the "r2," which shows what percentage of one fund's performance can be explained by the other fund. Thus, as you can see, Fidelity Blue Chip Growth (BlueChGr) fund's r2 when compared to Fidelity Growth Company (Growth Co) fund's is 84%; that's a high correlation—signaling that, in this case, owning two funds yields no greater diversification than owning one or the other of them. (A fund's r2 when compared to itself is 100%.) Fidelity Cap App and Fidelity Blue Chip Value, which are both invested in larger-cap stocks, have a lower r2 of 69%. Thus owning both offers some advantage in the way of additional diversification. The top row of the table shows each fund's correlation with the S&P 500 index—the best overall benchmark for US stock investors (although it does have its limitations as a benchmark for small-cap funds). Once you're clear on what you want your mutual fund investments to accomplish, take the following steps:

Step 1: Determine how much you can invest. Once you've determined what your investment objectives are, you'll need to figure out how much of your hard-earned money you can and are willing to invest.

Step 2: Figure the percentages. Once you know why you're investing and how much money you can invest you'll need to figure out how to divvy up your money among different types of funds. Why different types of funds? Because doing so will enable you to fit your investments to your goals, and take advantage of the benefits of diversification. Figuring out what percentages to place in which types of funds is asset allocation plain and simple.

Step 3: Select the funds you think will be best based on the prospectus, objective, and performance record as well as your individual investment means, objectives, and goals.

Step 4: Know what fees you have to pay. Fees really make a difference. Consider the following. If you invest $10,000 in a 4% load fund that turns in a 10% performance for the year, you earn the 10%, but not on $10,000. Instead, you earn 10% on $9,600. That's $400 short of a no-load fund investor. However, just because a fund says it's no-load doesn't mean that there are no fees associated with it. There may be a

	S&P 500	BlueChGr	BlueChVl	Cap App	Contrafund	Destiny I	Destiny II	Disciplined Eq	Discovery	Dividend Grow	Export&M	Fifty	Focused	Growth Co	Independence	Large Cap Growth	Large Cap	Large Cap Value	Magellan	Sp500Indx	SpTMI	Stock Sel	TaxMan	Trend
S&P 500	99	95	82	80	79	90	80	91	80	90	93	85	66	76	87	84	94	89	97	99	98	98	87	100
BlueChGr	85	80	83	76	86	81	64	94	65	71	86	81	87	70	87	88	85	88	82	85	89	86	100	87
BlueChVl	97	96	80	79	78	93	78	91	78	90	94	83	66	76	86	87	95	86	96	97	96	100	86	98
Cap App	99	94	80	83	81	90	76	92	76	86	91	82	68	80	86	86	94	89	99	100	96	89	98	79
Contrafund	100	95	82	79	75	89	78	89	78	90	92	80	63	74	83	83	93	88	96	100	99	97	85	99
Destiny I	96	95	80	78	74	88	76	85	77	91	92	81	61	75	82	82	93	93	84	100	96	94	96	97
Destiny II	88	76	83	67	78	74	70	87	71	76	84	75	72	58	79	74	79	79	100	84	88	86	88	89
Disciplined Eq	93	96	79	81	77	97	73	88	73	83	89	85	65	84	87	88	100	79	93	93	94	95	85	94
Discovery	83	87	71	76	81	85	59	90	59	69	84	81	80	80	87	100	88	74	82	83	86	87	88	84
Dividend Grow	83	84	76	85	80	84	72	86	72	74	86	97	77	80	100	87	87	79	82	83	86	86	87	87
Export&M	74	84	52	85	75	81	58	73	59	62	71	78	59	100	80	80	84	58	75	74	80	76	70	76
Fifty	63	61	72	65	84	63	49	82	49	48	71	67	100	59	77	80	65	72	61	63	68	66	87	66
Focused	80	81	71	81	72	83	72	79	72	75	83	100	67	78	97	81	85	75	81	80	82	83	81	85
Growth Co	92	90	83	77	78	90	77	87	77	86	100	83	71	71	86	84	89	84	92	92	91	94	86	93
Independence	89	87	66	69	58	81	83	73	83	100	86	75	48	62	74	69	83	76	91	90	86	90	71	90
Large Cap Growth	78	76	63	68	57	72	100	64	100	83	77	72	49	59	72	59	73	71	77	78	76	78	65	80
Large Cap	89	85	79	79	88	84	100	64	100	64	73	87	79	82	73	86	90	88	87	85	89	92	91	91
Large Cap Value	78	76	63	68	56	72	100	64	100	83	77	72	49	58	72	59	73	70	76	78	76	76	64	80
Magellan	89	94	73	77	74	88	72	84	72	81	90	83	63	84	85	97	74	88	89	90	93	81	90	100
Sp500Indx	75	74	68	79	100	74	56	88	57	58	78	72	84	75	80	81	77	78	74	75	81	78	86	79
SpTMI	79	82	62	100	79	77	68	79	68	69	77	81	65	85	85	76	81	67	78	78	83	79	76	80
Stock Sel	82	73	100	62	68	73	63	79	63	66	83	71	72	52	76	71	79	83	80	82	80	83	82	85
TaxMan	95	100	73	82	74	94	76	85	76	87	90	81	61	84	84	87	96	76	95	95	94	96	80	95
Trend	100	95	82	79	75	89	78	89	78	89	92	80	63	74	83	83	93	88	96	100	99	97	85	99

redemption fee, and every fund charges management fees in one form or another. The trick is to find the funds whose fees are (far) more reasonable than others and whose performance is still solid. To do this, you will need to do your homework—a task made easier by the list at step 6. For now, let's look at the range of mutual fund fees that can affect your investment dollars.

- Load. A load is an up-front sales commission charged and deducted from your initial investment amount. (Load charges range as high as 8.5% but are more commonly in the range of 3% to 4.5%.) There's little reason to purchase load funds when there are so many good no-load funds to choose from.
- No-load. No-load means no initial sales commission fee. No-load refers only to up-front sales commission charges. Many no-load funds have other fees (listed below). Nevertheless, no-load funds tend to be the best way to invest in mutual funds because more of your money is going to work for you.
- Back-end loads. Also known as "redemption fees," this is a fee charged to the net asset value of your shares when you sell them. Either your profit is cut or your loss increased. No matter how you look at it, this load sucks.
- Deferred loads (contingent deferred sales fees). On the surface, a deferred load seems as lousy as a back-end load. A deferred load is charged by some funds if and only if you redeem your shares before a specified time—typically a few years. While this may not be to your advantage if you're investing for the short term, the principle of discouraging investors from jumping into and out of the market in short shrift is a good one.
- Reinvestment loads. Some fund companies dock your dividend, interest, and capital gains should you decide to reinvest them. Any fund that does this is discouraging a very wise investment choice—reinvesting dividends. Drop any of these funds from your list of possible investments.
- 12b-1 fees. Some funds deduct the costs associated with advertising and marketing themselves from the fund's overall assets. The charge associated with such deductions is called a 12b-1 fee, and ranges as high as 1.25%. Some funds feed a portion of the fee to the broker who sold you the fund.
- Wrap fees. These are fees levied for bonding a group of investment products.

Step 5: Consider a fund network. If you want the simplicity of one statement and one phone number, but don't want to limit yourself to one fund family, consider a fund network such as those at Charles Schwab, Fidelity, or Jack White. Each has hundreds of funds available without any transaction fees, and many hundreds more with modest fees. (See page 278.)

Step 6: Open the account—either by investing directly or through the fund company or by opening a brokerage account. It's almost as easy as a click of your mouse. Just Google the following names if simply adding a *.com* to 'em doesn't do the trick.

Fund Family

20th Century Family	Meridian Fund
Artisan	Merriman Funds
Babson Fund Group	Montgomery Funds
Berwyn Group	Neuberger & Berman Group
Bramwell	Oakmark Funds
Cohen & Steers	Oberweis Funds
Columbia Funds	PBHG Growth Fund
Dodge & Cox Group	PIMCo Funds
Dreyfus Group	Robertson Stephens
Federated Funds	Royce Funds
Fidelity	Safeco Mutual Funds
Founders Funds	Schafer Value Fund
Gabelli Funds	Scudder Funds
Harbor Funds	SteinRoe Mutual Funds
Heartland Funds	Strong Funds
Invesco	T. Rowe Price Funds
Janus Group	Tweedy Browne
Kaufmann Fund	Vanguard Group
Lexington Group	Wasatch
Loomis Sayles	Yacktman Fund

Step 7: Keep accurate records of how much you've invested, and where. It's been a while since we mentioned the term "active file." Remember to set up a file for your investments, and to keep it current with statements that you receive.

Step 8: Keep tabs on your funds' performances. The quickest way to do so is to watch them online. But remember, the market is a fickle provider. That's why keeping track of your funds' performances is a necessary, ongoing process. You may not buy this, but it's kind of fun looking at the financial pages in your newspaper and seeing how your funds are doing. Of course, if they aren't doing well the fun goes out of the picture pretty damn fast. But don't let a bad day or two cloud your judgment. For that matter, don't let a few lousy months or even a year do so. If you've selected a good fund and still believe in its fundamental ability to succeed over the long term, then stick with it. Making a move based on short-term market fluctuations will only increase the likelihood of an overall poor investing performance.

Further, make use of the many good financial planning magazines available to you at your library, bookstore, and/or newsstand.

Step 9: Regularly increase your investments. Plan on investing regularly. Plan, too, on increasing the amount you invest as you get older and have more disposable income. And while chapter 16 details several ways to build an actual portfolio of mutual funds to suit your age, income, and objectives, the following is a "growth" portfolio for those with fifteen or more years to go before they retire:

Sample Investment Portfolio

Fidelity Dividend Growth	20%
Fidelity Select Technology	20%
Artisan Mid-Cap Value	20%
Fidelity Value Strategies	20%
Fidelity International Small Cap	20%

READY RESOURCES

As with stock investing, there's no shortage of fund information available to the avid reader. The following list of newsletters and books should be sufficient to get you going.

- *Mutual Fund Fact Book,* Publications Division, Investment Company Institute, 1401 H Street, NW, Washington, DC 20005, (202) 326-5800 ($15)

- *Keys to Investing in Mutual Funds,* Warren Boroson, Barron's Educational Publishing, 1992
- *Bogle on Mutual Funds,* J. Bogle
- *Hedge Funds,* J. Lederman

CHAPTER 15

Exchange-Traded Funds
from Scratch

Suddenly, as if they hadn't been in existence for more than a decade, and as if index funds and actively managed funds had become passé, everyone is talking about ETFs. And, no, "ETF" doesn't stand for "extra terrestrial funds"—it stands for "exchange-traded funds," an innovative investment vehicle that trades like a stock but is diversified like a fund.

Up front, there is more to ETFs than meets the general investing public's eye. And if well chosen, ETFs can provide low-cost performance, which is beautiful to behold—but, like any other investment, they can also deliver bupkes or worse.

The sense of the *sudden* emergence and *newness* of ETFs isn't too far off base; a large number of ETFs came to market in the early 2000s. And the sense of usefulness isn't off base either: ETFs can help you participate in the broader markets, for example the S&P 500 index, using something nicknamed the "Spider" (the ticker for this investment vehicle is SPY); or the Dow Jones Index using something dubbed the "Diamonds" (the ticker for this investment vehicle is DIA); or the NASDAQ's "Qube" (the NASDAQ 100—a basket of the largest one hundred stocks trading on the NASDAQ—ticker QQQ)— with lesser cost and greater tax efficiency than an S&P 500 index mutual fund. There are also hundreds of niche ETFs—ranging from biotech to wireless to dogs (dogs of the Dow, that is—the ten worst-performing stocks in the Dow 30 from the prior year). Some of these

are well-covered ground; some are opportunities your overall investment portfolio might not otherwise be likely or able to invest in.

While some ETFs may be mostly marketing sizzle without much
investment steak, make no mistake about the fact that exchange-traded
funds, or ETFs, are here to stay. Here's why. ETFs combine the strengths
of mutual fund diversification—both broad indexing and more narrowly focused market participation—with the day-to-day control of individual stock investing and trading.

The list of ETFs grows monthly; many more are on the way. The
most well known, the DIA (Dow 30), SPY (S&P 500), and QQQ (Nasdaq 100) mentioned above, are almost without exception the most
heavily traded securities on the AMEX every day. And aside from the
current crop of SPDRs, Qubes, and HOLDRs (don't worry, we'll come
to terms in this chapter with all of them), there's a slew of index-related
ETFs. Wed these facts to one other: Today's investors are clamoring for
better (and more) strategic investment instruments to fine-tune their
portfolios in bull and bear markets.

You need to know the ins and outs, ups and down, advantages and
disadvantages, as well as the best possible uses of ETFs for your portfolio. But you'll also need to find the best trees in the thickly growing
forest of ETFs. You'll need to know what stocks compose each ETF—
the fundamentals in terms of how such holdings differentiate one ETF
from another. Additionally, you'll need to be able to determine how,
where, and when they should be traded.

After a brief summary of what exchange-traded funds, or ETFs,
are, how they work, and why they may be appropriate choices for you,
I'll take a stroll down ETF memory lane to discover the history of the
birth of these securities. While they're coming of age today, they can
trace their genealogy back to a love-in at Berkeley back in the early
1970s. I'll also delve into more details relevant to determining their
suitability in their own right as well as in relation to index and sector
funds, which share similar investment objectives and holdings. I'll
end the chapter with steps you can take on your road to successfully
investing in ETFs. Let's get started.

ETFs: What Are They
and How Do They Work?

Exchange-traded funds are baskets of stocks, somewhat like closed-end mutual funds, that are themselves traded like stocks, virtually all of them on the American Stock Exchange. Since they are traded like stocks, they are priced continually throughout the day, and can be shorted or bought on margin—many even have put and call options (pages 263–64). Most have relatively low expenses compared to actively managed diversified and sector-focused mutual funds, but trading ETFs does incur regular stock commissions.

In order to understand what an ETF is, and how it compares to other pooled investments, we first must cover its two older siblings, the open-end mutual fund and the closed-end mutual fund.

An open-end fund is bought from and sold back to the fund manager, generally at the fund's net asset value, or NAV, but sometimes with a sales load or redemption fee levied. Almost all of the funds anyone has heard about are open-end, including the products of Fidelity, Janus, and Vanguard.

A closed-end fund, in contrast, is bought and sold among investors and brokers, but not generally bought from or sold back to the fund manager. Instead, the fund manager creates a relatively fixed number of closed-end shares and has a public offering of all of the shares. Closed-ends' market prices are thus set not by the fund managers' accountants, but by supply and demand among investors, and their price can thus go far—often 20% or more—above or below net asset value. In general most closed-end funds do go to a discount to NAV, and this makes it a lot harder to sell closed-end shares at the public offering, when at that time they're sold for a price exceeding the NAV by the brokers' commission, which is usually a lot higher than a normal stock trade commission.

Since savvy investors should generally avoid a closed-end offering, it's a lot harder to get a new closed-end started. So it should come as no surprise that in a typical section on mutual funds in *Barron's* magazine, closed-end fund tables take up about one page, while open-end funds take up ten pages. (And *Barron's* coverage of closed-ends is more comprehensive than its coverage of open-ends.)

The management of a closed-end fund does have some control over market prices. If a closed-end's market price gets so far below net asset value that investors become restless, management may buy back shares, but they're usually reluctant to do so because that means a smaller fund and lower management fees. Management can also add closed-end shares in a secondary offering, which they are somewhat more likely to do if the fund is popular enough to trade at a premium.

So why are closed-end funds created, and why would an investor buy one? The one place where a closed-end structure has real advantages is in a portfolio holding a lot of illiquid securities. Because the manager doesn't have to fear shareholder redemptions, he can feel free to load up on thinly traded, micro-cap, or foreign securities, including those based in emerging markets. In fact, if you want a single-country foreign fund, the closed-ends are often the best, or even only, place to go, excepting that many mutual fund companies do have open-end funds invested exclusively in Japan.

Enter the ETF

An exchange-traded fund, or ETF, is a hybrid, partway between an open- and a closed-end fund. Transactions are usually, but not always, made between investors via a stockbroker. The fund company doesn't continually buy and sell shares with most investors, but it will buy and sell large blocks of shares, called "creation units," primarily to institutions engaged in arbitrage.

If the market price of an ETF falls *below* net asset value, arbitrageurs can buy up a block of the ETF, sell it to the fund company, and get in return the ETF's component stocks, plus a small amount of cash, mostly from recent stock dividends. The arbitrageur can then sell the individual stocks for a profit. And if an ETF's market price *exceeds* net asset value, arbitrageurs can buy a basket of the requisite stocks and exchange them to the fund company for newly created ETF shares, again for a profit. Usually the fund company only does this for creation units of 50,000 shares, but Merrill Lynch's HOLDRs do not have this 50,000-share minimum. (More on that later.)

While the arbitrage profit is pretty much guaranteed, it is never a large one, as arbitrageur action keeps the ETF's price from getting far out of line with net asset value. ETF prices for the more heavily traded SPDRs (proxies for the S&P 500), QQQs (the NASDAQ 100), and Diamonds (the Dow) are generally well within a half percent of NAV, with the more specialized and thinly traded products frequently somewhat more deviated from their indexes.

So all in all, individual investors and their advisors can generally ignore the question of whether a given ETF is at that moment selling for slightly above or below net asset value, whereas with closed-end funds this discount or premium is a key consideration when making investments.

One final note on the topic of ETF premiums and discounts: Although regular stock trading ends each weekday at 4:00 PM Eastern time, many ETFs continue to trade until 4:15 PM, so published discrepancies between an ETF's net asset value, which is set at 4:00, and its market price, may reflect that fifteen-minute difference more than any real deviation between market prices and NAVs.

ETFs that trade until 4:15 PM Eastern time include most of those tracking broad-based indices, and the iShares sector funds.

ETFs that trade until 4:00 PM Eastern time include the Sector SPDR funds, foreign stock index funds, and HOLDRs.

Foreign-market ETFs have much greater than fifteen-minute closing time discrepancies, with Asian markets in particular never open when the American-traded ETFs are being traded. And so these ETFs' prices can reflect news that comes out well after the overseas markets have closed. For this reason, pricing discrepancies between foreign-market ETF values and published NAVs are far more likely to reflect timing discrepancies than any real failure of market pricing or liquidity.

What are the advantages and disadvantages of ETFs compared to stocks, mutual funds, and closed-end funds, you ask?

In sum one can say that ETFs have most of the advantages of closed-end funds, and most of the advantages of open-end mutual funds, with few of the disadvantages of either. The one major drawback of an ETF structure is that ETFs are pretty much limited to passive index investing.

ARE ETFs RIGHT FOR YOU?

To reach your destination, the vehicle you're in is less important than the road you're on. And in general, choosing ETFs, like choosing mutual funds, is mostly a matter of getting the underlying securities right. If we start with the premise that you are, or ought to be, interested in index investing with a portion of your savings, then the decision of whether to buy an ETF versus a mutual fund is pretty much limited to a consideration of relative expenses and tax considerations, unless you're interested in day-trading.

In general, ETFs have low expense ratios compared to mutual funds, even index mutual funds, but trading ETFs does incur stock commissions, so if you make frequent trades, or frequent purchases, such as in a dollar-cost averaging plan, you might find ETFs more expensive than many mutual funds. On the other hand, ETFs allow trades throughout the day, whereas most mutual funds are priced daily, and even Fidelity's Select sector funds are priced only on the hour, so if someone insists on day-trading the market or even sectors of the market, ETFs are the way to go, as is reflected in the very high volume of the QQQ, the ETF tracking the NASDAQ 100 index.

Also, many mutual funds do not welcome frequent trades out of the fund, so paying ETF commissions may be preferable to getting frozen out of a mutual fund account. And the mutual funds that do allow rapid trading usually charge for the privilege; notably, Fidelity's Select sector funds levy a 0.75% fee on all shares redeemed within thirty days of purchase. All in all, about the only customers who should have a significant cost preference for index mutual funds over ETFs are those who are dollar-cost averaging into their account. I'll get to ETF's tax advantages later in the chapter.

A Brief ETF History

Compared to mutual funds, which date to 1924, when Massachusetts Investors Trust came out, ETFs are a relatively new type of pooled investment. And if you want to impress your friends and neighbors with ETF facts, instead of their marketing fiction, this section is for you.

Building on the work of Berkeley professor Nils Hakansson, who in 1976 wrote of the possibilities of a SuperFund index that could be broken apart into securities with varying risk and return characteristics, in 1990, Leland, O'Brien, Rubenstein Associates (founded by two Berkeley business professors and an investment consultant) obtained permission from the SEC to create a new product called the SuperTrust. The SuperTrust was, in essence, the first ETF, an S&P 500 index fund that was traded like a stock, and also offered and redeemed shares. The permission required from the SEC came in the form of certain exemptions from the 1940 Act on the grounds that the new product was, among other things, in the public interest and consistent with the protection of investors. (The 1940 act made rigid distinctions about what a closed-end fund, open-end fund, and unit investment trust were, and exemptions were needed to create any hybrid product.)

But the SuperTrust was primarily sold as part of a portfolio insurance technique—a hedge against market declines. And the demand for market hedging was dropping off dramatically at this time. Ironically, this was in large part due to the October 19, 1987, market collapse, when hedging in general didn't provide the expected level of protection to investors, and dynamic hedging even took much of the blame for the market's sudden, one-day market decline.

The new SuperTrust came out in a market that was suspicious of one of its basic features: the fact that the shares could be divided into four separate products offering, essentially: first, the index's capital gains, to the extent they exceeded 25%; second, the first 25% of gains, plus any income from stock dividends; third, a downside hedge, receiving any losses up to 30%; and fourth, a residual of money market interest. While one could hold all four parts of the SuperTrust and have what amounted to an S&P 500 index ETF, the complexity of the product, its limited liquidity due to weak initial interest, and the fact that each created SuperTrust expired after three years conspired against its success. The first SuperTrust shares weren't sold until 1993 (after further regulatory and market delays), and the SuperTrust was killed off just three years later, in 1996.

While demand was weak for a hedging product backed by a market-index ETF, demand for index investments was growing, with the total of mutual fund and institutional index investments reaching $200 billion by the end of the 1980s. The American Stock Exchange took advantage of the legal groundwork laid by the SuperTrust, and in 1992 received SEC sanction for its Standard & Poor's Depository Receipt. The SPDR, generally pronounced "spider," was an S&P 500 indices ETF without the complex portfolio insurance features.

Love Spiders

Charlotte's web has nothing on the AMEX's SPDR. Since the creation of the SPDR, changes to the legal and accounting structures of ETFs have been modest, at least as far as the investor is concerned, and certainly not as significant as the increase in the number and type of indices that have been tracked, including narrow sectors and foreign markets.

In perhaps the most important accounting change, ETF managers now use the strategy of trading the lowest-cost-basis stocks in exchange for something dubbed "turned-in creation units" (don't ask!). This further reduces the odds that a given ETF will have to make a taxable distribution. And in another legal change, several ETFs, such as the iShares, Select Sector Spiders, and StreetTracks, technically are structured as open-end funds instead of unit investment trusts, or UITs. The open-end structure allows for the immediate reinvestment of dividends, while most UITs only reinvest dividends quarterly, which creates a cash drag on performance, albeit a very small one.

While ETFs organized as unit investment trusts do hold some cash from recent stock dividends, ETFs generally hold very little cash compared to mutual funds. Since ETFs are not really subjected to investor selling, they don't have to hold cash to meet redemptions. In contrast, actively managed mutual funds tend to lag the market in the long term because they tend to keep close to 5% of their assets in cash.

Even index mutual funds generally hold some cash for meeting redemptions. They offset this cash with positions in index futures or options; while this may mean slightly lower returns than for a "pure" stock position, it beats their two possible alternatives: First, if an index mutual fund just held some cash and avoided derivatives, it would have a lower beta than the index it was supposed to track, and would tend to lag over time; and second, if the fund instead held no cash, there would have to be perhaps five hundred tiny trades each day to cover exactly the net purchases or redemptions of the fund's shareholders, and that would of course add considerably to brokerage and other trading costs.

LEARNING MORE ABOUT A PARTICULAR ETF

All ETFs, like all mutual funds, have prospectuses. But while all the big investors who purchase creation units receive a prospectus, only some ETFs send prospectuses out to secondary (or market) purchasers, who probably have a greater need for such information than do the big Wall Street firms. But ETFs will send a prospectus to those who request one. Those ETFs that are technically open-end mutual funds also have "statements of additional information" and must provide shareholders with semiannual reports. Those ETFs that are unit investment trusts (UITs) are not so required.

ETFs Online

A lot of ETF information is readily available on the Internet. Go to Marketwatch.com and Google the topic.

Morningstar.com, a site that emphasizes mutual funds, has a link to ETFs from its main page. The area contains news on fund launches, free articles, and basic information on each ETF. For example, when the iShares MSCI EAFE index fund came out in August 2001, Morningstar pointed out that the fund's low expense ratio of 0.35% was matched by similar Fidelity and Vanguard offerings, and that the latter two funds didn't charge the commission that would apply to each iShares transaction, meaning the mutual funds would be better for many, but not all, investors. The ETF's likely greater tax efficiency gave it the edge for the investor planning to buy it once and hold on for the long term. All in all, Morningstar has a lot of useful commentary and information, even before you consider the fact that the bulk of it is free.

There are also, of course, industry-backed websites with ETF info, like iShares.com and Amex.com, and these do include such things as prospectuses and returns and index information. But of course you can't expect such sites to give you the drawbacks as well as the advantages of their offerings, any more than you would expect a mutual fund company's telephone rep to help you decide whether you should dump its index 500 fund and buy an SPDR.

Who Supplies ETFs

Several firms supply ETFs. But who sells an ETF is generally less important than what it is invested in, although the two are connected, since certain indices are proprietary or traded on one exchange. All ETFs are "passively managed" stock investments, and all are subject to the potential risks and rewards of other stock market investments. And all of the ETFs, even those sold by a bank, have normal market risks and are not insured by the FDIC or any other bank-related agency.

For most purposes, it pays to think of the ETFs as grouped by whether they are invested in broad-based indices, sectors, or international areas, rather than who is selling them, but here goes:

- **Diamonds** track the Dow Jones Industrial Average.
- **HOLDRs (Holding Company Depository Receipts)** are Merrill Lynch products that track relatively narrow sectors. HOLDRs are invested in certain aggressive, narrowly defined sectors such as biotechnology and the Internet, or even Internet architecture and B2B Internet! These concentrated-sector ETFs start with just twenty stocks, and this number can go down as firms merge. Needless to say, many got creamed in the 2000–2001 bear market in technology shares.

  HOLDRs have a few distinctions from other ETFs. First, you don't have to trade 50,000 share lots to break up your HOLDR. The minimum is 100 shares, so retail investors can easily make such a transaction, although since market prices do stay close to net asset value for all the ETFs, it's not very likely you'd want to do so. Also, there's a $10 charge for breaking up your HOLDR. And finally, that 100-share minimum applies to all HOLDR transactions—there are no odd-lot trades—so depending on share price you may have an investment minimum of $10,000 or more.

- **iShares.** Barclays Global Investors has numerous domestic style ETFs, tracking Russell and S&P value, growth, and combined indices, and also the broader Dow Jones sectors, Goldman Sachs technology subsectors, and also a Cohen & Steers Realty sector. Its Morgan Stanley Capital International foreign stock offerings were formerly known as WEBS (for World Equity Benchmark Shares, and continuing the spider metaphor), and run the gamut from the broad-based EAFE index of foreign established markets to individual country ETFs, including some emerging markets.

- **"Cubes."** The QQQ tracks the tech-heavy NASDAQ 100 index, which is essentially the one hundred largest nonfinancial stocks in the NASDAQ Composite, and is thus almost a pure technology index, albeit one not including IBM and other New York Stock Exchange–listed firms.

- **SPDR (Standard & Poor's Depository Receipts).** SPY tracks the S&P 500 index, and the Mid-Cap SPDRs, or MDY, track the S&P MidCap 400 index. Sector SPDRs track the broader sector groupings within the S&P 500.

- **StreetTracks** are State Street Global Advisors' ETFs tracking Dow Jones–style and global indices, Morgan Stanley technology indices, and the Wilshire Real Estate Investment Trust (or REIT) index.

- **VIPERs (Vanguard Index Participation Receipts)** are share classes of existing Vanguard open-end funds, the first being Vanguard Total Stock Market. Vanguard had plans to come out with an Extended Market Index ETF tracking the Wilshire 4500 in the fall of 2001, but the other obvious choice, an Index 500 ETF, is being delayed by bad blood with Standard & Poor's. Basically S&P wants Vanguard to pay it more money for the use of its index, while Vanguard wants to stick to the very cheap terms it got in a 1985 licensing agreement for its original open-end Index 500 fund.

How Are the ETFs' Prices Set?

Most ETFs have their net asset values set as a relatively even portion of the relevant index, but remember that NAVs will vary slightly due to index rebalancings and distributions, and also that market values will vary slightly from NAVs.

Cubes: The QQQ = 1/40 of the NASDAQ 100 index
SPDRs: The SPY = 1/10 of the S&P 500
Mid-Cap SPDRs: The MDY = 1/5 of the S&P MidCap 400
Select Sector SPDRs = 1/10 of the relevant index
Diamonds: The DIA = 1/100 of the Dow Jones 30 Industrial Average
Other ETF groups (such as HOLDRs and iShares) have varying index ratios depending on the fund.

Are There Any Exceptions to the Rule That ETFs Are Passive Indices?

Not really, but to understand this, one has to know that a so-called passive index fund still has some subjective or active management elements.

Even a "pure" index fund usually has some subjective human input about when to drop a stock if it moves a bit above or below a capitalization limit (or even how many shares are really outstanding, defining its market cap), which stock to replace it with, and what sector a stock properly belongs to. Index funds also must decide how much consideration to give to exactly matching index weightings versus minimizing transaction costs; and for funds that follow a broad index like the Wilshire 5000 or Wilshire 4500, there's a trade-off between getting every last stock versus minimizing trading costs, and when sampling stocks for such an index fund there are subjective decisions about sector and market-cap diversification.

That said, all ETFs are, and will likely remain, as pure in their indexing approach as index mutual funds are. For ETFs to maintain close to market prices, the market's major players have to know exactly how the ETF is constructed so that they can assemble or disassemble ETF creation units at will. Without the potential for this sort of arbitrage, ETF market prices could get significantly out of line with their net asset values, in the way closed-end funds often do.

An active manager wouldn't want to publish his exact holdings and trades in real time throughout the day, and so would not choose an ETF as his fund vehicle. We can imagine how other traders could take advantage of such information if a large actively managed fund were to do so. Moreover, even if the manager were willing to release the data, it would make the ETF arbitrageurs' activities far too complex to be practical, at least until the spreads between market prices and NAVs increased considerably.

Some of the sector "indices" tracked by ETFs are new creations tailor-made by the ETF marketer for just this purpose. They remain indices in the sense that the ETF manager does not make frequent stock trades, and those that are made reflect important or even existential changes in the stock: such as, it's merged out of existence, falls above or below a market-cap division, or changes its major industry. But in the very process of defining a new sector (such as B2B Internet, for example) and deciding it's a good time to offer it to the public, one has made a sort of management decision that amounts to sector market timing (and, in the case of some of those Internet-related sectors, disastrously bad timing at that). And further, when choosing the individual stocks that belong in a new proprietary sector, one can't avoid subjective judgments about each company's suitability and stability.

Expenses and ETFs

ETFs are usually cheaper than actively managed mutual funds, and even most index funds. Expense ratios range from as little as 0.09% for iShares S&P 500 index and 0.12% for the similar SPDRs, to about

1% for some of the iShares international products, which track Morgan Stanley Capital International indices.

Apart from some funds with temporary expense waivers, the cheapest open-end mutual fund is Vanguard Index 500, which currently charges 0.18% per year in fund expenses. Still, that's only about a tenth of a percent more than for the cheapest S&P 500 ETF, and 0.1% of even $50,000 is just $50, and remember that the Vanguard fund is bought and sold at NAV, with no commission.

With very small investment accounts there are two other considerations: fees and minimum investments. Vanguard Index 500 levies a fee of $10 per year on accounts under $10,000, and has a $3,000 minimum initial investment. In general it's hard to buy a mutual fund with less than that much money; Fidelity, for example, requires a $2,500 minimum initial investment on most of its funds. ETFs don't have such minimums, but they're no panacea for the truly small investor, as a $15 commission comes to 1.5% of a $1,000 account. An investor starting out with just $3,000 would probably be advised to buy a single, well-diversified option, such as an S&P 500 or Total Market Index mutual fund, rather than one or more funds or ETFs.

In addition to published expenses, ETFs and mutual funds also pay brokerage commissions on their own stock trades. But since ETFs make many fewer trades, here too they have the advantage over mutual funds.

TRADING COSTS WITH ETFS

ETFs are usually subject to commissions on the same or similar schedule as individual stocks. One can now make online stock trades for as low as $8, and even brokerage giant Fidelity now charges just $15 for a typical online stock trade. But even at $8, monthly purchases would mean $96 a year in commissions, and so for accounts under $100,000 ETFs would be more expensive for the monthly dollar-cost averager than Vanguard's Index 500 fund would be.

Compared to buying diversified portfolios of individual stocks, ETFs are of course much cheaper, as their diversification means fewer, larger trades than for trading individual stocks. Even at a rock-bottom $8 per trade, it takes $160 to buy or sell twenty stocks. With any kind of turnover in stock positions, that adds up to a lot of money compared to $8 for an ETF.

Bid/Ask Spread on ETFs?

As with stocks, in addition to commissions one may have to "pay" a bid/ask spread when trading ETFs. These spreads vary from zero for SPDRs and QQQ under normal market conditions, to close to 1% for the least liquid sector offerings, and even close to 4% for the most illiquid foreign markets, like the iShares MSCI Brazil index.

Note that the round-trip bid/ask cost of close to 1% on many sector ETFs is comparable to the 0.75% that Fidelity charges on Select funds, but Fidelity only levies its charge on positions sold out within thirty days. So for rapid sector traders, Fidelity's Select funds are comparable to sector ETFs, provided the trader doesn't mind being limited to hourly pricing, and doesn't need unmanaged indices or multiple Internet sectors. For sector traders who flip positions after a month or two, Select funds would be the cheaper option, while those who are apt to hold on to a sector for the long term will likely prefer ETFs in order to avoid paying the much higher expense ratios of Select funds.

Taxes and ETFs

ETFs offer much lower capital gains distributions than most mutual funds, and lower distributions than even index mutual funds.

A fully invested mutual fund is forced to sell stocks whenever investors make significant net redemptions from the fund. And an index fund has to sell its positions proportionately; it can't just sell the positions being held for a loss (while it may have shares in, say, IBM, that were bought at different times and have different cost bases, and it can sell those IBM shares that are showing the smallest gains or even losses, it can't sell out IBM while holding on to GE, or else its returns would start to deviate from the unmanaged index). In contrast, ETF shareholders mostly buy and sell among themselves, and even when ETFs are broken up, the fund company delivers individual stocks, not cash, so there is no capital gain or loss realized.

ETFs do sometimes have capital gains distributions, but generally only to the extent that they have sold stocks to account for changes in their underlying index benchmark, and even then, any previous ETF turnover via creation units would have already allowed the ETF to get rid of its lowest cost basis shares, and thus reduced the taxable gain realized from later selling a stock.

There have been occasions when ETFs with very narrow portfolios of a few stocks had to sell a winning position because it had exceeded the regulatory limit allowed in a single stock. Most notably, this meant big capital gains distributions for the iShares Canada and iShares Sweden funds in the summer of 2000. But outside of some of the smaller single-country markets and the narrowest of the sector funds, this should not be a factor for most ETFs.

ETFs also distribute stock *dividends*, of course, but those are very low now for most indices (for example, just under 1.5% for the S&P 500 index as of December 2005). And more to the point of judging the ETF concept, mutual funds similarly have to distribute any stock dividends.

Advantages of Mutual Funds

Mutual funds do continue to have advantages over ETFs. First, mutual funds can be actively managed, with many able to change holdings and even styles at the manager's will; of course, most fail to beat their fixed benchmarks anyway. Almost all mutual funds offer free telephone customer service—as well as comprehensive websites. Many mutual funds offer systematic purchase plans, without paying any commissions, and often with the initial investment minimum waived. Mutual funds settle in one day, while ETFs take three days. There are many more mutual fund choices (although ETFs do have the index bases covered). Even mutual funds' higher expenses may have a silver lining, as they mean more money for marketing. And that can be a good thing, as new sales mean more fees and perhaps drive up the stocks held by the fund.

ETFs vs. Index Investing

The argument for indexing is largely premised on the axiom that the stock market, especially the US large-cap stock market, is *efficient*. Efficiency here means that stock prices generally reflect what a stock is truly worth, and that stock prices respond so quickly to new information that no one can consistently outthink the market and achieve above-average returns. However, even if this theory of efficiency were perfectly true, some managers will still show better returns than others, but this will be due to luck. Hence, a manager with a great record one year will be no more likely to outperform the market in the following year than will any other manager.

Even if you don't think that the efficient market theory is perfectly true, it's hard to argue against these two facts:

1. Investors in general can't beat the market. For every investor who beats the market averages, another must lag the market. (Actually, the dollar amounts must balance out, not the number of investors.) Looked at another way, on average investors will match the market as, taken together, they are the market. And in fact, they must on average slightly lag the market due to brokerage commissions and other expenses. And further, most actively managed funds will further lag the market in the long run because they tend to hold 5% or more of assets in cash or equivalent income securities in order to meet redemptions.

2. It is very hard to beat the market over the long run. And for any finite period of time, outperforming the market can be due to luck. Over a short time period (say, a year), outperforming is almost certainly due to luck. Over a long time period (say, twenty years), significantly outperforming, while relatively more likely to be due to skill, might still be due to luck.

What about Peter Lynch? In every discipline, a few outstanding individuals will emerge from the crowd. That goes for money management as well as for music. Despite having retired years ago, Peter Lynch is perhaps still the best-known fund manager and stock picker in the country. Lynch ran the Fidelity Magellan fund for thirteen years, from 1977 to 1990, achieving an average annual return of 29.2%, versus 15.7% for the S&P 500 index.

But even if efficient market theory is wrong, and Peter Lynch was skillful, not lucky (which I'll grant is probably true), there's still the question of whether you can spot the next Peter Lynch before he's recognized as such. If you pick a young fund manager with a great record over the last three years, is that enough time to ensure that his performance wasn't due to luck, or to being in the right kind of fund at the right time? And if you wait until the manager has a great twenty-year record, can you ensure that he's not slowing down, playing lots of golf and anticipating a rich retirement, while letting the fund "run itself," or be run by interns from Wharton Business School? And over whatever time period, if many investors discover the hot manager and invest in his fund, isn't it likely that he'll have a much harder time putting a lot of new money to work than he had investing the smaller amount of money he managed early in his career?

Okay, you say. If no one can accurately pick a winning stock fund, what is there to be done? The index investing folks argue that the best way to take advantage of the stock market's long-term growth potential is to construct a portfolio that resembles that overall market as closely as possible, and the best way to achieve this goal is through index funds.

Currently, funds that mirror the S&P 500 index are the most common vehicles for achieving this "full investment" goal. The companies in the S&P 500 generally represent about 80% of the entire value of publicly traded US stocks, which is fairly complete market coverage. If you want to own literally every publicly traded US stock, the Wilshire 5000 index is your ticket to investment performance, and now there are Wilshire 5000 index funds, often called "Total Market" funds, to provide you with a close approximation to this index.

There are some rebuttals to arguments regarding the long-term performance superiority of index funds. Some industry advocates claim that one reason that S&P 500 funds have done so well relatively is that their rapid growth has driven up the share prices of the stocks that make up the index. But given how long this has gone on, and how major a part of the US market the index represents (namely, 80%), this argument isn't very compelling. But the fact that the S&P 500 has, for whatever reason, beaten smaller-caps for most of the past decade would to some extent reduce the meaningfulness of comparisons between active stock funds and S&P 500 returns. No matter what the rebuttal, however, ETFs have a decided edge over their index fund competition.

Expenses and Taxes

Wherever you come down in the indexing debate, the technique's advocates do have an indisputable claim to superiority in one department: cost. The index fund manager is basically a caretaker. All he or she needs to do is make sure that portfolio weightings do not stray from the index being tracked. Trades are made only to keep the portfolio in balance as stocks are added or removed from the index (generally once or twice a year, although sometimes a change is due to a corporate merger or spin-off), and when new money comes in or redemptions are made.

The index fund sponsor doesn't need to pay a bunch of analysts to search for good buys. With comparatively low brokers' commissions and research costs to cover, index funds can charge much lower management fees than their actively managed brethren. How much lower? The expense ratio for a good no-load larger-cap index fund will be around 0.2%, versus about 1% or more for an actively managed stock fund. And these incremental differences in fund expenses can make a big difference when compounded over the long run. (But they're already factored into the return statistics comparing funds to indices.)

But index funds' greatest cost advantage comes into play when we take a look at taxes. When a fund manager makes trades that result in capital gains, the law requires that these realized gains (minus any realized capital losses) be passed on to shareholders. This is the dreaded capital gains distribution, and you will be taxed on it even if you automatically reinvest those distributions in the fund. But since an index fund makes only the bare minimum of trades required to keep the portfolio in balance and meet redemptions, it tends to make much smaller capital gains distributions, if any. This is especially true of total market and large-cap indices that are market-weighted (such as S&P 500 index funds) and thus have little need to sell positions as part of a rebalancing or other change in index composition. (A small- or mid-cap index fund has to sell a stock if the company's stock has had a big enough run-up to move up to the large-cap indices, and a Dow index fund has to sell shares after a stock split, because that index is share weighted, not market capitalization weighted.)

Because most gains in an index fund are not distributed, leaving only small stock-dividend distributions, index funds have some of the tax-deferral advantages of holding your fund in an IRA, or of buy-and-hold investing in individual stocks. But unlike IRAs, index funds don't limit your investment to $4,000 per year, and there's no 10% penalty if you make a withdrawal—just normal taxes on any gains you realize by selling the fund. There's nothing wrong with holding an index fund in an IRA (or other retirement account), but if you have stock fund investments in a retirement account, and others in a taxable account, it's best to put any index fund positions in the taxable account, and any actively managed funds in the retirement account. That way you'll defer the most taxes.

INDICES, INDICES, STILL MORE INDICES, AND, OF COURSE, ETFs

One rule governing the ETF industry is that if a product proves popular, everybody rushes to copy it, and everybody tries to think up new, more exciting variations. While I think the index investing idea has a lot going for it, those who wonder how many different types of index funds we really need can find intriguing new avenues for investing thanks to ETFs.

But before you turn the key in your ETF vehicle, you need to map the indices, classified by their construction—i.e., how they are designed—and by the market capitalization of the companies they track. You also need to understand a few fundamentals about what makes your engine tick or stop dead as a brick. (I'll deal with the risk of investing in ETFs immediately following this section—and therein help you check under an ETF's hood to see what makes its financial engine run.)

TRACKING THE MARKETS USING ETFs

Using a selected group of ETFs, you can make your own daily map of the market in real time. To do so, you could use the following ETFs:

DIA	Dow Diamonds
SPY	S&P SPDRs
MDY	S&P Mid-Cap
QQQ	NASDAQ 100
XLB	S&P Basic Industries
XLP	S&P Consumer Staples
XLV	S&P Consumer Services
XLY	S&P Cyclical/Transport
XLE	S&P Energy
XLF	S&P Financial
XLI	S&P Industrial
XLK	S&P Technology
XLU	S&P Utilities
BBH	Biotech
BDH	Broadband

BHH	B2B Internet
HHH	Internet
IAH	Internet Architecture
IIH	Internet Infrastructure
PPH	Pharmaceutical
RKH	Regional Bank
SMH	Semiconductor
SWH	Software
TTH	Telecommunications
UTH	Utilities

To map the indices that form the overall mosaic of the global market, classified by their construction (how they are designed) and by the market capitalization of the companies they track, I have organized the mainstream indices by market capitalization. Then there are the specialized indices, some of which track specific industry segments, some which are idiosyncratic, but all the above relate to a better understanding of investing in any ETF.

Large-Cap Indices

Dow Jones 30 Industrials. The venerable Dow Jones 30 Industrials Average remains synonymous with "the market" although it is in fact a very narrowly based index: a mere thirty companies form it. Of course, there is nothing "mere" about giant corporations like McDonald's or GE. And despite the small number of stocks in this index, it has done reasonably well as a measure of the market's overall health. Still, its annual returns can easily deviate from those of the broader S&P 500 or Wilshire 5000 by 5% or more. The DIA, or Dow "Diamond," is the ETF way to invest in the bluest of the blue chips.

S&P 500 Index. While the Standard & Poor's 500 index is somewhat less venerable than the Dow—it began life in 1926—the S&P 500 index fund is the oldest index fund category. John Bogle, the foremost prophet of low-cost mutual funds, launched the first one in 1976, and although it now has about twenty competitors, his Vanguard Index 500 remains one of the cheapest ways to invest in the S&P 500. Most investors consider this index (which is basically, but not exactly, composed of the largest five hundred stocks in the United

States) to be a perfectly acceptable stand-in for the market as a whole even though its large-cap focus leaves out about 20% of the publicly traded stock market. The ETF of choice? The SPY, or "Spider."

NASDAQ 100 Index. The one hundred largest stocks on the NAS-DAQ can be invested in by using the QQQ. While some think this market exchange is a fairly arbitrary way to divide stocks, the truth is that the NASDAQ does have the distinction of being heavily weighted in technology stocks.

Wilshire 5000 Index. The Wilshire 5000 is a market capitalization–weighted index covering all the publicly traded companies in the United States. Despite its name, this index, tracked by Wilshire Associates, now actually consists of over seven thousand companies. Not surprisingly, since the S&P 500 represents about 80% of the country's market capitalization, the Wilshire 5000 usually tracks the S&P 500 pretty closely (although the Wilshire did lag by 5% in 1998's large-cap–dominated market). Like funds tracking this index, as well as those tracking the Wilshire 4500, and most small-cap index funds, ETFs do not buy every single little stock in the index. That's because the smallest companies are very illiquid (expensive to trade) and make up a very small portion of the index. Still, these funds do a good job of tracking their indices due to careful selection of stocks to match index capitalizations and industries.

Mid-Cap Indices

S&P MidCap 400 Index. This is the premier mid-cap index, composed essentially of the four hundred US stocks ranked between 500th and 900th largest in terms of market capitalization. There are iShares ETFs covering this index, as well as its separate Growth and Value halves.

Wilshire 4500 Index. Wilshire Associates' Wilshire 4500 index tracks every US company *except* those included in the large-cap S&P 500. While it holds mid- and small-cap stocks, the larger mid-caps of course make up a larger portion of this market capitalization–weighted fund.

Small-Cap Indices

All of these small-cap indices, including Growth and Value divisions, are offered as iShares ETFs.

S&P Small-Cap 600 Index. This index tracks the six hundred US stocks ranked between 900th and 1,500th largest, so it's slightly larger-cap than the Russell 2000 (below), and a bit easier to track completely.

S&P/Barra Small-Cap Value and Growth Indices. As with the S&P 500, Barra has divided the S&P Small-Cap 600 into Growth and Value "style" subindices.

Russell 2000 Index. Perhaps the best known of small-company indices, this index tracks the two thousand US stocks ranked between 1,000th and 3,000th largest.

International Indices

Morgan Stanley Capital International Europe, Australasia, and Far East (MSCI EAFE) Index. The EAFE is the industry-standard benchmark for the established international markets. The iShares ETFs cover both this broad benchmark and a number of individual countries tracked by Morgan Stanley.

Sector Indices

Use the sector ETFs that make sense—but if you can't make sense of the sector ETFs, you can instead use any number of sector funds, such as Rushmore American Gas, American Century Natural Resources, American Century Global Gold, Aon REIT, Vanguard REIT Index, Galaxy II Utility Index, Rydex Precious Metals, and Fidelity Select Technology.

INVESTMENT RISK WITH ETFS

Investing in ETFs is no more risky—and could prove to be less so—than investing in stocks and stock mutual funds. On the one hand, to get the needed diversification from direct ownership of individual stocks, you'd need to own a bare minimum of forty different stocks—with all the attendant risks of analysis, selection, and execution. With an ETF, you can own a basket of forty to five hundred or more stocks—just as with one mutual fund you may own five hundred–plus stocks in one investment vehicle. But typically, just as owning one stock isn't the most prudent route to take for long-term investment success, owning one ETF or one fund isn't likely to be the best way to go—since it would bias your portfolio toward a single investment style and/or a manager's focus, which, in turn, would no doubt favor some industries over others. How many ETFs is enough? Similar to mutual funds, you don't need thirty—in fact, don't go overboard with the number of ETFs in your portfolio; instead, concentrate on how and where each fund is invested. Four or five ETFs should cover most of the investment territory.

The stocks in which your ETF is investing hold the key to the ETF's investment success and underlying risks. The following will help bring you up to speed on the types of stock investments that your ETFs are most likely to invest in. Once you familiarize yourself with them, you'll be better able to check under the hood of each and every ETF you own. You should also refer to the section on the indices your ETFs are most likely to concentrate in—in this way you will have both a bottom-up and top-down perspective on an ETF's portfolio and likely performance.

Stock Risks

The underlying risks of investing in ETFs is the stocks the ETFs are investing in. Fortunately, the underlying risks of stocks are straightforward (and they hold as true for you as they do for your ETF): the stock's price may decline and/or the dividend income may be reduced or even eliminated. If you bought the stock at $10, loss occurs when you sell your stock for $9.99 or less. Selling may still make sense—and it may not. In fact, since most stocks fluctuate in price, it may be best to hold tight and ride out the downward curve if you have reason to believe that there will be an upside. Doing so may enable you to see the stock price rebound to over $10.

THREE MAIN STOCK TYPES

The following three types of stocks are the most common in ETFs—be aware that in each type there are likely to be a few poorly performing individual stocks. Knowing what to look for and diversifying with a selection of ETFs will help ensure that one dud doesn't ruin your ETF holdings.

1. Growth stocks. Growth stocks present investors the opportunity to invest in companies that promise to increase their stock's market value through earnings growth. They tend to be smaller companies and/or in rapidly growing industries. (But they could, like Wal-Mart, be large players expanding market share in a mature industry.) Because investors expect their earnings to grow, growth stocks tend to be expensive relative to their current earnings. Growth stocks typically rise in value more than other stocks, but they are far more volatile and subject to greater declines in price too. ETFs concentrating in growth stocks, such as a technology ETF, can be more rewarding over the long term, so long as you can afford the greater risk for the potentially greater reward.

2. Value stocks. Value stocks are stocks that are cheap relative to earnings or assets. Value stocks tend to be stodgier players in slower-growing, mature, defensive, or cyclical areas—basically the opposite of a growth stock. Value stock are often cyclical: stocks in companies whose earnings fluctuate more than average with business cycles. Examples of cyclical industries are housing, automobiles, paper, and steel. Correct timing is the key to successful cyclical stock—and cyclical ETF investing. As with growth versus value, the cyclicality of stocks is a continuum. Some stocks are in the middle, and might be considered cyclical by some investors but not by others.

3. Income stocks. Income stocks are those paying a substantial or above-average dividend income. Income stocks are most often value stocks: stocks in companies that are typically in more stable, mature industries. An ETF concentrating in the S&P 500 would be one example. The stability enables these companies to provide steady dividends—a source of income for many retirees or, more relevant from your vantage point, a source of reinvestment capital. Examples of income stock industries would be

utilities, telecommunications, and energy—but even many pharmaceutical companies (not exactly a stodgy industry), and an ETF like the PPH, fall into this camp.

SUCCESSFULLY INVESTING IN ETFs

As always, begin at the beginning. Determine proper asset allocation—i.e., which areas of the broad global market you want to invest in, as well as what percentage you want to invest in each category.

To start, you'll need to make a geographical decision: the percentage of domestic (US) and foreign assets in your stock allocation. Foreign markets are often far more volatile than ours, especially for dollar-based investors (like you). With currency movements and frequently illiquid markets, some foreign stock markets will rocket twice as much in a given time period, while others will plummet twice as far—or further—than the US market. But foreign markets don't always move in the same direction as the United States. For example, over most time periods, portfolios with an 80% stake in US common stocks and a 20% stake in established foreign market stocks (like the UK and Germany, as opposed to Thailand or Mexico) have actually shown reduced volatility or risk compared to all-US portfolios. On the other hand, for the past decade the all-US portfolio would have shown a higher total return than the internationally diversified portfolio, as few foreign markets have matched the United States.

Now, you need to decide how you want to allocate your investments in each stock fund subcategory (here defined by investment style and market capitalization, as well as country allocation). For example:

Large-Cap	30%
Mid-Cap	20%
Small-Cap	20%
Sector	20%
International	10%

Make sure your objectives mesh with your ETFs' objectives and risks; allocate into both growth- and value-oriented ETFs, and diversify as previously suggested along capitalization, sector, and geographical fronts.

Find out each individual ETF's investment style and performance record benchmarked against appropriate indices. Investment style tends to divide itself into two camps: value and growth. As you move from the forest to the trees, you'll want to know about each ETF's industry concentration, as well as each ETF's ability to deliver solid results in different markets and economic environments. And while past performance is no guarantee of future results, average annualized one-, three-, and five-year returns will help you get a sense of how the ETF has done, and might continue to do. Be sure to compare the returns of each ETF with those of other like-invested ETFs and funds—you may be surprised to find that, for example, an actively managed sector fund has fared significantly better or worse than a sector-focused ETF. What if the ETF is new to the market area you're thinking of buying? Find out what the ETF is made of—and see how the sum of those parts would have fared over the past three years.

Determine what types of industries and stocks each ETF typically invests in. This may take a lot of research—but not a lot of time. In fact, you can go online or call and ask the prospective ETFs you're thinking of buying (or the ones you own) for this information (found in the prospectus). True, the info may be a bit stale—three months old or so—but it's still relevant. Or you can look online at Morningstar.com, for example, or research past issues of the several personal finance magazines out there. Chances are your ETF, or one like it, has been profiled somewhere.

Establish how the ETFs in your current (or potential) portfolio correlate with each other. One of the most common mistakes fund investors make is thinking that owning many funds automatically guarantees diversification. Ditto for ETF investors. Two ETFs that own similar stocks will tend to move up and down together, and provide little more diversification than either ETF held alone. How can you tell if the ETFs you currently (or potentially) own are more or less likely to behave similarly? All the above steps (i.e., in choosing ETFs by objective) will come into play in a general way when it comes to distinguishing between ETFs' potential performances.

Don't chase hot ETFs, any more than you would chase a hot mutual fund. Last year's best-performing ETF may not be this year's darling. Better to buy an ETF you believe will perform reasonably well over two or more years than to buy one that has only recently rocketed skyward.

Don't buy ETFs simply because your friend says to, any more than you would buy a stock just because your friend said to. Just because your friend owns a good ETF doesn't mean it's the best for you. And just because your friend doesn't like an ETF doesn't mean it's not a good one.

Don't buy more than one ETF for one role in your portfolio. Why own two of the same thing when one will do? (If we were talking about wine or beer, then two of the same thing might make sense. But when talking about investing, this isn't the case.)

Do buy more than one ETF for your portfolio. Rarely can one ETF serve all your investment needs. In fact, I can't think of one ETF that does.

Finally, continue to learn as much as you can about ETFs. As with all other types of investments, ETFs live in a dynamic, ever-changing environment. Be sure to keep up your learning pace in order to stay in the race for long-term investment success using ETFs.

CHAPTER 16

Your Portfolio from Scratch

An investment portfolio is like a painter's palette. And, in a sense, being an investor is like being a painter. Your chances of creating a success of your overall work depends to a large degree on your range of skills and experience, as well as the potential materials you can apply to the canvas where you ultimately express your potential for failure or success. An investment portfolio is the palette from which you bring your investment objectives to life. And, as selecting the paints for the palette is potentially limiting or liberating for a painter and his work, so selecting the types of investments for your portfolio's palette will prove to be either restrictive or rewarding. Fortunately, your investment portfolio is a work in progress, and you can learn to quickly adapt and revise so as to secure a better total return picture for yourself.

Whether you have $100 or $1,000 to invest, you can plan a portfolio that will help you achieve your investment objectives. In fact, even if you have $0, zip, nada, zilch, you can profit today by planning your investment portfolio of tomorrow. Planning a portfolio requires prior knowledge of several investment-related steps—from knowing where you stand (financially speaking), to coming to terms with how the economy and securities markets work, to understanding and selecting the best types of investment vehicles to get you to where you want to go. That, of course, is what the first three sections of this book are all about. In fact, like rungs on a ladder, sections one, two, and three have brought you to a higher plain—the next level of investing wisely and well. From this vantage point of knowing the many investment alternatives that are out there, you can begin to contemplate the process of applying what you know in order to create a better world for yourself.

You still feel overwhelmed? No wonder. With over 6,500 mutual funds, and over 11,000 publicly traded stocks (plus hundreds of bonds and real estate opportunities) to chose from, the mind boggles. But you can always go back to a particular chapter to refresh yourself on a given subject or investment vehicle. Moreover, when it comes to building a portfolio of investments for yourself and your objectives, there's more than one way to keep a clear head in order to focus on the best investment alternatives for you. To begin with, you'll need a plan.

PLANNING YOUR PORTFOLIO

Planning your portfolio requires reviewing, and potentially revising, your life. That's the only way to ensure that your investment objectives make sense for you, and that you can achieve them.

Age

Your single biggest hidden asset is your age. Sure, you may feel that being older would make you somehow automatically richer—but just ask anyone who worked for Enron, and they'll tell you that ain't necessarily so. In fact, with the uncertain job market that exists today and is likely to persist throughout your lifetime, you need to be prepared for the loss of a job or, even more likely, for your desire to change careers or place of employment. Part of your portfolio planning will require you to view your investments in light of your overall financial planning, so that both are working in harmony to achieve your desired ends of a financially secure life from start to finish.

Because you are still young, you can afford to take on more risk in terms of the types of investments you select for your portfolio—and, as long as you have selected the right type of investments, more risks have, over time, delivered more rewards. In short, you have more time and a greater ability to create a sizable cushion to retire on. (Perhaps even retire early on.)

Lifestyle

If you're spending everything you make on fun, believe me, you're heading for some very depressing times in the not-so-distant future. If you don't start saving today, and you haven't started investing yet, the longer you wait, the more sacrifices you'll have to make just to stay in the game. What do I mean? Let's take a look at two twenty-five-year-olds. One invests $100 every month in a 401(k) plan, starting at age twenty-five, but he stops at age thirty-five and never invests another penny. The other doesn't start investing until age thirty-five, but he keeps plugging $100 per month into his account until he retires at age sixty-seven. Who wins? The early bird of course!

Current Income

Your current income obviously affects the amount of money you have to invest. But don't make the common mistake of thinking that postponing investing until you make more money is the best way to go. Maybe a refresher course on getting older will.

At twenty-seven, earning thirty grand, you're barely making ends meet. After all, there's the rent, the car, the student loans, the bars. So you say to yourself that in a few years, around age thirty or so, you'll be earning $35,000, maybe even $40,000. Since this is a reality check, let's not use the rosiest sum. Will that amount guarantee more disposable income for you—you know, more money to invest? Not likely.

First, taxes. Taxes on your $30,000 run approximately 28% federal and 5% state. Let's say that remains constant, so you go from $20,000 after taxes now to around $23,500 in three years—a $3,500 lift. But now you'll want to calculate into the equation the toll inflation will take. Let's say inflation remains under control at around 3% per year. Further, let's say that your salary moves from $30,000 to $35,000 in $1,666 increments ($1,666 × 3 years = $4,999). By the end of year one, your $30,000 loses about $900 worth of purchasing power. By the end of year two, your $31,666 loses about $950 of its purchasing power. Year three, your $33,333 loses $1,000. By year four, the year you were going to begin to invest, your $35,000 has lost $1,050 in purchasing power for the year, and a total loss of purchasing power of nearly 10%—or your total supposed advance. And if graduate school is part of the scenario, you've been set back big time. Add into this equation the likely changes in lifestyle that will occur, and the increased expenses to boot—you no longer buy wine by the screw-top jug, you want better skis and bindings, and, of course, your credit debt has skyrocketed.

Am I getting through to you? Don't panic. I've been there myself. But for those who have opted for real-life learning, as opposed to real-costly higher learning, and who haven't yet begun to invest, the message is: Just do it. Once you have a clear idea of your overall investment objectives, you can develop an investment plan designed to help you achieve those objectives. Your investment plan is based on your ability to determine:

1. What you can invest. Many of us feel as if we have little or nothing to invest. More of us, however, are beginning to invest in our future, through retirement plans like 401(k)s. The benefits of doing this are inarguable—so long as you view your 401(k) or other tax-advantaged, retirement-oriented investment as an active portfolio in its own right, as well as a part of your overall investment plan. (Section 5 has more information on retirement-oriented investment plans.) But you also need to focus on investing for your shorter-term objectives. What's an optimal percentage of your income to invest? A minimum of 5% of your take-home pay, for starters. But you'll need to ramp up your participation to 10% within one to two years—once you've got your overall financial house in order.

2. What you're investing for. If you're investing for your retirement, you can afford to be far more aggressive in terms of the investments you select for your portfolio. If, on the other hand, you're investing for a short-term goal like the down payment on a home, then you'll need to be far more fiscally conservative.

3. What rate of return you'll need to achieve your objectives. You'll need to invest in order to stay ahead of inflation and in step with the market. Using 3% as an inflation rate, and 8% as a conservative market standard, you need to find investments that will deliver an average annual return of at least 8%. Where does history tell you to turn? Stocks, and stocks alone, can generate returns of 8% or higher in the long run.

4. What asset allocation will optimize your chances of success. What percentage of your hard-earned savings should you place

Investing 101

- Stocks have returned 11% a year, on average, since the 1920s. Since 1982, their average annual return has been better than 13%.
- Bond funds return about 5% a year on average.
- Treasuries, or government bonds, return about 3% a year, and are like cash.

in each fund category, e.g., growth stock fund, small company fund, and international fund? If history can be repeated, concentrating your assets in stocks—in particular in large-cap growth and small-cap value stocks—is your best bet.

I like to think of asset allocation as the bones of the portfolio, and individual investments as the flesh. Asset allocation begins with your determination of which main categories of investments (stocks, bonds, and real estate) you want to allocate your assets in. Determining the percentage of your investment within each category leads you to a decision about how you want to allocate your assets within your chosen investment category. For example, you will most likely be better served by concentrating your assets in stock mutual funds (to begin with), and perhaps gradually moving into some individual stocks. Once you have made up your mind about this step, you need to take another: determine within the investment category how much of your investments should be placed in higher- and lower-risk investments. From that standpoint, you can move into the realm of selecting the individual investments you want to include in your portfolio.

There's a detailed portfolio-building design below. For now, what you need to know is that your asset allocation decisions are critical to the overall performance of your portfolio—not simply as it stands today, but, going forward, how well it will fare in tough and robust markets.

When coming to terms with asset allocation, you'll need to factor in much of what you already know: economics, stock markets, interest rates, inflation, investment vehicles, taxes, and your career. This is part of what makes investing interesting, but it can also frighten some individuals away from investing altogether—or in part. Either move is in the wrong direction, since, after all, you're in the driver's seat when it comes to ensuring that your investment decisions are in line with your personal objectives. Of course, you can work with a financial adviser to further your own interests. But even there, you'll want to know enough to make informed decisions—and to be certain that your adviser is at least as informed as you.

PORTFOLIO EXHIBIT

Whether you have just started investing or you have been investing for some time, you will need to review your portfolio periodically to ensure that it's allocated appropriately. Chances are, you'll need to make some adjustments. You may find that one or more of the individual investments (a stock or fund, for example) could be replaced with one that is more in keeping with your allocation decisions, which, in turn, reflect your investment objectives. I'm not advocating changing your asset allocation often. In fact, if you've done your allocation job well, you will have to review it only on an annual basis—or when sudden and dramatic lifestyle changes (marriage, children, career changes) occur. On the other hand, you will want to be more attuned to the performance of the individual investments that make up your portfolio. Again, making many changes isn't on my top-ten list of things to do with your portfolio. But keeping up-to-date on your investments, and their related industries, makes sense.

The following steps will take you through a core asset allocation plan from start to finish. Once you cross the asset allocation finish line, you begin the second leg of the investment biathlon—selecting investments for your portfolio.

To begin with, determine your objective. In this instance, let's say it's building a retirement war chest. Your objective (given your young age) determines the investment categories you want to invest your assets in. Before you even begin to do this, however, you'll need to make a geographical decision: the percentage of domestic (US) and foreign assets in your overall allocation. Here, the younger you are, the more you may want to invest overseas. But this is only true to a point. In fact, foreign markets tend to be far more volatile than ours—which means some will rocket twice as much as the US market in a given time period, while others will plummet twice as far—or farther. Solution? Get the mix right. From the efficient horizon chart on page 202, recall that most commonly the lowest volatility comes when about 30% to 40% of a portfolio is invested overseas.

Step One: Stocks vs. Bonds vs. Real Estate

At home, or abroad, the younger you are, the more important it is to concentrate on categories that have the highest growth potential. There's one: stocks. With that in mind, consider the following allocation:

Stock	Bonds	Real Estate
100%	0%	0%

Step Two: Stocks Funds and ETFs vs. Stocks

Since you're not investing in bonds or real estate, you have leapt ahead of the need to determine the percentage of your assets you want to invest in each category, and have landed on the need to decide how you want to invest in stocks. There are two options: direct ownership of individual securities, and indirect ownership through stock mutual funds. Unless you have amassed over $25,000 (and possibly even if you have), investing in stock mutual funds makes the most sense. Why? You easily get the benefits of being fully invested in the stock market with the benefits of broad diversification.

Stock Funds and ETFs	Stocks
100%	0%

Note: To get the diversification you need through direct ownership of individual stocks, you'd need to own an absolute minimum of a dozen stocks. (But these would have to be chosen very carefully, and primarily from the standpoint of diversification; thirty stocks is a more practical minimum to diversify most investors' portfolios.)

One fund, on the other hand, can offer you well over one hundred stocks in one basket. But owning one fund generally isn't the way to go—since it would bias your portfolio toward a single investment style and manager's focus, which in turn, would no doubt favor some industries over others. How many funds is enough? You don't need thirty—in fact, don't go overboard with the number of funds in your portfolio; instead, concentrate on how and where each fund is invested. Five funds should be more than sufficient. One more note: You probably shouldn't invest all your money in a single family's funds. Again, doing so could bias your portfolio to one way of participating in the markets the funds are invested in.

Step Three: Major Stock Fund Categories

Determine which major stock fund category you wish to invest in—as well as what percentage you want to invest in each category. As you learned in chapter 14, mutual funds come in several different packages—and stock funds come in several different flavors. Selecting the ones that best meet your objectives is crucial to your overall investment success. The following is one allocation among major stock fund categories, together with percentages of assets allocated to them, that could potentially suit your longer-term objective:

Aggressive Growth	Growth	Value	Multi-Cap	International
20%	20%	20%	20%	20%

Step Four: Stock Fund Subcategories

Now you need to decide how you want to allocate your investments in each stock fund subcategory (here defined by investment style and market capitalization, as well as country allocation).

Aggressive Growth	Mid-Cap Value	Small-Cap Blend	Multi-Cap	International
20%	20%	20%	20%	20%

Step Five: Your Mutual Fund Portfolio

Selecting the funds to match your percentages is the next step, but not the final one. In fact, there is no final step to this process—it's ongoing until the day you die (and, if you plan your estate well, you can control your investments from beyond the grave). To begin with, you'll need to build a fairly aggressive portfolio. Let's see how it's done.

1. Know your objectives and risk tolerance. You will need to build a portfolio that offers you both the (somewhat conflicting)

benefits of industry diversification and the potential rewards of asset concentration, while not overstepping your own ability to tolerate the inherent risks.

2. Know your funds' objectives and risks. (To help determine a fund's objective and risk level, turn to chapter 14.)

3. Find out the fund managers' investment styles and performance records. Investment style tends to divide itself into two camps: value and growth. Each camp has a history of performance that is well reflected in the Russell Growth versus Value Index, which we saw on page 164.

As discussed, investment style is a macro concern, while capitalization is a more focused one. You'll want to have a blend of small-cap value funds and mid- and large-cap growth funds—in addition to a well-diversified international fund (i.e., one that resembles the country weightings in the EAFE index; see chapter 8 for details).

As you move from the forest to the trees, you'll want to know about each fund's industry concentration, as well as each manager's ability to deliver solid results. And while past performance is no guarantee of future results, average annualized one-, three-, and five-year returns will help you get a sense of how the manager has done, and might continue to do. Be sure to compare these returns with those of other like-invested funds. What if the manager is new to the fund you're thinking of buying? Find out what his or her record was at a previous fund.

4. Determine what types of industries and stocks every fund and each manager typically invests in. This may take a lot of research—but not a lot of time. In fact, you can call directly and ask the funds you're thinking of buying (or the ones you own) for this information. True, the information may be a bit stale— three months old or so—but it's still relevant. Another way to pursue the question is to research past issues of the several personal finance magazines such as *Money, Kiplinger's,* or *Mutual Fund* magazine. Your fund and its manager might have been profiled in one or another.

5. Establish how the funds in your current (or potential) portfolio correlate with each other. Thinking that owning many funds automatically guarantees diversification is perhaps the most common mistake fund investors make. How can you tell if the funds

you currently (or potentially) own are likely to behave similarly when the market rises, flatlines, or falls? The easiest way is to look at the factors mentioned above (i.e., if the funds' objectives and holdings are similar, the funds are likely to perform similarly). There's also a more technical way to derive correlation. This will require some doing, since you'll need to accumulate monthly returns for each fund over a thirty-six-month period. If you can plug these numbers into a Lotus or Excel spreadsheet, it's fairly simple to determine their correlation. Correlation can tell you how closely the funds' performances move together—as well as against an index that best reflects them, like the S&P 500 for growth funds, the Russell 2000 for small-cap funds, or the EAFE for international funds.

FINAL STEP

Review your portfolio's composition and performance on a regular basis. Reviewing your investment portfolio is the only way you'll know whether or not it needs to be revised. It's also fun. Staying in touch with your investments helps keep at least one of your fingers on the pulse of a very real, as opposed to ideal, world. Don't panic over sudden market moves. Don't get overconfident on upswings. Do learn from history that investing wisely and well will, in the end, help you meet your objectives—no matter how tough the going gets, investing will help ensure that you can achieve a secure financial future.

SECTION 4

Smart Investing Moves You Can Make

CHAPTER 17

Your Best Investing Moves
from Scratch

He was the one who was always coming up with new ways to strike it rich. Whether it was buying a load of oranges off a truck whose refrigerator had gone berserk and frozen the lot ("I'll make a killing in frozen orange juice") or throwing his whole month's paycheck into a sure-thing stock in a company that sold parcels of land on the moon, this guy was the one who had a "gift" for discovering unique markets and ways to invest in them. But every time you saw him coming, you turned and headed in the other direction. In fact, when it came to his more down-to-earth investments, you actually found a good use for his "insights"—you simply did the opposite of whatever he said, and so far, you've come out ahead. The trouble is, he's doing so many things these days, it's hard to commit them to memory so that you can act accordingly.

There's a better way to school yourself in the best ways to invest. In fact, the following are among the best ways to get into the market and regularly add to and protect your investments. But don't try to commit them to memory. Act on them.

THE BEST WAYS TO INVEST IN TODAY'S . . .
AND TOMORROW'S MARKET

1. Automatic investing. Automatic investing is a great way to begin and to stick with a regular investing program. You can have a set

amount deducted from your bank savings or checking account and placed in an investment account with a mutual fund company or brokerage. The logistics of setting up an automatic investing account are easy. All you need to do is request an automatic investment account from your brokerage or mutual fund company. The rest is as easy as spelling out your name, address, and bank account number.

2. Dollar-cost averaging. The prime directive of successful investing is to buy low and sell high. Dollar-cost averaging's aim is to do just that by investing a fixed sum of money at scheduled intervals. In this manner, you are automatically buying more shares when the prices are low, and fewer when the prices are high. But don't look to it to guarantee a dramatic increase in the performance of your investments. Instead, look at dollar-cost averaging as the tortoise's strategy for winning the race.

Here's how dollar-cost averaging works:

	Amount Invested	Price	Number of Shares Purchased
1st period	$260	$ 9	28.88
2nd period	260	8	32.50
3rd period	260	6	43.33
4th period	260	8	32.50
5th period	260	10	26.00
	$1,300		163.21

Total amount invested over five periods: $1,300
Number of shares purchased: 163.21
Average market price: $8.20
Average cost: $7.97

Like automatic investing, dollar-cost averaging is also a great way to discipline yourself to invest on a regular, scheduled basis. The effect of both is basically the same. However, dollar-cost averaging is an investment method, whereas automatic investing refers to a method of withdrawal and deposit. The discipline of dollar-cost averaging helps you keep your cash flowing into your investments, which, in turn, you've chosen because they stand an excellent chance of providing you with a brighter financial future. There's no way to predict when to buy low, but dollar-cost averaging gives you your best overall shot at doing so. How? As the example above illustrates, investing on a regular basis can average out in your favor. Of course, if the stock is a dog that won't get up—or worse, one that keeps going down—then dollar-cost averaging won't help you.

3. Lump-sum investing. Is it better to invest your money in a lump sum or, given the market's recent heights, to gradually invest that sum in regular increments? The answer is that, historically, investing the lump sum right away is your best move—but the answer isn't always easy to swallow, because doing so naturally makes many investors nervous.

If you receive money in a substantial lump sum (e.g., an inheritance, or you were injured in an accident and your lawyer has made good on his ambulance-chasing TV promo), or you've been hoarding money in a savings account and are now ready to invest it, then you'll need an investing strategy that can help you cope with short-term market uncertainty. You're in luck. There are two ways to proceed: invest it all at once or invest in increments over a short time frame.

The most aggressive form of investing your lump sum would be to invest it all at once, 100% in the market if your objective is growth. In fact, this is generally the best way to invest because it puts your money to work immediately—but it is also psychologically a difficult way for many investors to act.

Why? Let's say you inherited $10,000 from your grandmother and put it all in the stock market, only to watch the market immediately slip from the high point of your investment. Watching your inheritance diminish isn't exactly what you had in mind when you invested the money—and many investors, especially those who are relatively inexperienced with the markets, panic and sell after a few down months. But historically this has been the wrong move to make. Investing a lump sum even at a market high puts you ahead of those who invested at the high and then sold out lower. The key is to stay invested.

If you think your tolerance for risk might be less than meets the eye, don't worry. Investing your lump sum in scheduled increments will still deliver the goods (and may even let you sleep better at night). The following incremental lump-sum investing strategy is designed for the more cautious investor, but nonetheless should help you remain steadfast to your goal of investing no matter how the short-term market moves. But it suits your age and ability to reap the rewards from taking some additional risk.

This is, in essence, a form of dollar-cost averaging (discussed above). The following timetable should help you get into the market in a relatively painless way. As the timetable indicates, you go from 100% cash (invested in a money market mutual fund) to being fully (100%) invested. Within the first twelve months of this investment program, your stock exposure is increased from 0% to 100%.

Investment

Category	Now	At 3 Months	At 6 Months	At 9 Months	At 12 Months
Stocks	0%	25%	50%	75%	100%
Cash	100	75	50	25	0
Total	100%	100%	100%	100%	100%

4. Value-averaging. This is another "automatic" investment method. Value-averaging's principle idea is to keep the value of your investment growing by a constant dollar amount. Rather than a set amount each month, you put in just enough to keep your investment on target. If the value of your shares goes up during the month, you put in less (or even take some out). If it goes down, you put in more.

However, even though your percentage return may be greater with value-averaging than with dollar-cost averaging, total profits may be lower, because you invest fewer dollars. In short, since you put less money in as the share prices go up, you inhibit yourself from taking full advantage of a bull market. To be able to keep true to the method, you'll need cash in reserve for the months when your portfolio goes down. Since this reserve money won't be in the market, you'll need to include what happens to the backup money in order to calculate a meaningful total return.

Value-averaging can outperform dollar-cost averaging in times of great market volatility combined with the lack of a sustained upward or downward direction. When the market trends up or down, however, you're better off putting fixed amounts in at regular intervals.

5. Stock purchase plans. You may work for a company that offers a stock purchase plan as part of its overall incentive package. A stock purchase plan enables you to buy stock in the company at a discount. In this way, you automatically come out ahead. But how long you stay ahead depends on the company's performance over time. You will need to do the same fundamental research on your own company's

strengths and weaknesses as you would for any company you're thinking of investing in. For now, consider this option a double-edged
sword. It does provide a great way to cut the cost of investing. But it
also can cut your investment legs out from under you, especially if you
put all your investment dollars into the stock purchase plan. Putting
all your eggs in one basket is a recipe for potential disaster.

6. Stop your losses. Using stop-loss orders can help you limit your
losses on stocks. They enable you to set a floor in a given stock's price
below which you are unwilling to go. For example, you buy a stock
at $8, and you place a stop-loss order at $6 to avoid too much damage
from any sudden market downdraft. (On the other hand, if the stock
fluctuates to $6 you'll sell out at that low price, and maybe miss
the bounce back to $8 or higher.) But stop-loss orders can also help
discipline you on the upside, to lock in a profit. For example, say
the stock you bought at $8 more than doubles to $20 per share,
and you put a stop-loss order in at $16 to lock in your double. (But
if the stock dips to $16 temporarily, then surges forward to $23,
you won't be able to participate in the gain.) In times of increased
market uncertainty, a stop-loss is a walk on the safer side and could
wind up saving you from some deeper loss. On the other hand, if the
stock's price falls quickly enough, you may not get out at your stop-
loss price, but rather may have to accept a lower bid. Typically, for
every seller, there's a buyer—but not every seller will get the price he
or she wants.

7. Buy and hold. If you've done your research, and you're not trying to time the market with the stocks or stock funds that you've purchased, then you should be able to buy and hold for the long term,
since high-quality stocks (like the market in general) have tended to
gain ground over time. What about small companies? Here you may
find yourself buying and selling more frequently, but the same truths
apply: if you have carefully selected your small company holdings,
then chances are you'll fare well over time—namely, far better than a
merely inflation-beating return.

Conversely, studies have shown time and again that trading in and
out of the market on a regular basis not only (a) racks up numerous
brokerage fees and/or taxable gains and (b) increases your stress level
remarkably, it also (c) tends to deliver worse results over the long haul.
This isn't to say that you shouldn't be actively managing your portfolio. Instead, it is meant to be a lesson in diligence (to begin with) and
patience (to profit by).

8. Revise the "7 and 7" strategy. Many long-term investors swear by this old standby for purchasing stocks. It's based on the principle of buying low-P/E (price-to-earnings ratio) stocks with relatively high-dividend yields. It's called a "7 and 7" strategy since the original P/E target was a ratio of 7 or less with a dividend yield of greater than 7%. This discipline helped investors buy out-of-favor stocks in companies that they had determined were fundamentally promising (i.e., no major long-term problems like producing asbestos as your main product). The dividend yield of such stocks (which you will reinvest) is relatively attractive, and the company may increase its dividend to maintain an attractive yield when (and if) the P/E rises. But few stocks in today's market have a P/E as low as 7, and most stocks with 7% yields are too conservative for younger to middle-aged investors. Is "7 and 7" unrealistic in today's market and for your time horizon? Probably—even if you want to try a more conservative value-oriented strategy, a "12 and 5" strategy would probably suit you better.

9. Buy stocks in companies that issue stock dividends. Buying shares in companies that pay stock dividends in lieu of cash is another way to realize a profit since you can turn around and sell your newly issued shares. But watch out. Wall Street doesn't take kindly to overly large dividend payouts. In fact, such payouts reduce the stock's market price, meaning that your overall holdings will decline to the level where you don't really benefit from your dividend sales. Most nonretired investors shouldn't seek big dividends to cash out.

10. Plan on dividend reinvestment plans (DRIPs). Many companies offer investors who already own their shares a bonus for doing so—some in the form of a discount on the price you pay for new purchases of more of their shares, others by enabling you to eliminate brokerage fees when you use the automatic reinvestment of your dividends to purchase new shares of their stock.

Just because a company offers the DRIP option doesn't mean you should invest in it. You'll need to scrutinize such companies the same way you do any other company whose stock you're thinking of buying. However, among the hundreds of companies that offer DRIPs, some clearly stand out over time as top performers, including name brands that you know and most likely use on a daily basis: 3M, Caterpillar, Coca-Cola, General Electric, HJ Heinz, Johnson & Johnson, McDonald's, Merck, Procter & Gamble, and Rubbermaid, to name a few.

How can you research DRIP companies? Get your hands on the "Directory of Companies Offering Dividend Reinvestment Plans" available at Dripinvestor.com. Other DRIP options? *Buying Stocks without a Broker* by Charles Carlson is the classic book on this type of investing strategy. (Your local library will likely have a copy, or you can go to Amazon.com and plug in the title to find this and related books on the topic.) *Moody's Handbook of Dividend Achievers* used to rate over three hundred companies that have increased their dividends over the past ten years—but it ceased publication in 1999 at the height of the last bull market's bubble, when no one was interested in dividends. That's too bad since, as they have historically done over long-term periods, these stocks came swiftly back into favor and even received a significant tax advantage just a few years later. Peter Lynch used to tout this source, and I still look at the last volume for investment ideas—but have to wed the information there with what I can find out on Valueline.com. Also, both Fidelity and Schwab, among other leading brokers, can provide you with dividend reinvestment plans.

Think positive. In a bear market, companies with a consistent history of paying generous dividends have tended to decline less in price than companies that pay little or no dividend. Investors are clearly more confident that such companies will continue to repeat their pattern of largesse—no matter how thin the overall market gets.

DRIP drawbacks: The best DRIP companies are pricey, meaning it will be hard for you to accumulate a lot of shares in them. However, you are buying quality and, more importantly, doing so at a discount, which is the best way to buy quality that I know. Record keeping can be a more lasting nightmare, since every dividend will mean another mailing to you. But more importantly, if you need to sell a DRIP, you won't be able to do it over the phone—or even overnight. Well, that's not quite right as long as you have a fax. That's because when you sell a DRIP you'll be required to present written authorization that it is in fact your intention to sell. Some DRIPs won't take any old written authorization—they'll require that your signature be notarized (which can add another day to the process). One more DRIP drawback is that you'll have to pay income taxes on the reinvested dividends (as if you had cashed them), and you'll also have to pay taxes on the amount of discount you received. But, in my opinion, these drawbacks are more than offset by the benefits of investing in a solid company that offers you the advantage of a DRIP.

11. Forget options (puts and calls). Investing in options may sound like a cool thing to do—but it's an essentially speculative way to bet on the direction of a stock's price. Think of it as being your own bookie,

and creating the spread. Most bookies know one thing very well: namely, how to make money off the suckers who use them. In this case, you're the sucker, and you're using yourself—unless you think you have suddenly acquired the ability to predict the near future of a stock's price (and if you think this, then you shouldn't have any trouble becoming the world's richest person in a matter of months).

There are two basic types of options: "puts" and "calls." Buying a call option gives you the right, but not the obligation, to purchase a set number of shares in a common stock at a specific price at any time during the life of the option. Buying a put gives you the right, but not the obligation, to sell shares of stock at a specified price at any time during the life of the option. So buying a call is a bet that the stock will go up, while buying a put is a bet the stock will go down. All options have a "strike price" (the price at which you may exercise the put or call) and an expiration date (the last day you may exercise the option to buy or sell the stock).

Options can be "written" on individual stocks and more: the NYSE Composite index, Standard & Poor's 100-Stock and 500-Stock indices, the AMEX index, the Nikkei 225 index, as well as foreign currencies, US Treasuries, and commodities futures contracts (to name a few). Options are not written on all issues of common stock, only on the most popular ones. In fact, one of the interesting figures to come out every morning ahead of the market's opening is the quantity and direction of people buying S&P futures. It's taken as a sign of the day's trend—and traders are trendy by nature. You, on the other hand, are not.

SCAMS AND SCHEMES

When it comes to money, scoundrels abound. And they come in all shapes and sizes—from the highfalutin to the lowdown, boiler room, cold call crush. But fortunately we are born with an innate warning system that can still alert us to the presence and dangers of predators in our midst. The problem is that, when it comes to investing, some of us allow the cheese to mask the mousetrap.

The following scam alert is brought to you by your own brain—listen to it. If it sounds too good to be true, it probably is. If it sounds too simple to be believed, it probably is. If you feel you're being pressured, you are. If you think you are being misled, you are. If you think the investment opportunity is less compelling than the person trying to sell it to you, you're right. If you can't understand it, don't buy it.

If the obvious isn't sufficient, steel yourself against the following MOs:

- You're asked for a little (or, worse, a lot) of cash up front. If the investment was truly worth it, there wouldn't be the need for a lot of your cash, since other investors would also see the merits of the investment and flock to it.
- The pressure is on to close the deal immediately. Good investments always last longer than one week—as does the opportunity to invest in them.
- You have never heard of the company trying to sell you the investment.
- You have never heard of the company you're being asked to invest in.
- The salesman is unwilling to send you information about his or her company in the mail or via e-mail.
- You can only deal with the firm over the phone. (Try checking it out at its office, and find out how long it's been in business there.)
- You're told there's no way you can lose money in the deal.
- You're promised you'll get rich quickly.
- It's undeveloped land.

Most of us have probably been solicited by a scheme at least once in our lives. A chain letter is a scheme—promising untold riches that will materialize if only you will participate and pass it on. Pass it up.

The Ponzi scheme is a classic investment scam that recently replayed itself in the 1995 New Era scandal (which saw some of the world's wealthiest and smartest investors get burned to the tune of hundreds of millions of dollars). It's named after its most famous practitioner, Charles Ponzi, a 1920s scamster par excellence. In a Ponzi scheme, an investor is asked to invest a sum of money today with the promise of huge (above-market) returns. The scamster then apparently delivers the goods, with substantial "interest," just as he said he would. The same investor is then asked if he or she would like to invest in another project. Naturally, since the investor has just been given proof positive that this is a legitimate investment—after all, how else could the money have grown so quickly, and why else would this person have paid off?—the investor consents. Filled with confidence, the investor often puts in more money the second time around. However, how the money grows so quickly isn't discussed. (And here's where you can spot a Ponzi scheme from the outset—ask for specific details about how, when, and where the money will be invested, then track down the investment at its source. No luck? Walk.) How does the money grow so rapidly? Simple. The scam artist's ability to grow your money depends on his or her ability to recruit other investors—whose money he then uses to pay you off. This can go on for many levels, until the scamster has accumulated enough dough to make it worth his while to move on (often to a country with rather lax extradition laws). You may have invested five or more times—but it's the one time the scamster doesn't make good that can make clear your financial folly.

Before you invest in anything, be sure you understand what you are investing in and more. For example, if it's a stock in a company you have never heard of before, track down the company's whereabouts, ask for its annual report, and call a few other brokers to ask what they might think about it. (Or ask other investors online.) Diligence in determining whether or not an investment is legitimate is as important as determining whether and to what extent it is appropriate for your objectives. Likewise, when it comes to those who would advise you about where to invest your money, you need to know who you are dealing with. Chapter 19 will help you do just that.

READY RESOURCES

- cnn.com
- Bloomberg.com
- Economist.com
- Forbes.com
- Fortune.com
- Kiplinger.com
- Marketwatch.com
- Money.com
- Smartmoney.com
- Worth.com

CHAPTER 18

Buying Stocks, Bonds, and Mutual Funds from Scratch

Okay, you've got it. You want to invest. But you don't want to have to open up a Swiss bank account and establish residency offshore in order to shelter your $327 from fee-hungry brokers. But when you asked your best friend if he was investing, all he could do was smirk and tell you that thanks to Uncle Donald, not only will he never have to work again, he won't have to worry about investing either—some guy in a pinstripe suit will do it for him. Your dad and mom are still arguing over whether or not they should purchase a new car or take advantage of the sale on twin cemetery plots (a guaranteed inflation-beating investment). You don't know where to turn.

Talk is cheap. (Unless you're calling your psychic at her 900 number.) But while actions may speak louder than words, they can also, when it comes to actually investing your money, put you and your savings at risk. And I'm not talking about the risks associated with the various types of investment vehicles we've been exploring. I'm talking about the more subtle risks of the cost associated with investing. Whether it's a front-end load on a mutual fund, a commission charged by your broker on a stock or bond purchase, or a percentage charged for services rendered by your money manager, there are several ways in which you can lose money before a single dime gets invested.

As the markets and the types of investments offered have grown dramatically over the last decade, so too has the potential for complication and cost for investors. Fortunately, today's individual investor (you) has several cost-cutting advantages over our predecessors—thanks to keen competition among the brokerages for our business. Simple to learn. Easy to implement. You don't want to miss out on the following cost-cutting investing strategies. After all, the reward of learning what follows is that more of your hard-earned money goes directly to work for you.

Not surprisingly, buying stocks, bonds, and mutual funds isn't all that difficult. After all, what kind of a product would it be that failed to enable its buyer easy access to ownership? But there are some basic mechanics involved in the purchasing of each category of investment just mentioned (and real estate is another category with its own rules of buying and selling). How do you begin?

PART ONE: OPENING A BROKERAGE ACCOUNT

When it comes to buying stocks and most types of bonds you'll need to open up a brokerage account—and it's as easy as the click of the mouse. But, while you don't have to leave your house and go to the brokerage office in person, the process will probably be easier if you do. Like opening a bank account, opening a brokerage account is relatively easy once you know the ropes. And like opening a bank account, different types of brokerages will offer you more or less for your money, both in terms of the services they offer and in terms of the price you'll pay for those services.

Fees

Large or small, brokerage firms all charge you a fee for just about any service they perform for you. That's why you need to know the fees you will be charged for every service that your brokerage (or mutual fund company) offers. Periodically review those fees, comparing them with what you were charged last year by your existing firm—and with what other firms are charging now for similar services. That's the only way you can rest assured that your firm's fees aren't outlandishly high. (If they're outlandishly low, keep it quiet.)

As we discussed earlier, for younger investors, mutual funds will probably be the way to go. So, for example, you will need to figure out which mutual fund companies offer you the best investment alternatives and low-fee deals. (Chapter 14 will help you sort this out.) Once you have accomplished this, you can simply dial the fund company and request an account application, the prospectuses for the funds you are interested in, and, if you believe in the company but don't know the names of specific funds they offer, you can also ask the investor representative to send you several fund prospectuses that relate to your investment interest and objectives. You can also ask if the fund company has any investing pamphlets or brochures that help explain mutual fund investing. Many do—and many are well-written and objective when it comes to discussing the mechanics of mutual fund investing. You can do the same thing with brokerage firms for stocks and bonds. However, you need to be sure that such pamphlets aren't your only source of information about investing.

There are three types of brokerages—full service, discount, and deep discount. Like a gas station, it's in your savings' favor to avoid full service. Full-service brokers cost you more money in fees and commissions every time you buy or sell (or even hold) a stock, bond, or mutual fund. You may like to pay more for the luxury of someone filling your own tank—but you get the same amount of gas in your tank for less money if you opt for self-service. Discount brokers offer you the opportunity to service your account yourself while, at the same time, providing you with many of the services that full-service brokers offer—from research to monthly account statements. Not only does opting for a discount broker make smart money sense, it also gives you a more direct involvement with your money and your investments. Deep discount brokers offer no frills, but more buy for your investable buck—as long as you know that you're the only one calling the shots.

If you're able to make reasonable investment choices, the more involved you are in your investment decisions, the better off you're likely to be in terms of making moves that relate to your objectives and goals. (You'll certainly never sell yourself a doggy stock just because the brokerage is sitting on a big pile of it.)

Before you choose a broker, be sure to contact the National Association of Security Dealers, or NASD (nasd.com), to receive a background check on any broker you're thinking of hiring. The NASD will notify you as to whether or not the broker has a bad record—which is well worth knowing in advance. Failing to do so, after all, could have you singing the blues.

Full Service Costs You More

Traditionally, full service offered you the most "service"—from fulfilling your requests for analyst reports on stocks you were interested in buying or selling to actively managing your account for you to making purchase and sale recommendations. But such services don't come cheap. Fees and commissions could run in the neighborhood of 3% or more for every purchase, or sale, of a stock, bond, or mutual fund.

While it's clearly in your savings favor to avoid full-service brokers, there are some strengths that full-service brokerages feel should be noted—although you should scrutinize them. Foremost among the strengths is the amount of research you'll be able to get your hands on by calling your broker. But there's a catch: this research will be done in-house, by the brokerage's team of analysts who, naturally enough, won't diverge dramatically from your broker's point of view—not to mention the broker's list of stocks he's under pressure to sell. Moreover, while this kind of research is among the best the Street has to offer, it's no longer as proprietary as it once was. In fact, thanks to the Internet (see chapter 22), you can set up your own hot list of investment sources, for free, that can prove to be at least as useful to you in your investment-making decisions.

Don't Discount These Advantages

If you don't like to pay more for the luxury of someone doing a job that you can do for yourself, discount brokers are for you. Moreover, today's discount brokers provide many of the same services that full-service brokers offer—from research that's specific to your individual investments to monthly statements of your account and transactions. It costs you less primarily because you'll be making the investment decisions and calling your broker to make your trades, whereas a full-service broker will be calling you with suggested trades. Self-service gives you more direct involvement with and control of your investments to achieve your objectives. Discount brokers are user-friendly. Convenient. Reliable. Hey, they're the smart way to invest. So where's the catch? Not all discount brokers are created equal. In fact, the difference between some discount brokers (in particular those between discount and deep discount ones) can be as significant as the difference between a discount and full-service brokerage. In fact, where a discount brokerage firm can save you in excess of 50% on commissions (the fees charged to your account for buying or selling an investment), a deep discounter can save you as much 90% on the same transaction but there will be no service perks. And today, trading your account online can save you an additional 10% or more off regular full-service and discount brokerage commissions.

The following brokerages are among the leading discounters: Fidelity.com, Schwab.com, and Ameritrade.com.

Comparing the Costs

The services and the charges for everything from placing a phone call to placing an order differ widely from one full-service broker to the next—and from one discounter to the next. As a result, you'll need to do your own cost comparison, similar to the one described in chapter 6 when it came to selecting the best type of bank account and best type of bank for you and your needs. Create your own comparison using the following checklist as your guide:

[ ] How long has the firm been in existence?
[ ] Does it have an office in your area?
[ ] How many offices does it have?
[ ] How many brokers does it employ?
[ ] How many institutional accounts does it manage?
[ ] How many retail (individual investor) accounts does it have?
[ ] How many retail (individual investor) accounts did it have two years ago?
[ ] What commissions are charged for:
  • 1,000 shares @ $25
  • 1,000 shares @ $5
  • 500 shares @ $25
  • 500 shares @ $5
  • 100 shares @ $10
  • 10 shares @ $20
  • 1 share @ $50
[ ] What is the minimum commission charged?
[ ] Is there a dividend reinvestment plan you can participate in?
[ ] Do they offer IRA accounts?
[ ] What is the fee for starting, maintaining, and closing an IRA account?
[ ] Can you buy no-load, no-transaction-fee funds?

Opening the Account

You don't need a brokerage account to invest. You can invest, for example, in mutual funds by directly contacting the fund company. But if you're going to buy individual stocks or bonds, or if you want to participate in one of the best innovations in the mutual fund industry in the last decade, namely, mutual fund networks (more about this later in the chapter), then you'll be better off with a brokerage account. With this in mind, selecting the best brokerage and type of account for you is obviously an important thing to do.

Opening a brokerage account is mechanically as easy as opening up a checking account at your local bank. (For that matter, many banks offer you the option of buying stocks, bonds, and even mutual funds—for a fee. But chances are the performance record of your bank's mutual funds isn't nearly as great as their marketing is designed to have you believe.) But, it is somewhat more intimidating psychologically. After all, you're taking a giant step toward admitting that, at least in some sense, you've grown up. However, just because the mechanics of opening up a brokerage account are easy, it doesn't mean the task of selecting a suitable firm to meet your specific investment needs is a no-brainer. Here are steps you'll need to take.

Step One: Your Nature. Before you open a brokerage account, quiz yourself. When it comes to making a decision about what's best for you:

[ ] You like to be in total control, even if it means having to spend extra time learning about the best avenues for getting you to where you ultimately want to be.

[ ] You seek others' counsel when it comes to making decisions, but ultimately make up your own mind as to what is best for you.

[ ] You feel better listening to someone else's advice and judgment about what is best for you.

[ ] You would rather pay someone to do a job that you could do yourself, but don't have the time to learn right now.

[ ] You would rather learn some basic skills to ensure that you can at least judge whether or not the person you hired to do a job is, in fact, doing a good job.

[ ] You have a bookshelf full of the Time-Life do-it-yourself plumbing, home wiring, and roofing books, and all of them are dog-eared from overuse.

While these questions may seem unrelated to the simple step of opening up a brokerage account, think again. If you're the type of person who likes to be in total control, even if it means having to spend extra time learning about the best avenues for getting to where you ultimately want to be, then chances are you will fare well with a deep-discount brokerage. If, on the other hand, you would rather pay some-one to do a job that you feel you don't have the time to learn right now, then chances are a full-service brokerage is the road to take—at least until you get the hang of it. The bottom line is that deciding upon the type of investor you are planning to be—active, semiactive, or hands off—directly affects the type of brokerage you should select.

Step Two: Account Ownership. You'll need to determine the type of ownership of the account:

1. Single account: The account is solely in your name. You have sole authority to purchase and sell investments in your account.
2. Joint account: This allows either of two signers to authorize the purchase and sale of investments in the account.

Step Three: Type of Account. Once you've decided who has access to your money, you'll need to establish the type of account that you want to open. You can choose from among the following:

1. Cash account. My recommendation. In a cash account, all your transactions must be paid for in cash. This doesn't mean you'll have to trot down to your bank, withdraw a wad of cash, cross town to get to an investor service center, plunk down the cash, and so on. Instead, when you open your account, you'll open a money market account or set up an automatic withdrawal through your existing checking ac-count at your bank. Transfer of funds will be done electronically—as long as there are sufficient funds to cover your moves. The best way to cover your bets is to be able to pay them in full.

2. Margin account. In contrast to a cash account, a margin account enables you to buy "on margin." Buying on margin is similar to taking out a loan to place a bet. Sound stupid? Well, some hot shots think they've got a sure thing and margin their bet—by as much as 50% of their brokerage account balance—to place that bet. But since none of us is infallible, it's clearly a risky way to invest. Not only that but, as with a loan, you're charged interest on the margined amount

(typically based on the prime rate plus 2% or more). What happens if the bet fails to materialize? Talk to Rocco.

3. Discretionary account. What could be worse than you risking up to a 100% loss of your savings by investing on margin? Letting someone else do it for you! A discretionary account allows your broker to invest your money at his or her discretion without getting your authority for each trade. Wrong!

Step Four: Investment Plan. You need to match your investment plan with an account that can put your plan into action. Will you be making annual lump-sum payments, monthly payments, or weekly payments into your account? How will your funds be allocated, when will they be disbursed, and at whose command? With these general facts and figures in mind, you can begin to examine what kind of brokerage account fits your unique situation.

• • •

Once you've figured out what type of brokerage and account are best for you, what amount you want to invest, and how you want to invest it, chances are you can do the rest of the work by simply picking up a phone and requesting the necessary paperwork. Or you can do it online in some instances (for more on this see chapter 22). No matter what the sales pitch, however, don't lose sight of the fees you'll be charged. They add up—to no good.

Bad Brokers

There are always rotten apples—sometimes they come in a bunch. You will need to keep tabs on your brokerage account much the way you do your bank account and loan statements. You should scrutinize every statement you receive from your broker to ensure the following:

- Confirmation of all transactions (should be received within twenty-four hours since you have a maximum of five days to settle the trade)
- Authorization of all transactions
- Shares bought and sold at number and price agreed on
- No unauthorized trades
- (In any discretionary accounts) no excessive trading (known as "churning," which is, basically, one way a broker can generate

more commissions for him- or herself by trading your account often—too often)
- What's in your account is what you expect to be there

If there's any disagreement on one or more of the above, get a specific explanation from your broker. If you can't get satisfaction, try a higher level in the firm. Still no dice? You may have to contact the NASD for further advice.

PART TWO: HOW TO INVEST WITHOUT OPENING A BROKERAGE ACCOUNT

You can invest directly through the company or agency that issues the security or fund. Doing so can save you money, if not time. The following are some of the most straightforward ways to bypass the middleman, and put more of your money to work for you.

Stock Purchase Plans

If you work for a company that is publicly traded, chances are you have the opportunity to participate in something called a stock purchase plan. (Why am I telling you this, since, if you already work for such a company they'll surely have made this point clear? Simple. While most of us aren't working for such companies now, we may be in the future.) What exactly is the benefit of a stock purchase plan? For one thing, you get the convenience of buying the stock directly (no brokerage hassles whatsoever). For another, you can often purchase the stock at a discount to the listed purchase price of your company's stock. Good deal! And there's more.

Such plans also provide you with an opportunity to reap some of the benefits of the future profitability of your firm—if, that is, you stay employed long enough to accumulate a sizable stake in the company stock, and provided that your company is profitable. The last point should be your foremost concern when it comes to your participation in a stock purchase plan. If your company ceases to be profitable, or worse, goes belly up, then you kiss all the advantages of this option good-bye. Your stock may be worth less than the change you've accumulated under your car seat. Is it worth the risk? You have the best inside track when it comes to being able to forecast your company's future worth. I think it's well worth considering, but I wouldn't let my investment in a stock purchase plan exceed 15% of my overall investment portfolio. Remember the benefits of diversification? (No? See chapter 14.) Putting too many eggs in your company's stock purchasing basket is one way to scramble your plans for a safe and secure retirement.

Dividend Reinvestment Plans

Many companies offer dividend reinvestment plans (or DRIPs, as they're more commonly known). What is a DRIP? It has nothing to do with pocket protectors and endless discussions of late nights in some lab lobotomizing mice. A DRIP is one of the best ways to purchase additional shares in a company whose stock you already own. (See pages 262–63.) Participating in a DRIP can enable you to reinvest the dividends automatically in new shares of the stock. Doing so will help you avoid paying out a commission to your broker (or at least sharply reduce the commission you'll pay). Some companies offer shares through such plans at a slight discount to you. You'll need to be sure that you want to continue not to simply hold shares in the company, but that the company's stock will most likely continue to do well. To do so, you'll need to review and, possibly, reassess the reasons that led you to buy the stock in the first place.

Investment Clubs

Investment clubs are an increasingly popular way to invest—either as a group that meets on a regular basis and invests by consensus, or in a more informal way, through online groups that serve more as further resources (and plenty of opinion) about which way to invest in a market, industry, or stock. Strictly speaking, however, the former group is the one that most people think of. The definition is elastic, but an investment club, like the famous Beardstown Ladies, is a group of individuals (few if any professional investors among them) who meet regularly to review and revise their investments and investment strategies by pooling their knowledge and analytical resources to determine what to invest in.

Today, investment clubs (as detailed in chapter 20) surely number in the tens of thousands, and for good reason. They offer the benefits of talking money: encouraging investment ideas and sharing research with others, and, unlike the book club you tried to start last month, this club can reward you with more than an existential longing for a concrete understanding of what Jean-Paul Sartre meant by the transcendence of the ego. Moreover, such clubs provide the ability to lower transaction, purchase, and sales costs and provide the potential for a greater diversification of investments through pooling money with other members. But be careful out there. While I haven't yet heard of an investment club that got swindled by a supposed friend, I'm sure it's happened—and will happen again. (For more on investment scams see pages 264–66.)

PART THREE: HOW TO BUY MUTUAL FUNDS

There are two great ways to purchase mutual funds (beyond those funds in your retirement plan): direct from the fund company or through a fund network. (There's also one lousy way—through a broker who will charge you for the privilege. Forget about it!) Like purchasing stocks and bonds, for the most part, buying shares in a mutual fund requires due diligence on your part. Some fund companies more closely resemble full-service brokerage accounts, with fees to match or best even the most greedy brokerage. Others provide you with ways to get more of your money working for you from day one. For now, let's look at the mechanics of buying shares in a fund.

One option is to buy directly from a fund company. Once you have figured out the type of funds that are best for your portfolio, as well as the specific funds that interest you most, all you need do is contact the fund company by phone or e-mail and request the prospectuses and applications of the funds that match your needs and interests. The list on page 214 will certainly speed up this process, but you can always dial up 800-555-1212 and ask for the fund company's toll-free number. Moreover, there are a host of fund families online that are hot to fill your needs for prospectuses, annual reports, and investment guides. You'll simply need to fill in some blanks and let the fund company and the post office (or e-mail) do the legwork for you. Either way, once you receive the prospectuses and applications (which you'll be able to complete in short order), you can either locate and visit a branch office of the fund company or mail your paperwork back. Also, be sure to take advantage of setting up an automatic investment account to transfer funds directly from your checking account on a regularly scheduled basis, so that your investing process is both specified and seamless.

It's easier to buy funds from several fund families today than it was just a few years ago, due to the introduction of fund networks. Fund networks are basically supermarkets of funds, offering hundreds of funds from over fifty fund families. While there are several fund networks that you can choose from, the two front-runners remain Fidelity's FundsNetwork and Charles Schwab's Mutual Fund Marketplace. Likewise, the two front-runners in virtual mutual fund marketplaces, TD Ameritrade and E-Trade, are worth clicking into.

Fund networks offer a menu of funds from different fund families, which enables you to tailor your overall portfolio. For a complete list of the specific mutual funds available through either network, call them directly or visit them online for more details. Be sure to get and read the prospectus before investing in any fund, and research the fund relative to its peers and your own portfolio.

Why is investing in funds from different fund families advisable? As with investing too much of your money in one fund, or in funds that are very similar to one another, investing your money in funds belonging to one fund family can hinder your portfolio's ability to achieve diversification. How? Though many fund companies will deny it, groupthink is a pervasive and persuasive influence on fund managers under one family's roof. Also, some fund families have historically delivered better results in stock selection, while others have surpassed their peers with bond selection, while still others have a better record abroad than at home. Participating in a fund network will enable you to select funds from those families that have delivered superior results in the past, as well as enjoy access to lesser-known and newer funds.

With the advent of the networks came a new fee designation for mutual funds—the no-transaction-fee, or NTF, fund. Basically, an NTF fund has no up-front transaction fee associated with your purchase. Funds charging loads are not NTF funds, although some load funds may waive their loads for fund networks.

Mutual Fund Network Comparison

Remember when comparing networks to consider the number of funds, fees, and minimums that are subject to change. While opening up a fund network account is a great idea for most fund investors, in particular for you since the initial investment can be as low as $500 for an IRA account or $1,000 for a taxable account, there are differences between networks you will need to know about.

You're sold on investing. Now you are also able to decide which is the best way for you to buy your investments. What's next? Where to turn to for financial advice.

CHAPTER 19

Financial Advisers
from Scratch

Even if you don't know much, chances are better than even that you know that selecting a financial adviser isn't as easy as changing your shorts. In fact, it's a difficult task and the difficulty is compounded by the obvious—few of us really know what we're looking for in an adviser, and few advisers are willing to get to know who we are (since we haven't yet made big money). Which points to one basic fact—that we ought to be able to do this for ourselves, at least in the beginning. But let's say you just have to have an adviser. Chances are you don't—but let's say you think you do. This chapter's for you.

PROFESSIONAL DESIGNATIONS

A matter of degrees. You could hang your shingle out tomorrow and be a financial adviser. Of course, a certificate won't guarantee investment success—any more than past performance will. Anybody with a fairly good background in accounting, or even somebody with a self-taught ability to read financial statements, can do value investing. Some think that when it comes to investing, a number of advanced degrees don't necessarily add a lot of value. But you'll want to know whether your adviser and his or her firm are momentum-driven or strictly bottom-up stock pickers. Take a look:

Certified Financial Planner (CFP)

This certificate, issued by the Institute of Certified Financial Planners, signifies that the individual who has earned it has passed a series of tests showing his ability to advise clients on a host of finance-related concerns including banking, estate planning, insurance, investing, and taxes. Be advised that tests are no substitute for experience, intelligence, and integrity.

Certified Public Accountant (CPA)

A rigorous examination process, coupled with relevant experience and state licensing, makes this certification one of the more meaningful professional designations for those whose career is focused on accounting, auditing, and tax preparation. This designation is an excellent indicator of a level of proficiency in the aforementioned fields, but is less indicative of the person's ability to advise you on non-tax-related investment matters.

Chartered Financial Analyst (CFA)

Like the CPA designation, this one requires a person to pass through a rigorous (three-year) examination process with relevant experience in economics, ethics, financial accounting, portfolio management, and hard-core securities analysis. Among those who would proclaim themselves qualified to analyze an investment's fundamental worth and appropriateness to particular portfolios, those with CFAs typically stand out.

Chartered Financial Consultant (ChFC)

An excellent addition to the CFP designation, this charter is offered to those who are CFPs and who have successfully passed a four-year program at the College of Bryn Mawr covering economics, insurance, investing, and taxes.

Chartered Mutual Fund Counselor

A new designation offered by the National Endowment for Financial Education, showing a financial adviser's enhanced ability to advise clients on their mutual fund questions and concerns.

Question Authority

Asking an individual adviser or any representative of an advisory firm about their qualifications will naturally net you, by the strangest coincidence, a series of parameters, conditions, and standards which they meet perfectly. Of course, this would be amusing if it weren't for one thing: it's a necessary partnership (no matter what the self-help money-management gurus try to sell you in their books, newsletters, or TV spots), and one that could dramatically affect your life. Moreover, just like any significant relationship, there's no guarantee that you'll get out of it what you put in. Comforting, isn't it?

Always get a second and third opinion from people who know better.

If you do find an adviser who is willing to help you manage your money, don't get into bed with the first adviser you meet—or with one you've just met. Remember, behind the vertical pinstripes lurks a horizontal interest—getting into your sack of money. A socioanthropologist could tell you the ways in which investment advisers mimic what car and real estate salespeople do every day. It's the deal of a lifetime, raised to a highbrow art form.

Typically, in under one hour, you'll be convinced that you have to make a decision that could dramatically affect the rest of your life. In a matter of a meeting or two, you'll need to assess your level of trust in the relationship with both the individual adviser and the firm, based on your general impression of their expertise and depth of knowledge. Their experience in the business of investment management. Resources. Tenure of the manager with whom you'll be working. Both the manager's and the firm's experience with clientele of your particular net worth. The firm's dedication to and experience with a specific field you need (such as tax and estate planning—you name it). Avoid firms that don't have that knowledge in spades.

Don't be seduced by short-term performance, but for goodness' sake, pay attention to it. While it's easy to be seduced by performance, it's also the quickest way to cast yourself in the financial equivalent of *The Crying Game*—the one where you wind up needing even more counseling. Surprisingly, however, when it comes to selecting a financial adviser, performance isn't the most important criterion. In fact, it's often way down the list according to Sanford Bernstein's *Future of Money Management in America,* which provides an annual study of the investment management industry. This is the start of the list:

1. Manager's overall expertise.
2. Care manager takes to identify needs.
3. Trusting the manager.
4. Discretion of the manager.
5. Attentiveness of the manager.
6. Manager's desire to establish long-term relationship.
7. Manager's reputation.

Note that nothing has been said about performance. In fact, it's not until you get further down the list that investment track record gets a mention. (And it's not rated as being very important.)

Are you only in it for yourself, or for a wider group? It could be your spouse, children, grandchildren—all of whom have separate but important needs. A good adviser can work with different generations and other investors with different needs.

Is your adviser's pay based on commissions or fees? You'll need to decide between fee-based investment counselors and those that charge a percentage of your money for their business. Here's a hint: fee-based is typically the best way to go. A fee-based counselor will charge you an hourly fee (typically $150 an hour), while a commission-based adviser charges a percentage of your investment return. The larger your account becomes, the more compelling is the fee-based structure.

They work for you. Is your adviser listening to you—or just lumping you into a computer model which, in turn, spits out a "personal" portfolio that bears all the family resemblance of a police composite sketch? How much quality time can he devote to you? The better he can understand your needs, the better he can appreciate what is left unsaid by you—reading between the lines to better react to your changing circumstances and objectives. Your objectives can't be something that can be measured on day one so you can live happily forever after. Fat chance.

Question the size of the firm. (While the size of the firm is not even on the Bernstein list, at one time, it was.) Is the firm too big to pay attention to you and your investment needs? Do you feel like a hapless soul in Kafka's *Castle*? (Run, don't walk to the nearest exit.) Does the person answering the phone recognize who you are? No? How about your adviser?

Unfortunately, going with a smaller firm may not be a better bet. For one thing, the head of the firm—you know, the one who is going to run your account—will more than likely be doing many things besides managing your money. Chances are, he's out pitching his business to prospective clients. You don't want to end up with a chief cook and bottle washer.

No matter what the size of the firm, try to determine what the other diverting, distracting activities are that could potentially impinge on your adviser's overall workload. Ask to be shown the research room of the firm—and ask to speak directly with the analysts. After all, having plentiful resources in-house could mean that your counselor is focusing more on your investments than on office politics.

Research the research. Know your firm's research capabilities. Resources clearly contribute to the quantification of overall expertise of management. So the extent to which there are broad and deep resources would be a measure of potential expertise. However, a brokerage firm's research department, whose reports can be very good, have an ulterior purpose—to create transactions for the brokerage firm. Not so with an investment counselor who is fee-based, i.e., not trying to sell you anything other than his or her service. (Think of your hair salon: they cut your hair for a flat fee—but do they also try to sell you some overpriced styling gel?) Does your adviser do his own research? Are the facilities to do the research on the premises? Even if you don't intend to invest globally, knowledge of global competitors is useful. An adviser with a worldwide perspective understands the global competition that even domestically oriented companies now face.

Are the people you'll be working with experienced in your type of account? Have they been with the firm for one year, or for an average of ten or more years? How long have they been in the business of managing other people's money? How did their portfolios fare on October 18, 1987 (the day after the crash), and how did they finish up the year? You can ask the same question about 9/11—the effects were immediately negative, but soon turned positive. But the most meaningful numbers in the last fifty years of market activity, as far as I'm concerned, come from performance during the five-year period from January 1, 1999, to December 31, 2003. During that time we saw a bull market in both stocks and bonds, as well as a bear market in both. We saw unprecedented volatility, geopolitical unrest, and of course the new terrorist toll on the financial marketplaces at home and abroad. During that time period, the S&P 500, the bellwether index of the US markets, fell 2.8%. Any adviser or fund manager worth his or her fee would have to beat that number by more than 10% with less risk to fit my bill. Those who trail that mark will try to tell you that everyone fared poorly, and will likely try to blame it on everyone but themselves. The truth? Hundreds of mutual fund managers beat that number by a wider margin—and they're not hard to find as long as you follow the steps in this book.

Why tenure is significant: One of the least desirable situations you can face as a client is constant turnover in your representative. Will you be meeting someone new every two or four years or will there be a continuity of relationship? Look for somebody who has at least a ten-year record. The reason for that is, you can have five-year records that constitute a fairly attractive period in the market. Sometimes you don't get a full market cycle unless you go through ten—a period in which you're more likely to see someone who has managed money in both a difficult market and a strong one.

Find the person who is responsible for that ten-year record. In other words, if the management or the senior participants of the firm have changed and yet the firm is showing you a ten-year record, perhaps that ten-year record is not reflective of the current management. (When a mutual fund changes managers it's a new fund.) Finally, the average tenure of a counselor at a firm establishes to some extent the firm's ability to provide a setting and an environment that keeps its good managers—and culls the bad.

Quality of the personnel and their experience is probably the single most important factor. But make sure that the adviser can describe in a commonsense, straightforward manner how he or she buys stocks and bonds and sells securities. The explanation ought to be coherent and easy to understand. Also ask how much of that manager's marketable net worth is invested in the same manner he or she is suggesting your money ought to be invested. If you're talking to a financial adviser who uses mutual funds as investment vehicles, for example, you would want to know that adviser had a significant portion of his or her marketable net worth invested in those same funds. That way, your financial adviser should ideally share your downside as well as your upside.

References? Try asking your accountant and attorney. Ask your estate planning attorney. Even your divorce attorney.

Do you want one-stop shopping? Are you looking to find trusteeship services alongside investment counseling? Do you want your adviser to be able to counsel you in noninvestment areas like estate planning? If so, you'll want that expertise either within the actual counselor or the firm. But be forewarned that there are financial planners who hang out shingles as qualified advisers who can do everything and be all things to all people. If they sell insurance, or if they do wrap fees (fees levied for bonding a group of investment products), they're doing it to you, all right.

Do you want significant input in the management of your money? Some firms will let you steer the ship; others won't take accounts except on a fully discretionary basis. If you are prepared to give up day-to-day control of your money, be sure that you ask for an investment memorandum outlining the adviser's understanding of your objectives and the general approach to be used in managing your account. You needn't go into specifics initially, but do set up the framework. Make the adviser understand what your objectives are, where the portfolio is now, and where you plan for it to go over the next six months, year, five years, and ten years. Some kind of a written understanding of how the account is going to be managed makes good sense.

Is the firm research or marketing driven? Is the firm built one investor at a time—or more than one successful investment over time? A long history of solid performance is more impressive than a long history of a company's existence.

Performance: don't be seduced by it. In fact, you'd be better off resisting spectacular numbers. What's a reasonable range? Rates of return in the 8% to 12% compounded range on an annualized basis are fine. Advisers producing returns in excess of 20% compounded should ring alarm bells in your head! Bottom line: if the pitch sounds too good to be true, step back from the plate. If, on the other hand, you think you have received satisfactory answers to your questions, try a short-term relationship on for size. It might fit your needs forever and a day—or just for this stage of your life. And remember, too, that when it comes to investing wisely and well, you can advise yourself!

READY RESOURCES

- Director of Arbitration, New York Stock Exchange (212) 656-3000
- Director of Arbitration, National Association of Security Dealers (212) 480-4881
- American Arbitration Association (212) 484-4000

For broker/planner background checks:
- abika.com/Reports/Samples/FinancialAdviser.htm
- Institute of Certified Financial Planners (cfp.com)
- National Association of Personal Financial Advisers (napfa.org)
- SEC-Registered Investment Advisers (sec.gov)

CHAPTER 20

Investment Clubs
from Scratch

Remember how cool it was to create a club among your friends? Secret passwords, ripped-out maps from your mom's *National Geographic,* the close air in the attic where you met to build model rockets— a world made woozy with model glue and chalk dust from the wall where you wrote out the day's agenda? Investment clubs aren't too different from the clubs we formed as children. Although this time the goal isn't the moon, it's down-to-earth profit making. And profit making, as the Beardstown Ladies have so finely demonstrated, is within the grasp of a disciplined club. The flip side? A poorly managed investment club can be a great way to self-destruct both your friendships and your finances. However, as you have no doubt gleaned from the preceding chapters, if you fail to take risks, you'll also fail to make profits—and, as with investing itself, setting up a club can be done so that both the risks and the potential returns are managed in proportion to one another.

Starting an investment club is a smart move. Why? Simple. Not only can you pool resources and so diversify a portfolio in stocks, bonds, and mutual funds—but you can probably do so at a discount (relative to the size of the club's account and the brokerage service you jointly decide to use). Another benefit is knowledge. With several club members researching, analyzing, and sharing their insights in their specified industry or general market observations, you stand to learn and know more about both.

Investment clubs are an increasingly popular way to share friendship and profit. In fact, there are over 50,000 investment clubs in existence today, with more than 25% of those clubs active members of the National Association of Investors Corporation (NAIC) (betterinvesting.org). The NAIC individual membership is over 250,000 investors.

Does starting or joining an investment club make sense for you? While you may not have either a lot of money or market know-how to your credit, you may be an asset to an existing club or, if you start your own, the source of inspiration. The following checklist will help you determine whether or not an investment club might make sense for you:

[ ] Do you like making decisions on your own, or do you find other opinions helpful to your overall decision-making process?

[ ] Will you be disciplined enough in your own research and analysis on a regular basis to be able to say with certainty why you have selected, held, or sold every stock, bond, and mutual fund in your overall portfolio?

[ ] Do you enjoy talking with others about investment opportunities?

[ ] Does the thought of sharing the management decisions that affect your money make you feel better or worse about investing?

If, after answering the above, you find that you really are the type of person who likes to make decisions on your own, then, have no fear, you're completely normal. In fact, it's probably better at least to start on your own, first, in order to sort out the type of investor you are (i.e., determine through trial and error the investment style and investments that suit you and your objectives). If you decide that this is the path you will take, you will find that there's an association designed for the individual investor—the American Association of Individual Investors.

If you decide that joining a club would be worth a try, then don't be intimidated by what you don't know. True, stepping into your first meeting will be like stepping into a gym for the first time where everyone seems to have been pumping iron since birth and genetically programmed to have washboard abs. In the club, people will no doubt be quite animated in their discussions of various industries within the overall market, as well as particular stocks that they love, hate, or love to hate. Relax. It's your first time. They've all been there before. They'll welcome you in. Just listen and learn—then take the plunge into the conversation.

By joining an existing club, you can lend your time and ability to research and analyze stocks. How? For one, you will have read this book. Beyond this primer, however, you'll find numerous other sources (many of which are listed throughout this book) as well as specific ways the club members themselves proceed to dissect particular investments. Some clubs will be biased toward a value investment style, others toward a growth investment style, and still others toward an amalgam of both. Some clubs will be biased toward the dominant age group, which, naturally, will affect their investment objectives and, accordingly, the types of investments they consider most attractive.

How to Form or Join a Club

Contact the NAIC for a list of clubs in your area. While club members are likely to be as suspicious about you as you are about them, you might find a familiar face or common ground (shared work history or schooling) that can help each of you feel more comfortable. Be sure you get to the bottom of the club's policies, procedures, and investment style and objectives before you overcommit yourself to it. Chances are that you will find most clubs are slanted toward a much older age group—whose investment style and objectives, as well as the type of investments they select—simply don't relate to your own. Nevertheless, you can make good use of an existing club in terms of learning how they set it up—from membership to research to the brokerage account they use, to what problems they had to overcome. Knowing these in advance may help you circumvent the same problems if you were to start your own club.

Perhaps the best way to start your own club is to join the NAIC and pore over the materials they send you. These materials will help you decide between creating a club—which takes up-front time, and long-term (five-plus years) commitment—versus investing on your own. If, after due deliberation, you decide setting up a club works for you, you'll need to begin the process of designing the club's investment principles and objectives, as well as initiate your search for members.

You may already know who you want. If not, you can consider colleagues at work or among your friends and neighbors. (Faith in the almighty dollar has an interesting way of bonding people together.) But don't let anyone join for the asking. Be selective. Be up front. Be prepared for questions concerning how the club works, what time and money commitments have to be made, who makes the ultimate investment decision (regarding what to buy, sell, hold), and much more.

The first meeting can be informal, but you'll need to ensure that it is also informative. You can bring your package of NAIC material, for example, to the meeting in order to show potential members what's in store. Open the meeting to discussion about the direction, operation, and objective of the club. Keep the mood light but the minds focused on the benefits of investing long term. If you have PowerPoint at home, create a little show on the benefits of investing in stocks and stock mutual funds versus other types of investments. You'll set the tone for potential enjoyment and profit making. Investing is fun; losing money never is. It's up to you to make certain that each member has a seriously good time. To make certain everyone is on the same level, bring NAIC application forms with you to the first meeting, and basically insist that everyone become a member. (No. I don't work for the NAIC. But, I do think that if you are going to start a club, you and your potential members will benefit from this membership. I also strongly recommend that you purchase *The Investment Club Book* by John Wasik—the best book on investment clubs on the shelf.) And, of course, don't forget to set the time and date of your next meeting (typically within two weeks).

You might even consider giving potential members a pop quiz—which you will take, too—just to gauge how much (or little) each individual knows about investing. Don't make it too highbrow, but do point out the strength of knowing one's weaknesses. The following quiz might help you on your way.

- What is the difference between value and growth investment styles?
- How do you calculate the P/E of a stock?
- What is a dividend yield? How is it calculated?
- What is a growth stock?
- What is the difference between a 12b-1 fee and a load?
- What would you consider to be an adequate allocation among stocks and bonds for your age group (twenty-five to thirty-five)?
- What is the advantage of a discount broker over a full-service broker?

- How many individual stocks do you own?
- How many mutual funds do you own?
- What number of funds would you need to create a diversified portfolio?
- How long have you been invested in the market?
- When will you need the money you invest with the club?
  — within five years
  — five to nine years
  — ten or more years

It's worth knowing who is and isn't up to speed on investing basics before you meet again. For one thing, it will help those individuals who are lacking to shift into high gear and prove to themselves and you that they're committed to working in the club's (as well as their own) best interest.

The first formal meeting will need to accomplish three things: (1) establish operational procedures and roles; (2) determine the initial investment amount as well as how you plan to take your initial plunge into the market as a club; and (3) draft the partnership. You will no doubt need to elect a scribe (to take down notes about the meeting—and this can be rotational, since it's a bore), perhaps a president, and more. You'll also need to set out the basic agenda for meetings going forward. The following agenda will help you on your way to running an efficient meeting.

- Elect officers and a president. Decide what happens if there are an even number of votes for and against a specific investment. Someone will have to be the tie-breaker.
- Elect someone to take notes of each meeting and write up a brief summary for ensuing meetings. This is necessary since, after all, agreements on the club's most valuable assets (not the members, the money) are being made and transacted during this time.
- Review company, industry, market, and economic news. You might want to assign members specific "beats" to report on. But every member ought to be vigilant in terms of the markets and the club's investments.
- Review your core list (actual investments) and watch list (potential investments). Creating a core list will no doubt be the order of many of your initial meetings. You can turn to chapter 16 for some

details on how to build a successful investment portfolio. But be sure everyone is up to speed on basic economics, markets, and industries, too. And always keep your club's objective in mind.

- Proceed to a particular portfolio; in the first year you'll be building this portfolio. Portfolio building is a dynamic and fluid activity. But this doesn't mean it's unfocused. Be sure that members are in agreement from the outset as to what the portfolio's main investment objective is.
- Ensure open-mindedness. New ideas, new industries or companies, the possibility of investing in international as well as domestic stocks and funds. You name it (or someone else nominates it) and, for the next meeting, prepare a brief analysis that will portend further research or the end of the idea.

SERIOUS PARTNERSHIP

Setting up a club is serious business. Part of the sobering side is setting up the partnership. The partnership will be the legal entity that represents the club in the real world—from its banking to its brokerage and investment accounts. Setting up a partnership will be explained in detail in your NAIC club kit (get it), but the following pieces of the overall partnership puzzle should be in place before you advance the club from investing theory into investment practice.

- Name and date of the partnership formation
- Signature of partners
- Contribution agreement
- Disbursement of profits and losses to partners
- Bank and brokerage accounts
- Value of partnership share
- Tax identification number of club

INVESTING IN THE MARKET

Once you've got the basic agenda set, and the partnership down, you will need to establish the club's reason for being: investing. How much should each member contribute on a monthly basis? Start small. Twenty dollars should do. And when should the club make its first investment? When you've built up $1,000—purchase shares in a money market mutual fund. From there, build into the market.

Of course, investing in the market requires that you select a brokerage, perhaps a broker, as well as the range of potential mutual fund investment opportunities. Chapter 18 and 19 examined the types and roles of brokerages in your overall investment process as an individual—and the rules generally apply here as well. Be sure that, no matter what type of brokerage you select, you can invest in a wide range of securities including DRIPs (see chapter 17) and no-load funds (chapter 14). Also, be sure that when you hire a broker, you keep tabs on him or her. The following checklist will help:

[ ] Confirmation of all transactions (should be received within twenty-four hours since you have a maximum of five days to settle the trade)
[ ] Authorization of all transactions
[ ] Shares bought and sold at number and price agreed on
[ ] Any unauthorized trades
[ ] Excessive trading (trading more often than necessary, to generate more commissions)
[ ] What's in your account is what you expect to be there

If there's any disagreement on one or more of the above, get a specific explanation from your broker. If you can't get satisfaction, try a higher level in the firm. Still no dice? You may have to contact the NASD for further advice.

MEMBERS ONLY

Clubs aren't for everyone. But, by the same token, they are not just for the older set. In fact, the average monthly contribution from NAIC club members is under $45 per month. The advantages—from research to commitment—may help you stay invested and learn more about investments that you would otherwise not be inclined to do on your own. While there are drawbacks—the collapse of a club could wreak havoc on a friendship—you'll have to weigh them against the potential benefits.

READY RESOURCES

National Association of Investors Corporation (NAIC) (betterinvesting.org)

- *The Beardstown Ladies' Stitch-in-Time Guide to Growing Your Nest Egg: Step-by-Step Planning for a Comfortable Financial Future*, The Beardstown Ladies' Investment Club
- *The Beardstown Ladies' Common-Sense Investment Guide: How We Beat the Stock Market—and How You Can, Too*, The Beardstown Ladies with Leslie Whitaker
- *The Investment Club Book*, John F. Wasik
- *Starting and Running a Profitable Investment Club: The Official Guide from the National Association of Investors Corporation*, revised and updated, Sr. Kenneth S. Janke and Thomas O'Hara
- *Investment Clubs: A Team Approach to the Stock Market*, Kathryn Shaw
- *Investment Clubs for Dummies*, Douglas Gerlach
- *Getting Started in Investment Clubs*, Marsha Bertrand
- *The Complete Idiot's Guide to Starting an Investment Club*

CHAPTER 21

Ethical Investing
from Scratch

Perhaps the most controversial area of investing is the one that's supposed to do the most good, namely, ethical investing. The problem, in short, lies in the fact that few people can seem to agree on what constitutes an adequate definition for ethical investing. In fact, coming to ethical terms with investing is like trying to order dinner with a casual vegetarian who sometimes eats meat, a vegetarian who eats fish, and an ovolactarian who shies away from everything but a bean burrito (where the beans are definitely not fried in animal fat).

While ethical investing can mean several different things to several different investors, there are some recurring themes that most ethical investors share. Foremost among these is a concern over the role their invested dollars will play in terms of supporting companies and their products. Most ethical investors also focus on the way in which a company treats the people who produce its products. This focus typically examines whether or not a company exploits a labor force in order to minimize the expense of producing a product, which it in turn marks up in order to increase its profits, as well as what types of employee benefit plans are offered.

Ethical investors (as a group) also tend to see themselves in contrast with another group of investors—those who invest in "sin" stocks like tobacco and alcohol companies. Other ethical investors seek to impart their political as well as their ethical take on the world by avoiding stocks in companies that produce (in whole or in part) products for the defense industry.

If ethical investing sounds restrictive in nature, it should also, by now, be sounding restricted in scope. Surprisingly, however, there are many solid stock, bond, and mutual fund investment opportunities for the ethical investor to choose from. The trick, as it is for all investors, is to select the best investment opportunities so that you can profit by doing good.

COMING TO TERMS
WITH ETHICAL INVESTING

Take the following quiz to find out if you've got the right stuff to be an ethical investor. Note: being an ethical investor doesn't guarantee that you're either a good investor or a good person.

1. Do you know the difference between "ethics" and "morals"?
   [ ] yes   [ ] no
2. How much of your recyclable trash do you recycle?
   [ ] all   [ ] most   [ ] some   [ ] none
3. Describe your bank's community involvement:
   [ ] active   [ ] passive   [ ] too global to act locally
4. Do you know where your clothes are made?
   [ ] all   [ ] most   [ ] some   [ ] none
5. Do you know where your clothes' materials come from?
   [ ] all   [ ] most   [ ] some   [ ] none
6. Do you know who makes the cans your soda sits in?
   [ ] yes   [ ] no
7. Did you look up the difference between "ethics" and "morals" yet?
   [ ] yes   [ ] no
8. Do you know where your over-the-counter drugs are made?
   [ ] all   [ ] most   [ ] some   [ ] none
9. Do you ever think about not buying a product because it is:
   [ ] made out of a material from another (previously) living being
   [ ] made from a natural resource as opposed to an available synthetic resource
   [ ] made by a company that also makes products designed to do harm to others
   [ ] made by a company you know nothing about

[ ] made in a country where human rights violations are
common

[ ] made to further a cause that you wouldn't send a charitable donation to

10. Have you ever discussed ethical investing with your:
[ ] friends
[ ] parents
[ ] colleagues
[ ] broker
[ ] investment adviser

11. Have you ever felt remorse for purchasing a product that you
found out was made by a country where freedom to invest as
we do is limited or nonexistent?
[ ] yes   [ ] no

12. Do you think the following are true:
[ ] In China, laborers are often paid less in one week than
you're paid in one hour.
[ ] In Norway, hunting whales is celebrated.
[ ] In Japan, ordinary investment clubs are illegal.
[ ] In Mexico, exploiting cheap laborers threatens US
workers.
[ ] In Thailand, prostitution is among the country's most
profitable industries.

13. Would you ever invest in a company that either resides or does
business in a place you would consider unsafe to visit?
[ ] yes   [ ] no

14. Do you ever choose to buy things at a local independent store in
order to support it, even though you know you could just as easily and more cheaply purchase them from a national chain store?
[ ] yes   [ ] no

15. Have you looked up the difference between "ethics" and "morals" yet?
[ ] yes   [ ] no

16. Did you just look up the difference between "ethics" and
"morals"?
[ ] yes   [ ] no

17. Would you refuse to buy a product that you knew was made
by child labor (aside from the roadside glass of lemonade
for 50¢)?
[ ] yes   [ ] no

18. Do you know which companies your mutual fund(s) invest(s) in?

[ ] all   [ ] most   [ ] some   [ ] none

19. Do you know which countries the companies you invest in do business?

[ ] all   [ ] most   [ ] some   [ ] none

20. Have you ever exercised your shareholder rights?

[ ] yes   [ ] no

21. Is the goal of your investments more than to make more money?

[ ] yes   [ ] no

22. Would you consider an investment that would make less money but would, in return, more closely match your own personal values?

[ ] yes   [ ] no

23. Given the chance to, would you decline to invest in a company that makes a product that is illegal?

[ ] yes   [ ] no

24. Would you prefer not to invest in a company that promoted a product to a specific age group, even though that product would cause health problems for that age group?

[ ] yes   [ ] no

25. Have you ever volunteered to work for a political campaign?

[ ] yes   [ ] no

26. Have you ever volunteered to work on a project for no money?

[ ] yes   [ ] no

27. If you could own the house of your dreams by investing in one company whose only product was the detonator for a neutron bomb, would you pass it up?

[ ] yes   [ ] no

28. Would you decide not to invest in a company that produced substances essential to the manufacture of chemical weapons even if you knew that if you *did* invest, you could amass a sizable enough fortune to successfully lobby against all such weapons?

[ ] yes   [ ] no

29. Do you use only cleansers that are nontoxic to you and the environment to clean your house and car?

[ ] yes   [ ] no

30. If you could only get a mortgage from a bank that is known to provide little or no minority lending, would you:

[ ] wait a few months and try to requalify at a bank with a better record

[ ] take the mortgage, no questions asked

[ ] take the mortgage, but ask to speak with the bank's president about its restrictive lending record

31. Do you give change to people on the street:

[ ] often

[ ] sometimes

[ ] never

32. Do you send a small charitable donation to a local shelter for homeless people or battered women?

[ ] often

[ ] sometimes

[ ] never

33. Are you a registered voter?

[ ] yes

[ ] no

34. What type of bag do you ask for at the grocery store?

[ ] paper

[ ] plastic

35. Do you recycle your wire hangers instead of tossing them out?

[ ] yes   [ ] no

36. Would you consider taking one week of your vacation time to volunteer in an urban renewal project?

[ ] yes   [ ] no

37. Would you be more inclined to invest in a company that provided solid medical and retirement benefits for its employees even if doing so meant cutting into its profit margins?

[ ] yes   [ ] no

38. Do you consider yourself to be an ethical person?

[ ] yes   [ ] no

39. Do you consider yourself to be an ethical investor?

[ ] yes   [ ] no

40. Would you consider ethics as a viable investment consideration when thinking about buying or selling stocks, bonds, and mutual funds?

[ ] every time   [ ] sometimes   [ ] never

Scratch Scorecard

Answering the above questions may have (a) heightened your sense of your potential role in responsible investing, (b) increased your ire concerning those who would tell you how you go about your own business, (c) made you more inclined to read the rest of this chapter, and/or (d) made you less inclined to read on. Reading on is strongly suggested, since, after all, you took the time to fill out the above and now might want to know just how well you scored. Not that scoring well means anything, especially if you're a cynical quiz taker—you know the type. They think about which answer is most likely to score well, regardless of their true first response. If you fall into this camp, the following won't do you much good. If, however, you answered the questions about ethical investing honestly (i.e., ethically), then you might benefit from the following scorecard.

To rate yourself, first total the number of the various answers from the questionnaire.

Total of *yes, often, all,* and *most* (and the like) responses:

Total of *no, never,* and *none* (and the like) answers:

Total number of *some* and *sometimes* (and the like) responses:

50 or more. You're good. You're real good. I bet you don't even cross a sandbox without checking for ants (which you then sidestep). Chances are you won't be shaken from your path of living and investing well within your definition of ethical means. Since this is the path you've chosen, you should pay particular attention to the remainder of this chapter since it will help you review your current investment portfolio in light of your ethical and investment objectives as well as present you with some of the best ethical investment strategies and opportunities in the market today.

40 to 49. You tend to be better at being good than you give yourself credit for. You might not have ever considered yourself to be an ethical investor, but in effect that's what you are. After all, look at the way you steer yourself away from products and companies that participate in doing harm (to the environment or to other living beings), and steer yourself toward those that help raise the standard of good business practices. Since this participation is, on some level, unconscious when it comes to your actual investments, you can benefit from this chapter's explanation of how to discern the level of ethical intent and action on the part of a company or mutual fund (that invests your

money in several companies). You'll also learn how to be more pro-
active in your future investment decision making so that you can wed
your profit with your own well-developed ethical practices.

30 to 39. So you never really thought about investing and ethics in
the same boat. Relax. It's a big boat—and one in which most of us find
ourselves. (The problem is, this boat has all the earmarks of being the
next *Titanic.*) As a result, your investment portfolio might be jam-
packed with companies that exhibit characteristics that, were they to
be present in a friend or colleague, would give you reason enough
to reevaluate your estimation of them, and your feelings as well. Igno-
rance used to be bliss, but now that you've taken this quiz the only
way to return to the state of bliss is to actively turn your back on the
question of ethical investing. Reading this chapter will help you come
to terms with your own quandary, as well as demonstrate that being
an ethical investor isn't nearly as constricting as you might think.
After all, the definition of ethical investing is, in reality, a question of
morality and not ethics at all (as you would know by now if you had
checked the definitions of "ethics" and "morals"). Morals are socially
defined, malleable, flexible, open to interpretation and challenge. This
chapter will help you stretch your thinking about investing to the
point of returning to your existing portfolio with some potential
changes in mind.

Less than 30. Okay. Maybe the devil makes you do it. Chances are
you could care less whether you are even reading this blurb. You invest
to make money—period.

A MORAL DECISION

Most people confuse ethics with morals. This gets in their way of their
being able to determine between questions concerning what is basically good and evil, and what the majority interprets to be acceptable
and unacceptable. That's why, aside from the financial merits, when it
comes to investing in companies that are solid citizens, it's easy to find
yourself questioning whether or not the company is a good company.
For one thing, it may have just donated a new playing field to your
town, while, at the same time, its manufacturing plant is located in an
area where pollution controls and labor regulations are virtually nonexistent. While a company may be a good citizen, it can also be a bad
neighbor. By the same token, if you're investing in a company that

participates in actions that you don't find acceptable, the company may not be unethical.

The decision as to how great or little a role the question of ethics will play in your overall investment decision-making process isn't up to you—the way we'd all like to think that it is. If ethics were up to us, we'd have to rename it morals. The reality is that ethical investing is really a form of social responsibility made manifest through investing. Sound confusing? Well, in a sense it's a good thing that it is—since it makes you think twice about the kind of company you're invested in from a wider angle than a profit perspective alone. In short, asking yourself more questions about a company's business practice is a great way to be more diligent and vigilant about your research and investments.

Too much of a good thing? Well, there are those who argue that ethics and investing shouldn't be in the same equation. I advocate a more profitable middle ground—one that seeks companies based on their financial and business ethic merits together. But what exactly does this mean? The following might be a likely conversation with yourself: "Do I invest in tobacco companies (or in mutual funds that do)?" Your response might be, "Not knowingly, although I do invest in funds that could easily do so since, as far as I know, there's nothing written in the prospectus about not doing so." Does this make you an unethical investor? I don't think so.

Ask yourself the following:

Am I conscious of what companies I invest in are up to in terms of their labor and business practices? Not necessarily, but I can find out more.

Do I want to take the time and effort to do this? Not really. But a quick glance at my funds' holdings should help me answer, in general, whether the overall investment picture is good or bad. Besides, I know I own stocks in a company like IBM, which surely manufactures some of its parts in some fairly questionable regions in the world.

Does that make IBM a bad company—or me an unethical investor? I don't think so. By the same token, I don't own R.J. Reynolds since I do believe its product is harmful to the health of those who use it—and of those who are around those who do.

Does that make me an ethical investor? To a certain extent, I guess it does.

Figuring out the ethical intent of a single company can be simple, as in the case of a tobacco company. Figuring out the ethical makeup of a large, diversified company requires that you dig deeper. For example, IBM makes parts for defense systems, and the parts themselves may be manufactured in areas where human rights violations and labor regulations are lax. But does this make IBM a bad company? It has one of the better employee-benefit structures going in corporate America. It's an excellent, tax-paying citizen. It does the right thing by its employees and shareholders. You'll have to think about it. The same negatives hold true for most manufacturers, while the same positives don't. So, on a relative basis, IBM wins. On an absolute basis, it's your call.

Mutual funds pose a particularly difficult problem for the ethically inclined investor, since your qualitative concerns can be overwhelmed by the quantitative reality that there are more companies in a fund's portfolio than you can shake a stick at. In fact, some funds invest in hundreds of companies. Getting to know each one up close and personal may not be in the cards—and the fact is that some funds sell and buy faster than you can get to know the companies they hold. Solution: determine the top five industry weightings of the fund's current portfolio. This can be done by glancing at the most recent semiannual report or prospectus. (For more on dissecting a fund, turn to chapter 14.) Figuring out which industries your fund emphasizes can give you an essential clue as to the fund's overall ethical intent. For example, the following industries might be considered dubious by a peace-loving, animal-rights-oriented vegetarian: agriculture, biotech, chemicals, defense/aerospace, and energy.

You can also determine the top fifteen company holdings in terms of their percentage of your fund's overall assets. Not only will that give you an idea of which companies the fund manager has bought, it will also serve as an indication of the types of companies he or she will be willing to buy.

AN ETHICAL INDEX

There is an index composed of companies that meet specific ethically minded and socially practicable criteria. Created in 1990, it is designed as a competitive standard to the S&P 500. Known as the Domini Social Index 400 (DSI 400), it's named for the woman who invented it, Ami Domini; she also manages some "ethical" funds. This market capitalization–weighted common stock index monitors the performance of four hundred companies that successfully pass the following screens: positive record on the environment; employee benefits; community action; safety and usefulness of the products. Companies that won't pass muster on this index are those with significant military contracts; significant involvement with the nuclear industry; commitment to the tobacco, alcohol, and/or gambling industries.

ETHICAL INVESTMENT OPPORTUNITIES

How has the DSI compared performance-wise to the S&P 500? Let's take a look:

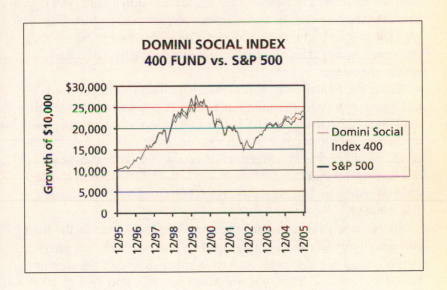

Bottom line: You can make good money investing ethically—but not great money! And that gets to the heart of the matter: the difficulty in life is not to be great—it's to be good.

YOU'RE A SHAREHOLDER, YOU HAVE THE RIGHT TO TRY TO CORRECT A WRONG

There are basically two ways in which you can apply your social investing inclinations: avoidance and engagement. Avoidance can come in two forms: either you never invest in or you sell stock in companies whose ethics you come to question. But is there a better way? Well, it's an age-old problem—to avoid or to work from within. If you think that you can make change happen (and, you can at least try), then I would recommend that you become familiar with your shareholder rights, and activate them.

Shareholder rights are not just for the fat cats. In fact, if you invest, you have them. As a shareholder (in a stock, or mutual fund) you own a piece of the corporation. In doing so, you create the opportunity for yourself to stand up and be counted. Granted, you may be the only one standing, but at least you can begin to raise the level of consciousness in the room.

Becoming an active shareholder is easier than you might think. In fact, one way to start becoming an active shareholder is through the mail—sending letters to the CEO, CFO, CFA, and board members will let them know where you stand on your belief that the company, while good, could become much better. Of course, it's only your personal opinion. And there is no guarantee your letter will be read by the person you send it to. Is there a way around this problem? Of course. It's called a proxy.

Always vote your common stock proxies. They come in the mail and you simply fill them out. If you don't, the board will vote for you. Do you let other people vote for you in other spheres? I thought not. So, get involved and fill out the proxy. Want to take it to the next level? As long as you have owned $1,000 worth of stock in the company for more than twelve months prior to the company's annual shareholders' meeting, you can stand up and be counted—directly, by sponsoring a resolution for a vote on a subject near and dear to you.

There's more that you can do. You can also submit a proposal for changing corporate policy. You'll need to do this by the book, however, since a proposal of this kind is strictly regulated by the SEC. The best way to proceed on this front is to get ahold of "The Shareholder Proposal Process," a sixteen-page guide that's put together by the National Shareholders Association and available at no cost to you. In a matter of minutes, you learn how to propose change.

Another way is to transfer your proxy to an organization that you believe in. The drawback to doing this is that it takes your vote out of your hands. If you want to pursue this course of action, but don't know where to turn, contact the First Affirmative Financial Network. FAFN will help you unite with institutions or coalitions that are sponsoring resolutions on issues that match your own agenda.

SOCIALLY RESPONSIBLE INVESTMENT FUNDS

One of the great ways to build a list of companies you might consider investing in is to request a prospectus and semiannual report from a socially responsible fund. First, you'll need to build a list; it will take some time to research those companies to discover which ones you deem acceptable—and which you don't. And this leads to the second accomplishment, namely, coming to see that there are different interpretations of what ethical investing is, and which companies count. Or, you could cut to a list of socially responsible funds put together by the Washington, DC–based nonprofit Co-op America (coopamerica .org), a group dedicated to wedding the goal of profit with the ideal of a better world.

ENVIRONMENT-FRIENDLY FUNDS

Some funds focus on one specific industry in order to provide investors the opportunity to concentrate their assets in a focused, as opposed to diversified, investment vehicle. While doing so can set you on a collision course with risk, it can also serve as a beneficial piece of an overall portfolio's pie.

When it comes to socially responsible funds, some concentrate on a theme that is near to the heart of many like-minded investors: the environment.

But keep in mind that investing in a fund that concentrates its assets in one theme can be as messy as investing in one that only invests in a single industry. You'd be well advised to consider a more diversified approach to your ethical investing. But if you think you'll clean up by investing in the environment, try limiting your commitment to under 10% of your overall portfolio.

RESPONSIBLE PARKING PLACES—FOR YOUR CASH

Money market mutual funds are a great place to temporarily park your cash. But, to an ethical investor, parking that cash in certain money market funds can be like illegally parking in a handicap zone. Such investors might prefer one of the money market funds listed on coopamerica.org.

AN END IN ITSELF?

Some people view money as the root of all evil—but it would be hard to build a church or temple without it, just as it would be hard to keep a roof over your own head and food on the table. But the flip side is that you can do well by doing good (to a greater or lesser extent). And, perhaps more importantly, if you invest in accordance with your conscience, you just might be more inclined to stay fully invested—no matter what temporary tempest the market is tossing your way.

READY RESOURCES

- The Clean Yield Newsletter (cleanyield.com)
- The Social Investment Forum (socialinvest.org)
- Co-op America's Socially Responsible Financial Planning Handbook (coopamerica.org)

CHAPTER 22

Online Investing
from Scratch

In a word, Google it! The world of investments hasn't changed all that dramatically in the last century—but the realm of investment research, as well as your ability to access it, is changing minute by minute. In addition, the ways of requesting, and receiving, annual reports, prospectuses, and applications for brokerage accounts, mutual funds, and more is changing daily. Investing has become a dynamic, interactive, online event for individual investors like yourself.

Unplugged? Let's start with a basic distinction between online services and the World Wide Web. Online services differ from websites in that they offer you a range of sites to browse and members to converse with, whereas the Web is open to anyone with access to a server—either through an online service or a lower-cost server. Generally, an online service will cost more but will provide a larger menu of services. The Web will cost less to access but, by the same token, takes some knowledge to navigate and to separate the investment wheat from the chaff.

Online investing isn't the wave of the future. It's here and now. And while many people may use a paid online service or server to participate in areas of interest to them, the truth is there's one area that can return the favor in a more rewarding manner than idle chat. It's the virtual world of investing. That world is divided into two distinct, but unequal halves—online services and the World Wide Web—but there are dynamic links between the two that enable you to cruise back and forth on a superhighway of real-time information and data. If you prefer, you can pull off the infobahn and park at hundreds of dead-end repositories of historical investment data, charts, and commentary. No matter which way you turn, however, one thing is clear. When it comes to investing, there's no need to take a back seat. In fact, your keyboard can put you in the driver's seat when it comes to researching your own investments.

There's a catch with the info highway. New sites are built every day. An increasing number of free sites are changing into paid services. It's hard to tell the wheat from the chaff—and even finding the wheat doesn't guarantee you'll net gains. No matter.

Chances are, some of the sites that you'll find named in this chapter may no longer exist by the time you read this. However, there are several main sites that will be around for a long time to come. The point is to get used to feeling your way around the Web to locate the sites that are most useful to you and your investment decisions. When it comes to the online services, the process is even more streamlined.

How to Get There

Online services: Online services continue to grow, some faster than others—and some better than others. Fortunately, you can test-drive each site, free, in order to select the service that best suits your needs. Concentrate your time exploring the investment sites already in existence on the online service. That in itself could take ten hours.

If your Mac or PC didn't come equipped with preloaded trial runs of every major online service, it's not hard to come by them. For one thing, they're in the mail and in the shrink-wrapped issues of *PC Week* and other computer-related magazines—including a growing number of online and Web-specific magazines. For another, they're online.

They're a snap to install and work, since prompts along the way tell you what to do next. In fact, they're kind of fun and, more importantly, add value to any investor's research capabilities.

The Web: People talk about the Web as if it's free. The truth is, for most of us it isn't since we at least pay for the DSL or cable line.

As with your decision between a full-service broker and a discounter (which weighed in favor of the discounter), you need to assess your level of literacy with the medium, as well as your desire and need for service. Online services provide comprehensive market coverage, research libraries, real-time quotes, discussions of the market and every category and type of investment, as well as the ability to tap into areas of interest to investors who are like-minded (and contrary). The online services provide excellent investment resources plus the ability to link to websites. They're a best of both worlds but you'll pay a premium price for them. True, by themselves, the online services would pale in comparison to the volume of information available on the Web. Also true: websites are becoming increasingly dynamic in terms of being interactive, useful, user-friendly, and easy to find.

Online services moved swiftly from an increasingly generous menu of investment sources and market commentaries to a flood of information. So long as you use Google as your Noah's ark, you can navigate the torrent and find your way to some meaningful market insights. Since you can't jump onto the Web with a six-gun at your side, you'll have to learn to tame it in more peaceable terms. The following reminders should help you do just that:

- Be patient.
- Don't be intimidated.
- Be persistent.
- Don't allow yourself to get sidetracked.
- Know why you're going online and where you're heading.
- Keep an accurate list of the pathways to sites you like (create a hot list, and save that hot list in a hard-drive file so that you can retrieve it if your online file gets corrupted).
- Review your research process for possible streamlining.
- Don't give out your name and address willy-nilly.
- Never reveal your account password. (And do change it often.)
- Avoid giving any information about yourself—most websites are set up to get such information since the site can then sell your name and address to other businesses.
- Avoid hot investment tips.
- Always scrutinize everything you read or are told online.
- When it comes to online banking and investing, review the security checklist in chapter 6.
- View the Web as a wide net that yields potential for fun—and profit.

YOU ONLINE

You know the drill. Type "investing" into your Google toolbar. Click enter. Net: 10,600,000 matches. Type "funds." Click enter—29,600,000 matches. Type "stock funds." Click enter—5,270,000 matches. Type "Help." Click enter. Get 315,000,000 matches. Type "What am I doing here?" Click control, alt, delete. Scream. Break the last remaining pencil on planet earth. Grab yourself an Ultra. No. Grab two.

Today, there are those who proclaim that we live in an informed age. The truth? We live in an age of information—overwhelming information—where smart guys finish first and losers suck dust. This is perhaps most true in the realm of online investing, where there's an avalanche of information about mutual funds that's just waiting to bury you. There are also a handful of fund sites that you simply can't afford to do without. This guide will help you sort 'em out.

Let's face it, the smart investors (that means you) will know how to rule the information that is most relevant to them—whereas the foolish investors will let the information rule them. In these turbocharged fund investing times, survival of the swiftest (both in terms of getting the right information at the right time, and in knowing how to apply it) determines who will thrive in the market—and who will merely survive it. One key: get plugged in.

Gotta get plugged in. Otherwise, you'll be left to the mercy of someone else's research, recommendations, and timing of your trades. (It's only money.) On the other hand, plugging into online investing can give you total control over your own investments. It's easy once you know how.

It's no secret that the Internet and online services like America Online provide a way to keep fully current with your fund investments, as well as the range of themes that affect them. But beyond the fund investment info glut, the Net also provides the most efficient way to invest in funds (and the most cost-effective—most fund families offer Web traders substantial trading cost cuts since they're doing all the work). Sure, there are some disconnects along the way—a busy day in the markets can leave you left out of the action (as many customers on most online trading sites have already discovered at one time or another)—but who said the world of web was perfect?

Despite the glitches, no one I know of can afford to remain clueless when it comes to online investing. To get (and stay) ahead of the dead heads, you'll have to become a net head. Clicking into the following will get you your digerati diploma.

If you are completely new to the Web, perhaps the best way to begin is to select one of the major online services: America Online (AOL), Microsoft Network, Verizon, or Earthlink. Online services are cost-competitive with straight Web servers (around $20 per month for unlimited access time), and offer a more tailored, user-friendly environment in which to pursue research-related work. Also, such services also provide access to the Web itself. The major online services generally provide a good start, with financial news and quotes, articles providing general money-management and investment advice, and live forums where you can participate in question-and-answer sessions, often with participating money-management experts and investment notables, such as mutual fund managers, market gurus, and authors.

The Internet servers provide access to the wider array of investment sources off the bat—and many investment sites on the Web are mimicking the online services' chat format. Growing in number, the basic difference between such servers is cost and accessibility. Many servers are behind the times in terms of speed and user-capability. This can translate into busy signals, disconnects, and slow searches. Once you've selected your server you'll need to choose a searcher. You know the names: Google wins—but Yahoo contends—and both are now name brands as familiar to most of us as Coca-Cola, McDonald's, and Game Boy.

Hot-listing a handful of active financial news sites creates a virtual resource room that can rival a business library's stacks—and it puts you in the driver's seat rather than at the mercy of whoever is pushing information your way. Such websites are modeled on magazines or newsletters, but they're on the Internet, where each page is a screen on your computer. Some are virtual mirrors of their hard-copy progenitors, while others are distinctly unique siblings with novel ideas all their own, like filling out worksheets wherein the Web server performs calculations and dishes out answers or advice. Very cool and, on the plus side, most are free to visit, and none of them has any magic way of charging you money without your knowledge. On the minus side, more and more sites are starting to charge customers, in exchange for a password needed to access the most interesting or most recently published parts of the site. Fortunately, right now, you can still access some of the best sites at no cost.

Bottom line: Access to information doesn't guarantee successful use of it. Investing with these sites in mind does.

MAJOR PLAYERS AND NICHE SOURCES

Nothing new under the sun? Check out "sun" using your Web browser and you will see there's plenty that's new. But don't stare at the sun too long. You've come this far; the next level is up to you. And that's learning where some of the most significant investment sources on the World Wide Web are located. You can always start a search by using Google or Yahoo (yahoo.com) and typing in the word for the subject matter (e.g., economy, stocks, mutual funds) or specific name (e.g., the name of a company, security, or mutual fund) in which you are interested. Or you can review the hot sites discussed below that shouldn't be missed.

STOCKS, BONDS, AND MUTUAL FUNDS

Use your browser to help locate any sites that are exchange specific. As of this writing, all three major US stock exchanges (NYSE, AMEX, NASDAQ) are on the Web. However, by the time you read this, chances are all the major exchanges will be out there—in virtual space awaiting your cursory glance. Fortunately, the Web isn't all that constrained by what it lacks—since it offers so much. Take a look at one or more of the following:

Ipodata.com is a unique website that offers investors the ability to track initial public offerings—plus a searchable database of those IPOs. Although bonds shouldn't be a large part of your portfolio (see chapter 11), if you want information about them you can click into bondsonline.com and also be sure to visit the Federal Reserve Bank of New York site for quotes on US Treasuries and bonds (ustreas.gov).

Some leading full-service brokerages offer free sites worth visiting, but you might have to yield your name to enter, which could translate into never having an uninterrupted dinner again in your lifetime— since brokers love to call when you're home. Still, the information available on the following sites is first-rate:

Merrill Lynch (ml.com)
Morgan Stanley (morganstanley.com)

Many fund companies have done their Web work. Some of these sites offer full-blown financial and investment resource centers, while others provide fund-specific details and prospectuses. The following list is by no means exclusive. However, the following fund families have done a better than average job at providing investors with some serious investment tools and information:

Fidelity (fidelity.com)
T. Rowe Price (troweprice.com)
Vanguard (vanguard.com)

COMPANY RESEARCH

If you're thinking about buying stock in a company, and you want to know some deeper details than its name, check out EDGAR (Electronic Data Gathering and Retrieval). This is the SEC's database of electronic corporate filings. Here you'll find filings from most publicly trade companies—from large-caps to small-caps. EDGAR provides customized company reports as well as bulk data. To get there: edgar-online.com.

MARKETS AND ECONOMY

The following sites will yield a bountiful crop of hard data on the overall markets and economy. Each online service has a market center with updated market statistics, commentary, and related news. On the Web, you can quickly locate current news of investment note by heading directly to the *Wall Street Journal* site (wsj.com). You can also move to one or more of the following sites for further information:

Bank of America Capital Markets, for economic news and data
 (economy.com)
Bloomberg, for economic and market statistics (bloomberg.com)
Census Bureau, for demographic stats and studies (census.gov)

INVESTMENT E-ZINES

What is an e-zine? It's a live magazine—live on the Web, that is. Most of the major finance magazines, from *Fortune* to *Smart Money* magazine, are available on the Web as well as through the several online services. Ferreting them out is easy: just type their name in your browser and go. E-zines are worth looking at—even if you've never cracked their hard copy cover. Which ones? For starters, try one or more of the following:

The Economist (economist.com)
Fortune (fortune.com)
Smart Money (smartmoney.com)

TRADING ONLINE

More than any other investment-related area, trading online has transformed itself from a poor relation of the traditional method of investing to a user-friendly, resourceful way to invest. The leaders of the tech pack:

Fidelity (fidelity.com)
Schwab (schwab.com)

SCRATCH'S E-GUIDE TO THE BEST OF THE INVESTMENT WEB

Bloomberg.com

A more conventional and more comprehensive means for financial facts and an overall market view is found at Bloomberg.com. But you get much more than mere coverage—you get in-depth analysis, market quotes, and access to a range of market experts and money managers that frequent Bloomberg's site on a daily basis. You can also zip into a number of market and industry comparison charts for a snapshot of how your overall portfolio is doing.

CNNfn.com

A comprehensive one-stop shop for the daily planet. Here you'll find all the news headlines, as well as a comprehensive market watch. Keeping in tune with the daily pulse of regional and international markets may leave you crying in your beer. But staying fully informed is one way to stay ahead of the herd—and it's not hard to do. Of course, if you're only interested in regular checkups, you can turn to the weekly overviews.

EIU.com

EIU stands for Economist Intelligence Unit. If you invest in foreign stocks or international stock funds, you can't afford to overlook this site. EIU.com covers 190 countries including emerging and newly emerging markets. EIU's core value is its consistent, objective analysis of trends in those 190 countries, with uniquely informed commentators and commentary. EIU's network of more than five hundred analysts, consultants, and researchers provides reliable and accurate intelligence to a client base that consists of the world's leading businesses, financial institutions, and government agencies. If another site offers more expertise, greater coverage, or a stronger reputation for accuracy and insight, it's hard to find.

Fundalarm.com

This site provides unique "sell" recommendations on funds.

Morningstar.com

There's nothing new under the fund sun that these two sites don't know about first. Completely reversing the old way of gleaning fund info, such as waiting for a monthly magazine or newsletter, these sites offer you the ability to leap-frog ahead of the unplugged investor. In fact, these two leading mutual fund–focused sites deliver more than you need for your fund investing maneuvers. Each provides an informed and efficient way to judge the funds you're investing in and the funds you might want to check out—or check out of.

Mutualfundsinteractive.com

More fund info, manager interviews, and commonsense investment advice.

Marketwatch.com

If you only want one site to hot-list for all your investment resource needs, you could choose this one and rest assured that your investment-related bases will be well covered. If you're looking for the top- and bottom-performing mutual funds, the best and worst fund managers, the largest funds, fund ownership of stocks, as well as sector and fund-by-sector performance numbers, you got 'em. If you want to look beyond a single rating system for funds, and for more commentary on individual funds in relation to their peers, it's all here.

Together, all the above sites provide the most efficient, comprehensive sources for fund information on the Web. But there's much more you'll need to learn about the Web before you can consider yourself its master.

YOUR PORTFOLIO ONLINE

Sometimes, even the World Wide Web doesn't get it. And when it comes to tracking one portfolio of funds (let alone a multiple-mutual-fund portfolio or a portfolio composed of funds, stocks, and bonds), there are plenty of placebos to be found—but no real solution to the problem. So, while you can look for more advanced, comprehensive, friendly portfolio trackers in the near future, today, if you want to track model portfolios at home, Marketwatch.com and Smartmoney.com are your best current options. If you want to do it in real time, chances are wherever you have your investment account you can do so online. Are some firms better than others? Definitely. Fidelity is state-of-the-art—Vanguard is known for its online black-outs. (In fact, Vanguard was on the wrong end of a lawsuit over just this issue in 2004.) The cost is the same for the use of these online services: free. But the end result can be starkly different.

The Net is often at its best when it provides a niche service that the megasites have overlooked or when the megasites provide a comprehensive toolbox to tackle your specific investment problem. Surprisingly, this isn't as clearly the case with a subject that's near and dear to our hearts—tracking multiple portfolios. In fact, if you're looking for a niche on the Net that is being tapped but has yet to be fully filled, creating a comprehensive multiple-portfolio analysis site could be your ticket to virtual success. Why? No matter what the hyperlinks suggest, there isn't a site that fits that bill, yet the demand for fund portfolio tracking (let alone a portfolio of multiple investment instruments) is clearly here today—and to stay.

YOUR OWN ONLINE FUND TRACKING SYSTEM

If you want to get really *technical* and be in greater control of a broader number of funds (and the markets, industries, and stocks they invest in) you'll need to move beyond the obvious fund sites and create your own spreadsheet.

Now I know that the very word "spreadsheet" probably has the hair on the back of your neck standing on end. But it's easy to do. It enables you to gain a broader and more meaningful picture of your funds' performance. And, after taking ten minutes to read this, and ten minutes to set it up, it will only take you ten minutes a day to update a top-level tip sheet.

Creating your own fund tracking system recognizes that the Internet is our friend. In fact, it's a crowded house of them: resources all designed to make our professional life more efficient and informed. But while most advisers and journalists (I include myself in both camps) focus on the latest and greatest sites that you and I can use to enhance our insights into the markets and personal financial planning issues that are the yeast in our daily bread, the truth is that most of us are still not using the Web to the degree of personalized proficiency that would mark it as an invaluable tool. Valuable, yes. In this chapter, I thought we could look at a simple way you can use the Web daily to help you keep up-to-date on your fund investments—and even your roommate's. Doing so may fall short of all the whiz-bang technology you can click into, but it provides a low-tech way to view your actual investment landscape each and every day.

Although there are many portfolio management programs available, I have long preferred the flexibility and control that comes from working with raw data and a spreadsheet program. All I use to keep track of the daily performance of two hundred or so funds, their top fifty stocks, and the most relevant market indices is a Web browser to cull the data (I use Yahoo) and Microsoft Excel to manage the data.

True, CNBC's right here in my office. But I like to see the daily, weekly, monthly, and year-to-date performance of each and every fund in my universe—not in the total fund universe—and I like to be able to view each part and the sum of their whole for my real and model portfolios. The best way to do this—and, remember, this is the Web according to me—isn't solely to rely on one of the many solid portfolio trackers that are available. With the amount of data I'm looking to catch, I need to cast a broader net. I find the browser to be essentially the best tool in my kit. Think of the browser as a net—once you know how to cast it, it is indispensable netting your daily analysis of the markets and funds you invest in. You can refine it even further to track the top fifty stocks that your funds invest in—giving you an early warning signal of potential pitfalls—or, hopefully, showing you why your funds are outperforming the markets.

There are many sources of free pricing data. I use Yahoo, which allows me to track multiple portfolios (of up to two hundred securities each), and whose data is easy to copy into my Excel spreadsheet. With a stock symbol (or five-letter fund code) I can get prices on just about any security. Ten minutes a day and I have a broad view of how every pick I've made is faring relative to an array of appropriate broad market and narrow industry and regional measures. (A few of the newest and smallest funds are not listed, but they're within a click or two once you know where to find 'em—more on that below.) Yahoo also lists news articles that mention any of the funds and stocks I track—new news that I can and do use every day in a way that keeps me ahead of the herd and up-to-the-minute about each piece of my portfolio's pie.

Here's how I do what I do. Call it a minilesson in how to excel on the Web. To show returns I use a spreadsheet that keeps track of a month's worth of daily prices. The spreadsheet includes the investment's year-to-date return through the end of the previous month, and its share price (or net asset value, NAV) on the last day of the previous month.

Total returns for the day, week, and month-to-date are simply derived from the last share price divided by the end-of-month share price, multiplied by a factor for any dividends within the month. So if a fund's share price has gone from $10.00 to $10.45 during the month, without any distributions, then its return is 4.5%: 100 × ([10.45 ÷ 10.00] − 1) × the distribution multiplier; in this simple case the distribution multiplier is just 1. Year-to-date (YTD) returns are shown by compounding the previous end-of-month YTD return by the present month-to-date return.

Distributions can be hard to keep track of and, as a result, are a potential glitch in my system, but I've learned to look for them, and integrate them when they occur. Fortunately, most are on a fairly regular schedule available from the fund companies. *Barron's* also shows distributions after the fact, and sizable distributions can usually be spotted by an unexpectedly negative one-day return for a fund, and then the size can be confirmed with a call to the fund company or a check of its website.

In the spreadsheet, the aforementioned distribution multiplier is simply 1 + (dividend ÷ reinvestment price). My "daily report" spreadsheet has separate distribution multiplier columns for the month-to-date, week, and day returns. The dividends of the month-to-date multipliers are of course cleared out at the beginning of each month, the others more often as the affected time periods elapse.

For bond funds, which have gradually accrued interest instead of occasional share-price-lowering distributions, there is a further multiplier that estimates income accrued for the month-to-date, using the fund's yield and the date of the month. I do not bother with showing week-to-date or one-day income accrual, as these small numbers will rarely affect returns much.

Return errors are almost always the result of a missed distribution or stock split. To make sure I'm not carrying forward errors from one month to the next, I do check my end-of-month YTD returns against another published source such as the newspaper listings and/or the relevant fund company.

Stock splits, like dividends, lead to unexpectedly negative returns. Splits are generally easier to catch, because most are two-to-one or greater, leading to one-day returns on the order of minus 50%. Usually a check of company news by ticker will quickly confirm the split (or will mention the stock's devastating decline!). There are many such sources for recent company news. I tend to use ones found at Smartmoney.com and CBSmarketwatch.com. There are also websites featuring stock split news, for example, 2-for-1.com, or search Yahoo with "stock splits" for other sites.

Yahoo has many indices in its database, (e.g., the S&P 500, Dow 30, NASDAQ Composite), but these are raw index values, not total return numbers. You'll either have to forget about index income or, like me, estimate accruing income intramonth, and correct for exact figures on a monthly basis. Barra.com shows exact monthly total returns for the S&P 500, 400, and 600 indices, including Growth and Value indices, usually on the second business day of the month.

On the Morgan Stanley site (msci.com) go to MSCI (for Morgan Stanley Capital International). There you'll find daily index values for its famous EAFE index, as well as all the country and regional indices you could possibly desire. They're generally available each weekday by 9:00 AM Eastern time, but are sometimes several hours late, especially with crucial end-of-month data. Be patient. Be persistent.

If you have one or more model portfolios, it's a relatively simple matter to track their values, and thus returns, with a row of your spreadsheet. For each day, the value of the portfolio is simply given by a formula summing up the number of shares in each relevant fund or stock. These formulas will of course have to be updated to account for any distributions and trading.

Check out my daily report on pages 324–5.

That's it in a nutshell—or should I say a web shell? Ten minutes a day can provide a low-tech way to ensure that I'm on my way to being able to see strong and troubling signs in every investment I own and track. If one stock or fund takes a significant nosedive, I first look for a distribution or split. If that hasn't been the culprit, I review Yahoo's daily news and also click into Bloomberg.com for the thin read. If the fund or stock is losing ground relative to the industry benchmark over five trading days, even if there's no punishing news, I know my manager isn't making the grade. And I need to review (see Fundalarm.com) the possible reasons for this. One other advantage of my fund daily report: I have found it to be a constant in the ever-changing Web universe—a reliable constant by which I still measure most others.

YOU, TRADING ONLINE

Beyond information lies action. After all, what good does a bunch of investment news do you if you can't turn it to your money-making advantage? Today, you can create your own trading desk—without having to pony up nearly $1 million to secure a seat on the New York Stock Exchange. Not bad. However, there are several online trading sites worth clicking into: Fidelity.com, Schwab's E-Trade, and TD Ameritrade. Each site offers differing price structures for your trades, as well as differing investment menus. The quickest way to assess which one is for you is to compare them. But before you do, make a mental note of the following: Fidelity and Schwab currently offer the most comprehensive (and within the low-cost universe, the most expensive) cyber floors for all types of trades and analysis. All these deep discounters are moving in the direction of bountiful research, trendy analysis, and efficient, real-time quotes and trades.

When viewing the online investing board, be sure you know both the advantages and the limitations of the sites you're considering. The checklist will help you do this at a glance, but be sure you also get answers to the following questions before you make your final move.

[ ] Ability to trade stocks, options, mutual funds, and bonds.

[ ] Cost per trade. For example, what is the cost per trade for up to 5,000 shares, applying to market or limit orders conducted over the Internet? Is there a discount for using the Internet as opposed to your touch-tone phone?

[ ] Hidden charges. Are additional charges imposed, such as inactivity fees and postage and handling fees?

[ ] Are the accounts protected? For example, one site offers up to $50 million per customer ($500,000 under SIPC, including $100,000 for cash claims) and an additional $49.5 million in protection provided by Aetna Casualty and Surety Company—which means that if you strike it rich and they go belly up, you're covered. (Note: this coverage isn't for market losses; it's more like FDIC insurance at your bank.)

[ ] When do you get confirmation of orders—within seconds of execution, with portfolio updated automatically, within hours, within days?

[ ] Free real-time quotes, and how many (some sites offer up to 100 per day)?

[ ] Free unlimited portfolio access and the ability to create charts as well as monitor investments in real time.

[ ] Free company news, market news, and other information on stocks, bonds, and mutual funds.

		%	YTD %	MTD %	Week %	Day $	Day 31	Mar
^SPX	S&P 500	3%	4.2	1.3	-0.6	-0.4	-5.43	1294.82
^DJI	Dow 30	333.3	4.3	1.2	-1.5	-0.4	-41.38	11109.32
^IXIC	NASDAQ Comp		6.3	2.6	1.2	0.0	-1.03	2339.79
^MID	S&P 400		7.6	2.5	0.7	0.0	0.26	792.11
^RUT	Russell 2K		13.9	4.8	1.5	0.3	2.55	765.14
^SML	S&P 600		12.8	4.9	1.3	0.4	1.62	394.83
^DWC	Wilsh 5K		5.5	2.0	-0.1	-0.2	-28.06	13155.44
	MS EAFE		8.8	2.9	0.5	-0.8	-14.09	1827.65
	MS Europe		10.2	3.5	-0.3	-1.0	-16.25	1616.91
	MS Japan		6.3	2.1	2.2	-0.4	-13.62	3243.41
	AC Far East Free ex Jpn		7.7	1.0	2.6	0.9	3.06	356.37
	AIM ETF Global Growth		7.3	3.0	1.2	0.1	60.22	107302.19
	AIM ETF Growth		6.5	2.6	1.0	0.0	9.05	106543.21
	AIM ETF Growth & Income		4.9	1.9	0.6	0.1	60.39	104905.79
	AIM ETF Strategic Income		4.2	1.5	0.3	0.0	3.66	104227.41
	ETF Sector Model		2.4	0.6	0.0	-0.1	-72.19	130911.16
	ETF – Consumer		1.5	0.4	-1.5	-0.6	-106.61	18516.01
	ETF – Cyclical		-3.8	3.5	1.0	0.5	78.83	17516.57
	ETF – Finance		4.7	0.8	-0.8	0.3	51.39	19149.72
	ETF – Health		6.7	-2.1	0.1	0.4	80.32	19460.55
	ETF – Technology		6.9	0.3	0.1	-0.7	-133.57	19511.54
	ETF – Utilities		-2.8	-0.8	0.1	-0.1	-13.70	17720.66
	ETF – Internatl		4.0	2.2	1.0	-0.2	-28.84	19036.12
	ETF Total Market		8.4	3.2	1.3	0.1	167.52	136400.66
	ETF – Large Cap		3.8	2.1	1.5	-0.3	-124.57	43525.23
	ETF – Mid Cap		8.0	2.5	0.6	0.1	47.81	45235.03
	ETF – Small Cap		13.5	5.0	1.6	0.5	244.29	47640.41
	ETF Aggressive Trader		6.9	-0.9	0.1	-0.7	-1001.89	146356.02

FSI Aggressive Growth			8.2	0.8	0.5	0.0	40	98,567
AG – Service			12.0	1.4	0.8	0.3	88	34,025
AG – Technology			4.1	-2.3	0.2	0.3	85	31,575
AG – Telecom			8.6	3.2	0.4	-0.4	-133	32,967
FSI Growth			5.0	3.3	0.7	0.0	-65	150,787
FSI – Consumer			3.1	3.1	0.2	-0.1	-12	21,123
FSI – Cyclical			14.0	6.6	1.3	0.6	147	23,378
FSI – Finance			12.0	1.4	0.8	0.3	60	22,999
FSI – Health			-0.6	-2.3	0.2	0.3	55	20,383
FSI – Technology			9.7	2.9	1.8	-0.4	-81	22,494
FSI – Utilities			-2.5	5.5	-0.5	-0.6	-123	20,159
FSI – Internatl			-1.3	6.1	1.0	-0.5	-111	20,250
FI Aggressive			10.0	3.4	1.6	0.1	140	220,029
FI Growth			9.1	3.1	1.2	0.0	-117	269,522
FI Grow & Inc			5.7	2.1	0.6	0.0	-3	228,315
FI Cap & Inc			4.8	1.6	0.5	0.1	155	190,079
FI VIP Growth			5.5	2.2	0.6	-0.2	-355	150,339
FI VIP Growth & Inc			4.9	2.0	0.5	-0.2	-308	150,942
Kob Aggressive			7.7	2.5	0.9	-0.1	-85	159,759
Kob Growth			5.3	2.0	0.8	-0.1	-1460	1,050,625
Kob G&I			3.5	1.3	0.0	-0.2	-1896	780,415
Kob I&P			2.1	0.6	-0.2	-0.2	-786	476,492
Bow Select			8.8	3.1	0.8	-0.4	-1416	343,998
Bow Growth			5.0	1.8	0.8	0.2	315	180,494
Bow G&I			4.2	1.1	0.0	-0.1	-115	163,170
Large-Cap	fbgrx	312	Blue Chip Growth	2.3	1.1	-0.1	-0.3	-0.13	44.17
2.1	fbcvx	1271	Blue Chip Value	5.6	1.4	-0.1	-0.2	-0.03	14.25
MTD	fdcax	307	Capital Appreciation	8.8	3.1	1.3	0.0	-0.01	27.32
5.4	fcntx	22	Contrafund	4.8	2.1	0.6	-0.2	-0.12	66.54

[ ] Free access to fundamental, technical, and earnings estimates, charting services oriented to technical investors.

Putting your money where your mouse is is no easy task—it tests one's nerves as well as one's wires. But the time saved, the research gleaned, the advice pooled and sifted all make the advent of online investing much more than a cool trend. In fact, with the mere flick of your wrist, you can take control of your financial life.

SECTION 5

Your Future Is in Your Hands

CHAPTER 23

Your 401(k) from Scratch

When the discussion shifts from the latest *Curb Your Enthusiasm* episode to retirement-oriented investments (and if it hasn't happened to you yet, wait a month or two and I guarantee it will), most people start talking in codes: "My IRA's so much more efficient than the SEP I used to participate in, but I've lost the tax-deductible status ever since my husband started to participate in his company's 403(b), since a 457(c) was out of the question. But my company is offering a 401(k), with matching funds . . ." You could be sitting there counting sheep or the unopened Zima bottles in the fridge for all you care.

Well, it may surprise you to learn that, when it comes to investing for retirement, so-called slackers do a better (that's right, better) job than their parents. This fact would probably surprise your parents even more! The facts are as follows: over 60% of those aged twenty-five to thirty-four have a savings account and invest in mutual funds; over 70% of this group already participate in a retirement investing plan; over 75% set retirement savings as a priority. About 70% already participate in a 401(k) plan, compared to around 60% for boomers.

This good news is most likely the result of several main factors. The job market is tight, meaning you're well aware of the hardships you face in making ends meet today, which, in turn, doesn't exactly bode well for tomorrow. So you're looking to safeguard yourself from financial collapse in more concrete ways. Second, you see how many of the boomers before you, the glamour-pusses of the 1980s, are having to downsize in order to keep a roof over their heads. Third, you don't believe Social Security will be around when you retire (okay—7% of you think so). (And why should you? Today, there are seventeen taxpayers for every Social Security recipient. By the year 2030, there will be only two taxpayers for every Social Security recipient!) This, coupled with the fact that there's much greater media coverage of issues relating to retirement and the need to create your own cash reserves for it, no doubt creates a motivational response to financial angst.

Now, you and I know that our retirement days are far, far away. You're not sitting in some bar bemoaning the fact that you have thirteen more years to go before you can hang up your mailbag and retire to Tampa. You're sitting in the bar thinking about Manhattans, not the sunset years, which are thirty-plus years down the road. You're not stuck in a yes-man rut of needing the income you currently earn in order to afford to retire within the next decade. You can still be your own boss. And, who knows, maybe an early retirement from your current career path is just what you have in mind—in order to start a second career, of course.

Since retirement is a certain financial hurdle you must overcome, and since it's the single largest financial hurdle on your road to overall financial independence and security, it's in your best interest to figure out the best options when it comes to investing for it.

Don't kid yourself. The 2004 comprehensive survey of "retirement confidence" completed by the Employee Benefit Research Institute (ebri.org) revealed some interesting facts about our preparedness for—and confidence in—retiring. (The survey is updated annually.) The vast majority (over two-thirds) of those surveyed said they were confident regarding their retirement income prospects, but 42% of the same group admitted to having nothing saved for their own retirement—and 58% hadn't attempted to calculate how much they would need to save to fund a comfortable retirement (one that would enable them to maintain a similar lifestyle). Now, of course you don't want to be stuck in the lifestyle you're living today—since you're young and working toward a better lifestyle.

The respondents are workers in your age group as well as far beyond: the study thus provides an interesting lens through which you can view the potential pitfall of being overconfident when it comes to investing today for that distant tomorrow. In fact, in contrast to the rosy scenario pictured above, this survey reveals that among those aged twenty-five to thirty-four who responded that they were very confident about their retirement income, 36% had no money set aside. (The survey didn't ask about debt levels, which, as you can imagine, are likely to be very high.) The good news is that there are several retirement investment options to choose from. But, as with other types of investment vehicles, the more choices you have, the more effort you must devote to finding the right one. Furthermore, it's true that the sooner you begin, the less money it will take to accumulate a solid financial reserve for your retirement days. It's also true that some options will deliver more than others. No matter what, there is a retirement plan to suit your particular situation.

Whether you are self-employed or working for a gigantic corporation, don't allow the fact that dealing with the present absorbs so much energy to delay you from planning for the future. And, while it's clearly important to keep your eye on your present goals and objectives, it's also easy enough to reward yourself for your current efforts by creating a plan that will positively affect your future.

OUR CHANGING FUTURE

Things are not what they used to be. It used to be that planning for retirement was a fairly straightforward proposition—you tallied your pension and Social Security benefits to ensure that you could maintain a modest lifestyle. Nowadays, neither pensions nor Social Security is a sure thing. Add to this troubling news the fact that inflation has to be factored into the mix (an inflation rate of 4.5% means that the cost of living will double every fifteen years). No wonder so many people are discouraged, rather than encouraged, from becoming more knowledgeable and active in terms of funding their own retirement.

For example, do you know why 401(k) plans and other self-funded retirement plans have become so popular? Increasingly, employers and the federal government expect that you are responsible for the lion's share of your retirement income. While, for your employer, this is a good thing (it beats the expense and liability of funding a traditional pension plan), it means that, for you, there's no guaranteed amount of income that you can rely on for your retirement.

There are attractive retirement investment alternatives available to you—but it's up to you to understand and select the most appropriate one(s) for yourself. And, while it is difficult to predict the level of retirement income you'll need (since it's hard to know how to predict the level of living and sundry expenses you'll encounter when you join the pink flamingo, shuffleboard set in thirty-plus years), now is the best time to start taking advantage of a tax-advantaged investment plan, as well as determining an appropriate investment strategy, so that your retirement years will be truly golden ones.

Chances are, you haven't yet accumulated a substantial nest egg for retirement. If you are like most people, you have more pressing and immediate concerns, such as buying a home and raising and educating children. Whatever your circumstances, however, you should regularly direct some attention to planning for your retirement—and then some of your resources.

Invest for a Better Tomorrow Today

You can develop a sound retirement plan today. True, there are many details that need to be worked out—and worked on. But, the sooner you start, the better—and the sooner you review the plan you've got, the sooner you can rest assured that it is the best one for you. If you have neither plans nor savings nor retirement investments in the works, relax. You've got time—as long as you begin right now—to develop a plan that will work for you. And remember that, with no plan, you're only working against yourself.

Estimating how much you will need to accumulate by the time you reach retirement age can be startling. (See pages 383–84 to find out how to do that.) If you are still young, this amount may seem more like the gross national product of a small country, but it is attainable. Caveat: Don't include the value of your home in your retirement-related assets unless you plan to sell the house and become a renter when you retire.

Take action to close the gap between the resources you now have and the resources you will need to retire. Figuring out how much you need to retire in comfort usually leads to the realization that you don't yet have enough money to meet your needs. If misery does love company then there is some solace in the fact that very few people achieve financial independence until they are very near retirement. But what is most important is to make sure you take action today to provide for your financial needs throughout your retirement.

- Get started on planning your retirement investment strategy today.
- Learn about the available retirement-oriented investment plans as well as the types of investments best suited to your objective.
- Regularly review your retirement investment strategy and investments' performance.
- Revise your retirement investment strategy and investments to keep pace with the benchmarks you establish.

Gauging your retirement expenses in order to establish an overall investment goal isn't as hard to do as you might think. In fact, it's easier (and less painful) to do than to create a livable budget! The tricky part is that your current lifestyle is probably not the lifestyle you'll rise to in the next five to ten years. Given that you're just starting out, the old rule of thumb (current gross annual income – amount of annual savings $\times$ 80% = an adequate amount of income that your investments will have to provide for up to thirty years or more) simply doesn't work. For example, if your current income is $30,000, and you save $1,500, that means you spend, including taxes, $28,500. The annual income in current dollars necessary to maintain this living standard during retirement years would be 80% of the $28,500—or $22,800. Not exactly living high on the hog. To project your necessary retirement income when you reach retirement age, adjust the results of this calculation upward to 100% of your current income, assuming that in the next five to ten years you will increase your income 20% to 25%. When that happens, scale back to the more conservative 80%.

Figuring out the amount of income your total retirement package (including pension, investments, and yes, Social Security) will have to generate on an annual basis for a span of at least two decades is perhaps the simplest part of the overall equation. The more difficult part is to estimate what you need to save today in order to achieve your very distant objective. The good news: almost everywhere you click (as long as you're clicking on financial sites), there's a financial projection calculator. Interactive worksheets will help you determine what you need to save today in order to reach a more financially secure tomorrow—based on your changing fortunes.

There's also a basic rule you should invest by. You will need to invest a minimum of 10% of your gross income in a portfolio that delivers an annualized return of at least 8% in order to maintain your current lifestyle.

That's it. You now know what you need to save today to brighten your financial future. Don't worry if you can't muster the money immediately. Chances are you do have some significant debts to pay off and a home's down payment to save for, too. But, on the other hand, don't postpone your retirement planning—or investing. Start small. Start today. Don't delay.

PART ONE: 401(K) FOCUS

401(k)s are here to stay. Whether you participate in a 401(k) or other type of employer-sponsored retirement plan (see page 48), or are about to, you need to know how to make the best moves within the plan. To do so, you'll need to learn more than the mechanics of investing in them. This chapter is divided into two sections: 401(k)s and other types of pension plans. While there are similarities and differences between each type of plan discussed in detail below, there is one basic truth you can't afford to forget: no matter how good the plan is, it's up to you to select the best way to invest in it.

Participating in a 401(k) couldn't be easier. If you already do so, or if you have the opportunity to do so, read on. If, on the other hand, you don't currently have the option of investing in a 401(k), don't feel too left out. For one thing, you may be able to participate in a 403(b) plan. And if that isn't an option, you still have a host of retirement investment plans to choose from—from company-sponsored pension plans (later in this chapter) to individually sponsored ones (covered in the next chapter). Still feel left out? Well, even though you can't open a 401(k) the way you can an IRA (i.e., by picking up the phone and calling a mutual fund company), you can certainly suggest that your company create a 401(k) plan. It's worth a shot.

401(k) plans are available among an increasing number of companies, large and small. To participate in a 401(k) plan, you designate a fixed portion of your pretax salary to be deducted in order to be invested in your company-sponsored investment plan. It's a great start—especially if your employer matches part of your contribution to your 401(k)s. How great? Let's take a look.

401(k)s are tax-advantaged. Participating in a 401(k) saves you federal (and most likely state) income taxes in several ways. First, the money in your 401(k) is known as deferred compensation, meaning it doesn't appear on your W-2 form and thereby escapes both federal income tax and Social Security taxes (unless your gross income after the 401(k) contribution exceeds the maximum income for which Social Security is withheld). Also, depending upon where you reside, your 401(k) contribution may escape state and local income taxes. Say you earn a taxable $30,000, and contribute 8% ($2,400) of that to your 401(k). As you'll note on your W-2 form next year, your earnings subject to federal (and most state) tax will be $27,600. Second, reducing your federal income taxes means that the $2,400 you contribute goes directly to work for you. Moreover (assuming you're in the 28% bracket with a 5.5% state tax), doing so reduces the amount you pay to Uncle Sam by $672 federal and $132 state—a savings of 33.5% on money you earned and put to work for yourself. Now that's a bargain! Another tax benefit is that the money you invest in your 401(k) can grow tax-free— until you begin making withdrawals. Dividends, interest, and capital gains won't be taxed as long as you reinvest them in the plan.

As you can see, participating in a 401(k) has some tax advantages for you. Naturally, if your employer matches your funds (in whole or, as is far more likely, in part) it's an even better deal—perhaps the only source of found money for those without a silver spoon. And participating in a 401(k) plan is easy and convenient; as with a regular investment account, the automatic withdrawal of a specified sum from your paycheck will help you remain steadfast on your self-funded retirement course. But, that said, don't make a common mistake of thinking that investing in a 401(k) is a no-brainer. While opening an account is clearly the right thing to do—and while it couldn't be easier—that's the bare beginning of your 401(k) planning. Like any potential portfolio of investments, the vehicles you select in your 401(k) portfolio can get you where you want to go or set you on a collision course.

When the cherubic human resource department guy or gal knocks on your cube inviting you to attend an informational meeting about 401(k) plans, attend—even if you already have one. Why? Chances are you'll be brought up to speed on a number of issues that affect you and your money! Examples? The rules and contribution limits governing your 401(k) change. Your company may change the number and type of investments that you can select from for your 401(k). Your company may change the way in which you can participate in managing your 401(k) fund by changing either its matching amount or the frequency with which you can make trades.

How to Invest in Your 401(k)

When it comes to selecting how to construct your 401(k), you may be surprised to find that you're either limited in terms of the types and number of investment vehicles you can choose from or presented with a dizzying menu of choices. Most plans offer stock funds, bond funds, and money market funds. Others may offer guaranteed investment contracts (GICs) and the option of purchasing shares of the company's stock. No matter which camp you fall into, the fact is that, when it comes to selecting the best way to construct your 401(k) portfolio, you're the boss. You decide how you want to invest your 401(k) funds, and you select from the available menu the best way to satisfy your appetite for a financially secure retirement.

Treat your 401(k) like you would any other long-term investment plan (for further discussion on creating portfolio strategies that work, turn to chapter 16). Since you've got a long time before you retire, you can take on some added risk in order to potentially increase your returns. Doing so will entail building a portfolio of predominantly small-cap value, large-cap growth, and international stock funds. Forget about cash or bonds for now—they're too conservative and, in the case of cash, the stock funds you select will already have a small position in cash (meaning that your overall portfolio will have a cash position—a position you need to watch to ensure that it doesn't ramp up, leaving you out of the market when you thought you were fully invested in it).

Remember: diversifying across industries, stocks, and countries is one of the best ways to deliver solid returns. How can you ensure that your portfolio is well diversified? Well, forget about the fund names—they'll lead you down a primrose path, but reveal little about their actual objectives. (For a thorough review of mutual funds, turn to chapter 14.) Instead, get thee to a library, which will likely have recent issues of *Morningstar* or *Value Line,* wherein you'll find a host of information about the funds that reside in your 401(k) plan. You can also request (from your employer or human resource person, or the funds themselves) copies of prospectuses that will describe the various investments and overall objective of each fund.

Chances are, your plan offers some growth, balanced, bond (income), and cash reserve options. Which should you concentrate on? Growth and more growth. You're young, and you're in the business of growing your capital—not trying to preserve it (yet). Moreover, since this money is earmarked for your retirement—an event that's twenty or more years away—you can afford to take on some additional risk in the form of an aggressive small-cap value or large-cap growth concentration with some foreign exposure added to your mix. Remember that the risk of taking no risk (i.e., putting your 401(k) money into a money market account) is that, over the long run, you'll likely lose to inflation.

Note: preretirement needs should be provided for outside of your 401(k) plan. Funds invested outside the 401(k), particularly those slated for your current or potential children's college education, should be invested much like your 401(k) plan investments—aggressively at the starting gate for maximum growth.

Reviewing is essential. Some people will go out and buy the *Star Wars* trilogy—and watch it over and over again. But when it comes to reviewing their 401(k) statement (which typically arrives on a quarterly basis) do they even view it once? Many don't—and that's a mistake. Every time you receive a statement involving your finances you should review it to ensure that: (1) it's your account, (2) it shows the right amount of initial investment, and (3) it reflects any trades that you authorized—or reveals trades that you did not authorize. I also keep a running portfolio of my 401(k) funds, checking their performance on a daily basis by turning to the fund section of my local paper. I like to know how the funds I have selected are performing relative to certain meaningful benchmarks—like the S&P 500 (for my large-cap growth funds), the Russell 2000 (for my small-cap growth funds), and the EAFE (for my international funds).

This is a great way to stay up to speed on the overall market as well—after all, the stocks each fund invests in come from different industries. By keeping track of each fund's performance, I can follow wider industry and economic trends in terms of how they affect my own financial well-being. If the performance of a particular fund or stock is steadily deteriorating over several quarters relative to similar funds or stocks (i.e., within the same industry), then it's probably time to consider an alternative fund.

Of course you should not trade in and out of funds on a regular basis. In fact, market-timing (trying to time the best time to buy and sell, and frequently trading in and out of the market) doesn't work. What does work is selecting the best funds available for the long haul; these may well not be the funds with the best short-term performance. Since some 401(k) plans provide a limited menu of investment possibilities, this may prove to be very difficult indeed. What you'll need to do is look for investment style (value versus growth—and small-cap value versus all else) and country allocation (established versus emerging market) in order to identify the best among your limited lot. If, on the other hand, you've got a menu that's a mile long, you'll need to sift the wheat from the chaff. And once that's done, you'll need to establish a way to determine (on a regular basis) whether and when to readjust your 401(k) portfolio.

The long-term portfolio allocation in chapter 16 shows how a typical 401(k) might be arranged at your stage in life.

Some employers may restrict your ability to actively manage your own 401(k) investments, while others encourage it. The more you know about your plan's rules, the more likely your 401(k) will perform in accordance with your expectations and objectives. You have the right to trade the investments within your 401(k) up to four times per year. Of course, you're restricted to the preset menu offered by your employer. The rules regarding such trades are specific to your company's plan. Your employee benefits department is the best place to go for all the details.

What Not to Invest in in Your 401(k)

Avoid tax-free investment vehicles (like a muni bond fund) since the 401(k)'s tax advantages render others null and void. Nix on GICs— there's nothing truly guaranteed about them (insurance companies that offer these products can fail, just like S&Ls but without the $100,000 federal guarantee), and they are not the best investment alternative for you (rarely delivering a better performance than a conservative stock fund). True, when you buy a GIC, the insurance company promises to pay a specified interest rate over a specified period of time. Don't believe everything you hear.

I would also avoid placing shares of your own company's stock in your 401(k). As one of my personal finance mentors was fond of saying, as optimistic as you might be about your company's financial future and fortunes, you never know what's going to happen to its stock price. Instead, hold those shares in a separate account—and don't let them account for more than 20% of your overall retirement portfolio. The last thing you want to have happen if the bottom fell out of the company's stock price is for it to fall out of your 401(k), too.

When Not to Invest in a 401(k)

Not all 401(k)s are created equal—and some are downright danger-ous. For one thing, many 401(k)s don't provide you with a menu of potential investments that are suitable to your age, income, and objec-tives. So, for example, your plan might not offer an aggressive growth fund or an international fund—or it may provide funds with poor per-formance records in those market areas, or worse, load funds. If you think that your plan is too restrictive, don't be afraid to just say no. True, 401(k)s are addictive—and, if the menu of investment choices is solid, then it's worth getting in the habit of contributing. But just be-cause everyone says 401(k)s are the best thing to invest in doesn't mean that your particular plan is. Scrutinize the plan the way you would any menu of potential investments. If there isn't a way to build a portfolio you can live with and prosper by, consider opening an IRA.

When to Question Your 401(k)

Fraud happens. And where large sums of money are involved, fraud happens more. The increase in plans may bring about an increase in the number of employers who might dip into this retirement pool. Here are some clear warning signs that can alert you to potential problems with your 401(k):

- You notice a steep drop in the value of your account that can't be explained by the market activity of the last quarter or the perfor-mance of the funds (or other types of investments you hold).
- The deductions from your paycheck don't match the contribu-tions on your 401(k) statements.
- Your 401(k) statements should arrive on a regularly scheduled date, four times per year. If your quarterly statement arrives late or at irregular times during the year, get an explanation from your benefits administrator—and be on guard.
- You have heard of former employees having difficulty when it came to receiving their benefits.

If any of the above problems seem to be occurring in your plan, and you can't get a reasonable (and understandable) explanation from your plan administrator, then by all means contact the Employee

Benefits Security Administration (dol.gov/ebsa). Be discreet, since you don't want to be in the position of angering a thief or wrongly accusing someone for an honest mistake.

Borrowing from Your 401(k)

When determining how much of your salary you want to go to your 401(k), keep in mind that early withdrawal of funds in your 401(k) is not simply frowned upon—it's punished. There's a 10% penalty tax for early withdrawal. As a result, you need to be sure that your investing budget doesn't collide with your living budget. Plan ahead so that the amount you slate for your 401(k) won't impact your current lifestyle.

If you absolutely, positively have to access the money in your 401(k) plan, there are ways to do so without incurring the penalty tax:

- You retire.
- You die.
- You become disabled.
- You leave or lose your job.
- Your plan is terminated and no successor plan is established.
- You demonstrate extreme need.
- Other unusual situations may also cause early distributions.

You must demonstrate both an immediate and substantial financial need as well as your inability to meet that need with any other resources. Purchasing your principal residence, meeting deductible medical expenses that exceed 7.5% of your adjusted gross income, and paying postsecondary tuition are demonstrations of such need, as is demonstrating need related to the imminent foreclosure of your principal residence. But think of your 401(k) as a last resort. If you have planned well, you shouldn't have to use it until you retire— which is what it is for!

Loans from 401(k) funds are permitted for up to 50% of your account balance up to $50,000, though loans of less than $10,000 may exceed 50% of your balance. Such loans must be for a stated interest rate and have a predetermined repayment schedule. Except for home loans, the maximum loan period is five years. If you don't repay the loan within the specified time period then the (outstanding) balance is taxable and subject to the 10% penalty (if you are under age 59½). Interest on such loans is not tax deductible.

Rolling Funds Over into an IRA

If you leave your job—for any reason—you can take your 401(k) with you. But if you don't reinvest the money in a similar tax-advantaged plan, you'll be taxed on it. And you'll most likely spend your retirement money. For some of us, the sum can be downright tempting—in the $10,000-plus range. Just enough for a year off in Europe. For others, with smaller amounts, the thought may be that the amount is incidental—but don't forget about the long-term benefits of compounding. Spending your retirement money is a huge mistake that can take years to recover from! So play it smart, avoid paying the penalty tax—and avoid spending your retirement resources prematurely: roll over your 401(k) money into an IRA within sixty days. You must roll over at least 50% of your balance. But if you don't roll over 100%, you're just cheating yourself. Also, be sure that the IRA you open is a new IRA, so that your tax-advantaged investments aren't commingled with your taxable investments—a paperwork nightmare. Moreover, if you commingle your funds with an existing IRA, you may not be able to roll the funds over again into a new 401(k) down the road. (For more on IRAs, see the following chapter.)

PART TWO: PENSION PLANS

Some people don't have the option of investing in a 401(k), but do have the choice of participating in a pension plan. (For the most comprehensive source on pension plan questions and answers, click on the Department of Labor's web page dol.gov/ebsa/consumer _info_pension.html. If you work for a company that has its own pension plan, and you plan on being there for the duration (or at least a minimum of ten years), and the company itself lasts through your tenure, then you may be able to retire with a pension that provides for the lion's share of your retirement needs. But be aware of the fact that fewer and fewer employees can rely on their place of employment either for their career or to still be there ten or more years down the road. While pension plans used to be the parachute most employees counted on for their golden years, we face a new corporate climate in which the top level is provided with golden parachutes, while middle managers and below are often asked to jump with little or no parachute.

Company pension plans usually require you to make after-tax contributions, which are either wholly or partially matched by your employer's contributions. And while this means that there are no immediate tax benefits (as there are with 401(k) plans), you are getting your employer's contribution, and your investments will enjoy the benefit of tax deferral.

Is a pension plan your only option? Well, chances are good that if you answer yes, you're thinking about it being the only option with the potential for matching funds, since you are free to open an IRA (which isn't deductible if you or your spouse currently participates in a retirement plan at work) or, if you're self-employed, you can consider an SEP or Keogh (all of which are explained in detail in the following chapter). In fact, I would recommend doing both—so that your retirement money isn't restricted to what could be a narrowly defined stable of investment opportunities through your pension at work, and so that you can take advantage of opening an IRA through Fidelity, Charles Schwab, or Jack White, wherein you can buy funds from over forty different fund families.

Most pension plans provide the following: defined rights, benefits, eligibility standards, and predetermined formulas to calculate your benefits. You'll need to get a handle on all of these by contacting your employee benefits administrator.

There are two basic types of pension plans: defined benefit and defined contribution plans. A defined benefit plan establishes a predetermined retirement sum. While this may sound like a dream come true, the results are less than spectacular, even risky. For one thing, your employer sets the amount and, while it may seem like a generous amount to you today, remember that you've got another thirty years to go—thirty years that are prone to the toll inflation takes. Moreover, expecting a specific amount of benefits is a far cry from actually receiving them. You're putting a lot of faith in your company, which could, like so many businesses before it, fail to last as long as you—taking your pension plan down the tubes with it.

A defined contribution plan is even less secure. Here, your employer makes a certain contribution to the pension fund each and every year. When you retire, you receive a monthly amount based on whatever happens to be in the fund at the time.

If I sound fairly skeptical about such pension plans, then you're hearing me loud and clear—but it is only my opinion. Many current pensioners would chase me down with their walkers and club me into silence with their four-pronged aluminum canes. But things change, and nowhere is this more evident than in corporate America, where downsizing has been (and is likely to continue to be) the rule—not exactly the kind of playing field I'd want to be playing on with my retirement funding! Nevertheless, there's one solid benefit to a pension plan—and it's called being vested in one.

Vesting

Simply put, vesting is the rate at which your pension contributions permanently accrue to your account. A typical vesting schedule: 100% vesting upon completion of five years of service or an alternative, seven-year, graduated vesting schedule, usually 20% after three years of service and 20% for each year thereafter for four years.

If you are out of work because of a prolonged illness or disability, your vesting will most likely be affected. In fact, you can lose all benefits accrued to a certain point.

Should you terminate your employment with a company and receive vested benefits, the benefits must be put into a rollover IRA within sixty days, or they will be regarded as taxable income for that year—and they will usually be subject to a 10% penalty tax for distributions received before age 59½. You may also have the option of keeping your vested pension benefits in the company until you reach retirement age, at which time you can draw a small pension. But don't let someone else have control over your retirement money or even a portion of it. Again, you should go for a rollover IRA.

Of course, if you have suffered an unplanned layoff, you may need to use some or all of these retirement benefits to meet living expenses—which means you didn't have a sufficient emergency account set aside. As with using any money earmarked for retirement, do it only as a last resort.

Plan Benefits

Unlike a 401(k) or an IRA, where you designate your spouse as your beneficiary, your pension plan probably won't include an option that will pay your spouse in the event of your untimely death. Why? Such benefits typically are available only if you have become eligible for early retirement or are within ten years of normal retirement age—neither of which is likely to be the case for you.

Permanent disability could impose severe financial hardship on you and your family. Some pension plans provide for disability by allowing for the distribution of a reduced income previously slated for your retirement. Others provide a disability plan that's separate from the retirement plan. Another option to hedge against the unexpected accident is to take out a disability insurance policy on your own. If you are your household's sole or primary source of revenue this is a must.

Chances are that you will have the ability to invest in one or more of the company-sponsored retirement investment plans. Chances are that doing so will be beneficial. However, you need to ensure that the benefits are there, in terms of the merits of the investments offered. The merits of the tax advantages are clear and present. But what happens if you don't have any of the above retirement investment plans at your present place of employment? Consider the next chapter as your immediate future's source of retirement investment plans.

READY RESOURCES

- *Getting Started in 401(k) Investing,* Paul Katzeff

CHAPTER 24

Your Individual Retirement
Accounts from Scratch

Whether you know it or not, when it comes to creating your own financially secure retirement, you're an entrepreneur. In fact, while you may work for someone else for your whole workaday life, when you retire, you're your own boss, like it or not. The benefits? You can be in control of your way of living. That is, as long as you sow the financial seeds for funding your retirement today. Drawbacks? If you aren't slating money for retirement, you not only won't be able to enjoy your present lifestyle for too much longer (since you'll be forced to save more), but you will also fail in the single most important entrepreneurial test of your life: securing an independent life for yourself.

Whether you are an entrepreneur or not, you need to take matters into your own hands when it comes to saving for your retirement. But if you don't have a 401(k) or other type of employer-sponsored retirement plan at your disposal, you'll need to figure out a tax-advantaged way to build your own retirement savings war chest. The best way is to create a tax-advantaged plan that enables you to invest in a range of investment vehicles, specifically, a range of stock mutual funds from different fund families. The following plans fit the bill.

Individual Retirement Accounts (IRAs)

More than just an old standby, participating in an IRA is an excellent idea. What exactly is an IRA? An IRA is a type of investment account, not an investment in and of itself. Like a 401(k), an IRA is a tax-advantaged investment account that can help you achieve your objective of a financially secure retirement.

IRAs used to be the best-known form of tax-advantaged investment accounts. Today, 401(k) plans may be more talked about. But there's no denying that millions of Americans have invested billions in IRAs. Should you invest in one? What are the advantages and disadvantages of doing so for you? And how can you make the most of your IRA account? Let's take a look.

Participating in an IRA involves three main aspects: opening the account; selecting and managing the funds you invest in it; and (way down the road) planning how you will withdraw from it. Bottom line: The benefits of tax-deductible and tax-deferred IRAs versus non-tax-advantaged or tax-deferred investments is that more of your money goes to work for you—and more of your money reaps the rewards of compounding.

Two IRA Stones, One Investment Bird

Whether you invest in a Roth IRA or a regular IRA (also called a "traditional IRA"), many of the same rules apply. However, there are significant differences you need to know about. This chapter will help you leap into the thick of the debate about which type of account is the most appropriate one for you. Suffice it to say, however, that even if you're participating in your employer's 401(k) or other employer-sponsored retirement plan (and thus, at incomes as low as $85,000 for 2006, lose some or all of the deductibility of a traditional IRA), you should consider placing any money you have left on the table in one or the other plan. That's because both provide deferral of taxes owed until the day (way, way down the road), when you decide to make a withdrawal.

THE DEBATE

Ask a simple IRA question, get a Roth answer. The Roth IRA, named for the late Senator William Roth from Delaware, is the IRA that everyone talks about but few understand. And while you should talk directly with your accountant to decide whether a Roth is for you, I think it's important to understand its basic advantages and disadvantages.

The difference between a Roth IRA and a regular IRA amounts to paying your taxes now or later. All IRAs offer tax-deferral, which means there are no tax consequences for any kind of fund or other securities trading. But for all IRAs you are taxed once on the money, either when you take it out in retirement (regular IRAs) or when you earn the money before you put it in (Roth IRAs). For a deductible regular IRA, withdrawals are taxable as income. For a nondeductible regular IRA, a portion of the withdrawals are considered "return of contributions," and are therefore exempt from tax, but most of the withdrawals are taxable as income. But for a Roth IRA (whose contributions are nondeductible, and thus were taxed like your other income), withdrawals are generally not taxed at all.

IS THE ROTH IRA BETTER?

There are really two different questions here.

1. If you already have an IRA, is it a good idea to roll the money over into a Roth IRA?
2. For new money, is a Roth IRA better than a traditional IRA?

The answers to these questions have more complications than you might imagine. And no matter how carefully considered, they will always be uncertain because they depend in part on unknowable factors like what income tax rates will be like in the future. So those who are prone to worry may never relax with the decision they make, no matter how many lawyers they hire to help, and those with a more devil-may-care attitude are not likely to regret either decision. Certainly, the question of what type of IRA to fund is much less important than the decision to fund your IRA, 401(k), or other retirement account in the first place.

In general, the Roth IRA's advantages do not come from the fact that there's an advantage to paying your taxes now, rather than after retirement, when you'll (hopefully) have much more money due to market gains. (A 28% tax payment cuts your assets by exactly 28% whether it happens at the front end or after investment.) The Roth advantage really comes from the Roth IRA effectively being like a *bigger* IRA. (More on this below under the heading "Is Bigger Better?")

The Roth IRA is generally superior to the regular IRA, except for people who will be in a lower marginal tax bracket after retirement. For example, under the current tax code, many working people at the lower end of the 25% marginal tax bracket will likely fall to the 15% bracket after retirement. They should probably stick to a deductible regular IRA, deferring taxes now but paying them upon withdrawal. On the other hand, many younger workers who are now in the 15% or 25% tax bracket can expect to be paying a higher tax rate in retirement. They should generally choose the Roth IRA.

Of course, no one really knows what will happen to tax rates more than a few years from now. If, to take an extreme example, we move from an income tax system to a "consumption tax" system, then all investments will essentially act like a deductible regular IRA, with contributions deductible, but withdrawals subject to tax. But even then, it's highly improbable that people would be taxed on their "consumption" of proceeds from Roth IRAs, because hordes of seniors would then vote out the offending members of Congress. In short, the Roth IRA is likely to become as sacred a cow as its more established brethren.

1) Roth Rollovers

The conversion, or rollover, from a traditional to a Roth IRA is a taxable event. That means if you move a $100,000 traditional IRA into a Roth IRA, that $100,000 is taxable income. Sounds bad, but of course, it also means you won't have to pay taxes on the (hopefully much higher) amount you'll be withdrawing after retirement.

If your modified AGI (adjusted gross income) is under $100,000 in a given year, you may roll regular IRA money over into a Roth IRA. You don't need to have earned income, and it doesn't matter how old you are or how much money is in your IRA (the conversion amount does not count toward the $100,000 AGI limit). The rolled-over IRA money is taxed like income, as it would be if you were withdrawing from your IRA now, but without the 10% penalty. Nondeductible IRA contributions are not taxed on the conversion, but earnings and deductible contributions are.

This may be worth doing if you have—outside of any retirement-type account—enough money to pay the taxes. In essence, the effect of paying taxes now with nonretirement money is to increase the effective amount you have invested in your IRA. But if, in order to pay the taxes on the Roth conversion, you have to withdraw some of the money, paying a 10% penalty in addition to income taxes now, then conversion probably does not make sense for you. (Better to convert just a part of your IRA each year, to keep tax payments down and perhaps avoid bumping yourself into a higher marginal tax bracket.)

Note that if you pay the income tax on a conversion from within the IRA funds, you are effectively making no real difference to the size of your IRA, since you will have eliminated tax owed on withdrawals. But if you are under age 59½ you will also owe a 10% penalty on this tax-driven withdrawal. For this reason, you should consider delaying any conversion until you're beyond that age or until you can afford to make the income tax payment with other funds. If you use other (taxable money) resources to pay the income tax on a conversion, you will in effect be making a large contribution into your IRA moneys, even though the government doesn't describe it that way. (This is related to the issue of a Roth IRA effectively being a *bigger* IRA, as discussed below.)

To avoid having to take IRA distributions after age 70½, you may convert to a Roth IRA. However, you will be paying the same taxes as with other IRA withdrawals; the advantage of the Roth conversion is that you will continue avoiding taxes on future growth, whereas if you move your IRA money into a taxable account, all future income and realized capital gains are taxed each year.

Both the taxable and the tax-free portion of a regular IRA may be rolled over to the Roth IRA. This can be a little complicated if you have made nondeductible contributions to a regular IRA, and you're not rolling over all of your regular IRA money. In that case you'll need to follow the standard IRA basis recovery rules (requiring a prorated calculation on all your regular IRA assets) to determine the taxable amount of the transaction.

Convert if all the following are true:

- You can pay the conversion taxes with money that is not in a retirement plan.
- You can leave the money in for at least five years.
- You expect your retirement tax rate to be the same or higher. This depends on guesswork, generally including the assumption of an unchanging tax code. It's hardly a certainty unless you're in the 15% tax bracket this year.

2) New IRA Money

In a given year you can make contributions to any combination of regular IRA (nondeductible or deductible) and/or Roth IRA, as long as the total amount does not exceed $4,000 (going up to $5,000 for the 2008 tax year), and as long as you have made at least as much earned income as you are contributing. (Married couples can make a full $8,000 contribution, as long as their combined earned income is at least that much.)

The ability to contribute to a Roth IRA phases out for singles at an AGI (adjusted gross income) of $95,000 to $110,000, and for married couples filing jointly at an AGI of $150,000 to $160,000. Above these levels, you must use a regular IRA instead (which at these income levels would be nondeductible if you also participate in a retirement plan at work).

Is Bigger Better?

If you expect to be in the same tax bracket after retirement, then the Roth IRA is still probably the best way to go. That's because in essence, a Roth IRA is like a *bigger* deductible regular IRA. Here's why: the IRA is limited to $4,000 per year ($8,000 for married couples). Most people should be putting away more money than that if they can. If you're paying 33% in combined federal and state income taxes, and pay the same rate in retirement, then a $3,000 Roth IRA is just like a $4,478 deductible regular IRA. The $3,000 Roth costs you $3,000 out of pocket. Say it grows tenfold, to $30,000. You get the $30,000 tax-free.

If instead you have a $4,478 deductible regular IRA, it also costs you $3,000 out of pocket (since it will cut your income taxes by $1,478, or

33% of $4,478). It grows tax-deferred by tenfold, to $44,780. After you pay the 33% taxes on that money, you're left with the same $30,000. So the Roth IRA is just as good as the regular IRA in this example. However, the Roth has the following advantage: You can make a bigger effective contribution; a single person can make a $4,000 Roth IRA contribution, but she simply cannot make a $4,478 regular IRA contribution as in this example.

If you're comparing a Roth IRA to a nondeductible regular IRA, the Roth is favored even more. In each case, you deposit $3,000, which is $3,000 out of your own pocket. If it grows to $30,000 in a Roth IRA, you get the $30,000 tax-free. If it grows to $30,000 in a nondeductible regular IRA, you'll owe taxes on the gains ($27,000) upon withdrawal. After paying $8,910 in taxes (again, assuming a 33% tax rate), you're left with $21,090. So if you cannot deduct your contribution to a traditional IRA, you should definitely contribute to a Roth IRA if you can.

ROTH WITHDRAWALS

A distribution from a Roth IRA is completely tax-free if you meet the following rules:

- At least five years have passed from the time of your Roth contribution or conversion; withdrawals are considered to come first from your oldest contributions.
- The distribution is made because of an approved reason; generally because you're over age 59½, or you're taking out up to $10,000 for "first-time" home-buying expenses, or you're disabled or dead.

Note that if you don't meet these rules, you're generally subject to normal taxes on any gains and a 10% penalty on withdrawals. The penalties for not following the rules can thus be more severe with a Roth IRA than with a regular IRA, since with a regular IRA only a 10% penalty is at stake, and income taxes are generally due regardless of your age or reasons for withdrawal.

Because older-age distributions from a Roth IRA are not taxable, the government has no financial interest in forcing you to make Roth withdrawals, so it doesn't. (Regular IRAs have withdrawal requirements after age 70½.) You can keep your Roth IRA intact no matter how old you are. Indeed, with a Roth IRA you can make new contributions or conversions at any age!

Of course, while the Roth IRA (and the regular IRA) are pretty certain to remain in effect in close to their present form, details in the law can change, often unpredictably. But since so many voters use IRAs, and thus nobody in power seeks votes by calling the IRA a "loophole," or a "tax shelter," most of the changes to IRA plans have been improvements (i.e., the Roth IRA itself, and more recently the increase in annual maximum IRA contributions from $2,000 in 2001 to $3,000 in 2002, $4,000 in 2005, $5,000 in 2008, and inflation indexing after that). Bottom line: Politicians aren't likely to put the screws to either kind of IRA investor, so don't wait for the lights to change, just put your pedal to the Roth IRA's metal.

TAX-FREE PROFITS

Anyone with job-related income (i.e., not that trust fund you've got) can contribute to an IRA. You can contribute up to $4,000 of this income to an IRA each year. Married couples can contribute up to $8,000, as long as their combined earned income is at least that much.

IRA profits are always tax-deferred until you make withdrawals. But your IRA contributions may or may not be tax-deductible as you make them. What determines your ability to deduct your IRA investment? If you are an active participant in an employer-sponsored retirement plan, and your income exceeds $95,000, the IRA contribution is not fully deductible. (For married joint filers the income level is $150,000 for an active participant, and $150,000 for the spouse of an active participant.) The deductibility phases out evenly over the next $10,000 of income, so for a single who participates in a company's retirement plan, and whose income exceeds $50,000, the IRA contribution isn't deductible at all. (These figures are for 2006 income.)

Even if you can't deduct your IRA contributions, it can still make sense to put as much money as you can afford into an IRA. Regardless of deductibility, IRA money still grows tax-free, and this keeps more of your money at work for you.

However, don't make the common mistake of thinking that tax-advantaged, tax-deductible, or tax-deferred means "tax-free." They don't. When it comes time to withdraw the money you've stowed away in your

IRA, as with most investments, you will be taxed. But by that time, no doubt you will have read all about the best ways to minimize such taxes, and you'll have established dozens of trust accounts for yourself, your children, your children's children, and so on. For now, let's focus on how you can build the chest that you'll put your treasure in.

Opening Your IRA Account

As with the types of investments we've talked about in previous chapters, getting started, in terms of opening your IRA account, is easy. To do so, you can call or walk into your local bank, brokerage, mutual fund investor center, or insurance company and request an application.

While opening an IRA account is as easy as opening a brokerage account or purchasing shares in a mutual fund, choosing the holder of your IRA account (bank, brokerage, fund company, etc.), and selecting the type of investments that will compose your IRA portfolio, is as complex a task as selecting the best brokerage, stocks, bonds, and mutual funds for your actual portfolio. Where you open your IRA affects the range and type of investment options available to you. Hint: If no-load mutual funds from several different fund families aren't an option, move on to a place that does offer them.

Is an IRA right for you? Basically, if you are employed but don't have the ability to participate in a 401(k), 403(b), or other type of employer-sponsored plan, and you are not self-employed (either full- or part-time), then, yes, by all means open an IRA. If, however, you have these or other options to invest in your retirement, then you'll need to weigh their strengths and weaknesses against those of an IRA.

Timing

If you decide that you will be best served by opening up an IRA account, the sooner you do so, the better—literally. Waiting until the last minute is rarely a good way to do anything with your money (unless you're feeding a parking meter). And when it comes to investing in an IRA, the benefits of doing so earlier in the year—as opposed to at the tax-time deadline of April 15 the next year—are substantial. If you make your $4,000 2006 IRA contribution in April 2007, and you also make your 2007 contribution in April 2007, that is, from an investment standpoint, just like making two contributions in one year—you've effectively doubled your $4,000 annual contribution to $8,000.

Looked at another way, you'll get an extra year of tax-deferred growth out of your 2007 contribution. Either way, moving up your $4,000 annual contributions by twelve months can mean more than $40,000 extra when you retire (at 8% annual growth over thirty years). This effective "extra payment" is all perfectly legal; in fact, you could make your 2007 contribution as early as January of 2007, or as late as filing time in April 2008. Of course, you can't make a "double contribution" in this way more than once.

PERFORMANCE AND YOUR IRA PORTFOLIO

After setting up your IRA account, you'll need to figure out what types of investments you want to put in it. In doing so, you'll need to create one portfolio that can accomplish two things. First, you'll need to ensure that your IRA performs in accordance with your return objective. Ensuring that this is the case will require you to relate your IRA's performance to your other retirement-oriented investments. Second, you'll want to be certain that the investments you've selected for your IRA portfolio are the best possible choice.

You can put just about any type of investment in your IRA portfolio, including: CDs, US Treasury bonds (or bills or notes), money market funds, stocks, corporate bonds, mutual funds, zero coupon securities, unit investment trusts, limited partnerships, options (for self-directed IRAs only), and US gold and silver coins. My preferences: stocks, taxable bonds, and mutual funds holding the same. (There's no sense putting a tax-free investment, like a municipal bond or muni bond fund, in a tax-free account!)

As with your other investment portfolios, you will be best served by actively managing your IRA portfolio. What does active management mean? Among other things, it means reviewing the investments in your IRA, especially looking at their performances compared to other available investments. Doing so isn't all that difficult. For one thing, most banks, mutual fund firms, and insurance companies issue monthly or quarterly statements that allow you to track the performance of your IRA account. And tracking the constituent parts of your IRA portfolio has never been easier, thanks to the increased coverage in even local papers of mutual funds—which are the best way to build your investment portfolio from scratch.

Making changes to particular parts of your overall portfolio in order to account for changes in the overall market is a good idea. But don't confuse changing your mix with changing your overall portfolio—if you've done the job right, you shouldn't have to make dramatic changes to the overall objective that your portfolio was originally designed for. Also, be careful of chasing after this year's winning stocks, bonds, and mutual funds. While there are legitimate reasons for selling and buying new stocks, bonds, and mutual funds to enhance your IRA portfolio's return, buying a highflier is not one of them.

What parts of your IRA portfolio might need to be adjusted? For example, if you want to increase your exposure to international markets, you may want to add an additional international fund or up the ante in the one you've got. (For optimal portfolio allocations, return to chapter 16.) How do you do this? If you haven't exceeded the contribution limit for the year, you can purchase the fund for your account outright, or, if you have reached the maximum, you can consider selling another investment or reducing your money market amount in order to purchase the international fund with the proceeds. Some plans restrict the number of trades you can do in a given time frame—per quarter or per year. You'll need to be sure that your IRA account enables you to make at least one trade per quarter. Not that I'm advocating active trading. Far from it. Instead, I'm advocating your right to react to changes in the market.

To shift money from another retirement plan (a 401(k) from a previous employer, for example) into a new or existing IRA, there are two ways to do it: direct transfer and rollover. In order to pursue a direct transfer, you will need to lend the custodian of your old account the right to transfer those assets directly into your new account. Typically, this entails having to physically sign a specific form. Once signed, the old custodian can then transfer your money (and whatever investments it's invested in) into your new account. You may encounter some delay between the time you sign the form and the time the money gets transferred. Stay on top of your old custodian to ensure that it is working on your behalf (rather than its own; after all, the longer your account stays with it, the more fees it receives).

When it comes to rollovers, be sure that you are in charge. Rollovers typically happen when you transfer funds from an existing retirement plan or when your existing IRA funds are transferred to a new IRA. For example, if you decide to change jobs from a company that currently provides a 401(k) plan, and you're taking a job at a company that doesn't offer any retirement plan, you'll need to roll the funds from your old 401(k) plan into an IRA (the rollover must occur within sixty days of the withdrawals, lest taxes and a 10% penalty be incurred).

Note: You should not roll over money from an employer-sponsored retirement plan into an existing IRA, and you should not make your annual IRA contributions into a rollover IRA. Why? If you do, the resulting "commingling" of rollover IRA money and ordinary IRA money means you will never be able to roll this IRA back into another employer-sponsored plan. (Something you might want to do if a future employer's plan has attractive features, such as the ability to loan oneself a house down payment.)

Instead, set up a new IRA account as the repository for your 401(k) or other employer-sponsored savings. Should you again become employed by a company that offers a 401(k), 403(b), or other plan—and chances are great that you will do so before your toes turn up—then it's in your best interest to safeguard the savings you've already accumulated. Also, if you're a job hopper, keep in mind that you're entitled to one personal rollover per each twelve-month period (whereas direct transfers may be made as often as you want).

WITHDRAWAL PENALTY!

If you withdraw before your time, you'll get the hangover without the wine. That's because withdrawing funds from your IRA before you reach age 59½ makes them subject to a 10% penalty tax in addition to being fully taxed as regular income. (On the other hand, you will have to begin withdrawals from regular IRAs by April 1 of the year after turning age 70½ or you'll be subject to a whopping 50% penalty from the IRS.) Exceptions? Disability. But be careful. This is your retirement money—nothing save a dire emergency should push you into using it. Of course, once you near retirement age—59½ at the earliest, unless you become permanently disabled—you will need to plan on the best way to withdraw funds.

You can make personal use of your IRA funds for up to sixty days per year while rolling over your account. Don't do it. It's simply too easy to fritter away the money, leaving you holding less than zero (as the IRS will want those taxes and the 10% penalty!).

RETIREMENT PLANS FOR THE ENTREPRENEUR

If you are self-employed and earning income—i.e., you're getting paid to play your guitar in the bar on Thursday nights and not just toting it around for the Antonio Banderas look—then you can create your own self-employment retirement plan, even if you currently participate in your full-time employer's pension plan. The benefits of doing so are threefold: your contributions may be fully or partially tax deductible, you'll enjoy the benefits of tax-deferred growth of your investments, and you'll build a better retirement stash for yourself. Even if you stop playing at being a musician later in life, you'll have established an additional source of retirement revenue for yourself.

We'll look at three types of plans: the SEP, the SIMPLE, and the more complicated Keogh plan. The well-known 401(k) plan is expensive for smaller businesses, but prevails. Like other retirement plans, the threefold benefits of these plans come with some strings attached. There are specific maximum contributions and deadlines for those contributions, and the money you invest won't be available to you (without generally paying 10% penalties on top of taxes) until you reach 59½. But, since this is part of your retirement savings, these shouldn't be drawbacks. Just don't look to these plans as a source of funds for preretirement financial expenses, like college tuition or the down payment for that vacation home on the Vineyard.

You can do this at home. You can set up a self-employed retirement plan if you fit the following bill: you are self-employed (full- or part-time). That's it. No big character check or profitability analysis. You work for yourself. You get paid. You can participate. (And chances are you should.) Even if you are a full-time employee and participating in a pension plan, as long as you have income from one source of self-employment, chances are you'll qualify for one of the following self-employed retirement plans. (What's better, contributing to one of these plans won't prevent you from also contributing to a Roth IRA, if you're otherwise eligible.) Note that if you run a business with employees, you generally have to include your employees along with yourself in any of these plans.

SEPs (Simplified Employee Pensions)

Simplified employee pension plans (called SEPs) are a non-CPA's answer to self-funding a retirement plan. Why? Ease. Instead of maintaining a separate pension plan (as is required with a Keogh, detailed below), your SEP contributions are deposited directly into your IRA account. (If you have employees, consider a SIMPLE IRA—detailed below—to enable your employees [and yourself] to fund their own retirement plans at lower cost.)

How an SEP works in your (and your employees') favor: If you own a small business, closely held or otherwise, and not necessarily incorporated, you can use it to create an employer-funded pension plan for your eligible employees. If you're an employee in search of a retirement plan at your place of work, you can suggest this viable option.

How SEPs work: First, you'll need to set up an IRA account (see above) into which your contributions can be placed—or your employer can establish one in which you can deposit your contributions. Your employer can then make contributions in accordance with specified limits. Once an SEP is established, your employer must contribute to the accounts of each employee who is over age twenty-one who has performed services in at least three of the five preceding calendar years.

Tax advantages: Contributions to an SEP are basically tax-free income paid by an employer to an employee. Employers can contribute to each employee's account the lesser of $44,400 for 2006 (up from $42,400 in 2005) or 25% of pay (or a lesser percentage, but the same percentage for each employee). Each employee is always 100% "vested" (has total ownership of) the money in his or her SEP IRA. Employees can't put their own money into an SEP (not that that's a real impediment when it comes to self-employed people), but they can still contribute to an IRA. (The SIMPLE plan, below, allows employer and employee contributions.)

As with an IRA, plans can be set up, and contributions for a given tax year can be made, until April 15 of the following year. If you're an employer, your contributions are not subject to FICA or the Federal Unemployment Tax Act (FUTA) tax withholdings, although state income tax usually will have to be paid on your contribution amount.

As with a traditional IRA, withdrawals are taxed as income, and premature withdrawals (those before age 59½) are generally subject to a 10% penalty.

SIMPLE Plans

The SIMPLE plan (Savings Incentive Match Plan for Employees) has replaced the Salary Reduction SEP. It offers sole proprietors and businesses with one hundred or fewer employees an affordable and yes, simple plan for funding retirements through employee salary reductions and matching employer contributions (similar to a 401(k) plan, but with lower administrative costs). Employees can generally contribute up to $6,000 per year through payroll deductions and employers must offer matching contributions equal to employee contributions (up to 3% of employee wages) or fixed contributions equal to 2% of employee wages (up to $3,200).

A SIMPLE plan can be sponsored by most types of organizations, including C- and S-corporations, partnerships, sole proprietorships, tax-exempt employers, and governmental entities, as long as they don't already sponsor another retirement plan. The employer may allow each employee to choose a financial institution, or the employer may choose the financial institution that will receive all contributions under the plan. In the latter case only, employees have a right to transfer contributions to a SIMPLE IRA at another financial institution without penalty.

Keogh Plans

A Keogh is a plan designed to provide the self-employed (and principals in unincorporated businesses) the opportunity to make tax-deductible and tax-deferred retirement funds for themselves and any employees. If you work in a company through which you participate in a pension plan, you may still set up a Keogh plan if you also have self-employment income.

Drawbacks: Keoghs aren't all that easy to set up if you're trying to go it alone. They're subject to changing, complex, confusing rules. Fortunately, many financial institutions offer an easy way to open a Keogh (since they do most of the technical work for you). Banks, brokerage firms, and mutual fund companies can help you understand and open a Keogh. But, like most things in life, the more you know about a Keogh before you start asking questions, the more meaningful your inquiry will be. The following Keogh primer should help you cover the basics and then some. That way, you can better determine if a Keogh may be right for you, and if so, you should proceed to consult your attorney or tax adviser before choosing a Keogh over an alternative plan.

Types of Keoghs

The most common form of a Keogh is, like the other plans mentioned in this chapter, a defined-contribution plan, which is just what it sounds like: contributions are a set percentage of compensation or fixed regular sums (more on this below).

A second type of Keogh provides a defined-benefit plan, one set up to pay a defined (predetermined) series of retirement payments to ex-employees during their retirement years. If your income stream is strong and well in excess of your needs, and you're at least into your forties, this type of plan can allow the highest annual tax-deductible contributions, well in excess of the cap on a defined-contribution Keogh. (Contributions are limited to the extent calculated to result in a given maximum retirement benefit; this benefit is generally the lesser of the participant's average compensation for the highest three consecutive tax years as an active participant.) But setting up a defined benefit plan requires a lot more work and administrative (indeed, actuarial) expertise, and since contributions are based on actuarial determinations, not your profits or ability to pay, such plans can be problematic during business downturns.

Whichever Keogh plan you choose, you must set it up by December 31 of the year in which you want to begin taking the deduction. However, once you have set up the account, you don't have to make the actual contribution until your tax return is filed, or April 15 of the following year. (Of course, the sooner you contribute, the sooner the positive effect of compounding can begin to work for you.) Note: if you want to set up a retirement plan but missed the Keogh deadline for last year, and it is not yet April 15, you can consider setting up an SEP, detailed above.

For a defined-contribution Keogh plan, in 2006 the maximum contribution is the lesser of $44,000 or 100% of employee compensation (that compensation limited, for the purpose of this calculation, to $205,000 in 2004). Apart from these dollar limits, all employees must receive the same percentage of their compensation, and in reality an employer is likely to limit contributions to 25% of compensation, as employer contributions are deductible only up to 25% of the participants' aggregate compensation.

There used to be a separate higher limit in the less flexible "money purchase" Keogh, which required the same portion to be contributed every year, but now that the "profit-sharing" Keogh can be deductible at up to 25% of compensation, there's every reason to stick to a profit-sharing Keogh since it allows you the flexibility to reduce or eliminate contributions during business downturns.

For the self-employed, deductible contributions to a Keogh plan are limited to 25% of your net income after your Keogh deductions are accounted for. How can you calculate the amount of deductible contributions you can make? Your deduction percentage is determined by dividing 25% by 125% (i.e., the maximum percentage divided by your total income plus the Keogh deduction) to arrive at 20%. (In other words, if you're the boss, 25% of your gross income equals 20% of your net income.)

As with a deductible IRA, withdrawals generally can't be made without paying taxes—and a 10% penalty before age 59½—and distributions must begin before age 70½. Nevertheless, unlike with an IRA, you can lend yourself money from your Keogh nest egg—you can, that is, if you're an employee of a business that offers such a plan. Owners can't.

If you don't own more than 10% of the business you're not considered an owner, and you can lend yourself a sum that can't exceed $50,000 or 50% of your vested Keogh plan value, whichever is less. You have five years to repay the loan, unless you use it to buy your residence, in which case the repayment period can be longer. If you leave your job, your ex-employer may require you to repay the loan immediately. Note the penalty attached to failing to repay the loan: the outstanding balance will count as a withdrawal; you'll owe income taxes and, if you're under age 59½, an additional 10% penalty.

• • •

As you can see, SEPs and Keoghs make investing in IRAs look easy. There are distinct advantages to each plan—beyond the ease with which one can or can't participate in them. For the successful entrepreneur, saving the maximum tax-advantaged amount (i.e., the SEP or Keogh route) may make the most sense. On the other hand, for those just starting out, an IRA is the best place to start.

Ready Resources

- Fidelity Investments (fidelity.com) has an IRA evaluator to help you pick the right type of IRA (Roth or deductible or nondeductible traditional IRA).
- Roth IRA website (rothira.com) contains more technical information.
- A helpful pamphlet, "Choosing a Retirement Solution for Your Small Business," can be found at the Department of Labor's website at dol.gov/ebsa/pdf/choosing.pdf. Or call the IRS at 1-800-TAX-FORM and ask for it (catalog number 34066S).
- IRS Publication 560, "Retirement Plans for Small Business," can be found at the IRS site at irs.gov/pub/irs-pdf/p560.pdf.

Tax Strategies Investors Need to Know

CHAPTER 25

Your Tax Strategies from Scratch

Nothing, not even the Ice Capades rendition of "Michael Jackson on Trial," could be as mind-numbing as taxes. Forms and more forms. And more forms. Numbers—that don't add up. Annual, quarterly, monthly statements from hell. You might as well give up, move to a place where taxes don't exist.

If only such a place did exist—but then, how would they be able to afford to build roads, finance schools, and foster religious freedom, not to mention paying for all those haircuts and parking spaces at national airports that our politicians make such good use of?

Knowledge versus legwork—that's what tax strategizing is all about. But who has the time to do either? Not you. I mean, let's face it, there are movies to be seen and coffee bars you've yet to blow the froth from. And while I can't offer you individual tax advice, I can make sure that you are up to speed on some of the more essential areas relating to taxes and your investments. Reading the following can help you both save a bundle and maximize the earning power of your hard-earned money. Now we're speaking a language that isn't dead. Let's take a look.

Basically there are a few definitions you need to know, and several sources and several strategies that can help you master the tax-related issues of your overall investment plan. But first, always evaluate the tax consequences of your investing (and all finance-related) moves. Never invest in something solely for the tax benefits of doing so. Instead, weigh the merits of the investment in light of several factors—

from your personal objectives to the inherent quality of the investment to the potential tax ramifications of it.

Defining Moments

When it comes to investing, there's a defining moment at year-end. It's the moment when you determine just how well your investments have done over the year. If they've done well, then chances are you have capital gains to account for. If they have done poorly, you may have capital losses, which, once accounted for, can help you reduce the overall tax burden of your capital gains.

Capital gain: The difference between an asset's (for example, a stock's) purchased price and selling price, when that difference is positive. Taxes must be paid when that asset is sold. Selling an asset that has capital gains is known as realizing the gain. As long as you hold on to your investments, you don't pay any capital gains taxes on the increase in value of these investments. That's one benefit of buying and holding, although eventually you will have to learn some fancy estate-planning footwork.

Capital loss: The difference between an asset's (for example, a stock's) purchased price and selling price, when that difference is negative. In this case, a negative can be a positive—come tax time. That's because of your ability to take advantage of a "tax loss." Doing so is relatively easy. You simply exchange shares in a losing stock or fund into a similar stock or fund. This method of exchange is known as a "tax swap." You can apply the loss against any capital gains plus $3,000 of income. (Moreover, if you have suffered more losses than your swap can swallow in a given year, you can carry the excess loss over to future years.)

Wash sale rule: If you just sold a stock (or fund or other security) for a loss you want to deduct, but you want to buy the stock back, be sure to wait thirty-one days before switching back into it. If you do it sooner, the IRS will consider it a "wash sale" and disallow the loss.

Distributions: When it comes to investing in mutual funds, you lose the ability to control your capital gains, since the fund manager will be the one who is buying and selling shares in the securities that constitute his or her portfolio. Mutual funds are corporations, but they have special dispensation from paying corporate income tax, provided they distribute (pay out to shareholders) virtually all of their realized gains and after-expenses income. Distributions are made up of long-term capital gains, short-term capital gains, and dividend income. Starting with 2003, taxes on long-term (held for over a year) capital gains are now capped at 15%, while if you're in a higher tax bracket (25% to 35%) you'll pay that higher rate on short-term gains and income. Distributions do not affect tax-deferred retirement accounts. The whole point of an IRA, 401(k), SEP, annuity, or other tax-advantaged account is to allow for tax-free compounding of interest and capital gains.

Tax Planning from Scratch

- Coordinate your investment tax planning with other important personal financial planning areas, including investments and retirement planning.
- Keep meticulous tax records. (See chapter 5 for details.) It's the only way to stay ahead of the flood of forms—from your investments and beyond.
- Don't be sold on an investment solely on the merits of its tax advantage—do be sold on the merits of investing in a tax-advantaged investment plan like a 401(k) or 403(b).
- Hold the stocks you buy—and let the capital gains work in your favor.
- If you're owed a refund, send in your tax return early. Filing late means you lose the ability to receive and invest the refund—meaning you lose interest on money you could have had sooner.
- If you owe the IRS money, don't send in your tax return early. Paying early means you lose interest you could have earned.
- If you overpaid taxes the previous year, amend your return and get a refund.
- Donate stocks, not cash. If you are looking for a way to avoid capital gains tax, and benefit a cause you believe in (and one that the IRS believes in, too), donate some appreciated stock instead of cash. You'll get a deduction for the stock's full market value at the time of the donation, without paying capital gains.
- Donate your clothing (not all of it) and other items you don't need or use—from a toaster oven to furniture to a car—to a charitable organization. (Sorry, your best friend who was just fired from that cool software company doesn't rate—in the eyes of the IRS.) Get a receipt briefly describing the goods. You can deduct

the fair market value of the items—which can translate into a great inverse investment.

- Delay buying a fund until after its distribution is made. Call your fund company to find out if and when it will be making a distribution—typically in December, but often additionally in some other month(s). Income and capital gains distributions create an immediate tax liability in taxable accounts, but don't really add to the value of your portfolio (share prices drop by the amount of the distributions).

- Note that you should receive 1099-DIV forms by the end of January. You should record "Ordinary Dividends" on Schedule B of your federal tax return as dividends. Naturally, capital gains distributions are recorded as part of your calculation of capital gains (or losses) on Schedule D.

INVESTOR TAX STRATEGIES

Maximize your 401(k), 403(b), IRA, or other tax-advantaged or tax-deferred contribution. This is a winner—and a no-brainer. Chances are you will qualify for one tax-advantaged retirement-oriented investment plan—and so much the better. It's especially advantageous if you can participate in a company-sponsored 401(k) or 403(b), since contributions are made with pretax dollars and you may receive the added benefit of matching funds from your employer. The maximum contribution ceiling is also higher in most plans than in an IRA. Bottom line: participate to the maximum—but realize that the maximum for you isn't necessarily the maximum allowable contribution. You need to ensure that your other living expenses are accounted for, too. Otherwise, you run the risk of dipping into your retirement fund for current living expenses. There is a substantial penalty for doing so.

Contribute to an IRA if you have maxed out on your 401(k) contribution. Even if the IRA contribution is nondeductible, it's a good deal since your money grows, tax-deferred, until withdrawal. Also, plan ahead so that you can contribute to your IRA as early in the year as possible. The earlier you begin, the more time your money has to compound tax-deferred.

Request and review your brokerage or fund company's tax reports. Full-service brokerages (and even most major discount shops) as well as some mutual fund companies (and many leading fund networks) provide you with most of the necessary tax information you'll need. This is a great help, but it's not perfect. Their reports showing capital gains and losses you've realized generally calculate gains based on the "average cost, single-category" method.

While a little more complicated, there are other calculation methods the IRS allows you to use, which could result in a lower tax bill if you make a partial sale of a fund position whose shares were bought at different times and prices. (The "last-in, first-out" method generally shows lower gains over time, as investments generally go up, while the "specific shares" method allows you to pick exactly which shares you want to sell; usually whichever have the highest cost basis—were bought at the highest price—and thus will show the smallest gains or largest losses.)

For those shareholders who elect to use the specific shares method, you'll need to prove to the IRS that you elected this method before you sold the shares, not after. The evidence you'll provide is the written instructions you sent your fund firm directing it to sell a specific lot of shares, which the firm should date-stamp and return to you. Some fund firms can do this after a phone or Internet transaction. Ask your mutual fund customer service representative. (Fidelity's Tax Center has a multitude of tax-related articles, including some on cost basis and different methods for selecting shares, at fidelity.com/tax.)

Municipal bond funds (see chapter 11) are potentially a solid tax-exempt investment. (Buying municipal bonds directly is expensive and risky in terms of your inability to invest in several and research all.) Consider that if the munis are issued in your state (or Puerto Rico), your income will be free of state (and often local) as well as federal income taxes. But also consider the risks: state-specific funds aren't well diversified, and if someday your home state sees serious budgetary or political problems, your fund could see losses despite previously solid-looking credit ratings.

Ready Resources

- irs.ustreas.gov (Here, you can download IRS forms and publications—a list of the most meaningful ones is found below. You can also click here to your state tax department sites.)
- securetax.com
- taxcut.com
- turbotax.com

The following IRS publications (free for the asking) can help you consider, evaluate, and file your investment-related taxable transactions. At irs.ustreas.gov you can search for them by number or title.

SECTION 7

New Family,
New You

CHAPTER 26

The Parent Trap
from Scratch

Whether you're about to propose to your better half or are advanced to the stage that you're expecting a baby, your life will fast become a whirlwind of clothes, room decorating, toys, binkies, and bottles. What's a binky? Trust me, unless you turn out to be the next "40-Year-Old Virgin," you'll find out.

If you're not there already, one day you'll find yourself wondering when your refrigerator swapped from bottles filled with beer to bottles filled with milk; when sleep deprivation became the norm and evenings out turned out to be a logistically insurmountable planning event; when the hard-won dinner out had you seated and eating before the other set with no teeth and diapers had even arrived. All the while, you know that you wouldn't swap a moment of your new family life—while at the same time, you're probably thinking about finances and the future more than ever before. You'll be pouring a lot of energy into making sure your children are healthy and happy and educated from day one. And I'm not going to play pat the bunny on this one: It's going to be challenging—and fun. This chapter can help you think about all the smart financial moves you can make now, to create the life you want for your family in the years to come.

And if you think you're not planning on having a family, I have two words of wisdom for you: Uh-huh. I bet you're also planning on living forever. Yup. And I bet you're also counting on winning the lottery to fund your retirement. Great! I hate to burst your bubble, but I'll take the bet that has you in the family way in under ten years' time.

THINGS CHANGE

Your priorities—financial and otherwise—may have changed significantly as you've made the leap from single to couple to family. You may be willing to give up some luxuries to stash more away for retirement. Perhaps you have your heart set on taking the family on a sailing trip every summer, or on sending your kids to private colleges. Or maybe you want to invest enough money to retire early and travel cross-country in an RV. Maybe having kids has changed your ideas about time and money. You might prefer to cut back on the rat race and live more modestly, so you can have more time with your family.

Before you go any further, take a few minutes to put those priorities in writing. Remember to include things like: paying off credit cards or student loans, buying a house, putting an addition on the house, saving for college tuition(s), getting a new job, saving, putting aside enough to retire by age sixty, or coaching a soccer team by the time your kid is in first grade.

PRIORITIES

Financial: **Time/Leisure:**

1. _____   _____

   _____   _____

2. _____   _____

   _____   _____

3. _____   _____

   _____   _____

4. _____   _____

   _____   _____

5. _____   _____

   _____   _____

And so on.

This book can help you get where you want to go. First stop on this new adventure: section I. (This note is a return-trip ticket if you bypassed it on your way here.)

REVISIT YOUR BENEFITS

Now is the time to take a look with fresh eyes at health plans, life and disability plans, and other important benefits offered to you and your spouse or partner at work. If a new baby is on the way—or has just arrived—you may have a different view on benefits than you did when it was just the two of you. We'll look at how you can make the best choices to keep your family healthy and well protected today, while also plotting the best use of your money, so you can save and invest for the future.

Health Plans

You may not have thought much about your medical benefits since signing up for them when you started your job. Perhaps you made changes when you got married. Either way, it's important to give those health benefits a close look again now. (Chapter 3 will help you accomplish this.)

If you and your spouse are on different medical plans, now may be a good time to enroll the whole family on one employer's plan. Compare premium costs, plan types, and out-of-pocket costs before you decide.

Let's say James and Melinda have each stayed on their own employer plans since they married three years ago. James contributes $50 a month to his health plan, while Melinda pays $40 a month (both payroll-deducted). Family coverage at James's office costs $90 a month; Melinda's would jump to $80. Not only is her family plan less expensive, but the doctors she's seeing for her pregnancy are in her HMO plan. James rarely goes to the doctor and wouldn't mind changing plans. They decide to enroll the whole family on Melinda's plan, and to drop James's coverage.

But don't you drop anybody's plan until you're sure he or she is enrolled correctly in the other person's plan. The last thing you want to do is leave somebody uncovered due to an administrative oversight. Also, make sure to have your new child added to the plan on the day he or she is born or, in the case of an adoption, on the date on which you take legal custody.

Premium rates tend to rise significantly when you go from single coverage to a family plan. There may be a rate for an employee with just one dependent, should you decide that works best for you. (For example, if James is in the middle of knee reconstruction, this may not be a great time for him to change doctors or plans. He needs to recover in time to chase the baby around! It's possible that it makes sense to put mom and baby on one plan, and leave dad on his plan for now.) Your company will be picking up the bulk of the tab, and you will be contributing a portion of your paycheck. The payments typically are deducted automatically by your payroll department, meaning one less bill for you to worry about. And health insurance premiums come out of your gross pay, before taxes, which saves you money.

In case you need a refresher on the types of health care available, refer back to chapter 3. You will probably need to choose between a traditional indemnity plan—with deductibles and bills split between you and the insurer—and a managed-care plan, such as an HMO (health maintenance organization) or PPO (preferred provider organization). As a parent, you should consider not only the premium costs, shown in the example we just saw, but also:

- Whether an HMO or other managed-care option works for you. Are your doctors and preferred hospitals on the list?
- The out-of-pocket costs you'll incur when you use the plan

It's a multipart decision, for sure. Make certain you're comparing apples to apples when you look at premium costs. And look at the out-of-pocket costs of using an indemnity plan. Should you decide an indemnity option best suits you—perhaps because the doctors or hospitals you prefer aren't part of the HMO option you're considering—make sure you're prepared to cover the bills that could come your way.

The good news in the example on the following page is that you're protected against having to shell out more than $2,000 in a given year under the Rx plan. If you choose an indemnity plan, consider signing up for a *flexible spending account* with the company. These accounts

	Rx Indemnity Plan	Alpha HMO
Monthly premium contribution	$90	$80
Annual deductible	$200	$0
Coinsurance (bill splitting)	80/20 (you pay 20% of every bill)	0
Co-pay per doctor visit/prescription	$0	$10
Annual out-of-pocket maximum	$2,000	n/a

let you set aside money on a pretax basis, to help cover out-of-pocket expenses more cost-effectively.

You can set aside as much as $5,000 if you're married. Remember not to overfund these accounts, however. Any money you don't use in the course of a year, you lose. Do the math to make sure it's worth your while.

As new parents, you may be grappling with issues of day care too, particularly if you both plan to work. Flexible spending accounts can be an effective tool for helping with the high costs of child or elder care.

Dependent care spending accounts can be used toward the costs of day care, summer day camp, preschool, or in-home child care for kids under age thirteen. Dependent care also includes adult day care, in the event you're one of many Americans caring for both children and elderly parents. It's easy to run through more than $5,000 a year on dependent care.

Quick tip: If you need to pay for day care, or if you know you'll need to set money aside for eligible health-care expenses, consider opening a flexible spending account. It will save you money, by allowing you to set aside money for expenses related to dependent care and medical care, before taxes. Failing to take advantage of this opportunity is leaving money on the table—money you could put to work for you.

There are some hidden benefits to all the health plans offered through your company. Many have twenty-four-hour health hotlines. If a child is sick in the middle of the night, or if you're traveling and not sure about some physical pain you're experiencing, you can call the hotline and get answers to your questions immediately from trained nurses. That can mean great peace of mind when you can't reach your own doctor, or when you're weighing whether you need to seek care immediately.

Dental Coverage

Review your dental coverage the same way you do your medical plans. While your child will be more interested in the tooth fairy than in the dentist for some time, you and your spouse will need dental care. And you'll want to make sure you can get a family plan when the time comes, if not now.

Dental care may seem like a luxury, but it's not. It's a necessity. While most plans don't cover all the expenses of dental work (unlike your medical plan), they do help foot the bills. And many plans cover two regular cleanings every year. People with no dental coverage tend to skip regular preventive care visits. This could cost them more in the long run—in looks, comfort, and the wallet.

Look at what you have to contribute in payroll deductions to have dental coverage. Is it less than the cost of twice-yearly cleanings for you and your spouse or dependents? Remember, too, that it's likely you or the kids will need fillings—or other more expensive dental care— along the way. Without any dental coverage at all, those bills can be hefty.

Most dental plans don't cover braces. Check to see if your company offers orthodontia benefits, to cover part of the expense of teeth-straightening when your kids are approaching their preteens.

Life Insurance

As parents, life insurance may become more important to you than it has been before. It can be a source of financial protection for your spouse and kids. And it's a financial tool to consider as you build your plans.

If you were to die, life insurance would put a lump sum of money (often a year's pay or a flat amount, like $20,000) into the hands of your beneficiaries. In some cases, if you were suffering from a terminal illness, you could get half your life insurance benefit while you were still alive, to help cover expenses.

To decide if you need life insurance, or how much, you need to look at who's supporting your household, and how large your savings and investments are. If only one of you is working, while the other takes care of the kids, then that one income source is very important. If the family were to lose that income stream for any reason, what would happen? Would the family have to move? Sell the house? Cash out some investments?

As far as planning for the future, you're probably better off investing money in stocks and mutual funds than stashing it in big life insurance policies that do no one any good until you're dead. But it's not a bad idea to have some life insurance, to tide the family over if you or your spouse were to die.

Take whatever life insurance may be offered by your company at no charge to you. It may not be worth buying additional life insurance, however. Consider the cost of any supplemental life coverage offered to you, and whether your money would be better put into investments for the future, whether for college tuition or for your own retirement. Also, keep in mind that the cost of life insurance in excess of $50,000 is added to your taxable income.

Example: For a thirty-three-year-old employee, life insurance might cost the company 29¢ per $1,000 of insurance per month. If an employer provides $90,000 of life insurance to that employee, that is $40,000 worth over the nontaxable allowance, and the employee must count as additional income the value of the difference:

$40,000 ÷ $1,000 = 40
40 × $0.29 = $11.60 per month

So this employee would have $11.60 per month, or $138 per year, in "imputed income" added to his or her income statement.

Term life insurance premiums don't accumulate for you to tap later. Only with group universal life and "whole life" plans does your policy act like an investment. If you or your spouse were to leave a job, you could convert a group life policy to an individual policy, without having to answer medical questions—an advantage if you are not well.

Be sure to designate your beneficiaries carefully on life insurance as well as investment documents. As you're planning to have a family, this is a good time to make sure your paperwork is in order. If you want your spouse or kids to receive the money if something should happen to you, make sure their names are on the documents.

Dependent life insurance is sad stuff. Here's hoping you never need it. The policies can cover a spouse or children. Policies on children tend to be in small amounts, say $5,000 to $10,000, and are meant to cover funeral costs in the instance of a child's death. For your spouse, you can often get the same coverage you get for yourself. This would clearly be most useful if you would need additional income in the event of your spouse's death.

Your company may offer free *accidental death and dismemberment* coverage. Not a pretty name, but it's a good benefit to have, providing a lump sum of cash in the event you died in an accident, or lost your sight or any limbs in an accident. It's not a pleasant thing to think about. But it's something to sign up for, and to know is there for you and your dependents if you need it.

Another benefit you should consider now that you're parents is *long-term disability.*

Particularly if one of you is earning the bulk of the family income, it may be important to insure that income. If you were to become sick or injured, and unable to work for several months, would you have enough cash to pay your mortgage or rent, electricity and phone bills? Would you deplete your savings? Run up credit card bills?

This is a serious issue. If both of you have jobs, you might be able to make ends meet on just one salary, on a temporary basis. If you couldn't make ends meet in an emergency, long-term disability coverage could be very important for you.

It's likely your employer pays for short-term disability, to cover part of your pay if you're out of work due to an injury or illness for up to three months or six months. But what if you're out for nine months due to a disability? Long-term disability typically covers up to two-thirds of your monthly income. Look at the cost of this benefit carefully, and consider what other income sources you could tap if you were sick or injured for a long period. You and your spouse may decide this benefit is a must for you, and that group rates at work make it affordable.

SAVING AND INVESTING

Now that you've done the important work of getting the most out of your benefits menu, you should feel good. You've taken a big step in ensuring health and financial protection for you and your family.

Now comes the part where you look into the future. Think hard about the priorities you wrote down above—the simple and the complex—and we'll work on how to get you there.

Handle the obvious first. If you're carrying credit card debt, you'll need to work that down, as we discussed in the first section. It's a rare investment that can beat the 9% to 20% interest you might be paying on revolving credit card debt. If you haven't done so already, make a plan to chip away at that debt—even if that means paying $100 per bill instead of the minimum. It's the best investment you can make. It's truly paying yourself.

If debt isn't an issue, congratulate yourself for a minute. Either you never spent beyond your means, or you conquered those bad habits and their resulting financial burdens. It's time to focus on your goals. If buying a house is your biggest goal, then you'll need to start stashing money in a savings or money market account. Don't put any money you'll need in less than three years at risk in the stock market.

Say you've got $7,000 saved and you need $5,000 more for a down payment on a house. You'd be much better off saving your money in the bank or in a money market account than to try turning a quick buck in stocks or mutual funds.

Just because some people you may know (perhaps even you) have recently reaped big gains in the market in short periods of time, you can't count on that happening all the time. And what if the market drops? You could fall months, even years, behind in your goal of saving enough to buy a house.

If you're like most parents, you have two big, long-term goals before you. One is saving to send the kids to college, or at least to help with tuition. The other is investing for your retirement. Both are important. One probably comes sooner—college. Depending on when you're starting, it's eighteen years away at best. It could be as near as five or ten years. Retirement may be twenty to thirty years away. But the chunk of money you need to amass for your retirement years is even bigger than the sizable nugget you may be hoping to pull together for college.

You need to think about both these targets at once. Don't put off one for the other—only to panic about the issues when it's too late to do anything about them.

Let's tackle retirement first.

By now, both you and your spouse have probably been enrolled in a 401(k) plan or an employer-funded ("defined-benefit") pension plan.

If one of you is planning to leave work, make sure you understand the "vesting" schedule of that plan, or how long you need to work for the company to reap benefits in retirement. This will factor into your other retirement planning. We'll come back to that in a minute.

If, for some reason, neither of you is enrolled in a 401(k) plan—and a plan is available to you at work—by all means, now is the time. Even if money is tight. The sooner you join, the better off you're going to be down the road, especially if your employer offers any kind of investment matching program. Failing to sign up means leaving money on the table. Would you walk over a $100 bill on an empty sidewalk? No. You'd pick it up and put it in your pocket. Passing up an employer retirement-plan match is like giving away $1 million—literally—over time. And now that you have two people to support in retirement, and lots of family expenses between now and then, time is truly of the essence.

If one of you is leaving work to be with the child or children, be sure to roll over his or her 401(k) plan assets within sixty days. Move the assets directly into an IRA, without ever touching them, and get the money back to work in mutual funds or other securities that you choose. Failing to do so will cost you dearly, in the form of a 20% tax and a 10% penalty for withdrawing the funds before age 59½.

With an IRA, you could continue to put money away in your spouse's plan, even when he or she isn't working—or if your spouse is working part-time and isn't part of a corporate plan.

Remember we talked about the power of compounding in chapter 1? Well, $1,000 invested today (assuming a 10% average annual return) would be worth $6,727 in twenty years. If you could invest it for thirty-five years instead, you'd have more than four times that amount, or $28,102. In forty years, it would be worth $45,259.

And that's without adding any more money to the pot.

The point is, you need to take advantage of every year you've got. Don't wait until you have more money, or until you get a new job, or until you finish that MBA. Do it now.

This is not to suggest you should use money slated for mortgage payments or food or any other basic necessities to invest for retirement. Far from it.

But as you look at your budget, and you've accounted for all the basics, look at where the additional money goes. Some may go to movies, dinners out, new clothes, vacations. Entertainment and leisure are important to the quality of your life. Investing is about locking in the quality of life you want for the future. Your new plan may mean modifying your lifestyle temporarily. Like taking a local beach vacation this summer instead of flying to the Bahamas in February. Or ordering pizza in on a night when you don't feel like cooking but taking the family out would set you back $50. Capture any money you can and put it to work for your future.

Ideally, you and your spouse will each set aside at least 10% of your pay in a 401(k) plan if you're in your thirties. If need be, that 10% could be made up of your contribution and your employer's match. You'll be even better off if you put away 10% and your employer matches 25%, 50%, or 100%. If you can afford it, many financial advisers say, the best investment you can make is to max out your 401(k) plan, by contributing 15% of your pay, to a maximum of $10,000 a year.

This money is deducted from your pay before federal and state taxes, which means a 10% contribution will feel like less than that in your paycheck. You'll also owe less tax on April 15, because you'll lower your income by the total amount of your yearly 401(k) contributions.

It's helpful to have a sense of how much you'll actually need in retirement. The numbers are big. Bigger than most of us realize we're capable of saving in our lifetime. But you can do it.

Let's calculate how much you'll need for retirement. People are living well into their eighties and even nineties these days. Assume you'll be retired for twenty-five years. There's inflation to consider. And Social Security, if you believe it will exist in your retirement in the same form it exists today. You'll see on table A that if you're earning $50,000 today, and you plan to retire in thirty years, you'll need more than $1 million to continue your current lifestyle. That may sound strange to you. But if you divide $1.07 million by 25 years, you come up with $42,654 a year. Add Social Security payments to that, and you're back to the income level you were accustomed to in your working years.

Let's make a plan to get you there.

First, answer a few questions:

1. At what age do you hope to retire? _____

2. How old are you now? _____

3. Subtract line 2 from line 1   _____

Line 3 is how long you have to invest—or your retirement "time horizon."

1. Write the amount from table A here (how much you'll need to retire):
   $_____
2. Figure your current retirement savings, then see table B for how much that will be worth by your retirement:
   $_____
3. Plug in how much you expect to get from any traditional pension plans your employer may offer:
   $_____
4. Subtract lines 2 and 3 from line 1. This is how much you need to save to reach your goal:

   $ [   ]

We'll use the example of Dan, thirty-five, a software engineer making $65,000 a year. He and his wife, Kathryn, a thirty-four-year-old architect, are expecting a baby in a month. He has $10,000 in a personal IRA account. She has $12,000. They bought a house last year. They hope to help their child with college tuition, and they might try to have a second baby in a couple of years. Their dream is to retire by age sixty and travel. Both are enrolled in 401(k) plans at work. Neither company offers a traditional "defined-benefit" pension plan. Kathryn, who makes $80,000 a year, plans to take a nine-month leave to be home with the baby.

1. From table A, amount Dan and Kathryn need to retire in twenty-five years: $3,249,359
2. Their combined IRAs, earning 11% a year for twenty-five years, will be worth: $309,143
3. How much they need to save, on top of the IRA money (subtract line 2 from line 1): $2,940,216
4. Table C amount that they need to save per month to get there:

   $1,949 per month

That's a pretty big chunk of money, no question about it. But it's less daunting when it's broken down into weekly contributions. That comes out to about $219.26 a week for Dan (assuming he's responsible for 45% of the total, based on his pay). Kathryn, saving 55% of the total, would set aside $267.99 a week.

Those calculations are before considering any employer contributions to their plans.

If they can afford to set this much aside every paycheck, plus reap an employer contribution, great. They'll have an even bigger nest egg in retirement. They may even be able to retire a few years earlier than they'd hoped.

On the other hand, if those contributions are a stretch, between mortgage payments and college savings, and their firms are both contributing, say, 5% of their pay, Dan could reduce his contribution to $156.76 and count on $62.50 per week from the company to his plan. Kathryn could cut her contribution back to $191.07, knowing her company was adding $76.92 per week.

Of course, they could also decide to cut back one plan but not the other. Indeed, during Kathryn's leave, that would be nine months in which she wasn't adding money to her plan. It could also be a time when Dan can't max out his 401(k) plan, because his salary is needed to pay the mortgage and all the household bills.

Remember that companies can change their 401(k) contribution levels, so there's no counting on what you get today as a guarantee of what you may get five years from now. Depending on the economy and how your company is doing, you may get more or less in the years to come.

Now back to the vesting issue we touched on above. This is important as it relates both to any traditional company-sponsored pension plans and to your 401(k).

Vesting is a tool companies use to build employee loyalty. The longer you stay with a company, the more you'll get in pension or 401(k) matching payments (if the company matches).

- *Traditional pensions:* If you have to work for the company for at least ten years to earn benefits, there's a good chance you'll never qualify. Most workers change jobs as many as seven times over the course of their lives. Perhaps your career plan has you moving to a new firm within five to seven years.

  You should sign up for the plan in any case. You never know for sure how long you'll stay with a company. Be mindful of the vesting schedule, because you just might hang on for a tenth year, for example, instead of leaving in your ninth year, if it meant locking in substantial retirement money for later.

- *401(k)s:* All the money you invest from your own pay is, of course, yours, no matter when you leave the company. That money belongs to you. The employer's contribution, however, may become yours over a period of time. For example, you might be 25% vested in two years, 50% vested in four years, 75% vested in six years, and so on.

If one of you is leaving your job permanently to care for children, this vesting schedule will become a reality for you.

Take the example of Samantha. She's worked for a consulting firm for five years. She has put $25,000, or $5,000 a year, into her 401(k) account. Her company has matched 50% of that, with full vesting in ten years. If she leaves to have a baby now, she takes her own $25,000—plus market gains (or losses)—and half the $12,500 her company has contributed on her behalf. That's $6,250 on top of the $25,000, or $31,250, plus market gains.

If Samantha were to stay the full ten years, she would reap the full $12,500 match. That may not stack up to the importance she places on being home with her baby. But she and her spouse should figure this into their plans.

The same choice applies when one of you is changing jobs. In that case, take the vesting money left behind into consideration in pay negotiations at the new job.

Quick tip: Understanding your company's retirement plans could factor into your family and career planning. Even if you decide to leave a company when you're just shy of meeting a vesting hurdle, you need to know how much money you're walking away from.

Time is important when it comes to saving and investing. Years logged on the job—and retirement benefits accrued—are valuable.

• • •

Now you've got a handle now on how much you need to save for retirement. We're going to talk in a minute about how to invest to reach that goal. But first let's touch on the other expense you need to plan for: college tuition.

The cost of getting a college degree is skyrocketing. But so is the importance of having a degree. Not only is the degree a key to landing the most interesting jobs, with chances for advancement, it offers a big leg up in earnings potential. Studies show that college graduates earn twice as much as high school graduates. On average, college grads earn a stunning $750,000 more in their lifetime than people who finish high school only.

The cost of private colleges is jumping 5% a year, faster than inflation or wage growth. In the 1997–98 year, the average bill for private college was $19,213. That's $76,852 over four years, and the prices will be higher by the time your kids get there.

If you've got sticker shock, remember that there are lots of alternatives. Many state schools have excellent reputations, and some private schools cost less for in-state residents. There are scholarships for talented students and athletes. And there is financial aid, an all-important loan structure that half of all students take advantage of in some form.

You'll be doing your kids a great service by helping them with college in whatever way you can. While many young people exit college with loans to pay off, that burden will be smaller if you are able to help by investing for them in advance. In Dan and Kathryn's case, if they were able to invest $226 a month combined for fifteen years (earning 11.2% a year) they'd have $100,000 to put toward the baby's education. That's $3.77 a day each. About the price of a coffee and a scone.

Now let's talk investing. The way you handle both these long-term investments—retirement and college—will be similar at this stage in your life.

PUTTING YOUR MONEY TO WORK FOR YOU

At most companies, you'll invest your 401(k) assets in mutual funds. Your employer will offer a menu of funds from which you can choose. Study the fund options in your plan, in order to make the smartest investing moves you can. Keep in mind your time horizon (how long you plan to leave the money alone) and your risk tolerance. Then examine the historic performance of the funds in the plan.

You should be thinking long term. You're probably still twenty to thirty years from retirement. You should be mostly—even entirely—in stock mutual funds that shoot for growth over time. Don't be too conservative or worried about the short-terms ups and downs of the market. If you invest too conservatively, you won't reach your goals by retirement. Remember that many of the charts and assumptions we've used have assumed an 8% to 10% average return over time. That takes into account years when the market soars 30%, and the stomach-churning years when it slumps 20%.

Your investment should be spread out among large-stock funds and smaller-stock funds. You might consider putting a portion of your money, from 5% to 20%, in an international or global stock fund. You may want to own a small amount of a bond fund to reap possible upside gains when bonds do well and stocks falter.

Think of the money you stash in your 401(k) plan as funds you won't see for at least ten or fifteen years—and probably much longer if you're in your twenties or early thirties. You should be in stock funds because they give you the greatest gains, year in and year out. If you were to put your money in Treasuries, a cash equivalent, you wouldn't be outpacing the current rate of inflation. Inflation has been low in recent years, in the 2% to 3% range. Over time, it's likely to edge up. You need to make sure your investments are doing better than the rate of inflation.

Consider that your stock returns, if they average 11% a year, would feel like 8%, taking into account 3% inflation. If you held conservative bond funds, earning an average 5% a year, and if inflation rose to 4% in the coming years, you'd be netting a mere 1% gain.

So you can see the importance of beating inflation.

Another key to investing success is to put money away regularly—and not to try to time the market. Even the pros can't time the market right most of the time. How can you count on doing so? You can't.

By investing regularly through your paycheck, or dollar-cost averaging, you will automatically avoid buying on emotion. Your gut can be wrong, after all. And you won't get caught putting too much money in at the top of the market, or trying to guess where the bottom is. Sometimes you'll buy high, sometimes low. The money will add up quicker than you think, and it will go straight into the funds of your choice.

Here's a sample portfolio for a new family. Assuming you are at least fifteen years from retirement:

- 80% to 90% stock funds (10% of that slice may be a global stock fund)
- 10% bond fund (high yield; corporate; government)

There are thousands of mutual funds out there from which to choose. You'll want to zero in on your company's stock fund menu. From your twenties and well into your forties (at least) you should be looking to grow your money in diversified growth funds. Diversified funds buy a variety of stocks; they don't focus solely on a particular industry or geographical region.

Consider an index fund, if one is offered. Funds that track the Standard & Poor's 500 Index own the five hundred biggest US stocks and tend to have lower costs than funds run by managers who spend time actively researching and selecting stocks. Over time, index funds have beaten most active managers.

There are also plenty of actively managed growth funds worth owning. Too many to fathom, really.

Growth funds typically own fast-growing, profitable companies that the fund manager thinks will have strong revenue and earnings for the foreseeable future. The best funds don't hop in and out of stocks constantly, but rather stick with good names and monitor holdings to sell off companies that start to lag.

Look at the funds' record over one, three, and five years. Don't pick a fund just because it was last year's hot story. You want funds that have solid reputations over the past three years. New, untested funds aren't necessarily a great idea. Nor are funds with once-great records that may have faltered because of a manager change or change of style.

Examine the fund performance information your company gives you. Then do some additional research on your own to see how the funds you're considering have performed compared to similar funds. You can find these easy-to-use analyses online (see chapter 22 for investing sites worth clicking into) in consumer investing magazines and in quarterly reports in newspaper business sections.

If the funds you're mulling are in the top 20% of their peer groups, great. Don't assume that last year's number-one fund will be tops again this year—or next year. Once you're among the top funds in a category, you should feel comfortable that, barring disaster, they'll all produce results in the same range over time. The hot fund that pumps out a 38% return this year may be more volatile than the others if the group average is a 24% return. Next year, that fund could come in below its peers, especially if it's loaded with stocks that soared and could come crashing down.

Remember: We're talking long-term money here. The point is how you end up over time. You certainly don't want to own a fund that's not performing up to the level of other like funds. But having a comfortable—even wealthy—retirement isn't about owning the best fund in the market every year. It's about investing a portion of your pay deliberately and regularly, and earning competitive rates of return over time.

Look at funds that own small stocks or mid-sized stocks. These are commonly called small-capitalization ("small-cap") and mid-capitalization ("mid-cap") funds (capitalization simply means the market value of a company: its number of shares outstanding times the share price). Large-cap funds have been beating small- and mid-cap funds handily for several years now. Many people still believe it's smart to have some exposure to smaller stocks, for the cycles in which they do outrun big stocks.

You may also need to choose between growth and value funds. Value funds have been out of favor for several years now, as growth stocks have prospered. Value managers look for beaten-up, lower-priced stocks that they think will rise as the underlying companies post better profits and grab the attention of investors. If that's a style that appeals to you, it may be worth a look. But value tends to beat growth only cyclically. In your early stages as an investor, your best bet is to keep most of your money in growth.

Global and international funds are worth a look for you. Pick a fund with a strong three-year track record that invests around the world. Global funds can also invest in US stocks, if that's where the manager sees strong prospects, while international funds tend to invest overseas only.

Either way, a good fund that invests abroad will give you exposure to other parts of the world. Yes, that can be risky, especially considering that there's been no better market than America's for most of this decade. Sure, Russia soared one year, then it crashed. Latin America was red-hot for a while, then it tumbled. Parts of Asia were big winners—until the market collapsed in 1998.

A good fund manager will spread your assets in stocks or bonds around the world. He or she will do the grueling work of watching economies, taking advantage of positive trends like Europe's recovering economy and Japan's efforts to shrug off a ten-year stock slump.

Of course, you have to weigh the opportunity cost of taking money off the table in what's still widely seen as the world's best market, right here at home. It's probably risky to put more than 20% of your portfolio in global funds. But it could be very smart, as a diversification tactic, to put 10% overseas. Then when stocks soar in far-flung corners of the world, you'll benefit.

Bond funds will give you smaller returns than stock funds over time. You make money on bonds both by the securities rising in value (based on inflation, market forces, and the economy) and from the income, or interest, that bonds pay.

Sure, an 8% bond fund return looks great in a year when stocks are down. But an average 5% return on bonds over time is half what you can expect with stock funds over time. To reach your goal of accumulating a substantial nest egg by the time you retire, you'll be better off investing in stocks than bonds.

It can be strategic to have 5% or 10% of your money in bond funds, to reap those fairly steady, if modest, gains at times when stocks fall or are volatile. But again, you shouldn't try to time the market. By the time you figure out bonds are in a period of beating stocks, it's too late. As with other asset classes, you need to be there all the time to reap the gains.

And don't kid yourself: Bonds can fall too. When interest rates rise, bond prices fall. (The reverse is true too. Interest rates fall when bond prices surge.) In a period of quickly rising interest rates, most bond funds will perform poorly. If you want to have exposure to bonds, consider a fund that owns quality corporate bonds or high-yield ("junk") bonds. For young, aggressive investors, bond funds that own corporate debt (instead of just government Treasuries) can provide interesting returns.

As for municipal bond funds, they're not a great bet for a young investor. They are highly conservative bond funds that are best used in taxable accounts (your 401(k) isn't taxed until you withdraw the money) because they shield investors from certain taxes. Revisit these investment vehicles much further down the road.

As parents, if you don't have a 401(k) plan at work at all, you should consider opening an IRA (individual retirement account). A $4,000 annual contribution may be fully tax deductible for you, depending on your salary. And it will help you invest for retirement if what you're getting at work isn't going to get you there.

If you make the maximum contributions to your 401(k) and you still have enough money left over to stash away more for retirement, you could open a Roth IRA. There's no up-front tax deduction, but you don't pay taxes down the line either, when you withdraw the money. But make sure you have enough money to pay your bills and to save in your bank account too. You'll do yourself no favors if you put away every spare cent for retirement but save nothing for nearer-term needs like buying a house or saving for your kids' education.

BACK TO THE SUBJECT OF COLLEGE

Like all other investing, putting money to work in the market to save for college tuition is all about time.

Maybe you've got a newborn, and eighteen years to plan. Or perhaps your child is already eight, and you've got ten years. Maybe college is only five years away. How you invest depends almost entirely on the time horizon.

You can set an investing plan that suits your stomach for risk. Let's say your goal is to raise $50,000 in ten years. Under these guidelines, you'd meet your target with the following monthly investments:

- Conservative: $250 per mnth @ 9.6%
- Moderate: $228 per month @ 11.2%
- Aggressive: $217 per month @ 12.1%

A word on borrowing to finance college tuition:

Employers often permit you to borrow from your 401(k) plan, either to pay for a house or for other purposes. Under the law, you can borrow up to 50% of your vested account balance, to a maximum of $50,000. But don't enter into such a loan lightly.

A general-purpose loan—which would include loans for education—would have to be repaid, with interest, within five years. That's not a lot of time to repay a multithousand-dollar loan. On top of that, it's not a great idea to borrow from yourself. Even though you'd be paying interest on the loan to yourself, you would not be earning the investment rate you're counting on to meet your retirement goals.

Dos and Don'ts

Do:

- Investigate which health plan is most cost-effective for you and your family; decide whether to enroll the entire family in one plan.

- Add your new child to your health plan on the date of birth or the day you become legal guardian.
- Consider the advantages of a flexible spending account.
- Think about whether you need long-term disability coverage.
- Start investing in your 401(k) plan as soon as you can.
- If investing for your kids' education is a goal, start as soon as you can.
- Remember to check your 401(k) investment choices, quarterly or every six months, to be sure you're still happy with the investments. As you get closer to retirement, you may need to rebalance, to keep your risk in line with your time horizon.
- Be sure your beneficiary on any life insurance policy or investment documents is properly designated.

Don't:

- Short-change yourself for your future. Put some money away in your 401(k) plan, even if it's a modest weekly sum. Even saving $120 a month—$30 a week—earning 10% a year over thirty-five years would get you $250,000. That may not be enough to meet all your retirement needs. But it's a terrific start.

Ready Resources

- *Securing Your Child's Future,* W. Conkling
- *From Cradle to College: A Parent's Guide to Financing Your Child's Life,* Neale Godfrey with Tad Richards

CONCLUSION

The Most Important Investment You'll Ever Make

When it comes to living life on your terms, you're the only person who can decide what those terms are. Failure to do so will result in a compromise that can, sooner or later, become unlivable, or worse, tolerable. Why is living a tolerable life worse than an unlivable situation? Because when something is unlivable, you move on. When it is tolerable, you stay put and suffer the consequences.

We'll be able to see the majority of those one generation ahead of us living a tolerable retirement lifestyle—one they wouldn't have chosen for themselves from a Lifestyle catalog, but one which their lack of investing forces them to accept. If they had broken their backs sending their children to private school, encouraging learning and self-advancement and investing in their own offspring, then, yes, give them the benefit of the doubt. This small subsector at least invested in someone's future. But don't feel too terribly sad for the majority, at least not for those who charged their way through life, never saving enough. It's no wonder this group ate their way through their savings, since they probably blew at least one-fourth of their disposable income dining out. They probably spent over $150,000 on uselessly expensive cars, too. Self-indulgence, not self-discipline was the rule. *Make your life an exception to it.*

While many of us know that life is what we make of it, the siren call of spending what you earn now (rather than investing it in a distant future) can be overwhelming. And it's not just temptation of what we desire that can drive us to the poorhouse. It's also fear of the un-known. And when it comes to investing, the best way to ensure a bet-ter life for ourselves now and in the future, fear of the unknown can set us way back in terms of being able to reap the rewards that long-term investing can bestow.

In working your way through this book, you began on one side of what may have appeared to be an unscalable mountain. If you have read every chapter contained in this book, then you have scaled the peak, and seen the world of investing for what it is—a bountiful land-scape with some treacherous slopes that can be avoided or managed within reason. If you tunneled from the introduction straight through to the final section, you know the core theme of investing: to provide a financially secure future for yourself. No one else can climb a moun-tain for you. No one else can get you to prove to yourself that you have the stamina to invest regularly and often. But that's the only way you'll be able to overcome the most troublesome obstacle between you and living life on your own terms—call it the object of money.

Money won't make your life more meaningful. Nor should your life be bent by the pursuit of money alone—or merely the things that money can buy. There's far more to life than what money can buy. But, by the same token, a life lived in the quiet desperation of debts owed is unsettling. You know it is. By the time you retire, you'll not only need to have paid off all your debts, you will also need to have a war chest of easily $1 million—just to maintain your current $45,000 lifestyle of today. You know it. You can't get around it. But you can achieve it—as long as you begin to invest in your future today.

There are more immediate financial hurdles. Saving for a down payment on a home. Paying off your college or grad school loans. Your car is on its last rounds. There's always something in the here and now that can steer you away from your longer-term goals. There's no easy answer to any of the hurdles you face. But there is a significant advantage in knowing what they are, and what strategies you can use to win the race. That's what this book has been all about—winning the race of your own financial independence. Doing so opens up a world of opportunities that extends far beyond the horizon of mak-ing, saving, and investing. Taking care of your financial life (in the here and now, as well as for the future) will enable you to invest more meaningful time in yourself as well as those who mean the most to you. (A capital idea!)

As you have learned, the recipe for investment success is a simple one. You have the ability to invest wisely and well. You have the resources. You understand why it's in your best interest to invest, and to do so consistently and over the long term. There's no artificial substitute or minute method available. You need to make it on your own. In fact, the only way you can rest assured that you'll have your cake and eat it too is by *Investing from Scratch*!

GLOSSARY

Use this glossary to help you on your way to building a basic investment vocabulary.

advance/decline ratio. The number of stocks whose prices have advanced versus those that have declined over a given day. Typically calculated at the close of market, this ratio is used to represent the general direction of the market.

annual report. Yearly report of a company's overall financial condition (from operations to balance sheet), which, by law, must be sent to all shareholders.

asked price. A security's (or commodity's) price as offered for sale on an exchange or OTC (over-the-counter) market. (See, for contrast, *bid price*.)

asset. Value attributed to stocks, bonds, real estate, mutual funds, or, in terms of a company, the value of owned equipment or plants.

asset allocation. A strategy for diversifying money in major investment categories as well as particular types of investments within each category.

automatic investing. A method for investing in mutual funds that enables you to select a specific amount to be withdrawn from your bank savings or checking account on a regular, scheduled basis and invested in a mutual fund. It's a great low-cost way to start investing in mutual funds, since many funds are willing to waive their minimum in order to get what they hope will be your long-term participation in their fund.

automatic reinvestment. Typically, the automatic reinvestment of dividends in new shares of a company's stock or a mutual fund. Some companies and almost all mutual funds allow automatic reinvestment. A smart move, even though you will have to pay taxes on the dividend amount (whether you reinvest or receive it in cash).

average annual return. A measure of historical return. The amount per year you would have had to earn to achieve the same total return over the time period in question.

average maturity. The average maturity is the weighted average of the maturities of all of a fund's bond holdings. (The maturity of a bond is the date the debt is due and payable.) Typically, the longer a fund's average maturity, the greater its interest-rate risk. Not as meaningful as a bond fund's duration.

balanced fund. A fund that invests substantial portions in both stocks and bonds.

balance sheet. Company's accounting of its current assets, liabilities, and owner's equity at a specified point in time. Found in the company's annual report.

bear market. A sustained period of falling stock or bond prices. In the stock market, fear of economic downturn, and proof of it, tends to bring the bear out of hibernation. In the bond market, rising interest rates bring on the feared animal.

beta. The extent to which a fund or stock's value tends to go up or down as the market goes up or down. A growth fund with a beta of 1.5 would most likely go up 15% when the market as a whole is up 10%. (Or down 15% when the market is down 10%.)

bid price. The highest price a prospective investor (or market maker) is prepared to pay for a security, usually just under the asked price, the lowest price a seller is willing to accept.

blue chip. Large, well-known, established companies whose stock is considered to be a solid investment and safer than other companies' stocks, since a blue chip is unlikely to go bankrupt.

bond. An IOU issued by a corporate or government entity in return for a pledge of repayment of the original face value invested, plus interest payments to be paid on specified dates.

bond fund. A mutual fund that invests primarily in bonds.

capital gain. Profit made on the sale of securities or property. Federal capital gains taxes are currently capped at 28%, even for investors whose income is taxed in a higher bracket.

capital gains distribution. A mutual fund's distribution to shareholders of gains realized on the sale of securities within the fund's portfolio. Typically, the distributions are made once per year, and can affect the optimal timing of your own purchase or sale of the fund.

capital loss. When the amount realized on the sale of an asset is less than the amount originally paid for it, the investor has suffered a capital loss.

capital preservation. Investors who have already grown their seed money into a harvestable crop want to protect what they've got. Capital preservation refers to the objective of ensuring that the amount of capital doesn't become reduced over time, which in turn means that risks are avoided in favor of a defensive portfolio. Nevertheless, some growth of capital must ensue, if only to be able to safeguard the capital from inflation's toll, and some income is also usually sought, to allow periodic withdrawals without depleting principal.

cash. The most liquid asset, typically thought of in the form of negotiable currency, but inclusive of cash equivalents: interest-bearing short-term instruments like a money market fund or Treasury bill.

cash cow. A business that generates a continuous cash flow which, in terms of companies that issue publicly traded stocks, typically results in reliable dividends.

cash dividend. Taxable cash payments made to shareholders from a corporation's earnings. Some companies issue a stock dividend in lieu of a cash payout.

cash flow. A company's net income after expenses, but before accounting for abstract costs such as depreciation. Cash flow is one indicator used by stock analysts to evaluate a company's ability to pay off debt and keep paying dividends.

certificate of deposit. Better known as a CD, it is a specified-term, fixed-interest-earning debt instrument issued by a bank or savings and loan. A good temporary parking place for cash you will need at a specified date in the near future (CD maturities can range from three months to five years). Penalties apply for early withdrawal. Most are FDIC insured; forget those that aren't.

certified financial planner (CFP). This certificate, issued by the Institute of Certified Financial Planners, signifies that the holder has passed a series of tests showing the ability to advise clients on a host of financial concerns including banking, estate planning, insurance, investing, and taxes. Be advised that tests are no substitute for experience, intelligence, and integrity.

certified public accountant (CPA). A rigorous examination process, coupled with relevant experience and state licensing, makes this certification one of the more meaningful professional designations for those whose career is focused on accounting, auditing, and tax preparation. This designation is an excellent indicator of a level of proficiency in the aforementioned fields, but is less indicative of the person's ability to advise you on non-tax-related investment matters.

chartered financial analyst (CFA). Like the CPA designation, this one requires a person to pass through a rigorous (three-year) examination process with relevant experience in economics, ethics, financial accounting, portfolio management, and hard-core securities analysis. CFAs stand out among those who would proclaim themselves qualified to analyze an investment's fundamental worth and appropriateness to particular portfolios.

chartered financial consultant (ChFC). An excellent addition to the CFP designation, this charter is offered to CFPs who have also passed a four-year program at the College of Bryn Mawr covering economics, insurance, investing, and taxes.

chartered mutual fund counselor. A new designation offered by the National Endowment for Financial Education, showing a financial adviser's enhanced ability to advise clients on their mutual fund questions and concerns.

closed-end investment company. Contrasted with an open-end fund, which issues new shares per new purchase, a closed-end fund sells a fixed number of shares in its portfolio of securities. Closed-end fund shares trade on the major US exchanges and over-the-counter market. Their market value is determined by supply and demand, which leads to shares being sold at either a premium or a discount to the actual net asset value of the fund's portfolio.

commission. Percentage (based on selling price, amount managed, or service rendered) charged by a brokerage firm—be it real estate or investment.

commodities. Goods, from foodstuffs to metals, traded on several exchanges by traders speculating on supply and demand's effect on the goods' prices.

common stock. Share of ownership in a company. Stock prices can rise or fall with the company's fortunes, or even with stock market supply and demand fluctuations (which may or may not be entirely rational).

compound interest. Interest earned on previously paid interest as well as on original principal amount. Example: $500 principal at 10% annual interest would become $550 in one year, but going forward, that $550 at 10% would become $605, after realizing $55 in interest during the second year ($50 on the original principal, plus $5 on the first year's interest).

contrarian. An investor who examines the investments and trends consensus wisdom is buying into, and invests in their opposite. To a contrarian, the crowd is always wrong. But, you might ask, what happens if there's a crowd of contrarians?

corporate bond. Debt instrument (IOU) issued by a private or public corporation, as opposed to a government entity. Corporate bonds typically share the following characteristics: their income is taxable; they have a par value of $1,000; they have a specified maturity; and they're traded on one of the major exchanges.

correlation. The extent to which a fund and the stock market (usually as measured by the S&P 500 index) tend to move together. An S&P 500 index fund would have a correlation of 99% or 100%. A fund invested in smaller stocks not found in the S&P 500, or which makes big bets on narrow sectors, or which invests heavily overseas, would tend to have a much lower correlation (most likely less than 50%).

coupon. The original interest rate paid on a bond's face (or par) value. A $1,000 par bond paying $50 per year has a 5% coupon.

credit rating (bond). A letter grading of potential risk. Standard & Poor's (S&P) and Moody's are the top rating agencies, and both rate companies based on their ability to repay bondholders' interest and principal. Standard & Poor's ratings of AAA (Moody's highest rating is Aaa) to BBB (Baa) signify a range of "investment-grade" bonds, while ratings of BB (Ba) or lower denote "below-investment-grade" bonds, more commonly referred to as "junk bonds." A rating of D signifies the bond is in default.

credit rating (consumer). A report of a consumer's history of timely (and untimely) bill paying, used to determine potential credit risk for mortgages, new credit cards, and other loans.

current yield. Current yield is determined by dividing the bond's annual interest by its current market price. It differs from the coupon rate in that it accounts for the price paid for the bond (as opposed to its par value). So, for example, while the coupon rate of a $1,000 par bond paying $50 per year is 5%, the current yield of a bond bought at $950 with a $50 income would be 5.26%.

cyclical stock. A stock whose performance is closely tied to the health of the economy. In tough times, these stocks falter. In good times, they typically rise rapidly. Housing, cars, and "deep cyclicals" like steel manufacturers are directly affected by the consumer's (and industry's) willingness and ability to purchase goods.

debt-to-equity. A ratio, calculated by dividing a company's total liabilities by total shareholders' stock in the company, that is used to help measure a company's ability to pay its creditors if the company itself fails.

default. Failure of a company or other debtor to make principal and/ or interest payments on schedule. A bad thing.

defensive stocks. These stocks are the opposite of cyclical stocks, since the company's products tend to be staples (like food) that consumers can't or won't do without (unlike a new car). As a result, their performance is less affected by economic downturns.

derivative. A bet on the direction of interest rates or the price of some other security or commodity. Some funds and investors use derivatives aggressively to enhance the yield or potential return of their portfolio, while others use them in an attempt to reduce the risk of their portfolio. Derivatives aren't all bad—but, like a dark freckle, a proliferation of them is a potential warning sign.

discount. Just like what you find at Wal-Mart, discounts reflect a price reduction in the product or security you're buying at market. For example, relating to bonds, a discount is the difference between the bond's par value and its current market price where that price is lower than the par value. (In contrast, buying a bond at a premium would mean the current market price is higher than the par value.) For a closed-end fund, a discount is the amount by which the purchase price is less than net asset value.

discount broker. Broker who typically charges less (in comparison to full-service brokers) for services rendered—from trades transacted to reports and recommendations issued. There's a wide variance in such costs and services among discounters and deep discounters.

discount rate. The interest rate the Federal Reserve Bank charges member banks on loans. This rate in turn affects the interest rates on loans consumers will pay, since banks use the discount rate as the benchmark from which they mark up the rate on their loans.

distribution. A payment made to a shareholder. Except for income from municipal funds, distributions are taxable events. Distributions amount to a return of your capital because (except for monthly bond fund dividends) share prices are reduced by the same amount as the dividend. This share price reduction occurs on the ex-dividend date.

diversification. A strategy for reducing investment risk by investing in different categories and types of investments as well as (within the stock market) different industries and company market capitalizations.

dividend. A distribution of earnings to shareholders, either by an individual company or by a mutual fund.

dividend reinvestment plan. Like automatic reinvestment, the reinvestment of dividends in new shares of the stock or fund. A smart move, even though you will have to pay taxes on the dividend amount (even if you don't receive it in cash).

dollar-cost averaging. Investment method in which a specified amount of money is regularly invested on a scheduled basis. This method can reward the investor who employs it with more shares bought at lower prices than at higher prices.

Dow Jones industrial average (DJIA, or "the Dow"). A stock market index that has withstood the test of time by adequately reflecting the movement of the market as a whole. It's calculated by adding up the prices of thirty large-cap stocks, which results in a potential flaw (according to some critics), namely, its narrow definition and exclusion of newer industries and companies. Nevertheless, this index is the most widely used measure of the market—and it has certainly earned its place as a standard worth watching.

duration. A measure of a bond fund's interest rate sensitivity, based on the maturities of the bonds in the portfolio. A fund with an effective duration of 4 should lose 4% if interest rates rise 1%, or gain 4% if interest rates fall 1%.

earnings per share (EPS). Portion of a company's profit allocated to each outstanding share of common stock. (Total profits divided by number of shares of common stock.)

economic indicators. Statistics used to represent the current state of the economy and also to predict (with a meteorologist's accuracy) the direction of the economy.

efficient market theory. A theory that suggests that market price reflects market value, meaning that dart throwers and analysts have an equal chance of selecting the best stocks. Contentious, but hardly groundless.

equity. A fancy name for common stock. If you're in the habit of saying "*très* good," by all means call stocks "equities."

ex-dividend date. The date on which stocks (or mutual funds) effectively pay out their dividends. Shareholders who own the fund on this date receive the dividend, the share price tends to fall by the amount of the dividend on this date, and automatic reinvestments are made on this date. (However, actual dividend checks may be delayed by several days.)

expense ratio. The amount investors in a fund pay for expenses incurred in the operation and management of the fund during the year. This expense may be 1% or more. A higher expense ratio reduces the fund's total return; therefore, two funds of equal strength but with unequal expense ratios present a clear choice—opt for the one with the lower expense ratio.

face value. Worth of a bond or other security as stated on it.

family of funds. Group of funds "owned" (that is, managed and operated) by the same investment management company. (Technically, each fund is owned by its shareholders, who could vote to move the fund to another fund family.)

fixed-income fund. A mutual fund that invests in fixed-income securities such as corporate bonds or Ginnie Maes.

401(k) plan. Employer-sponsored tax-advantaged retirement plan that enables contributors to put pretax dollars in the investment vehicles offered by the plan. The employer often matches the contributions of participating employees.

403(b) plan. Equivalent to 401(k) plans, but for nonprofit employers.

fundamental analysis. Analysis of a company and its securities based on hard data from its balance sheet and income statements, sales, earnings, and management, as well as extrinsic economic factors that affect the company's ability to operate profitably. Such analysis can be used as a predictor of future potential. (See, for contrast, *technical analysis.*)

fund of funds. A mutual fund whose portfolio consists of other mutual funds.

futures contract. Written agreement to buy or sell a commodity or security for a specified price at a specified future date.

growth fund. A mutual fund that invests in growth stocks. In doing so, this type of fund seeks to deliver capital appreciation to its shareholders, rather than income. As a result, a stock's earnings growth is favored over its actual or potential dividends.

growth and income fund (G&I fund). A mutual fund that typically combines the objective of capital appreciation with the generation of some income. Note: some G&I funds are very close to growth funds, offering virtually no income; others look almost like bond funds, with little room for capital appreciation. Match your objective with a G&I fund's actual portfolio.

growth stock. A stock in a company characterized by above-average growth in earnings or sales. Growth stocks tend to have a high price relative to earnings, and provide little if any dividend. Growth stocks also tend to have a high beta (or risk), but can offer long-term investors the potential for solid capital appreciation. (See, for contrast, *cyclical stock* and *value stock.*)

hedge. Not a rhododendron. A hedge, or hedging, is a strategy used to neutralize the risk inherent in an investment. The phrase "hedging one's bets" accurately reflects the objective: to break even whether the hedged assets move up or down. Hedging, which is often accomplished with the use of derivatives, sometimes fails to protect against risks as planned.

index. A standard or benchmark against which the performance of a market, industry, company, or security (stock, bond, real estate, mutual fund, and more) is measured.

index fund. A fund whose objective is to match a specific market index (most commonly the S&P 500 stock index). Since most funds fail to beat their relevant index benchmark, an index fund is likely to perform slightly better than most funds in the long term.

inefficient market theory. This theory holds that an informed investor stands a better-than-even chance of picking stocks more effectively than a chimp with a dartboard. In contrast to the efficient market theory, this one encourages research, analysis, and the ability to beat a fellow investor to the punch—finding hidden profits or pitfalls in a given company.

inflation. The rise in the prices of goods and services as reflected in the consumer price index (CPI), which tracks consumer goods, and the producer price index (PPI), which focuses on industrial goods and materials. Inflation decreases the purchasing power of your dollar in the long run. The cause is usually attributed to an increase in the money supply.

investment company. An arrangement whereby investors pool their assets into a corporation or trust which then employs professional management to invest the assets according to a stated objective. Mutual funds are one form of investment company. (See also *mutual fund* and *closed-end investment company.*)

investment objective. A fund's aim, as stated in its prospectus. Investors should choose a fund whose objectives match their own—although they need to go beyond the stated objective and examine the fund's history of actually hitting what it says it's aiming at.

IRA (individual retirement account). A tax-deductible retirement investment plan—or, at least, a tax-deferred one. Penalties apply for early withdrawal.

load. A mutual fund's sales charge. See chapter 14 for a list of the ways a mutual fund can take a bite out of your investment.

mutual fund. A professionally managed portfolio of securities (one or a combination of stocks, bonds, cash, real estate investment trusts) that enables investors to pool their money and reap the potential rewards (or suffer the possible consequences). An excellent investment vehicle for getting you to your investment destination—the problem is, there are so many cars on the lot, and only a few of them have a full tank of gas.

net asset value (NAV). The market price of a fund (its NAV) is derived at the close of market every day by determining the value of the fund's total assets (the value of each security as well as cash and cash equivalents) less its liabilities, divided by the total number of its outstanding shares.

no-load fund. A mutual fund whose shares can be bought and sold at NAV without any sales charge—but be forewarned that there may be redemption fees (a fee charged for selling the fund, generally within a specified time of purchase).

offering price. The net asset value per share, plus the sales charge. Also called the "asked price." For no-load funds, the NAV and offering price are the same.

open-end fund. See *mutual fund.*

OTC (over-the-counter). The NASDAQ is the leading over-the-counter market in the United States. OTC stocks aren't listed on any exchange. Instead, they are bought and sold through a computerized network of traders.

par. The face value of a bond; the principal amount that should be paid when the bond matures.

portfolio. Term used to describe an investor's or fund manager's investment holdings.

premium. The opposite of discount.

prospectus. A fund's equivalent to a company's annual report. The Securities and Exchange Commission (SEC) requires every fund to provide to each shareholder a prospectus wherein the fund describes its investment objectives, investments, past performance, fees, and services. Get it. Read it. Know it—before you invest in it.

sector. Sectors are the constituent parts of an overall industry. For example, pharmaceutical companies and semiconductor manufacturers as distinct from health and technology.

sector fund. Fund that invests in companies in one defined sector or related group of sectors. Fidelity's Select funds are perhaps the best known of this rather speculative genre.

technical analysis. Using charts of a security's past price performance, technical analysts look for trends (and other, more abstract symbols) to tip them to an investment's future prospects. (See, for contrast, *fundamental analysis.*)

tenure. This term refers to a fund manager's time at the helm. Since managers are responsible for the performance of the portfolios they run, tenure is an excellent way to determine the manager's experience, the relevance of any performance history, and the potential for problems should he or she choose to leave the fund. Note that just because a manager may not have a lengthy tenure at the fund you're thinking of buying (the average tenure is under four years), it doesn't mean he or she didn't have solid experience elsewhere. Researching a manager's past history of performance at his or her present and preceding funds is a critical step in a comprehensive fund selection process.

total return. The annual appreciation of an investment (including its capital appreciation, dividends, and/or interest), thus a clear marker as to how much your investment has grown since you bought it.

turnover rate. Calculated by taking the value of all a fund's trades (buys and sells) and dividing it by twice the net assets of the portfolio, this figure indicates how aggressive a manager is being with regard to trading in and out of (or within) the market. A turnover rate in excess of 100% generally means a pretty aggressive manager.

If the manager's good, that's not a problem, but excessive turnover can drive up fund expenses and hurt returns.

value stock. A stock that is considered cheap relative to earnings or assets. Value stocks tend to be stodgier players in slower-growing, defensive, or cyclical areas. Contrast with growth stock. (Note that almost all fund managers at least pay lip service to the concept of value; even some aggressive growth players claim to be seeking "value-growth" issues!)

yield. The rate of interest payments on a bond. The current yield on a bond is the amount of yearly interest divided by the current value of the bond. A more useful measure of yield is the yield to maturity, which takes into account the fact that bonds selling at a discount or premium to their par value will get closer to par value as they near maturity. The SEC now requires that funds report yield to maturity.

yield spread. The difference between the yield on one kind of income investment and the yield on a standard investment, usually US Treasury bonds. The yield spread between a bond and the benchmark US Treasury would tend to indicate the degree of credit risk expected for the bond. Not surprisingly, yield spreads are much higher for junk bonds than for high-quality corporate bonds.

INDEX